Communities That Care

Communities That Care

Building Community Engagement and Capacity to Prevent Youth Behavior Problems

ABIGAIL A. FAGAN

J. DAVID HAWKINS

RICHARD F. CATALANO

DAVID P. FARRINGTON

OXFORD

UNIVERSITY PRESS

OXFORD
UNIVERSITY PRESS

Oxford University Press is a department of the University of Oxford. It furthers the University's objective of excellence in research, scholarship, and education by publishing worldwide. Oxford is a registered trade mark of Oxford University Press in the UK and certain other countries.

Published in the United States of America by Oxford University Press
198 Madison Avenue, New York, NY 10016, United States of America.

Library of Congress Cataloging-in-Publication Data
Names: Fagan, Abigail A., author. | Hawkins, J. David, author. |
Catalano, Richard F., author. | Farrington, David P., author.
Title: Communities that care : building community engagement and capacity to prevent youth behavior problems / Abigail A. Fagan, J. David Hawkins, Richard F. Catalano, David P. Farrington.
Description: New York : Oxford University Press, [2019]
Identifiers: LCCN 2018013293 | ISBN 9780190299217 (hard cover) |
ISBN 9780190299224 (pbk.) | ISBN 9780190299231 (updf) |
ISBN 9780190299248 (epub)
Subjects: LCSH: Juvenile delinquents—United States—Social conditions. |
Youth—Mental health services—United States. | Community health services—United States. | Behavior modification—United States.
Classification: LCC HV9104 .F334 2018 | DDC 364.360973—dc23
LC record available at https://lccn.loc.gov/2018013293

1 3 5 7 9 8 6 4 2

Paperback printed by Sheridan Books, Inc., United States of America
Hardback printed by Bridgeport National Bindery, Inc., United States of America

Contents

List of Figures

List of Tables

Foreword

MOST OF MY ACADEMIC career has been spent in a mean season of crime control, a four-decade era marked by crass "get tough" rhetoric, portrayals of offenders as irredeemable super-predators, inflexibly harsh sentencing laws unconnected to the advance of public safety, punitive interventions that amounted to correctional quackery, and mass imprisonment. Early on, this embrace of meanness struck me as an awful policy choice—one that, with Karen Gilbert, I opposed in my 1982 book, *Reaffirming Rehabilitation*. This volume was a criminological outlier because it was published at a time when virtually everyone—conservatives and liberals alike—were persuaded that "nothing works" to reform offenders. In fact, it was fashionable then to talk about the "decline of the rehabilitative ideal" and to ask, "Is rehabilitation dead?"

I thought it might be, at least in the public's mind. So, starting in 1979, I conducted surveys to explore just how punitive Americans had become and just how much they had abandoned the goal of saving the wayward. I was teaching at Western Illinois University, which meant that it was convenient to conduct surveys in this region. Illinois had a Republican governor, and the west-central part of the state was rural and conservative. I anticipated that evidence of a "punitive public" would be overwhelming and the embrace of rehabilitation minuscule. I was only half right.

Indeed, I have conducted numerous local, state, and national surveys over the past three decades. With only minor variation, they have all reported precisely the same finding. The American public is punitive; this is no myth. They favor exacting just deserts and locking up the dangerous and even the chronically bothersome. But the nation's citizenry is also highly supportive of treatment as a goal of corrections. So, I was right about punitiveness but wrong about rehabilitation. Indeed, the sustained embrace of offender reform should be seen for what it is—a remarkable criminological fact. Despite 40 years of rising prison populations and of politicians trampling over one another to see who could be the toughest on crime, the public simply is unwilling to forfeit the idea that corrections should be about correcting offenders. Notably, when asked how best to respond to youngsters involved in or at risk for crime, support for rehabilitation and for human service interventions is virtually universal—with surveys often showing more than 9 in 10 respondents endorsing treatment.

I have argued elsewhere that this advocacy of rehabilitation in general and of "child saving" in particular is an unshakable cultural belief—what Alexis de Tocqueville in his classic *Democracy in America* called a "habit of the heart." This phrase refers to the fundamental beliefs, sensibilities, and practices that constitute the American character—the very stuff that makes us who we are as a people. Whether for religious or secular reasons, we believe that lost souls can be redeemed and that everyone merits a second chance. To consign others to the scrapheap of life would be, in this sense, un-American.

In his treatise on the political psychology of Americans, *The Righteous Mind*, Jonathan Haidt captures this matter in another way. His research shows that "caring/harm" is one of the core "moral foundations" that underlies our political views—what Haidt calls the "universal cognitive modules upon which cultures construct moral matrices." This principle is at the heart of liberal or progressive politics, but it is still valued to a degree by most conservatives. In practical terms, this way of seeing the world lends legitimacy to policies that seek to limit harm or suffering through caring and kindness.

When it comes to offenders, moral foundations theory offers a mixed bag. Other core principles—such as "fairness/cheating" and "authority/subversion"—would evoke a punitive impulse and a preference for punishment. But more than one principle can be operative at a time. In the area of corrections, the caring/harm foundation can temper our sense of what is moral and lead us to impose sanctions that not only exact justice but also offer help. As Haidt notes, the caring/harm principle is especially powerful when we are confronted by children under duress. Even for those who are wayward, a moral response would require more than seeking an eye for an eye.

All this leads to the conclusion that a fundamental habit of the heart of moral foundation among Americans is that we care for one another—even those who go astray and even those who we must punish and restrain. Trite as it is to say, *caring is as American as apple pie*! This reality means that there is a strong cultural willingness not just to be mean but also to do good. The moral impulse to care is an important resource that needs to be appreciated—and exploited to advantage.

For much of my academic life, however, a key difficulty remained: We did not know *how to care effectively*. In the early part of my career—a time when labeling theory rose in prominence—most criminologists believed that efforts to do good masked coercive practices and made offenders worse off. In his classic book, *Radical Nonintervention*, Edwin Schur advised "to leave the kids alone whenever possible." I opposed this view on the grounds that caring about youngsters (and others) was better than explicitly trying to inflict pain on them, which became the official policy of American criminal justice. Still, critics had a point: A huge knowledge gap existed between our desire to care and our ability to care in a way that reduced recidivism and other human troubles.

In the early 1990s, two paradigm shifts occurred that did much to narrow the knowledge gap between aspiration and achievement in intervention. First, until this time, criminology in the United States and elsewhere focused mainly on inventing and testing theories of delinquency. However valuable this work was, it was based on the implicit and false assumption that all causes of crime were age-graded—that behavior occurring in the teenage years was caused by circumstances in this life stage (e.g., blocked success goals, peer pressure). This view ignored the obvious reality that youngsters do not arrive in adolescence as blank slates but as manifesting individual differences acquired in childhood or before.

Between 1990 and 1993, three works appeared that undermined this prevailing paradigm of adolescence-limited criminology (as I have called it): Gottfredson and Hirschi's general (self-control) theory of crime, Moffitt's developmental typology of antisocial behavior, and Sampson and Laub's age-graded social bond theory. Taken together, these path-breaking works showed that childhood experiences, including the early onset of conduct problems, were integral to whether youngsters were ensnared in a criminogenic life-course trajectory. Criminology has not been the same since. Suddenly, the developmental/life-course perspective was on its way to becoming the dominant theoretical paradigm in the field.

This novel focus had a critically important effect. Childhood and human development had long been the domain of psychology. Now, as traditional criminologists realized the importance of looking into the first stages in life, they discovered the writings of psychologists, many having a community focus. This body of research provided key insights into the risk and protective factors that caused life-course-persistent criminal involvement (e.g., David Farrington's prolific studies). Equally important, given the therapeutic mission of their discipline, some of these psychologists had developed early intervention programs aimed at preventing a variety of negative life outcomes, including crime (e.g., David Olds and his Nurse-Family Partnership program). These model interventions showed powerfully *how to care effectively*. Over the years, this intellectual marriage between psychologists and traditional criminologists has grown, creating a group of scholars steadily producing a range of blueprints for saving wayward youngsters.

Second, around the same time—by the year 2000 in corrections—a broad movement emerged in medicine, education, and other human service fields to make sure that interventions were "evidence based." Even baseball was not immune to this development as highlighted in Michael Lewis's *Moneyball*. This best-selling book (and later movie) chronicled how the renegade general manager of the low-budget Oakland Athletics, Billy Beane, used sabermetrics to outfox opponents and build a winning team. Today, it is hard to imagine what else other than evidence would be employed to justify an intervention. But informed by ideology and so-called common sense, the field of corrections is littered with programs that were formulated in a post-factual world (e.g., boot camps, scared straight).

The evidence-based approach was consequential because it led to two lines of inquiry regarding "what works" in interventions with kids and adults. The first approach, exemplified by the rigorous research of Mark Lipsey, was to meta-analyze hundreds of evaluation studies. This assessment demonstrated convincingly that human service programs with a caring orientation reduced problem behavior whereas punitive or deterrence-based programs did not. The second approach, exemplified by the contributions of the Canadian psychologists Don Andrews, James Bonta, and Paul Gendreau (among others), developed a theory of rehabilitation called the "risk-need-responsivity" (RNR) model. This approach was rooted in known predictors of recidivism and vetted empirically. Although it should not be sanctified, it has served as a powerful method for reducing recidivism and now dominates the field of correctional treatment.

All this is to say that those interested in intervening with offenders, whether younger or older, are now better equipped to do so. The knowledge gap is closed. We now have a substantial amount of evidence-based wisdom about how to care effectively. But another daunting gap exists: How to reach the many at-risk youngsters who need services that are caring and evidence based? That is, taking knowledge to scale is the challenge—not youth by youth or agency by agency but rather community by community.

It is within this context that Communities That Care is best understood. Lawrence Sherman has reminded us that criminology was developed as "a new way to reduce human suffering." Doing so, he observes, involves trumpeting criminology as a field not only of basic science but also of invention. In this regard, Communities That Care should be seen as a criminological invention that holds inordinate promise for reducing human suffering, both of troubled youths and of their potential victims. It is innovative precisely because it seeks to take extant knowledge and boldly address problems on a community-wide basis. It is thoroughly evidence based and expansive in its impact.

As Paula Smith and I observed previously, virtually all effective interventions have three core components: criminological, correctional, and technical. Not surprisingly, this trinity of components is found at the center of Communities That Care. First, the criminological component refers to the quality of the crime causation model that underlines the intervention. If the criminology component is limited or downright faulty, then the intervention will target the wrong risk factors for change and protective factors for enhancement. Notably, Communities That Care has a strong criminological component. It is rooted in J. David Hawkins, Richard F. Catalano, and colleagues' Social Development Model. This perspective is theoretically sophisticated and empirically substantiated. Most important, this theory serves as an umbrella for identifying and incorporating into the intervention the known predictors of problem behavior among youths.

Second, the correctional component is, in essence, the "medicine" that is delivered to fix the problems at hand. In correctional terms, the intervention must be "responsive" to or capable of changing the sources of the negative outcomes. One reason why deterrence-oriented programs are ineffective is because threatened or applied punishment does not, for example, cure family conflict or enable failing students to bond with their school. By contrast, Communities That Care starts by assessing what is leading to youth problems in a specific community. The community then selects the evidence-based programs that are best suited to diminishing risk factors or building protective factors in the local environment. In short, the effective treatments are matched to the sources of the problems that have been diagnosed.

Third, the technological component includes the instruments, surveys, training manuals, and procedures that are used to implement an intervention. The inventors of Communities That Care have been masterful in developing the tool kit that any community needs to carry out a community-wide strategy. As my mother used to say about something that was complete, the Communities That Care technical component goes from "soup to nuts!"

Let me end by drawing on insights from Steven Pinker, one of my favorite public intellectuals. In his 2011 *Better Angels of Our Nature*, he dismantled the notion that humans are driven strictly by selfishness and self-interest and argued that, building on our cooperative and kinder side, humans were becoming less violent and inhumane. In his 2018 *Enlightenment Now*, he extends these insights and cautions against doomsday thinking and asserts that progress is more possible than ever. Pinker advocates the Enlightenment as the best means for societal advancement—defining the "Enlightenment principle" as the application of "reason and sympathy to enhance human flourishing."

Communities That Care is remarkable precisely because it is informed by Pinker's Enlightenment principle. Foremost, its inventors embraced the view that troubled youths—often the most at risk and most difficult among us—have value. Ted Palmer, who I admire for all he has contributed to the cause of offender reform, put it this way to me: "People can change. Offenders are people." The point is that interventions have an impact when they are rooted in an ethic of caring. When caring is writ large at the community level, much good can be accomplished. But caring is not enough; it is how we care that matters. Reason must trump custom and ideology, and scientific evidence needs to inform policy and practice. Again, the genius of Communities That Care is that it brooks no compromise between heart and mind, between caring and science. It shows what is possible when reformers who care deeply about kids also are first-rate scholars with an abiding commitment to empirically validated truth. The pages that follow in this book chronicle the amazing story of their criminological invention. I have had the privilege of embarking on an excursion across these chapters. It is a trip well worth taking.

Francis T. Cullen
University of Cincinnati

Communities That Care

Overview of the Communities That Care System

Theoretical Basis, Development, Evaluation, and Comparison to Other Community-Based Preventive Interventions

I

Community-Based Prevention of Youth Behavioral Health Problems

The Prevalence and Consequences of Youth Behavioral Health Problems

Youth behavior problems are a serious public concern affecting large numbers of young people and resulting in many negative consequences for individuals and for society as a whole. Yet, as we describe in this book, these behaviors can be prevented, and the harms they produce can be minimized when communities take proactive and strategic actions to address the underlying causes of the behavior problems. Although community-based solutions to public concerns have been advocated for many decades, only recently have rigorous evaluations shown that community-based prevention efforts can be successful in producing community-wide reductions in what we refer to in this book as youth *behavioral health problems.*

Behavioral health problems are behaviors that compromise young people's mental, emotional, and/or physical well-being [1]. They include anxiety, depression, delinquency, violence, substance use, risky sexual behaviors, and school drop-out. The list is broad because research has indicated that these behavioral health problems often co-occur and that they share many antecedents [2–4]. In addition, the pattern of involvement in these behaviors tends to be similar, with an onset in early to mid-adolescence and a peak in prevalence during adolescence and early adulthood [5–7].

Although many of these behaviors have declined in prevalence in the past two decades [3, 8–10], young people continue to be disproportionately involved in health-compromising behaviors. A large-scale U.S. survey of 13- to 18-year-olds reported that 50% met criteria for experiencing any depressive, anxiety, behavioral, or substance use disorder, and 22% had experienced a severe disorder in their lifetimes [6]. Substance use and delinquency are also common during adolescence. In the United States, 22% to 33% of high school students report past-month use of tobacco, alcohol, and marijuana [11], and lifetime substance use is even higher, with 44% of 12th-grade students reporting lifetime use of marijuana and 66% reporting alcohol use [10]. The World Health Organization [12] reports that 11.7% of youth aged 15 to 19 years engage in heavy episodic drinking (i.e., consuming 4 to 5 drinks in a 2-hour period) and that these rates exceed those of adults. Worldwide estimates of substance use disorders and dependency among adolescents range from 6% to 16% [2].

Studies asking youth to report on their involvement in illegal behaviors indicate that a majority of teenagers engage in some form of delinquency during adolescence and that a significant proportion engage in violence [13–15]. For example, according to self-reports from males participating in the Pittsburgh Youth Study, about 75% had committed a minor theft by age 19, 50% had engaged in more serious theft, and 33% had engaged in moderately serious forms of violence [16]. A longitudinal study of youth from 24 communities in seven states indicated that by grade 12, 59% to 67% of participants had engaged in at least one delinquent or violent act (e.g., stealing, damaging property, beating someone up) [17]. In addition, of the high school students participating in the 2015 Youth Risk Behavioral Surveillance System, 23% reported being in a physical fight in the year preceding the survey, and 16% had carried a weapon in the past month [11].

Research also demonstrates that youth behavioral health problems vary considerably across communities [18–21], which supports the need for community-based prevention. For example, data from the 2016 Florida Youth Substance Abuse Survey indicate substantial variation in cigarette, alcohol, and marijuana use across Florida counties (see: www.myflfamilies.com/ service-programs/substance-abuse/fysas/2016). In 2016, the percentage of middle school students who reported past-month binge drinking ranged from a low of 1.6% to a high of 7.6% across counties, while the percentages ranged from 3.5% to 17% for any past-month alcohol use. Similarly, in a study of eighth-grade students living in 11 U.S. cities, the proportion of youth who reported committing one or more serious violent acts (e.g., aggravated assault, robbery, gang fights, and shootings) ranged from 13% to 38% across these communities [22].

Data on the prevalence of behavioral health problems provides some motivation for communities to take preventative action, but even more persuasive is the evidence showing that youth behavioral problems contribute to adolescent morbidity (i.e., non-fatal health problems) and mortality [23–25].

Internationally, violence is the fifth leading cause of morbidity and mortality among 15- to 24-year-olds when measured using disability-adjusted life-years (DALYs) [25]. In addition, drinking during adolescence can impair brain development and brain functioning, increase the risk of unprotected sex and sexually transmitted diseases, and lead to risky driving and motor vehicle accidents, including fatal crashes [26].

If they are not prevented, adolescent behavioral health problems also increase the likelihood of adult health problems and morbidity [2, 5, 7]. Data from the World Health Organization's Global Burden of Disease study indicate that depression and violence experienced during ages 10 to 24 are among the most important factors contributing to premature death and disability later in life [25]. Other research indicates that most adult mental health and substance use disorders have their onset during adolescence, and that the early initiation of behavioral health problems increases the likelihood of disorders in later years [5, 7, 27]. This pattern extends to criminal behavior as well [28, 29]. For example, data from the Pittsburgh Youth Study indicated that, of those whose onset of delinquency occurred during ages 10 to 12, 71% became persistent offenders compared to 32% of those whose onset was during ages 13 to 15 [16]. Data from this study also showed that early diagnoses of disruptive behavior, delinquency, and drug use predicted later perpetration of homicide [30], arguably the outcome of greatest concern to the public.

Youth behavioral health problems also have significant financial costs to society, especially because they can lead to persistent behavioral problems across the life course. Taking into account both the tangible costs incurred by crime victims (e.g., costs related to medical care, lost earnings, property damage/loss, etc.) and of operating the criminal justice system, as well as intangible costs such as the pain and suffering of crime victims, Kathryn McCollister and colleagues [31] estimate that a single property crime costs the United States $5,000 to $10,000. A single violent crime like robbery costs $100,000, while an assault costs about $240,000. Excessive alcohol use cost the United States $249 billion in 2010, with underaged drinking contributing $24.3 billion to this figure [32]. The majority of costs are related to lost productivity, but they also include costs related to the health care and criminal justice systems. In addition, the National Drug Intelligence Center estimated that misuse of illegal drugs and nonprescribed medications cost the United States $193 billion in 2007 [33]. In regard to mental health problems, Thomas Insel [34] estimated that such disorders cost the United States $317 billion in 2002. About two thirds of these costs were related to loss of earnings and one third to health-care costs.

Can anything be done to prevent these human and financial costs to society? Yes! Evidence from prevention science, a multidisciplinary field dedicated to preventing major health disorders, has demonstrated that *it is possible to prevent youth behavioral health problems and to promote healthy youth development* [1, 23, 35, 36]. In the last few decades, a growing number of programs, policies, and practices have been created, tested, and shown to be effective in reducing behavioral health problems including conduct disorder, delinquency, violence, risky sexual behaviors, teen pregnancy, substance use, anxiety, and depression [2, 7]. This is very good news and contradicts the often prevailing public opinion that such problems are inevitable and that nothing can be done to stop adolescents from engaging in risky behaviors.

However, it is also true that most current efforts to prevent behavioral health problems do not involve the use of evidence-based interventions (EBIs), defined in this book as programs, practices, and policies that have been subject to rigorous scientific evaluations and shown to reduce behavioral health problems. Instead, public agencies most often implement prevention strategies that have not been well evaluated, and in some cases, that have demonstrated harmful effects for their participants [37–39]. For example, the Drug Abuse Resistance Education (D.A.R.E.) program is one of the most widely used substance-use prevention curricula in public middle schools [40, 41], but evaluations of several versions of the program have failed to find positive effects in reducing adolescent substance use among students receiving the curriculum compared to those not exposed to the program [42, 43]. As noted by the Institute of Medicine [1], the Centers for Disease Control and Prevention [44], and the World Health Organization [8], the lack of dissemination of EBIs is a major barrier to improving public health.

Although increasing the use of EBIs is a formidable challenge, there is growing consensus that the solution to this problem is to improve community-based prevention systems [45]. To significantly reduce behavioral health problems requires building the infrastructure and capacity of local agencies, organizations, and systems to: (1) understand, assess, and prioritize for preventive intervention the predictors of youth behavioral problems, called risk and protective factors; (2) decide to use EBIs to reduce prioritized risk factors and strengthen prioritized protective factors; and (3) deliver these EBIs at scale and with adherence to their requirements [1, 2, 23]. Community-based prevention is expected to not only increase the use of EBIs but also foster stakeholder support for prevention and ensure that interventions are a good fit to the local context [46]. Together, these conditions should produce significant and sustained impacts on youth behavioral health problems [47, 48].

Overview of This Book

The goal of this book is to advance understanding of how to effectively engage in community-based prevention. We do so by describing the steps that communities can take to prevent youth behavioral problems and provide examples of many different community-based systems that have been developed and implemented by communities. We also describe in detail one specific community-based prevention system, Communities That Care (CTC), developed by Drs. David Hawkins and Richard Catalano when they were professors at the University of Washington. CTC is a comprehensive community-based system that assists community members to: (1) form broad-based and diverse coalitions whose goal is to prevent youth behavioral health problems; (2) understand, collect, and analyze local data on the risk and protective factors that research has shown contribute to these problems; and (3) implement with integrity a set of EBIs to target the most elevated risk factors and most depressed protective factors experienced by local youth [49]. As we describe in this chapter (and in chapter 8), a multisite randomized controlled trial has shown that communities that have used CTC, compared to similar communities not using this prevention system, are better able to delay the initiation and reduce the prevalence of substance use, delinquency, and violence among their local youth.[1]

In the remainder of this chapter, we provide an overview of the CTC system, including its foundation in prevention science, its implementation requirements, and its impact on community systems and youth behavioral health problems. We also discuss how CTC compares to other community-based interventions. In chapter 2, we describe how CTC, like other EBIs, was created based on theoretical perspectives regarding the development of youth behavioral health problems. We also discuss the importance of community-based participatory research and highlight the ways in which CTC has been developed and evaluated using this perspective. In chapter 3, we identify the types of research methods that can be used to evaluate community-based prevention systems and other types of EBIs. We then discuss how CTC has been developed and evaluated over the past few decades, from its early pilot studies to more recent and rigorous attempts to evaluate its effectiveness and potential for widespread dissemination.

In section two (chapters 4–7) of this book, we describe the five main components that should be included in community-based prevention efforts and that constitute the foundation of the CTC system. In the CTC system, these are referred to as the *five phases of CTC*, and they include: assessing readiness for prevention; building and sustaining broad-based coalitions;

conducting needs and resource assessments; identifying and selecting EBIs to address local needs; and monitoring EBI implementation. Each chapter provides a general overview of these concepts, illustrates how CTC builds community capacity to complete these prevention tasks, and summarizes the challenges and successes likely to be encountered when communities perform these activities.

In section three, we describe the research design and outcomes found in a randomized controlled trial examining the effectiveness of CTC in 24 U.S. communities (chapter 8), and in a quasi-experimental evaluation involving communities across the state of Pennsylvania (chapter 9). In section four (chapter 10), we summarize the lessons learned from CTC and other community-based prevention approaches about how to effectively prevent youth behavioral health problems. We also offer recommendations to help increase the use of community-based prevention systems in the United States and across the world.

We anticipate that this book will be of interest to scholars, policymakers, and practitioners who are engaged in or planning to undertake community-based prevention and community-based participatory research. To that end, we strive to provide content and insights that will appeal to all these audiences. We offer academics a model of prevention program development and describe how they can successfully partner with communities to develop, refine, and evaluate community-based interventions using community-based participatory research. We highlight the challenges of conducting community-based participatory research, as well as the resources that are gained when community members lend their insight, expertise, and passion to the research enterprise. In addition, we aim to provide enough information about CTC and its various components to assist practitioners and policymakers in planning, implementing, and/or sustaining community-based prevention efforts.

A *Public Health and Prevention Science Approach to Addressing Youth Behavioral Health Problems*

The fact that youth behaviors can significantly impair health during adolescence and adulthood supports the use of a public health approach to prevent these behaviors, similar to preventing health problems like cancer and heart disease. The public health perspective emphasizes the benefits of preventing a disease or disorder *before* it manifests [36, 50]. To do so requires, first, identification of the predictors, often called risk and protective factors, that are related longitudinally to increases or decreases in the likelihood of the problem [51]. This understanding of risk and protection means that actions can be taken before problems occur to minimize exposure to risk factors, reduce their impact, and increase exposure to and the influence of protective factors [36]. For example, medical research indicates that heart disease is related to an individual's diet and lifestyle. To prevent heart disease, individuals should reduce their intake of fats and salts (i.e., risk factors) and regularly exercise (i.e., a protective factor). The newly developed field of *prevention science* seeks to extend the public health perspective to the prevention of behavioral health problems. Like those working to prevent physical disease, prevention scientists emphasize the importance of understanding the risk and protective factors shown in scientific studies to influence later behavioral health problems, then advocate for the development, evaluation, and implementation of preventive interventions that reduce risk factors and enhance protective factors [36, 52].

Risk factors increase the likelihood of behavioral health problems. Although exposure to a risk factor does not guarantee that one will develop such problems, the chance of such outcomes increases as the number of risk factors experienced by an individual increases [53]. Table 1.1 provides a list of risk factors that have been shown in empirical studies (as indicated by the check mark at the intersection of a row and column) to be related to a behavioral health problem. These include characteristics of communities, families, schools, peer groups, and individuals. Examples of specific risk factors that increase the likelihood of multiple behavioral health problems include residence in low-income communities, family management problems like having parents who fail to effectively monitor and discipline their children, academic failure, peers who engage in crime, and personal attitudes favorable to violence or substance use [51, 53–55].

Protective factors are conceptually distinct from, and not simply the absence or opposite of, risk factors [51, 56]. They are often referred to as promotive factors [57] if they directly reduce the likelihood of behavioral health problems, and as protective factors [58] if they moderate the impact of risk factors on problems [see also 59]. Evidence demonstrates that a specific factor may have both promotive and/or protective functions. For the sake of simplicity, we refer to both promotive and protective factors as *protective factors* in this book. As shown in Table 1.2 (and indicated by check marks), research has identified cognitive, emotional, and social competence; belief in the future; self-determinism; pro-social norms; and spirituality as individual protective factors [60–64]. Social and environmental protective factors include having opportunities for positive social involvement, receiving recognition

Table 1.1 Risk Factors Associated With Youth Behavioral Health Problems

Risk Factor	Youth Behavioral Health Problems					
	Substance Abuse	Delinquency	Teen Pregnancy	School Drop-Out	Violence	Depression
Community						
Availability of drugs	✓	✓			✓	
Availability of firearms		✓			✓	
Community laws and norms favorable toward drug use, firearms, and crime	✓	✓			✓	
Media portrayals of violence					✓	
Transitions and mobility	✓	✓		✓		✓
Low neighborhood attachment and community disorganization	✓	✓			✓	
Extreme economic deprivation	✓	✓	✓	✓	✓	
Family						
Family history of the problem behavior	✓	✓	✓	✓	✓	✓
Family management problems	✓	✓	✓	✓	✓	✓
Family conflict	✓	✓	✓	✓	✓	✓
Favorable parental attitudes and involvement in the problem behavior	✓	✓			✓	

School

Risk Factors					
Academic failure beginning in late elementary school	✓	✓	✓	✓	✓
Lack of commitment to school	✓	✓	✓	✓	
Peer and Individual					
Friends who engage in the problem behavior	✓	✓	✓	✓	
Gang involvement	✓	✓		✓	
Early and persistent antisocial behavior	✓	✓	✓	✓	✓
Rebelliousness	✓	✓	✓	✓	
Favorable attitudes toward the problem behavior	✓	✓	✓		
Early initiation of the problem behavior	✓	✓	✓	✓	
Constitutional factors	✓	✓		✓	✓

Table 1.2 Protective Factors Associated With Youth Behavioral Health Problems

Protective Factor	Youth Behavioral Health Problems					
	Substance Abuse	Delinquency	Risky Sexual Behavior	School Drop-Out	Violence	Depression
Cognitive competence	✓	✓	✓	✓	✓	✓
Emotional competence		✓			✓	✓
Social and behavioral competence	✓	✓	✓		✓	
Self-efficacy			✓			
Belief in the future	✓	✓	✓		✓	✓
Self-determinism			✓			
Pro-social norms	✓	✓	✓		✓	✓
Spirituality	✓	✓				
Opportunities for positive social involvement	✓	✓				
Recognition for positive behavior	✓	✓	✓		✓	✓
Bonding to pro-social others	✓	✓		✓	✓	✓
Healthy and clear standards for behavior	✓	✓	✓	✓	✓	✓

for positive behaviors, bonding to pro-social individuals and institutions, and espousing healthy and clear standards for behavior [60, 65].

Following the public health model, prevention science stipulates that the most effective way to reduce behavioral health problems is by implementing EBIs that reduce risk factors and/or increase protective factors [36, 52]. Interventions that simultaneously target multiple risk and protective factors have the greatest potential for success, given that the more risk factors an individual experiences, the greater his or her likelihood of behavioral health problems, while the more protective factors experienced, the smaller the likelihood of these outcomes [53, 66]. As shown in Tables 1.1 and 1.2, it is also true that risk and protective factors predict multiple types of behavioral health problems, such as substance use, delinquency, teen pregnancy, school dropout, violence, and mental health problems [51, 67]. This overlap means that EBIs that change risk and protective factors can have beneficial effects across multiple problems [36, 68, 69].

Research indicates that different risk and protective factors emerge and/or become salient at different stages of life [28, 65, 70, 71]. For example, during early childhood, family factors such as poor family management and bonding to caregivers may be most important, whereas school and peer experiences become more influential during adolescence. This developmental sequencing of risk and protection means that, to be effective, interventions must address the risk and protective factors that are most salient for the participants' developmental stage [36]. That is, an intervention seeking to reduce the influence of delinquent peers should be delivered to teenagers because they are the age group most likely to be exposed to and negatively affected by delinquent peers.

During the past few decades, many interventions have been tested, evaluated, and shown to be effective in reducing youth behavioral health problems by reducing risk factors and enhancing protective factors [2, 7, 23, 29, 72, 73]. These EBIs take many forms. They can be programs and practices delivered to individuals across the life course, from the prenatal period through early adulthood and/or to groups of youth, parents, teachers, schools, and communities. They can also be policies that influence an entire developmental age, such as monitoring teenagers' access to contraceptives without parental permission [74] and raising the minimum legal drinking age [75].

The U.S. Institute of Medicine classifies EBIs as universal, selective, and indicated according to their targeted population [2, 76]. *Universal* EBIs are intended for the general public—that is, for all the individuals in a particular setting, such as all students in a middle school or all parents in a community. *Selective* EBIs are intended for individuals, groups, or areas considered to be at elevated risk for behavioral health problems because they have been exposed to one or more risk factors and/or because they have low levels of protection. Examples of selective interventions include early childhood programs targeting families living in low-income neighborhoods and tutoring programs for students with poor grades. *Indicated* interventions are offered to individuals who are already displaying some problem behaviors, but who do not have a diagnosed disorder and are engaging in these behaviors at relatively low levels. For example, some indicated EBIs seek to improve parenting skills and increase attachment to parents for young children displaying conduct disorder.

Community-Based Prevention

EBIs may address individual, peer, school, family, or community risk and protective factors, but currently, relative few effective interventions target community risk and protective factors [77–79]. In this book, we define community-based preventive interventions as those that take place in the community and that are intended to alter community levels of risk and protective factors in order to promote healthy youth development and prevent behavioral health problems community wide. These types of interventions differ from services that take place in the community but that seek to change more proximal risk and protective factors, such as youth mentoring programs that are designed to increase youth bonds to pro-social individuals. Instead, community-based prevention efforts seek to change features of the community that contribute to behavioral health problems. These characteristics may include, for example, structural problems like community socioeconomic disadvantage and social processes like residents' shared norms and expectations for behavior and collective efficacy, or the degree to which residents trust each other and are willing to take informal actions to reduce problems [80, 81]. Examples of community-based prevention efforts include making changes to local laws and policies related to behavioral health problems (e.g., limiting sales of alcohol to minors), promoting anti-drug and/or anti-violence norms among community members, and improving trust and cohesion between community residents.[2]

Because they are trying to alter community conditions and affect a large proportion of the population, community-based interventions should be undertaken at the community level and reach as many individuals and/or organizations as possible. These interventions are often undertaken by coalitions or groups of local stakeholders from diverse organizations and backgrounds who are committed to achieving a common goal [82], such as reducing youth behavioral health problems. The use of coalitions to prevent behavioral health

problems has several advantages. First, reliance on members of the local community to plan, implement, and monitor prevention activities should enhance
residents' investment in and support for prevention, which in turn should
improve the quality of implementation and sustainability of services [83, 84].
Second, community-led approaches should help ensure that actions are feasible to implement and are responsive to the needs, resources, and norms of
the community [49, 85]. Third, if coalitions include numerous stakeholders
representing all important sectors of the community, they should be better
able to offer multiple, coordinated services that address multiple risk and protective factors and reach a significant proportion of the eligible population
[47, 86]. This comprehensive approach should enhance the ability to produce
a significant collective impact [48] on behavioral health problems.

The advantages of community-based prevention have led to the development of several community- and coalition-based prevention models, as we
describe in this section. Not all these interventions have been rigorously evaluated, however, and not all have demonstrated effects on intended outcomes
[77, 87]. The lack of evaluation is probably related to the methodological
challenges associated with this type of approach, such as recruiting a sufficient
number of communities to participate in an evaluation [88] and collecting reliable and valid data on community-level processes, which are not easy to observe, quantify, or operationalize [81, 83, 89].

The failure of community-based prevention strategies to produce effects
could be due to challenges ensuring full implementation of these models. For
example, community-based prevention often relies on volunteers whose participation can be difficult to elicit and maintain. In addition, these stakeholders
are likely to vary in their backgrounds, skills, and views about prevention,
which can impede collaboration efforts [83, 90–93]. Efforts may also fail because they do not provide community stakeholders with enough guidance and
support to help them effectively prevent behavioral problems [94].

As an example of the last problem, consider the Chicago Area Project, one
of the first coalition efforts to target the prevention of youth crime. This initiative involved the creation of coalitions in impoverished and socially disorganized neighborhoods in Chicago. The use of community members to
prevent crime, a novel idea at the time, was based on the assumption that
community members would be better able than "outsiders" to reduce youth
crime and foster healthy youth development because they were more familiar
with neighborhood problems and resources. Coalitions were completely
empowered to identify and solve the problems they considered to be most related to crime; they received no instructions or support for their efforts from
the scientists who developed the initiative. An evaluation indicated that these

neighborhoods did not experience reductions in youth crime following implementation of the intervention [95, 96].

Two subsequent and larger scale coalition projects intended to prevent youth substance use also failed to achieve their goals. Evaluations of the Fighting Back [94] and Community Partnership [97] initiatives indicated that rates of youth substance use were not significantly reduced in communities using these coalition-based prevention systems, compared to communities not using these systems. The evaluations further indicated that the coalitions involved in these projects, like those in the Chicago Area Project, had insufficient knowledge of how to enact effective prevention strategies. They received very little guidance from project staff about interventions that had been tested and shown to be effective in reducing youth substance use. Without this information, the coalitions varied in the nature and amount of prevention services provided, and they largely relied on locally created prevention strategies that had not been previously evaluated and shown to be effective [98].

These evaluations and other prevention research indicate that community members are unlikely to have access to knowledge regarding the risk and protective factors that predict youth behavioral health problems and that they are not generally aware that EBIs exist to address risk and protective factors [86, 99]. As a result, communities often implement strategies that are easy or popular, such as one-time events meant to generate awareness and/or fear that a problem exists. However, these interventions may not target risk or protective factors, and they may lack evidence of effectiveness from well-conducted evaluations. To achieve desired reductions in behavioral health problems, community coalitions need to know what works to prevent these outcomes and be supported in their efforts to enact such strategies [77, 93].

Neighborhood Watch groups are another type of community-based prevention approach that rely on community members to work together to address crime. Common activities of such groups include regular meetings of neighborhood residents to discuss local crime problems, communication between residents and law enforcement officers, and citizen patrols of neighborhoods to prevent crime [100]. Neighborhood Watch groups have shown some effects in reducing crime. A meta-analysis of results from 18 evaluations of these programs indicated that, on average, crime was reduced by 16% to 26% in areas with Neighborhood Watch programs compared to neighborhoods without such interventions [101]. Although these findings suggest that Neighborhood Watch programs are effective, all the evaluations included in the meta-analysis were quasi-experimental; none randomly assigned communities or neighborhoods to implement the strategy or not; and in most cases, the intervention and comparison sites were not wholly equivalent at the start of the study [101]. As discussed in chapter 3, randomized controlled trials are preferable to other types of evaluation designs because they help ensure that intervention and control communities are equivalent at baseline, which increases confidence that effects are due to the intervention rather than to a preexisting difference or some other factor. Other reviews have suggested that Neighborhood Watch programs are difficult to implement, particularly in regard to eliciting participation by community members and sustaining these groups over time [100, 102].

The "pulling levers" crime prevention strategy relies more heavily on criminal justice agents to prevent crime, but it also includes citizen participation. First developed and tested in Boston, Massachusetts, to reduce youth homicides perpetrated by gang members, the primary change strategy is for police to communicate to potential offenders that they will "pull all available legal levers" to prevent these crimes. To do so, police increase their surveillance of gang members, make more arrests, and work with local prosecutors to increase the certainty and severity of legal punishments for offenders [103]. This practice also seeks to change community norms regarding the acceptability of violence. Community members participate in the police/offender meetings to help reinforce messages that violence will not be tolerated. They also provide information about social services available in the community to individuals considered at risk of committing violent crimes [104]. Sometimes, former gang members facilitate meetings with gang members to discourage gun violence [105, 106].

A quasi-experimental evaluation of the first "pulling levers" program in Boston showed reductions in youth homicides, gun crimes [104], and gang-related shootings [107]. Based on these positive findings, other cities implemented similar initiatives. A meta-analysis of findings from 10 evaluations of these programs indicated a fairly large reduction in crime rates, with an average effect size (Cohen's *d*) of 0.60 [103]. However, none of the studies included in the meta-analysis employed randomized experimental methods to evaluate effectiveness, which again means that the effects could be attributed to factors other than the "pulling levers" intervention [108]. It is also true that not all the studies showed significant crime reductions, which some evaluators attributed to implementation difficulties such as a lack of coordination between key stakeholders and failure to enact all of the required intervention activities [e.g., 106].

The "pulling levers" and Neighborhood Watch programs are considered to be community prevention strategies because they target for change community-level risk and protective factors such as community norms and collective efficacy. However, since youth behavioral health problems have many potential causes, preventive interventions may be even more effective in reducing these problems if they address multiple risk and protective factors in multiple contexts. Evaluations of some coalition-led interventions that target a variety of risk and protective factors using EBIs indicate that this approach has the potential to reduce youth behavioral problems [77]. For example, Project Northland and the Midwestern Prevention Project both involve the implementation of multi-year school-based alcohol- and drug-use prevention curricula to alter individual, family, and peer factors. They also include coalition-led activities designed to change community laws and practices related to substance use, such as increasing enforcement of underage drinking laws, increasing local taxes on alcohol, and creating drug-free zones and/or alcohol-free community events. Both these interventions have been evaluated using randomized controlled trials and both have been found to reduce adolescent substance use [109–111].

In contrast to these types of approaches, some coalitions focus solely on enacting changes to community laws or policies, without the additional implementation of EBIs for youth and families [77]. Policies are important prevention strategies, and there is evidence that policy changes that reduce the local availability of alcohol (e.g., increasing taxes on liquor, limiting alcohol sales, etc.) are effective in decreasing alcohol use and related problems such as driving while intoxicated and alcohol-related motor vehicle accidents [112; also see the Centers for Disease Control and Prevention's Community Guide at www.thecommunityguide.org/alcohol]. However, these effects have typically been found only among adults. Studies have either failed to demonstrate significant reductions in youth substance use [77] or have not examined outcomes for this population [7].

The Communities That Care Prevention System

The Communities That Care (CTC) prevention system was designed to build on the strengths of community-based, coalition-led interventions; avoid their implementation challenges; and target for change both community and individual, peer, family, and school risk and protective factors. CTC emphasizes the use of EBIs to address locally identified needs and provides coalitions with extensive training and technical assistance to assist with their implementation efforts. CTC also ensures local ownership of prevention efforts by empowering community members to collectively identify areas of concern; select interventions that they consider to be a good fit for their needs, resources, and populations; and provide opportunities for youth to be positively bonded to their communities.

CTC seeks to minimize implementation problems by providing a structured, step-by-step approach to community-based prevention that involves five phases, as shown in Figure 1.1.

In Phase 1 (*Get Started*), communities assess their readiness and support to undertake a collaborative approach to reducing behavioral health problems.

In Phase 2 (*Get Organized*), communities identify key leaders who will support CTC, hire a full-time paid coordinator, and begin to form a diverse coalition of community members who represent all the key organizations and stakeholders concerned about healthy youth development. All these individuals become familiar with prevention science and learn about risk and protective factors, the existence of EBIs to address these factors, and the five phases of CTC.

In Phase 3 (*Develop a Profile*), coalition members learn how to conduct needs and resource assessments. The needs assessment is based on data from the Communities That Care Youth Survey [113], a school-based survey in which students anonymously report their exposure to risk and protective factors, as well as their behavioral health problems. CTC community coalitions learn how to administer the survey and interpret its results. Using this information and data from archival sources (e.g., police or school records), they identify and prioritize for prevention action the risk factors that are elevated and the protective factors that are depressed in the community. The resource assessment involves surveying local service providers to identify the interventions currently in place in the community to address risk and protection.

In Phase 4 (*Create a Plan*), coalitions learn about the Blueprints for Healthy Youth Development website (www.blueprintsprograms.com/), an evidence-based registry that provides information on EBIs that have been shown in well-conducted research trials to alter risk and protective factors and reduce behavioral health problems. Coalitions select EBIs from this website that will

FIGURE 1.1 The Five Phases of the Communities That Care Prevention System

change the particular risk and protective factors prioritized in their communities and fill gaps in their resources.

In Phase 5 (*Implement and Evaluate*), local service providers implement EBIs and, with assistance from CTC coalitions, they monitor implementation processes to ensure that EBIs are implemented as intended and at a scale sufficient to produce community-wide reductions in behavioral health problems.

Recognizing that many community members will not have preexisting knowledge or skills to implement these phases, CTC includes multiple, interactive training workshops to allow community members to learn about, discuss, and practice methods to fully implement the system. All the goals to be achieved (called *milestones*) during each phase of CTC, and the actions that should be taken to achieve these goals (called *benchmarks*), are outlined for coalitions in written materials and reviewed during the trainings.[3] Coalitions also receive ongoing technical assistance in how to achieve these milestones and benchmarks during regularly scheduled telephone calls and in-person visits from CTC coaches who are well versed in CTC implementation processes. The five phases typically require 12 to 18 months to complete, but timelines can be adjusted according to community needs.

CTC does not mandate that coalitions choose particular EBIs or sets of interventions to implement. Rather, coalitions select EBIs that match their particular needs—that is, the risk factors that are elevated and the protective factors that are depressed in their communities. Ideally, communities using the CTC system will provide EBIs that reach youth of all ages, beginning in the prenatal and early childhood periods and continuing through high school and early adulthood. This approach helps ensure delivery of a continuum of prevention services, in which each EBI is directed at a particular age group/ developmental period, and the risk and protective factors targeted by the intervention match those identified in the needs assessment as elevated or depressed in that particular age group [115]. Coalitions may also select EBIs that are delivered to families, schools, and/or at the community level.

It is expected that the prioritized risk and protective factors, and the EBIs implemented to address these needs, will vary across communities [49]. How these services are delivered will also differ. Based on their knowledge of their community, coalition members make joint decisions regarding the number and types of populations to be targeted for services and the agencies and organizations responsible for service delivery. This flexibility is expected to increase local support for the EBIs and increase the probability that interventions will be well implemented and sustained over time. Recognizing that communities may face challenges implementing new EBIs, CTC also provides training and technical assistance to help coalitions and local agencies develop ways to routinely monitor implementation delivery and provide feedback to implementers to ensure high-quality implementation.

Throughout CTC implementation, coalitions encourage all adults in the community to create a supportive environment for youth. As we will describe in chapter 2, adults are encouraged to employ the Social Development Strategy [65] when interacting with youth so as to strengthen young people's attachment to the community. To do so, adults provide youth with increased opportunities to be positively involved in the community, help them learn the skills needed to take advantage of these opportunities, and recognize their achievements. For example, coalition members may invite youth to participate in the CTC coalition and related training workshops, where they can learn about prevention science and how to prevent youth behavioral problems. Or, business owners can provide young people with paid or volunteer opportunities so they can contribute to the community. If these opportunities are developmentally appropriate and provide adequate preparation, skills training, and positive reinforcement, then bonds between youth and their communities should be strengthened. When youth have greater attachment to their communities, they will be more likely to comply with the norms and standards espoused by adults living in those areas, which should emphasize pro-social behaviors.

By following all these guidelines, communities should be better able to prevent youth behavioral health problems, as depicted in the CTC logic model shown in Figure 1.2. Coalitions that receive coaching and support to implement all five phases of CTC should be better equipped to adopt a science-based approach to prevention, engage in collaborative prevention efforts, support the use of prevention strategies, promote norms that discourage behavioral health problems, and increase the use of the Social Development Strategy during adult–youth interactions. These community-level changes should lead, in turn, to increased use of EBIs that target local risk and protective factors. When EBIs are well implemented, the community should achieve reductions in risk factors, increases in protective factors, and decreases in youth behavioral health problems.

The Effectiveness of Communities That Care

We describe the effectiveness of CTC in more detail in sections two and three, but we summarize here the effects on behavioral health problems found in the Community Youth Development Study, the most rigorous evaluation of the CTC system to date. The timeline of this randomized controlled trial is shown

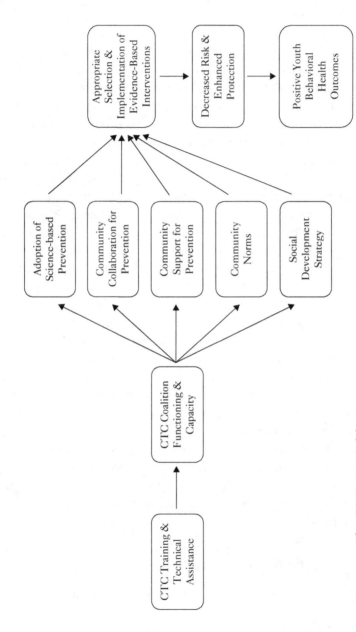

FIGURE 1.2 The CTC Logic Model

in Figure 1.3. In 2002, 24 small- to medium-sized cities in seven U.S. states matched in pairs within each state on size, poverty, diversity, and crime indices were randomly assigned to implement CTC ($n = 12$) or to serve as control communities ($n = 12$) in which prevention services were conducted as usual [116]. During the five-year implementation phase of the study, from 2003 to 2008, CTC communities received trainings and technical assistance to implement CTC and funding to employ a full-time coalition coordinator. They also received funding to implement EBIs from 2004 to 2008 [117]. The sustainability phase of the trial began in 2009. During this period, CTC communities received no trainings or technical assistance and no financial resources to support their coalitions or EBIs.

The degree to which use of the CTC system led to reductions in youth behavioral health problems was examined using data from a longitudinal panel of 4,407 students surveyed in all 24 communities beginning in grade 5 and continuing through age 21. Based on information from these participants, CTC had desired and significant effects in reducing the initiation of behavioral health problems beginning in grade 7 [118]. At that time, fewer students in CTC communities had ever committed a delinquent act compared to those in the control communities ($AOR = 0.79$). Delays in the initiation of substance use were first found when the longitudinal panel was in grade 8 [119]. At that time, students in CTC communities were significantly less likely than those in control communities to have begun to use alcohol ($AOR = 0.68$), cigarettes ($AOR = 0.67$), and smokeless tobacco ($AOR = 0.67$). According to their self-reports, 25% of 8th graders in CTC communities reported having ever used alcohol, compared to 17% of those in control communities; 12% reported ever smoking cigarettes, compared to 8% in control communities;

FIGURE 1.3 Research Design and Timeline of the Community Youth Development Study

and 6% reported ever using smokeless tobacco, compared to 4% in control communities [119]. In grade 8, those in the CTC communities were also less likely to have initiated delinquency (*AOR* = 0.71), with 21% reporting having ever committed a delinquent act, compared to 16% of youth in the control communities [119].

Intervention effects on the initiation of alcohol, cigarettes, and delinquency continued to be evidenced through high school [17, 120], and at age 19, those in the CTC communities were significantly more likely to have refrained from committing any delinquent act compared to those in control communities [121]. When the longitudinal panel was age 21, significant and desired intervention effects were found for the initiation of gateway drugs (i.e., tobacco, alcohol, and marijuana), delinquency, and violence [122]. According to self-reports collected at age 21, 10.1% of those in CTC communities reported never using any gateway drugs, compared to 6.7% of those in control communities; and 33.9% of those in CTC communities reported never committing a delinquent act, compared to 28.8% of those in control communities. In addition, 36.7% of respondents in CTC communities had ever committed at least one violent act, compared to 41.4% of those in the control communities. The adjusted risk ratios (ARRs) for these outcomes were 1.49, 1.18, and 0.89, respectively.

Effects on the prevalence of illegal substance use, delinquency, and violence were found when students in the longitudinal panel were in middle school and in the first years of high school. When they were in grade 8, a significantly smaller percentage of youth from CTC communities reported past-month alcohol use (16.4%) compared to those in the control communities (21.4%). They also reported less binge drinking in the past two weeks (5.7% of CTC youth versus 9% of control youth), and fewer delinquent acts (an average of 0.78 in the past year, compared to 1.13 for control youth) [119]. In grade 10, significant intervention effects favoring CTC youth were found for past-month cigarette use, but not for any other substance. In addition, the odds of engaging in any delinquent and violent behaviors in the past year were 17% and 25% lower, respectively, among CTC versus comparison youth [120]. Intervention effects on the prevalence of substance use, delinquency, and violence were not maintained at grade 12 [17], age 19 [121], or age 21 [122].

CTC has been demonstrated as cost beneficial. The Washington State Institute for Public Policy [123] conducted a benefit-cost analysis of CTC based on CTC effects shown when the longitudinal cohort was in grade 12. Using information about the costs to implement the CTC system [as estimated by Margaret Kuklinski and colleagues, see 124] and the Institute's estimations of tangible and intangible benefits, CTC has a benefit-to-cost ratio of $5.31.

Similarities and Differences Between CTC and Other Community Prevention Systems

How is it that CTC has produced desired effects on youth behavioral health problems when some of the other community-based prevention systems mentioned earlier in this chapter have not? As discussed, a common feature of CTC and other community-based prevention systems is their reliance on coalitions and/or community members to plan and oversee prevention activities. These models endorse the view that prevention efforts will be better supported, implemented, and sustained when local stakeholders are involved in change efforts. These systems create opportunities for community members to identify the problems that need to be addressed and allow some flexibility in the types of actions that will be taken to address needs, how prevention services will be delivered, and who will receive services. In addition to providing prevention services, CTC and other community-based prevention systems promote changes to community norms by encouraging all residents to promote healthy behaviors and minimize tolerance of adolescent behavioral health problems, like substance use, delinquency, and violence.

Despite these similarities, CTC differs from other community-based interventions in ways that may explain the differing findings of effectiveness. Unlike Neighborhood Watch programs, the "pulling levers" law enforcement strategy, and some other coalition-based initiatives, CTC emphasizes the use of EBIs to reduce youth behavioral problems. Like many coalition models, CTC allows for flexibility and empowers community members to select the prevention activities that will best address their particular needs and resources. However, instead of asking communities to "do their best" to develop prevention activities or determine on their own which existing prevention strategies are effective, CTC provides specific information, training, and technical assistance in how to target local needs with EBIs that have been shown in rigorous research trials to prevent youth behavioral health problems.

In addition, CTC encourages the implementation of multiple EBIs to address risk and protective factors from multiple domains. Neighborhood Watch programs, "pulling levers," and policy change strategies target fewer risk and protective factors. Compared to CTC, Project Northland and the Midwestern Prevention Project have a more limited and specific focus on the prevention of substance use. They also stipulate the implementation of one particular school-based curriculum, although multiple policy changes may be enacted. Unlike the "pulling levers" approach, which is led by law enforcement, CTC relies on a broad-based, diverse coalition of community members from all agencies concerned with youth behavioral health problems and healthy development.

"Pulling levers" also employs a more reactive and punishment-focused response to crime, whereas CTC seeks to prevent the development of future
problems among youth who are not already engaging in these behaviors.

CTC is most similar to a coalition-based prevention system not yet mentioned: PROmoting School-community-university Partnerships to Enhance
Resilience (PROSPER). Like CTC, PROSPER relies on community coalitions
to select and oversee the delivery of EBIs to prevent youth behavioral health
problems. PROSPER also provides coalitions with training and technical assistance to support the high-quality implementation of these interventions [125].
Also similar to CTC, PROSPER has been evaluated in a multisite randomized
trial and demonstrated positive effects, with adolescents in PROSPER communities having a delayed initiation of illegal substances and less substance
use and delinquency compared to those in control communities [126–129].
Because they have both demonstrated desirable effects on youth behaviors in
rigorous research trials, CTC and PROSPER are both identified as effective
(i.e., "Promising") by Blueprints for Healthy Youth Development (see: www.
blueprintsprograms.com/programs), a notable designation achieved by few
interventions.

Although they have similarities, PROSPER and CTC differ in their
approaches to community-based prevention. First, PROSPER has a more restricted focus compared to CTC. Its primary goal is to reduce substance use
among youth in early- to mid-adolescence. Second, PROSPER assumes that
adolescents in all communities will experience peer and family risk and protective factors (e.g., exposure to delinquent peers and family conflict). Given
this assumption, PROSPER does not require that communities conduct needs
assessments or collect information from youth on their exposure to risk and
protection. Third, PROSPER provides communities with a more limited menu
of EBIs and guides coalitions to implement one school-based and one family-
focused program selected from a list of six interventions. Fourth, the composi-
tion and leadership of coalitions differ. CTC allows communities to determine
the number and types of individuals who will constitute their coalitions, the
institutions in which they will be housed, and the individuals who will serve as
paid and unpaid leaders. PROSPER, in contrast, embeds coalitions in local educational systems and requires that they are co-led by a staff person from the
local land-grant university Cooperative Extension system and a staff person
from the local school district [125].

CTC is also similar to, but different from, the Strategic Prevention
Framework (SPF) developed by the Substance Abuse and Mental Health
Services Administration (SAMHSA). The SPF involves a coalition-based pre-
vention planning process similar to CTC, as communities are expected to

assess their needs (i.e., determine levels of youth substance use and the risk and protective factors contributing to substance use), build coalitions, and implement and evaluate prevention strategies (see: www.samhsa.gov/capt/about-capt/prevention-grants). However, the SPF has a more narrow focus than CTC, with coalitions focused exclusively on reducing adolescent substance use. In addition, the SPF does not require that coalitions use EBIs to prevent youth behavior problems. Although EBIs are recommended, coalitions may also implement locally developed prevention programs and practices, even if they have not been rigorously evaluated [130]. In recent years, SPF coalitions have been guided to focus on policy changes rather than EBI implementation.

Although communities receive some training and technical assistance to implement the SPF, these supports are less structured and extensive than those provided through CTC. The effectiveness of the SPF in reducing youth substance use has been tested in quasi-experimental evaluations conducted in three states [131–133]. These studies have shown minimal or no significant reductions in substance use among adolescents living in communities using the SPF compared to those living in communities not using the SPF. Although some evaluations have been conducted using information from coalitions in multiple states [e.g., see 134], these studies have not yet used rigorous research designs, such as randomized controlled trials, to assess impact and thus cannot conclusively demonstrate the effectiveness of the SPF in reducing youth substance use.

The Challenge and Promise of Community-Based Prevention

This brief review of community-based prevention systems highlights both the challenges that communities are likely to face when trying to reduce youth behavioral health problems and the gains they can realize when successful in their collaborative efforts. Throughout this book, and especially in section two, we identify the most common threats to high-quality implementation of community-based prevention efforts and offer solutions to these obstacles based on our experiences working with communities using the CTC prevention system. To preview these discussions, we summarize here some of the more frequent challenges communities have reported when implementing the five phases of CTC.

In Phase 1 (*Get Started*), the community considers its readiness to initiate a prevention-oriented approach to youth behavioral problems and to implement developmental prevention strategies (i.e., EBIs) that target risk and protective factors. If community members do not endorse a prevention approach and/or prefer to implement reactive strategies, such as increasing surveillance and arrests to reduce crime and providing drug treatment rather than prevention services, then CTC will be very challenging to implement [117]. If individuals and organizations do not trust each other and cannot agree to collaborate on prevention activities, then they will be less able to implement CTC. They will have to address these barriers prior to adopting the CTC system.

In Phase 2 (*Get Organized*), the greatest challenge will be mobilizing and sustaining commitment from key leaders and community members to participate in CTC [117]. CTC relies primarily on volunteers whose availability may wax and wane over time. This instability will necessitate ongoing and time-intensive efforts to retain members, recruit and retrain new members, and maintain positive relationships among all members. CTC also requires a paid staff person to manage the coalition, and it can be difficult to find individuals who have the requisite skill set (e.g., knowledge of prevention, experience with facilitation, ability to delegate tasks, etc.), as well as the local connections and credibility needed to build and sustain the coalition.

In Phase 3 (*Develop a Profile*), communities may find it difficult to convince school officials to administer the CTC Youth Survey to collect data on risk and protective factors and youth behavioral health problems. Similarly, they may struggle to obtain archival data (e.g., police or school records) that are specific to their community. Coalition members may also find it difficult to interpret these data and agree upon the priorities to address with EBIs.

In Phase 4 (*Create a Plan*), coalitions may be challenged to select a range of EBIs to target their prioritized risk and protective factors. As the field of prevention science has grown, the number of available EBIs has increased [23, 135]. However, high-income nations such as the United States have achieved much more progress than lower income nations, which often have few well-evaluated, effective preventive interventions [8, 23]. Even when EBIs do exist, individuals and organizations may be reluctant to adopt new interventions, given the financial costs associated with adoption, the need to (re)train or hire new staff to deliver them, and general reluctance to change the status quo [136–138]. In the randomized evaluation of CTC, many CTC coalitions found it difficult to convince schools to implement EBIs that they had not used before, and some communities spent as many as three years negotiating with administrators and/or teachers before they agreed to adopt school-based prevention EBIs [117, 139].

During Phase 5 (*Implement and Evaluate*), many coalitions struggle to engage enough individuals to participate in EBIs to produce community-wide changes in behavioral health problems. Although this obstacle may not be faced when delivering school-based programs to students, it can arise when implementing programs in which participation is optional, such as mentoring programs, after-school activities, and parent training interventions [140]. Communities must be prepared to make financial and human investments in participant recruitment. Last, sustaining CTC and specific EBIs over the long term is universally challenging for communities.

Although the challenges of implementing CTC and other community-based interventions are not to be understated, they are not inevitable, as we discuss in later chapters. Likewise, although relatively few effective community-based preventive interventions exist, evaluations of CTC, PROSPER, and some other initiatives indicate that community members can be effectively mobilized. Moreover, the growing list of EBIs means that strategies are available to reduce youth behavioral health problems, and communities have some ability to choose the interventions that are most compatible with their needs, resources, and populations. This flexibility serves to enhance local support for evidence-based prevention and, over the long term, increases the likelihood of a sustained, population-level impact on behavioral health problems.

The goal of this book is to demonstrate that successful community-based prevention is possible. In subsequent chapters, we describe the development, implementation, and evaluation of CTC to provide a template for how to conduct community-based prevention and achieve reductions in youth behavioral health problems. In doing so, we offer guidelines and recommendations for: (1) researchers who are interested in developing and evaluating community-based interventions, especially those who wish to do so using community-based participatory research methods; (2) policymakers who are interested in promoting widespread use of EBIs; and (3) community members who want to build their capacity to prevent behavioral health problems among local youth.

2

Theoretical Perspectives Guiding the Development and Evaluation of CTC

PREVENTION SCIENCE ADVOCATES that, in order to be effective in reducing youth behavioral health problems, preventive interventions must: (1) be guided by theories of human development; (2) seek to change the risk and protective factors specified in these theories to influence behaviors; (3) have clearly defined implementation procedures; and (4) be evaluated in high-quality research studies that examine implementation and outcomes under idealized and naturalistic conditions [1–3]. This chapter begins our discussion of how CTC has been developed and tested according to these principles. In this chapter, we describe the theories underlying the development and specification of the CTC system. We also begin our discussion, which is continued in chapter 3, of how best to evaluate community-based prevention systems. In this chapter, we discuss the benefits and challenges associated with community-based participatory research, in which scientists collaborate with community residents to develop and evaluate EBIs. In chapter 3, we review how CTC has been field tested, refined, and evaluated using a community-based participatory research approach that involves partnerships with policymakers and community members.

Theories Guiding the Development of CTC
Life-Course Developmental Theories

Life-course developmental theories describe the ways in which human behavior unfolds across the life span, from the prenatal period through adulthood.

According to this perspective, human development is characterized as a series of age-specific tasks to be accomplished and milestones to be met [4, 5]. For example, in the first few years of life, it is important for children to develop positive attachments to their caregivers [6]; in adolescence, teenagers must learn to be independent of parents [7]; and in early adulthood, individuals are expected to find steady employment and form families of their own [8]. Successful attainment of age-specific tasks denotes healthy development, whereas failure to achieve goals (e.g., dropping out of school prior to graduation) or being "off time" in their completion (e.g., having a child while in high school) indicates problems with development [5].

Life-course theory views the stages of life as closely linked; that is, what occurs in one stage has repercussions for the next stage [4, 9]. The early years of life are especially critical for healthy development, and the failure to achieve early milestones is likely to hinder the attainment of later goals and lead to a cascading of negative outcomes across the life course [10–12]. For example, young children whose parents are overly lax or harsh in their discipline practices are more likely to develop weak attachments to parents, which can impair their relationships with teachers and their school performance in adolescence, alienate positive peers, and attract deviant peers [13]. Each of these subsequent risk factors has been shown to increase behavioral health problems, and their accumulation contributes to the maintenance of these problems throughout adolescence and into adulthood [14].

Life-course research also indicates that: (1) many behavioral problems evidenced in adulthood begin during childhood or adolescence [9, 15, 16]; (2) the earlier in life that problems such as drug use or crime occur, the more likely they are to continue [17–19]; and (3) the onset or initiation of these problems during the first decade is especially detrimental and likely to lead to serious and persistent problems throughout the adult years [13, 20–22]. All this research indicates that the first two decades of life are critical for later development.

Life-course theory posits that individual development is influenced by the environment and that individuals must learn to navigate and successfully adapt to the new challenges and expectations faced in multiple social contexts [23, 24]. From a risk and protective factor standpoint, each environment may contain risk factors that can threaten successful adaptation and increase the likelihood of behavior problems and protective factors that can provide opportunities for pro-social behaviors and/or mitigate against behavior problems [17]. In addition, different risk and protective factors emerge at different developmental stages [4, 25]. For example, during early childhood, individuals spend most of their time in the family context, making family risk and protective factors such as child maltreatment, family management practices, and parent/child attachment most relevant for development [25, 26]. During middle childhood and adolescence, the school and peer contexts become more influential [27, 28]. For adults, experiences in the community (e.g., the work-place) take precedence, and the family context (e.g., romantic relationships and child-rearing) regains its importance [4].

According to life-course theory, individuals must successfully complete age-graded tasks to avoid behavioral health problems and attain successful de-velopment. However, their ability to do so depends on the degree to which they encounter and appropriately respond to risk and protective factors. The de-livery of preventive interventions can promote successful outcomes, assuming that these services are developmentally appropriate and provide the opportu-nities, skills, and reinforcements that are most critical for the positive develop-ment of the targeted age group. For example, drug-use prevention programs delivered to middle school students should seek to reduce substance use by enhancing individuals' cognitive and social skills, promoting healthy beliefs and clear standards against drug use, and helping youth resist peer influences to smoke or drink.

Consistent with life-course theory, prevention services should be delivered early in life to give children the best possible chance of attaining successful development. For example, home visitation programs are implemented in the prenatal period though ages 2 to 3 years to provide parents with skills to phys-ically care for and emotionally support their young children, prevent child abuse and neglect, and promote positive attachments with children [29, 30]. It is also important to offer preventive interventions at later ages to help individuals overcome newly encountered developmental challenges and risk factors, and to counteract the erosion of protective factors that typically occurs from childhood to adolescence [31]. Because behavioral health problems are most likely for those who face multiple risk factors and few protective factors [1, 32, 33], life-course theory would also suggest that interventions target mul-tiple factors in multiple social contexts across development.

Life-course theory has guided the development of the CTC system in sev-eral ways, as outlined in Table 2.1. Most important, CTC is a prevention system that recognizes the developmental progression of behavioral health problems and the negative consequences associated with the early onset of problems. The main goal of CTC is to prevent the onset of problem behaviors, and so CTC guides coalitions to focus their prevention efforts on children and adolescents. More specifically, coalitions select and implement evidence-based develop-mental interventions [34] that address risk and protective factors encountered

Table 2.1 Theories Guiding the Development of CTC

Theory	Tenets	CTC Operationalization
Life-course developmental	• Human development proceeds in stages, with each stage having specific tasks that must be accomplished • Behavioral health problems tend to have their onset during childhood and adolescence • Multiple social contexts provide risk and protective factors	• EBIs are implemented to provide youth with skills necessary to master age-specific tasks • EBIs are offered in childhood and adolescence to prevent behavioral health problems • EBIs are offered in multiple social contexts
Social Development Model (integration of social control theory, differential association theory, and social learning theory)	• Multiple risk and protective factors in multiple social contexts influence positive and negative behaviors • Social groups must provide healthy beliefs and clear standards for behavior and foster bonds to youth to promote positive youth development • Bonding is facilitated when individuals have opportunities to contribute to social groups, learn necessary skills, and are reinforced for their skillful contributions • The active involvement of community members in prevention efforts helps increase adults' commitment to prevention and communicates to youth that they are supported	• Coalitions collect data from youth of different ages to assess multiple risk and protective factors across contexts • Coalitions implement EBIs in multiple contexts to foster bonding and promote healthy beliefs and clear standards • Community residents take ownership for prevention planning and implementation by joining or supporting CTC coalitions • Adult residents promote healthy beliefs and clear standards and create bonds with youth in their daily interactions with young people

(*continued*)

Table 2.1 Continued

Theory	Tenets	CTC Operationalization
Social disorganization	• Rates of behavioral health problems vary by geographical region • Structural, social, and cultural features of communities influence behavioral health problems	• Communities collect data to identify local levels of behavioral problems, risk factors, and protective factors • Community-level risk and protective factors are identified and addressed with EBIs • CTC coalitions allow community residents to take ownership for prevention activities and foster collective efficacy and pro-social community norms
Diffusion of Innovations	• Dissemination, implementation, and sustainability of EBIs is difficult to achieve • Individuals and organizations need assistance to promote their adoption, implementation, and sustained use of EBIs	• Provides a structured process, training, and ongoing technical support to increase communities' awareness, adoption, high quality implementation, and sustainability of EBIs

from the prenatal period through late adolescence and early adulthood. These interventions should be shown in well-conducted evaluations to reduce risk factors, increase protective factors, and reduce behavioral health problems. Coalitions may offer these EBIs to children and adolescents, as well as to parents, teachers, and community members and organizations, since healthy development is affected by individual and environmental factors.

CTC does not dictate the delivery of particular EBIs in specific settings or to particular age groups but, rather, encourages coalitions to offer a coordinated set of services to address multiple elevated risk factors and depressed protective factors. Targeting factors in multiple contexts (e.g., families, schools, and communities) is encouraged to strengthen the overall impact of prevention efforts. Because different factors are likely to emerge at different ages, CTC trains coalitions to collect data on risk and protective factors for different age groups, such as youth in middle and high schools (see chapter 5). Ideally, these data will provide information on the full spectrum of risk and protective factors known to predict behavioral health problems described in chapter 1.

Social Development Model

The Social Development Model [25] is the main theory guiding CTC. It is an integrative theory that utilizes a life-course developmental framework to describe the onset, persistence, and desistance of behavioral health problems, as well as the development and maintenance of positive behaviors. The Social Development Model integrates criminology's social control theory [35], differential association theory [36], and social learning theory [37] to explain the mechanisms through which risk and protective factors affect positive and negative behaviors from childhood to young adulthood.

Similar to other life-course theories, the Social Development Model recognizes that many risk and protective factors affect behavioral health problems, that these factors change during the life course, and that multiple social groups and environments influence young people's development. These contexts are especially important in promoting bonds, and the theory explains both the formation of bonds and the impact of bonds on behavior. Bonds contribute to positive behaviors when youth bond with pro-social individuals and institutions. Negative outcomes occur when youth do not bond with pro-social others and/or when they bond with antisocial individuals and institutions.

The theory recognizes that the environmental contexts in which bonding and behavioral health problems occur change across development. Children first experience the family and preschool environments, then the elementary school context, then the middle and high school environments. EBIs should be delivered in the contexts most relevant for the developmental age of the individual and should address the risk and protective factors that are most prevalent and influential in those environments. The prevalence of behavioral health problems also follow a developmental course, from relatively low rates in elementary school, to increases in initiation during middle school, frequent and problematic engagement beginning in high school, and peak rates occurring in young adulthood.

The Social Development Model starts with the assumption that children learn both healthy and unhealthy patterns of behavior during social interactions and via socialization experiences in the home, school, peer group, and community as they encounter these contexts during the life course. The theory hypothesizes that opportunities for involvement and interactions in these environments affect youth behaviors, as do the rewards provided for involvement, efforts, and contributions in these environments. When youth show skillful involvement in these environments, they should receive positive recognition and rewards, which in turn leads to attachment, commitment, and bonding to the socializing groups.

Drawing from social control theory [35], the Social Development Model posits that the more youth are bonded to the individuals and institutions in these socializing contexts, the more likely they will be to adopt the values and conform to the standards of these groups. Consistent with differential association theory [36, 38, 39], the more children are bonded to pro-social groups that provide healthy beliefs and clear standards for positive behavior, the more likely they will be to engage in positive behaviors. Conversely, those who are not bonded to pro-social others or who become bonded to deviant individuals or groups will be more at risk for developing behavioral health problems.

The Social Development Model has guided the development of CTC in four ways (see Table 2.1). First, it provides a theoretical basis for the assessment of risk and protective factors across multiple socialization contexts and for youth of different age groups. Coalitions work with middle and high schools to administer the CTC Youth Survey so that students can report on their opportunities to be involved in primary socialization groups, as well as their mastery of skills, feelings of recognition, social bonds, and exposure to healthy beliefs and clear norms. For example, survey items ask the degree to which youth have chances to help decide on classroom activities (opportunities), would refuse a friend's offer to drink alcohol (skills), have been complimented by their neighbors for doing a good job (recognition), are praised by teachers for working hard (recognition), feel close to their parents (bonding), try to do their best in school (bonding), and believe that adults in their neighborhood think it is wrong for kids to use marijuana (norms). The survey also asks students to report on their exposure to risk factors in their social contexts; for example, they rate how much their neighborhood is characterized by crime and/or drug selling, if their family members or peers engage in drug use or crime, if they are committed to school, and whether they think they would be seen as cool if they smoked cigarettes.

Second, the Social Development Model provides a theoretical rationale for the implementation of EBIs to target risk and protective factors. Given the theory's emphasis on promoting strong bonds to pro-social groups, CTC recommends that communities select and implement EBIs that will (1) create strong bonds between young people and their families, schools, peer groups, and communities; (2) ensure that these groups communicate healthy beliefs and clear standards for behavior; and (3) provide youth with opportunities, skills, and recognition for making positive contributions to these groups. EBIs are also selected to reduce youths' exposure to risk factors in their families, schools, peer groups, and communities. For example, interventions may try to reduce conflict among family members or increase adolescents' skills to resist peer influences to use drugs.

Third, the Social Development Model is incorporated into the community mobilization and coalition development components of CTC. The theory recognizes that the social environment affects youth behavior and that the community as a whole should communicate clear standards and norms encouraging healthy behavior and discouraging problem behaviors. The more community members are involved in the CTC process and are helping to create a more positive environment for youth, the greater the likelihood of healthy youth development. By relying on broad-based coalitions of community members to plan and oversee prevention activities, CTC provides an opportunity for all interested community members to foster healthy youth development.

In the early phases of CTC, coalition members work together to develop a common vision for positive youth development based on the tenets of prevention science. This vision guides their subsequent actions and provides a common language that fosters collaboration across diverse community members and organizations. Through trainings and technical assistance, coalition members develop skills to engage in successful prevention. They learn to create and maintain high-functioning coalitions; conduct needs assessments; and select, plan for, implement, and evaluate the effectiveness of EBIs. The CTC process provides milestones and benchmarks to mark progress through each of the five phases and encourages coalitions to share their successes with the larger community and to recognize and celebrate the contributions of individual members and agencies. Providing opportunities, skills, and recognition for community stakeholders to work together to foster healthy youth development increases the likelihood that coalition members will develop strong bonds to each other and to their communities [40]. They also develop a stronger commitment to completing the CTC process and to promoting the healthy beliefs and clear standards promoted in the CTC initiative.

Fourth, CTC includes a component that asks all adults in the community to commit to operationalizing the theory by using the Social Development Strategy during their interactions with youth. The Social Development Strategy, shown in Figure 2.1, is the component of the Social Development Model that specifies how to build protective bonds between youth and positive adults and peers, and it describes how these bonds motivate youths to adopt clear standards for healthy behavior. Community members learn about the Social Development Strategy and discuss how they can provide local

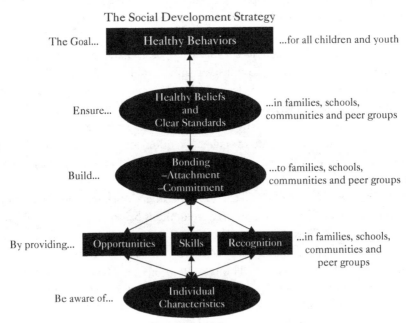

FIGURE 2.1 The Social Development Strategy

youth with opportunities, skills, and recognition to encourage bonding to the community and promote healthier youth development. Use of the Social Development Strategy provides a common orientation that community coalition members can share with other organizations and individuals to enhance their involvement in the CTC process.

Social Disorganization Theory

Social disorganization theory [41–43] has also informed CTC. One of the tenets of this theory, supported by empirical research, is that rates of crime and other behavioral health problems vary across regions, cities, and neighborhoods [41, 44, 45]. CTC endorses and extends this view by recognizing that communities are also likely to differ in the types and levels of risk and protective factors associated with behavioral health problems [40, 46, 47]. Also consistent with social disorganization theory, CTC is not a "one size fits all" approach that recommends the delivery of a particular intervention or set of EBIs in all places. Instead, it recognizes that, because problems and their precursors will vary across communities, different EBIs will be needed in different communities.

According to social disorganization theory, spatial variations in crime rates indicate that the community context itself influences behavior. Structural, social, and cultural features of an area are all expected to affect youth behavioral health problems, including factors such as poverty, high residential mobility, the availability of drugs or weapons, visibility of social problems such as crime, local resources and services, social cohesion between neighborhood residents, and shared norms and values regarding acceptable and unacceptable behaviors [41–43, 48, 49]. Collective efficacy is another community-level protective factor that can reduce youth behavioral problems [45, 50–53]. Collective efficacy is the degree to which adult residents of a community trust and respect one another, share responsibility for the well-being of their community, and are willing to intervene and take informal actions to address local concerns like youth crime [43].

Social disorganization theory provides a theoretical basis for two primary components of CTC (see Table 2.1). First, to capture variation in behavioral problems and risk and protective factors across communities, especially community-level factors, CTC coalitions administer the CTC Youth Survey to assess rates of problem behaviors, risk, and protection. The CTC Youth Survey asks youth to report on five community risk factors, including the availability of weapons and illegal drugs in their neighborhoods, how much crime occurs in their neighborhoods, the likelihood they would be caught by police if they engaged in crime, and the degree to which local adults think adolescent drug use is wrong (a measure of community norms). The survey also asks about three community protective factors: the availability of local recreational or volunteer service activities for youth, the degree to which adults encourage positive youth behavior, and how much youth like living in their neighborhoods. When youth report high levels of community risk factors or low levels of community protective factors, CTC coalitions select EBIs intended to address these concerns. Since behaviors and risk and protective factors may also vary *within* a community, CTC advises coalitions to disaggregate their data, to the extent possible, by geographical region and consider implementing different EBIs in different parts of the community [40].

Second, the implementation of the CTC system and activation of local coalitions are expected to directly affect community norms and collective efficacy. Following the Social Development Model, CTC provides residents with civic opportunities to be positively engaged in their communities. When adults participate in CTC coalitions, they learn how to engage in effective, collaborative action to foster healthy youth development, and they should be more likely to agree upon and communicate to youth standards and norms that promote positive behaviors and discourage problem behaviors. CTC also builds collective efficacy by increasing communication and positive interactions between residents, fostering trust and cohesion, and increasing collective action via the delivery of EBIs. When collective efficacy is enhanced, youth are expected to refrain from problem behaviors because they perceive greater levels of social support from residents, are more attached to the community, and are more likely to believe they will be caught and punished in some way for misbehavior [43, 54, 55].

Diffusion of Innovations Theory

A last theory upon which CTC is based is the Diffusion of Innovations theory developed by Everett Rogers [56]. It is well known that communities do not commonly use EBIs to prevent public health problems and that there are many barriers to the adoption and sustained use of EBIs [15, 57–59]. Rogers [56] was one of the first to provide a theoretical explanation of how and when EBIs are adopted and to offer recommendations for increasing EBI dissemination and sustainability. According to his Diffusion of Innovations theory, organizations of all types progress through five stages when considering whether or not to adopt a new "innovation"—that is, a program or practice intended to address a particular need such as the reduction of youth behavioral health problems. These stages include: (1) gaining knowledge about the innovation, (2) being persuaded to use it, (3) deciding to use it, (4) implementing the innovation, and (5) confirming the decision.

Many organizations interested in prevention never reach Stage 1. That is, they do not learn how to effectively prevent behavioral health problems using EBIs because, until recently, information about new and effective preventive interventions was primarily published in academic articles that were not likely to be accessed or understood by a lay audience [59–61]. In Stages 2 and 3, an agency must determine that the new innovation will address a prioritized need(s), has distinct advantages compared to existing services, can be feasibly implemented given available resources and infrastructure, and is culturally relevant for the intended population(s) [58, 62–65]. Even if these stages are accomplished, many challenges may occur during Stage 4 (implementation), and problems can lead to significant (mis)adaptations and/or discontinuation of an EBI so that Stage 5 (confirming the decision) is never reached [66–68]. Organizations need assistance during Stage 4 to monitor implementation efforts, correct problems when they are encountered, and evaluate the impact of their efforts. The completion of these tasks and the ability to demonstrate that a new innovation addresses the local need(s) promotes the long-term sustainability of the EBI and the completion of Stage 5 [68–70].

Research on the dissemination of EBIs has shown that organizations require external supports to help them move through all of these stages [15, 61]. CTC is designed to provide such assistance (see Table 2.1). It provides communities with a structured process with clearly identified goals and the specific steps and tasks to take to achieve these goals. In addition, a series of trainings and ongoing consultation and coaching help to guide coalitions through all the stages of innovation. In Phase 2 of CTC, key leaders (i.e., elected officials, as well as leaders of law enforcement, justice, education, health-care, public health, human services, and civic organizations) and the coalition members who will implement the CTC system learn through trainings that EBIs have been developed, tested, and found to address risk and protective factors and to reduce behavioral health problems, and that many EBIs are cost beneficial. In Phase 3, coalitions receive guidance to assess and prioritize their needs—that is, to specify the risk factors that are elevated and protective factors that are depressed in their community. They also conduct resource assessments to examine the provision of current services. The goal is to determine if any local organizations are currently implementing EBIs to address local needs. If not, they fill these gaps in service delivery with newly adopted EBIs.

In Phase 4, coalitions use the Blueprints for Healthy Youth Development website (www.colorado.edu/cspv/blueprints/) to learn about specific EBIs designated as effective. This website includes information on the risk and protective factors and outcomes impacted by a variety of EBIs, as well as their costs, implementation requirements, and the populations for whom they are intended. Coalitions move through Stages 2 and 3 of Rogers's [56] theory by learning about EBIs that could be implemented to address their local needs, identifying the advantages of these EBIs relative to current services, and considering whether or not they could be fully implemented given financial and human resources.

CTC provides training and technical assistance to help coalitions use information from Blueprints to develop comprehensive and detailed community action plans that identify their prioritized needs, current services, and new EBIs that will be implemented to address needs. The plan specifies all the actions and resources needed to fully implement newly selected EBI(s) in order to avoid or minimize challenges that would otherwise be faced during implementation and Stage 4 of the Diffusion of Innovations theory. The action plan includes information on how implementation will be monitored, including the steps that will be taken and actors responsible for documenting adherence to EBI protocols, hiring staff and providing them with feedback on their performance, and recruiting participants. The action plan also considers the long-term sustainability of the EBIs, including identification of needed financial resources, in order to promote completion of Stage 5.

Community-Based Participatory Research

A variety of theories have informed the development of CTC, but the various components that constitute the five phases of the CTC system were not developed simultaneously. Instead, as we will describe in chapter 3, the current CTC model has evolved over time, largely due to feedback from community stakeholders. As we discuss in this section, the CTC developers have used a community-based participatory research [71] to inform the development and evaluation of the CTC system.

Community-based participatory research (CBPR) is a methodological approach involving active collaboration between scientists and community members in defining, carrying out, and evaluating research projects [72]. As with similar research approaches (e.g., community-centered research, participatory research, action research, and empowerment evaluation), the goal of CBPR is to integrate research and practice [71, 73]. The community is not considered an object of research inquiry but, rather, an active and equitable partner [74]. Researchers recognize and respect the knowledge, strengths, and resources of community members, and community members recognize the skills and expertise of researchers; neither side is privileged and the contributions of both are deemed critical to success [71, 75]. CBPR can be advantageous in seeking to prevent behavioral health problems because it combines researchers' knowledge of the scope and causes of behavioral health problems, research methods, and EBIs with community members' knowledge of the local values, relationships, and resources that may affect EBI implementation and sustainability.

A goal of CBPR is to produce outcomes of interest to both scientists and community members [71]. To this end, it entails active participation by diverse and representative members of the community, including policymakers, administrators, practitioners, targeted participants, and any other community residents interested in preventing behavioral health problems. It is especially important to include community members who may otherwise be marginalized, so as to ensure that interventions do not produce or reinforce existing disparities [71, 72]. Community members and researchers must agree that the research methods to be used and the outcomes to be achieved are culturally relevant.

A related goal of CBPR is to build community capacity and empower community members to solve their own problems [76, 77]. Researchers are not solely responsible for creating desirable changes or "fixing" a community's problem. Nor should they provide a temporary solution that will dissipate once their involvement ends [78]. Instead, scientists seek to build the capacity of community members by providing them with knowledge, skills, and tools they can use to solve local problems in the current initiative and in future change efforts [71].

CBPR involves collaboration between scientists and community members in the development and testing of an intervention. During intervention development, community members share their views on the extent and causes of local behavioral health problems, the needs of community residents, the resources available to address needs, and the typical methods of service delivery used in the community. Researchers take this information into account to ensure that interventions target relevant needs and can be locally delivered [79]. During intervention testing, community members may serve as participants, assist with participant recruitment, and help to collect data. Scientists and community members should work together to analyze results, identify actions that should be taken based on these findings, and publicize the findings and their implications.

CBPR offers rewards but also presents challenges for both researchers and community members. Both parties may initially distrust and/or discount the perspective of the other, and it will take time and ongoing communication to create strong partnerships [71, 80]. There may be preexisting political, social, or cultural tensions in a community that researchers will need to learn about and navigate when working with local partners to promote equitable involvement [81]. Given their different backgrounds, scientists and community members may disagree on the outcomes, measures, and intervention methods to be utilized in the study [59, 82]. For example, one side may be more task oriented and the other more process oriented, or one side may expect quick results while the other has a longer term view of success.

These differing opinions may delay evaluation timelines and create tension between partners [75, 83, 84]. Each party must be willing to compromise to achieve mutually agreed-upon goals. In addition, they must jointly decide on the roles, responsibilities and decision-making authority of each group [71, 77]. Lastly, maintaining commitment from both parties is often difficult, given competing time demands. Community members are often volunteering their time after work hours, and researchers will be juggling other tasks, such as teaching, publishing, and other research/service [71, 72, 84]. Clearly delineating the project goals, the tasks to be completed, and the individuals responsible for achieving each outcome can help minimize conflict and ensure ongoing participation. Despite these challenges, CBPR can help ensure that interventions can be feasibly implemented and are responsive to the needs of the community, culturally relevant, and well supported, all of which should enhance their effectiveness [85, 86].

In chapter 3, and throughout section two of this book, we describe how the CTC developers have utilized a CBPR approach to create, refine, and evaluate the system. Consistent with CBPR, CTC recognizes that efforts to change communities must be owned and operated by community members. The role of the researcher/scientist is to provide tools, support, and guidance to community members, not to direct the effort. The community is responsible for enacting all five phases of CTC, from assessing community readiness for prevention, to conducting needs and resource assessments, to selecting and overseeing the delivery of EBIs. Because community members are unlikely to have all the knowledge or skills necessary to complete these steps, CTC provides training and technical support to build their capacity to do so. Moreover, CTC helps foster community capacity [87] for prevention by improving communication and resource sharing between individuals and agencies, enhancing individuals' commitment to the community, and providing a forum for community members to agree on norms and values.

The goal of CTC is to improve the well-being of all youth in a community, but it is up to community members to define the specific outcomes they wish to achieve within this very broad framework. Diverse and democratic decision making is another defining characteristic of CTC and CBPR. CTC guides communities to create coalitions representing all sectors, population groups, and levels of decision making in the community, but it is up to the community to identify and recruit the specific individuals who should be involved. Participation from positional leaders (e.g., government officials, school superintendents and principals, police chiefs or sheriffs) is considered critical because these authorities control resources and access to the systems necessary for achieving change [88]. They can also help influence local norms and hold individual community members accountable for prevention actions. At the same time, creating positive change across the entire community requires broad support and participation from all those concerned about youth development (e.g., educators, social service providers, health professionals, clergy, parents, youth) and who can support and publicize prevention efforts (e.g., civic groups, media, business). Those representing marginalized groups must also be included to ensure that change efforts are inclusive and equitable.

Summary

This chapter has described the theories guiding the development of the CTC system to illustrate how community-based interventions and other types of EBIs should build upon theory to create a model of change that is best able to prevent behavioral health problems. These systems should also be carefully evaluated, with pilot studies examining the feasibility of implementation procedures and more rigorous evaluations examining their impact of targeted outcomes, as well as their potential to be widely and well implemented in communities. As we have described, community-based participatory research can help ensure that interventions are developed and evaluated in ways that will be responsive to the needs of the community, are culturally relevant, and are well supported. In the next chapter, we describe how the CTC developers have used the CBPR approach and high-quality, systematic research methods to create, refine, and evaluate the CTC system.

3

The Development and
Evaluation of CTC

EVALUATING ANY TYPE of EBI is difficult and requires significant time and resources. The development and evaluation process usually proceeds in a series
of distinct and sequenced stages. The goal of the early, exploratory stages is to
create a logical, theory-driven intervention that will be feasible to implement.
The goal of the middle stage is to test the feasibility and acceptability of the intervention through community input, and the goal of later stages is to evaluate
the impact of the intervention [1, 2]. There is some disparity in the literature
regarding the specific number of stages or steps involved in the evaluation
process, and different terminology has been used to describe these steps. For
example, Type I and Type II research refer to, respectively, (1) basic/clinical
research that identifies the scope of a behavioral health problem, the risk and
protective factors associated with it, the development of an intervention based
on this information, and the initial testing of the intervention to determine
its effectiveness; and (2) research that investigates methods for disseminating
interventions shown to be effective [1, 3]. Some subdivide Type I research to
differentiate between efficacy and effectiveness research, and others, such as
Rogers's [4] Diffusion of Innovations theory, partition Type II research into
multiple steps.

In this chapter, we adapt a framework developed by Sussman and colleagues
[1] to illustrate the steps taken in prevention science research to create and evaluate interventions. As shown in Figure 3.1, we conceptualize the prevention
research process as including: (1) intervention development; (2) pilot studies
to examine the feasibility of the intervention; (3) measurement development;
(4) efficacy trials, which examine the impact of an intervention under carefully
controlled research conditions; (5) effectiveness trials, which examine impact

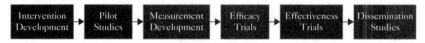

FIGURE 3.1 Stages of Prevention Science Research
Source: Adapted from Sussman and colleagues [1]

under more real-world conditions; and (6) dissemination studies that investigate the factors that facilitate and impede widespread use of the EBI. This chapter describes these steps in order to illustrate our thinking about how community-based preventive interventions should be evaluated. We also review how CTC has been developed and evaluated following these steps and using a community-based participatory research approach.

Evaluation Research

Intervention development, the first step in the evaluation research process, involves a review of theory and empirical research to ensure that interventions target the risk and protective factors shown to affect the development of behavioral health problems [5, 6]. Next, program developers must specify the methods, procedures, and duration of services that will be used to reduce the risk factors and enhance the protective factors identified in the guiding theories. They should also decide on the populations and/or areas to be targeted for services. These considerations should also be guided by theory and prior research. For example, multiple theories and research studies identify family factors as especially important in early childhood [7–9] and indicate that positive parenting practices will be more difficult to utilize with disruptive children [10–12]. This information suggests that interventions seeking to change family processes should be implemented in the early years of life. In addition, services for parents of children with behavioral problems like conduct disorder may need to be longer and/or more intensive than services for those whose children are not displaying such problems.

Once the intervention is specified, a pilot or field study can be conducted. Pilot studies are generally exploratory in nature and small in scale. They involve a process or formative evaluation that examines implementation procedures in detail to determine which parts of the intervention are feasible to deliver, which are not, and which may need to be altered or refined prior to conducting an outcome evaluation [13]. Process evaluations document, for example, the length of time needed to complete the intervention activities, staff skills and competencies, costs, and strategies for recruiting participants and ensuring participant responsiveness to the intervention [14]. Researchers can collect quantitative and/or qualitative data on these issues using observations; surveys of implementers, administrators, or participants; focus groups conducted with these groups; or all such methods [13]. Although process evaluations might include information on changes in participant outcomes, evidence of effectiveness will be preliminary, especially if the study involves only an intervention condition with no comparison group, which is often the case. Depending on the results of the pilot study, a developer will make changes to the intervention and retest the new version in a new pilot study or proceed to a more rigorous outcome evaluation.

Once the process evaluation has demonstrated that an intervention can be well implemented, its ability to produce desired changes can be evaluated. However, evaluators must first identify measures that will be used to assess impact [2]. They may draw upon existing measures that have been shown to be valid and reliable indicators of the intervention targets, or they may need to develop such measures. Measurement development is especially likely to be needed when evaluating community-based interventions because valid and reliable measures of community-level constructs are not common [15].

Outcome evaluations typically begin with an efficacy trial—an evaluation of the intervention's impact when it is implemented under tightly controlled, scientifically rigorous conditions [16]. The goal is to assess the degree to which the outcomes targeted by the intervention changed for those in the intervention condition relative to the control condition—that is, the individuals, groups, or places that did not receive the intervention. In addition to establishing the main effects of an intervention, efficacy trials may involve evaluation of the mechanisms that produce change (e.g., tests of mediation) and/or of variables that produce variation in effects across individuals or groups (e.g., moderation analyses) [17, 18].

Randomized controlled trials (RCTs) are typically recommended in efficacy trials because they are best able to ensure internal validity and rule out alternative explanations of intervention effects [17, 19–21]. In RCTs, developers randomly assign individuals, groups, or places/communities to two or more groups: those that receive the intervention and those that do not. Assuming that a sufficient number of units are assigned to study conditions, random assignment ensures that intervention and control groups are as similar as possible at study baseline. Having comparable groups increases confidence that observed differences are due to the intervention rather than to chance, preexisting differences between groups, or some factor other than the intervention [19, 21, 22].

Efficacy trials usually involve a larger and/or more diverse group of participants compared to pilot studies, but they are not as broad in scope as effectiveness trials. Effectiveness trials evaluate intervention impact when programs or practices are delivered in naturalistic conditions [16]. The goal is to evaluate whether or not an intervention produces intended outcomes when implemented by practitioners rather than by highly trained and closely supervised research staff, and when delivered in organizations to clients or students typically served by such organizations. As such, effectiveness evaluations help determine whether the intervention produces salutary effects across settings, in real-world conditions, and without the oversight of program developers [1]. These studies may also evaluate mediating mechanisms and moderating effects, including whether or not variation in implementation delivery affects outcomes [16].

Dissemination research represents the last step in the evaluation process. Dissemination studies examine features of the intervention, implementers, and/or implementing organizations that facilitate or impede the adoption, high-quality delivery, and/or sustainability of EBIs [1]. Like effectiveness trials, dissemination studies involve implementation in naturalistic conditions, but in these evaluations, developers may intentionally manipulate parts of the intervention or its delivery system in order to analyze effects on scale-up and delivery. For example, evaluations may compare different models of training and technical assistance in terms of their ability to achieve high-quality implementation [e.g., 23].

These staged steps, with smaller scale studies conducted under tightly controlled conditions preceding larger scale studies implemented in more realistic settings, are recommended in order to fully understand if and how interventions work *before* significant human and financial resources are spent taking them to scale [24]. In reality, however, the research process is often nonlinear,[1] and some interventions are widely disseminated before their effectiveness is fully established. As we will discuss, in CTC evaluations, an effectiveness trial of CTC was actually undertaken prior to an efficacy trial.

As noted in chapter 1, relatively few community-based interventions have been identified as effective in preventing youth behavioral health problems. The scarcity of effective community-based interventions, relative to other types of interventions, has been attributed to their greater scope and complexity, which makes them more difficult to evaluate [26]. For example, many community-based interventions allow for flexibility in their implementation components, with different actions undertaken by different communities based on their particular needs and resources. This variety can make it difficult to examine the overall effectiveness of the community-based system [27]. Collecting reliable and valid data on community-level processes is also likely to be difficult, especially when assessing constructs like collective efficacy (i.e., the amount of trust, cohesion, and willingness to intervene to improve the community that exist among residents) that are not easy to observe, quantify, or operationalize [15, 28, 29]. Finally, relatively few RCTs have been conducted of community-based interventions, likely because RCTs require that a sufficient number of units (i.e., communities) be randomized to allow adequate statistical power to detect significant intervention effects [30, 31]. It is always difficult to recruit participants for research studies, and community-based interventions are especially challenging given that multiple parties and key leaders will need to agree to random assignment [32, 33].

Despite all these challenges, it is possible to evaluate the effectiveness of community-based prevention systems using rigorous scientific methods and in collaboration with community stakeholders. The rest of this chapter illustrates how CTC has achieved these goals.

The Development and Evaluation of the CTC System
Intervention Development

As depicted in the logic model shown in Figure 1.1, CTC views the prevention of youth behavioral health problems as affected by multiple processes and factors operating at the community level and in the individual lives of youth. As recommended in prevention science, this logic model is based on theories and empirical evidence related to the prevention of youth behavioral health problems. As discussed in chapter 2, CTC was developed taking into account theories and evidence indicating that: (a) multiple risk and protective factors affect the development of youth behavioral problems; (b) communities vary in levels of these risk and protective factors and in levels of behavioral health problems, making community-specific approaches necessary; (c) EBIs exist and can be implemented to reduce risk, increase protection, and prevent behavioral health problems; and (d) involvement of community members is important to increase bonds between youth and their communities, increase local support for prevention, and ensure that EBIs are feasible to implement and culturally relevant. All this information is incorporated into CTC's coalition-based prevention system.

As discussed in chapter 1 and shown in Figure 1.1, CTC currently involves five phases with discrete steps to be followed and goals to be achieved in order to effectively prevent youth behavioral problems community wide. The system did not always involve all five phases. Rather, the logic model and primary components of CTC have evolved over time based on information from pilot studies and through community-based participatory research. The program developers learned during interactions with the community members who implemented CTC and the policymakers who funded these efforts what was needed, feasible, and likely to be successful when attempting to prevent youth behavioral health problems in communities.

When first developed, CTC was intended primarily as a system for preventing youth violence and delinquency [34]. In a partnership with the National Council on Crime and Delinquency, Drs. Hawkins and Catalano reviewed criminological theories and information from longitudinal studies that identified risk and protective factors. These sources indicated that delinquency and violence often co-occur with other behavioral health problems and share many of the same risk and protective factors [35–37]. The developers also reviewed evaluation research to identify preventive interventions delivered in various contexts with youth at different developmental stages and shown to impact risk factors and protective factors in family, peer, school, and community settings [38–41]. These studies showed that several interventions that addressed risk and protective factors prevented multiple behavioral health problems, even though they were usually developed to target only a single problem [42–45]. Information on these EBIs was summarized in guides intended for policymakers and practitioners [46, 47], including those who would be using CTC to select EBIs.

Drs. Hawkins and Catalano next conceptualized how this information might be packaged into an intervention system to assist communities concerned with the prevention of delinquency, violence, and other behavioral health problems. Although the developers had prior experience in developing and testing prevention programs delivered in schools, with families, in after-care programs used in juvenile corrections, and in adult drug treatment interventions, they had never developed a comprehensive, community-wide system like CTC. CTC was to be more than a program. It was conceived of as a method to build the capacity of communities to use the information from theories and research on risk factors, protective factors, and effective programs to organize, assess, and prioritize local needs, and to choose EBIs to address local priorities. Drs. Hawkins and Catalano consulted with several scientists who had implemented community-based prevention approaches across a spectrum of behavioral health problems to learn more about methods that would be effective when seeking to change communities and enhance community collaboration [48].

Although the initial conceptual model for CTC was developed with the goal of preventing delinquency and violence, CTC was first tested in multiple communities as a substance-use prevention system. As shown in the timeline in Table 3.1, the U.S. Department of Education and the Center for Substance Abuse Prevention (CSAP) provided funding for these early pilot studies. CTC

Table 3.1 Timeline of the Development and Evaluation of CTC

Year/Project	Community Partners	Funding Agency(ies)	Type of Research
1988–1990: Together! Communities for a Drug Free Youth	32 Washington communities	U.S. Department of Education	Pilot study
1990–1995: Oregon Together!	40 Oregon communities	Oregon State Office of Alcohol and Drug Abuse Program (OADAP) U.S. Office of Substance Abuse Prevention (now CSAP)	Pilot study
1993–2000: Title V project	400 communities in the U.S.	Office of Juvenile Justice and Delinquency Prevention	Pilot study
1993–1997: Six-State Consortium	State offices of alcohol and drug abuse services of Kansas, Maine, Oregon, South Carolina, Utah, and Washington	Center for Substance Abuse Prevention (CSAP)	Measurement development
1994–present: Pennsylvania project	120+ Pennsylvania communities	Pennsylvania Commission on Crime and Delinquency (PCCD) and other state agencies	Effectiveness evaluation
1997–2001: Diffusion Project	41 communities State offices of alcohol and drug abuse services of Colorado, Kansas, Illinois, Maine, Oregon, Utah, and Washington	Center for Substance Abuse Prevention, U.S. Department of Education, National Institute on Drug Abuse, and the U.S. Department of Justice	Measurement development
2003–present: Community Youth Development Study	24 communities State offices of alcohol and drug abuse services of Colorado, Kansas, Illinois, Maine, Oregon, Utah, and Washington	National Institute on Drug Abuse, National Cancer Institute, National Institute of Child Health and Human Development, National Institute of Mental Health, Center for Substance Abuse Prevention, National Institute on Alcohol Abuse and Alcoholism	Efficacy evaluation

was subsequently funded and evaluated as part of the Title V delinquency-prevention community grants administered by the Office of Juvenile Justice and Delinquency Prevention (OJJDP), a federal agency in the U.S. Department of Justice that supports state and local efforts to prevent delinquency and improve the juvenile justice system.

CTC was also incorporated into the OJJDP's Comprehensive Strategy for Serious, Violent, and Chronic Juvenile Offenders [46]. The Comprehensive Strategy represented an expansion of OJJDP's Title V prevention work with communities. In the Comprehensive Strategy, communities were guided to use CTC as a prevention and early intervention strategy that could be implemented along with other services, such as those designed to keep offenders out of juvenile correctional institutions, and after-care programs that supervised juvenile offenders who were released back into their communities following a period of incarceration [49]. As this brief history illustrates, the CTC developers were open to refining and expanding their intervention based on the needs of communities and federal policymakers.

Pilot Testing

The first evaluation of CTC was a two-year pilot study funded by the U.S. Department of Education and involved communities in Washington State [50]. The goals of the pilot study were to understand if CTC could be feasibly implemented and to identify the challenges faced by communities when enacting the CTC system. At this time, CTC involved four phases (community recruitment, team formation, team training, and implementation) and two training workshops, one to introduce key leaders to the CTC system and the Social Development Model (the Key Leader Orientation), and the second to train coalition members in how to identify and prioritize local risk factors and develop and maintain healthy coalitions (the Risk and Resource Assessment training). At this time, staff from the Washington State University Cooperative Extension offices, who were based in communities, facilitated the trainings, and they regularly communicated with the local coalitions to support CTC implementation.

To launch the Washington project, the CTC developers held focus groups with educational leaders, law enforcement officials, and other researchers who had worked on community-based projects in the state. This group discussed potential communities to participate in the pilot study and recommended that the project be named *Together! Communities for a Drug Free Youth*. Participants also suggested that the project's principal investigator, Dr. Hawkins, as well as Washington governor Booth Gardner and the University of Washington's president, William Gerberding, send invitations to the Key Leader Orientation to key leaders in Washington communities. Invitations were mailed to leaders in 43 communities. In order for communities to be eligible to participate in the pilot study, they had to commit to bring five or more of the following types of key leaders to the Key Leader Orientation: a mayor, police chief, school superintendent, judge, human service agency director, faith community leader, business leader, and/or a media leader. Representatives from 32 communities across the state accepted the invitation and attended this first meeting, which was held in Seattle at the University of Washington. They then returned to their communities to start organizing coalitions to implement CTC [50].

The process evaluation of the two-year study found that 29 of the 32 communities formed coalitions and sent team members to the second training workshop on needs assessment and coalition development [50]. A year later, 28 coalitions were still operating and 22 submitted implementation plans for preventive interventions to research staff at the University of Washington. Surveys of coalition members indicated that their knowledge about risk factors improved after attending training, and 14 of the 22 plans indicated the use of prevention strategies to address prioritized risk factors. These results indicated that the majority of communities were successful in implementing CTC. However, feedback from communities suggested that two training workshops were insufficient to ensure that coalitions were well organized, able to train new members, and proficient in matching prioritized risk and protective factors with new preventive interventions. Coalition members also reported that key leaders did not always hold coalition members accountable for their prevention activities and that membership turnover was frequent.

Based on these findings, CTC developers added a third training for coalition members that focused on matching prioritized risk factors with prevention strategies and creating community action plans that specified how, where, and when prevention programs would be implemented. A second pilot study evaluated this expanded version of CTC (see Table 3.1). This project, named *Oregon Together!*, occurred in Oregon in 1990 to 1995 [51]. It was jointly managed by research staff at the University of Washington and the Oregon State Office of Alcohol and Drug Abuse Programs and was funded by the U.S. Center for Substance Abuse Prevention. To initiate *Oregon Together!*, these partners sent invitations to a CTC Key Leader Orientation to all mayors, police chiefs, school superintendents, chamber of commerce presidents, and district attorneys in the state.

The process evaluation of this initiative involved surveys of key leaders, coalition members, staff reports, and qualitative data taken from coalition meeting minutes and action plans [51]. These data indicated that 40 communities sent key leaders to the first training, 37 created coalitions (with two communities working together), 35 had coalition members attend both trainings, 31 created action plans in the first year of the project, and 28 submitted action plans in the second year. Over the two years of the study, 25 of the 35 (71%) trained coalitions implemented programs considered to have prior evidence of effectiveness. A study comparing this project to a community-based drug prevention initiative in Washington that did not involve training for community members in risk factor assessment or EBI implementation found that CTC communities in Oregon were more likely than those in Washington to collect quantitative data on risk factors, create prevention plans, and implement effective interventions [52]. These findings supported the hypothesis that use of the CTC system increased use of EBIs.

While the Oregon study was in progress, the Office of Juvenile Justice and Delinquency Prevention developed its Comprehensive Strategy, and Congress established the Title V: Incentive Grants for Local Delinquency Prevention Programs to support local delivery of the juvenile delinquency prevention programs [53]. The OJJDP initiative funded communities to use the CTC system to plan for and implement delinquency prevention programs. Communities received the two trainings delivered in the Washington State project (i.e., the Key Leader Orientation and the Risk and Resource Assessment training), and Juvenile Justice State Advisory Groups in each state determined the communities to be selected and trained in each state. From 1994 to 1996, over $50 million in training and support was provided to about 400 communities in 49 states.

When the Title V initiative was begun, the CTC system had not yet been developed to the point where it provided coalitions with explicit tools and guidance on how to conduct needs assessments or on the types of EBIs available to address these needs. Although coalitions received training in risk and resource assessment, the CTC Youth Survey had not yet been created to collect comprehensive data on risk and protective factors and very few sources of such data were easily accessible to communities. Coalitions were advised to collect administrative data from archival sources such as schools, law enforcement agencies, and/or health department records. Coalitions could also hold focus groups with key informants in the community or create their own surveys to be implemented with youth, but it was up to them to decide how to collect such data [51]. Similarly, communities were provided with information on evidence-based programs in the *Comprehensive Strategy Guide* [46], but not all of these interventions were actually available for use (e.g., some developers had not developed training protocols or materials that could be used in community replications), and not all had been tested in rigorous research trials.

Prevention science was still in its infancy and the development and rigorous testing of EBIs was not common.

Several nonexperimental evaluations were conducted to assess the implementation and outcomes of CTC in the Title V project. The Office of Juvenile Justice and Delinquency Prevention [53, 54] provided reports to Congress describing the number of communities that received funds, evaluations of the trainings, the diversity of organizations represented in CTC coalitions, and the types of key leaders who attended the Key Leader Orientations. In an evaluation of CTC communities receiving Title V funds in Iowa, Jenson and colleagues [55] found that most sites did not conduct a comprehensive assessment of risk and protective factors but, rather, used whatever data were available to them. Many collected anecdotal information during community discussions or simply relied on coalition members' knowledge of their communities. Coalitions identified a variety of community, family, school, and individual risk factors, but a more limited number of protective factors—most commonly, opportunities for involvement in school and the community, family bonding, and commitment to school. Based on interviews with community members, an estimated 16,000 youth and parents received a variety of prevention services, but many were not evidence based. Nonetheless, the study indicated that CTC communities in Iowa saw desired changes in school behaviors, academic performance, refusal skills, and court adjudications.

The U.S. Government Accountability Office [56] reported that CTC coalitions receiving Title V funding across the United States implemented 277 delinquency prevention programs, and 90% delivered two or more interventions identified as evidence based in the *Comprehensive Strategy Guide* [46]. The majority of programs were delivered to youth aged 12 to 16 and included parent training, after-school programs, changes to community or school policies, family therapy, school behavior management strategies, and mentoring with behavioral management. Evaluations conducted by the Office of Juvenile Justice and Delinquency Prevention [53] and the Government Accountability Office [56] indicated that youth in CTC communities experienced improvements in protective factors and reductions in risk factors, behavioral problems in schools, and delinquency. However, these studies provided only preliminary evidence of CTC's effectiveness because the evaluation was conducted only in CTC sites and did not include control communities not using the CTC system.

Although they could not produce definitive evidence of CTC's effectiveness, all three pilot studies achieved their primary goal of providing information on CTC implementation processes that could be used to further refine the CTC system. As noted, many communities reported challenges when conducting local needs assessments and in selecting and implementing EBIs to address their needs. Communities voiced the desire for easier methods to assess needs, as well as information allowing an objective prioritization of needs so that they did not have to rely on subjective and sometimes conflicting opinions from community members about the risks facing local youth. Developers realized that data that allowed comparison in the levels of risk and protective factors using a single metric would greatly simplify the needs assessment process, which led to the development of the CTC Youth Survey.

Communities also indicated a desire for more information on evidence-based programs that provided implementation supports like training, manuals, and technical assistance. This request eventually resulted in the publication of the *Prevention Strategies Guide* [57], which provided detailed information on EBIs, and later to the recommendation that communities use the Blueprints for Healthy Youth Development website (www. blueprintsprograms.com/) to select EBIs since its information is regularly updated. It was also during these pilot studies that the CTC developers observed that coalitions usually formed subcommittees and workgroups to implement the different phases of the CTC system. Realizing that this type of organization improved coalitions' efficiency, the workgroup structure was built into the CTC system, and some of the trainings were redesigned so that only members of the relevant workgroups were expected to participate, which also eased the burden on coalition members. These examples further illustrate the community-based participatory research approach utilized in CTC's development and evaluation.

Measurement Development
The Communities That Care Youth Survey

Given the importance of needs assessments to the CTC process and the challenges faced by communities when trying to assess needs, CTC developers realized they had to provide better guidance and more user-friendly methods to assist communities in this work. During the time that the CTC Youth Survey was being developed, some scientists had created surveys to collect self-reported data from youth on behavioral health problems. However, few of these surveys measured their precursors comprehensively, and most included only a subset of the many individual, peer, family, school, and community risk and protective factors identified through research as predictive of youth behavioral health problems. In addition, most surveys were conducted with small groups for particular research projects, and no instruments or cost- and time-efficient methods of survey administration had been developed to collect data from a representative sample of youth in a community, using items shown to be equally valid and reliable across age, gender, and racial/ethnic groups [58, 59].

The goal of the Six State Consortium project (see Table 3.1) was to address these gaps—that is, to develop a reliable and valid set of indicators to measure a broad range of empirically supported risk and protective factors, and to create a standard methodology for communities to use to collect and analyze the data. This project, funded by the Center for Substance Abuse Prevention, involved collaborations between researchers at the University of Washington and representatives from state-level agencies responsible for drug and alcohol prevention in Kansas, Maine, Oregon, South Carolina, Utah, and Washington. These agencies had worked with communities to assess risk and protective factors using school-based surveys and wanted to broaden these instruments and ensure that these measures were valid and reliable [58].

The Six State group created the CTC Youth Survey by combining information from existing survey instruments. The result was a comprehensive survey that could be administered in a single classroom period with middle and high school students.[2] The survey initially included 350 items hypothesized to measure 21 risk factors and 11 protective factors. Each risk and protective factor was measured using two or more survey questions, with items typically asking students to rate their agreement with statements using binary (no/yes) or Likert scale response choices [58].

The survey instrument and classroom administration procedures were pilot tested in six Oregon school districts with about 1,000 students in grades 6 to 12 [58]. After assessing the correlations between items and distribution of responses, the survey was revised to eliminate redundant questions and ensure adequate variance in responses. The new survey was then administered to a statewide probability sample of over 11,000 Oregon public school students in grades 6, 8, and 11. Researchers again analyzed responses to determine the reliability and validity of the individual items. Factor analyses, run separately by grade and gender, were used to determine the reliability and validity of the composite risk and protective scales.

These analyses indicated that a few risk and protective factors had weak factor structures or low reliabilities. Once these were eliminated, the CTC Youth Survey included 121 items measuring 29 risk and protective factors. All but one of the 29 risk and protective factor scales had average reliabilities of over 0.60 (and most had reliabilities greater than 0.70), and these values were consistent across grade level and gender [58]. To determine the validity of these measures, average scores of all the items in the scale were calculated for all the risk and protective factors. These scores were then correlated with students' reports of substance use and delinquency. All the risk factors were positively correlated with the problem behaviors, and all the protective factors were negatively correlated with outcomes, with correlations ranging in size across domains [58].

A subsequent study involved administration of a slightly revised CTC Youth Survey with 133 items to over 170,000 public school students in seven U.S. states (Colorado, Illinois, Kansas, Maine, Oregon, Utah, and Washington) [60]. This project was designed to provide a confirmatory test of the reliability of the risk and protective factors in a diverse sample and to assess if reliability differed by students' grade, gender, or race/ethnicity. According to confirmatory factor analysis, the results indicated that the survey provided reliable measures of 31 risk and protective factors for students in grades 6, 8, 10, and 12. In addition, the analyses indicated that the risk and protective factor scales were equally reliable across grade, gender, and five racial/ethnic groups, including African Americans, Asians or Pacific Islanders, Caucasians, Hispanics, and Native Americans.

From a community-based participatory research perspective, the development of the CTC Youth Survey addressed the needs and goals of both practitioners and researchers. Coalitions had requested easier procedures to guide needs assessments, and the CTC developers responded by creating and validating a relatively short, low-cost, easy-to-administer instrument that assessed a broad range of risk and protective factors and behavioral health problems. In addition, several formats for the display of the risk and protective factors were developed, and community and researcher input was collected to determine the formats that were most interpretable by community members [61, 62]. By training community coalitions in the methods needed to administer the survey in local schools and to interpret its results, CTC enhanced local capacity and empowered local groups to be responsible for collecting and analyzing information from their own young people. The CTC Youth Survey is now a standard part of the CTC system and used in Phase 3 to identify needs and in Phase 5 to assess changes in risk and protective factors and behavioral health outcomes following EBI implementation. CTC researchers have also relied on data from the survey when evaluating the effects of the CTC system on youth behavioral health problems.

Measures of Community Norms and Processes

After the CTC Youth Survey was developed, the next step was to develop valid and reliable indicators of the community attitudes and practices that are hypothesized in the CTC logic model to lead to changes in youth behavioral outcomes. When CTC was first developed, relatively few such measures existed, and so the CTC developers had to create new measures to assess CTC implementation and its effectiveness. These measures are summarized in Table 3.2.

Much of this measurement work was conducted during the Diffusion Project [63], a naturalistic study of the spread of community-based prevention undertaken in 1997–2002 (see Table 3.1). The Diffusion Project involved partnerships between CTC researchers at the University of Washington and administrators from state drug and alcohol-prevention agencies in Colorado, Illinois, Kansas, Maine, Oregon, Utah, and Washington. At the start of this study, state partners identified 20 small- and medium-sized incorporated towns they thought were using an evidence-based approach to prevent youth behavioral health problems (e.g., assessing risk and protective factors, implementing EBIs to address these factors, etc.). These towns were then

Table 3.2 Measurement Instruments Developed to Assess Community-Level Processes in the CTC System

Instrument	Purpose	Respondents
Community Key Informant Interview (CKI)	Measure community adoption of a science-based prevention framework, collaboration on prevention activities, support for prevention, norms regarding adolescent substance use, and use of the Social Development Strategy	Positional leaders (e.g., police chiefs and mayors) Prevention leaders (local prevention experts)
Community Resource Documentation (CRD)	Measure the adoption, implementation quality, and sustainability of EBIs by community agencies	Administrators and staff (including teachers) who deliver prevention services
Community Board Interview (CBI)	Measure coalition functioning and perceived effectiveness	Coalition coordinators and members

matched within the states on population size, racial/ethnic diversity, economic indicators, and crime rates to 21 comparison sites (one town was matched with two comparison sites) that were thought to be lacking a scientific approach to prevention [63, 64].

The Diffusion Project involved the development and first administration of the Community Key Informant (CKI) survey to measure the community-level constructs in the CTC logic model. This survey involved phone interviews with positional leaders (e.g., police chiefs, mayors, school superintendents, etc.), as well as other community members identified by the positional leaders as knowledgeable about community-based prevention services. One of the first constructs measured using this survey assessed the community's adoption of a science-based approach to prevention, which corresponds to the stages of adoption described in Rogers's [4] Diffusion of Innovations theory (see chapter 2). This measure was based on key informants' responses to items asking about their community's understanding of risk and protective factors, collection of data to conduct needs assessments, and implementation and monitoring of EBIs to address prioritized needs [63]. Analysis of responses from about 500 individuals in all 41 communities indicated that communities could be reliably differentiated in terms of their adoption of a science-based approach to prevention [63].

The Community Key Informant survey respondents also provided information regarding community collaboration [65], support for prevention [66], community norms related to adolescent substance use [67], and use of the Social Development Strategy by adults to encourage youth bonding [66]. All these measures have been used in evaluation studies to determine the degree to which CTC improves community processes related to the prevention of youth behavioral health problems.

The Community Resource Documentation (CRD) was also developed and first used in the Diffusion Project to measure the degree to which community organizations use EBIs to prevent youth behavioral health problems. Prior to the development of this tool, few methods existed to document the implementation of multiple types of EBIs by community-based organizations [68]. A few studies had examined schools' delivery of EBIs, typically using mail or phone surveys of school administrators and staff [69–72], and sometimes by asking students to report such services [73]. These studies have noted challenges in ensuring the reliability and validity of the findings, particularly when relying on secondary informants (e.g., administrators) who may be too far removed to accurately assess implementation practices [71].

The Community Resource Documentation was developed in the Diffusion Project to overcome these limitations and provide a methodology and instruments for measuring the delivery of EBIs across all service providers in a community, including schools and other youth-serving agencies and organizations (e.g., YMCAs, Boys and Girls Clubs). The CRD relies on phone interviews with agency administrators who identify the use of particular interventions implemented by their agency/organization in the year prior to the survey, using both open-ended questions and by selecting named interventions from a list of EBIs identified as effective in the CTC *Prevention Strategies Guide* [57]. Respondents also indicated the number of individuals who participated in these programs [68].

A final instrument developed in order to facilitate CTC implementation and to measure its effectiveness was the CTC Board Survey. Researchers at Pennsylvania State University created the first version of this survey during the CTC effectiveness trial conducted in Pennsylvania (described in the next section and in chapter 9), with some collaboration from the CTC developers. Survey items and constructs were derived using measures created for other community-based efforts, including items from the Diffusion Project's Community Key Informant Survey, which were modified to be suitable for prevention coalitions [63].

The Board Survey was first developed as a phone interview with coalition leaders and members who were asked to rate coalition functioning, as well as a few community factors expected to affect CTC implementation and coalition functioning (e.g., community readiness to engage in community-based prevention). Measures of coalition functioning include directedness (e.g., having clear goals and objectives), clarity of roles, and member participation. The perceived effectiveness of the coalition, including how well coalition leaders elicit support for the initiative and promote prevention in the community, is also rated, as is the amount of financial and human resources available to the group.

CTC Effectiveness Trial in Pennsylvania

As discussed at the start of this chapter, in the typical evaluation sequence, an efficacy evaluation precedes an effectiveness study. However, the reverse was true in the evaluation of CTC. The first major outcome evaluation undertaken to assess the impact of CTC on youth behavioral problems, which occurred before the efficacy trial mentioned in chapter 1,[3] was an effectiveness trial conducted in Pennsylvania (see Table 3.1). CTC was first adopted in Pennsylvania in 1994 using funds from the Title V initiative, which were supplemented by funds from the Pennsylvania Commission on Crime and

Delinquency (PCCD) and other state agencies [74]. State funding continued to support CTC implementation and the delivery of EBIs well after the Title V initiative had ended, and eventually led to the formation of over 120 CTC coalitions across the state [75].

As described in chapter 9, researchers at the Pennsylvania State University designed an effectiveness trial to assess whether CTC reduced youth behavioral health problems. A quasi-experimental evaluation compared changes in risk factors, protective factors, and behavioral health problems reported by middle and high school students on the CTC Youth Survey in counties that had adopted the CTC system and those in counties that had not adopted the CTC system [76, 77]. The study also examined the implementation of CTC in Pennsylvania communities, particularly coalition functioning and sustainability [e.g., 75, 78, 79] and EBI implementation and sustainability [80–83].

The Pennsylvania evaluation can be considered an effectiveness trial because implementation was carried out in naturalistic conditions with little involvement by CTC developers. CTC staff provided initial training to communities, then trained Pennsylvania personnel to deliver subsequent training workshops and technical assistance [84]. Researchers at Pennsylvania State University conducted the outcome evaluation independent of CTC developers, a strategy recommended in effectiveness studies [17] to help guard against the potential for bias and/or conflicts of interest when developers evaluate their own interventions [85–87]. The Pennsylvania initiative also involved a diverse and large number of communities, with the largest number of CTC coalitions (over 100 in the study on coalition sustainability; see 75) and young people (over 100,000 in the study by Mark Feinberg and colleagues; see 77) involved in any CTC study to date.

Efficacy Trial

The Community Youth Development Study was an efficacy trial begun after the effectiveness trial was launched in Pennsylvania (see Table 3.1 and Figure 1.3). It was funded by the National Institute on Drug Abuse, National Cancer Institute, National Institute of Child Health and Human Development, National Institute of Mental Health, Center for Substance Abuse Prevention, and National Institute on Alcohol Abuse and Alcoholism. The study was initiated in 2002 following the Diffusion Project, and like that study, involved researchers at the University of Washington and administrators from state drug- and alcohol-prevention agencies in Colorado, Illinois, Kansas, Maine,

Oregon, Utah, and Washington. It involved 12 of the matched pairs of communities from the Diffusion Project, for a total of 24 communities. In these 12 pairs of communities, both communities in the matched pair had been found to have low levels of adoption of a science-based approach to prevention based on information from the Community Key Informant survey administered in the Diffusion Project. These communities were therefore deemed to be eligible for a randomized trial to evaluate whether or not CTC could enhance science-based prevention and reduce youth behavioral health problems.

Compared to the Pennsylvania study, the efficacy trial included fewer communities, more involvement by the CTC developers, more oversight of CTC implementation, and a more comprehensive and rigorous investigation of implementation and outcomes. It was a randomized controlled trial, in which the 24 communities were randomly assigned to implement CTC ($n = 12$) or to serve as control communities [88]. The project provided sites assigned to the CTC condition with training in all five phases of CTC and four years of funding to support EBI implementation, and weekly or biweekly technical assistance administered via telephone and occasional in-person contacts [89]. These contacts, along with reports from coalition members and staff delivering EBIs, allowed implementation procedures to be carefully monitored [89, 90]. When implementation challenges occurred, technical assistance providers worked with local coalitions to address problems and ensure high-quality implementation of the CTC system. Nonetheless, even in the efficacy trial, research staff embraced the community-based participatory research approach and viewed their role as helping to support, not dictate, community actions. Furthermore, local coalition members took ownership and responsibility for implementing all CTC phases; for example, they decided the needs to be addressed and outcomes to be achieved in their own communities, and they selected, implemented, and monitored the EBIs that addressed prioritized local needs and youth behavioral health problems.

The randomized study evaluated the impact of CTC on community processes using data from the Key Informant Survey and Community Resource Documentation survey developed previously [66, 91–93]. Short- and long-term changes in risk factors, protective factors, and youth behavioral health problems were assessed by analyzing data from a longitudinal panel of youth followed annually beginning in grade 5, and from repeated, cross-sectional surveys of middle and high school youth in all communities, all of whom completed the CTC Youth Survey [64, 94–101]. In addition, formal tests of mediation were conducted to identify the degree to which changes in community processes were associated with reductions in youth behavioral problems [102].

As described in more detail in chapters 8 and 9, the effectiveness and ef-ficacy trials both indicated that use of the CTC system improved community processes and reduced youth behavioral health problems. Importantly, these studies also provided useful information on implementation processes that led to further development of the CTC system. As discussed in chapter 9, during the first years of the Pennsylvania effectiveness study, researchers real-ized that many coalitions faced challenges when enacting the five phases of CTC and that more extensive technical assistance was needed to support their prevention efforts. Over time, the state increased its provision of technical assistance and eventually created a centralized agency, the Evidence-based Prevention and Intervention Support Center (EPISCenter; see www.episcenter. psu.edu) to provide training and consultation to CTC coalitions. Staff from the EPISCenter deliver both individualized and group-based support to coalitions across the state, which helps to ensure proactive and standardized technical assistance and creates learning communities and mutual support systems among those implementing CTC and selected EBIs [103].

In the efficacy trial, coalitions sometimes reported challenges in ensuring that key leaders and coalition members attended the six to seven in-person training workshops, which ranged in duration from a half day to two full days, that were part of the CTC training system at the time the study was conducted. These trainings were delivered by CTC trainers during the first year of the project to assist communities in completing all five phases of CTC [89]. As new leaders took office and new members joined the CTC coalitions in subse-quent years, they also needed training, but it was difficult for coalition leaders to arrange for and justify the costs of hiring CTC trainers to conduct formal workshops. As a result, new members often received only a brief orientation to the CTC system, which may have been insufficient to promote their full un-derstanding of the system and prevention science.

In 2013, with financial support from the National Institute on Drug Abuse, the CTC developers created a web-streamed training curriculum to address these challenges.[4] The web-streamed workshops include the same content as the in-person trainings, but they divide the information into 50 modules that can be completed more quickly than the original workshops and be sched-uled at times more convenient for local community members. As in the orig-inal trainings, the information is still presented using interactive methods, but the web-based system takes advantage of newer and more engaging tech-nologies. The core content is delivered in short (two- to five-minute) videos that include use of a "Ted Talk" style to explain the main idea of each preven-tion concept, as well as instructional videos to provide detailed descriptions of the specific steps needed to operationalize the concept, and examples and experiences from CTC communities. Participants discuss this information, take short quizzes to test their understanding of the CTC system, and complete worksheets outlining how their coalitions will use the information.

The standardized videos ensure that the core content is delivered in a consistent manner across sites, and the information can be accessed any time it is needed to refresh participants' understanding. Another advantage of the web-based system is that CTC coalition coordinators, not CTC trainers (now called "coaches"), facilitate the sessions. Coordinators receive a three-day orientation when first hired that provides them with the content and skills they need to facilitate CTC in their communities, including the web-streamed workshops. All the web-based modules contain instructions and discussion points to guide the coordinators' delivery of the trainings. By empowering local coordinators to facilitate these workshops, the web-based system exemplifies CTC's community-based participatory research approach. The method also reduces the costs of training and allows more workshops to be facilitated than was possible in the previous system, which should allow for greater dissemination of CTC. Coordinators are not left entirely on their own, however. CTC coaches provide an initial three-day orientation, then regularly communicate with coordinators to support their implementation of the CTC system. Together, the web-based workshops and coaching contacts are referred to as CTC Plus.

Summary and Introduction of the Next Section

This chapter has described the development and evaluation of the CTC system to illustrate how community-based interventions and other types of EBIs should build upon theory, empirical research, and participant input to create and evaluate a model of change intended to prevent behavioral health problems. We described different stages of evaluation, including pilot studies that examine the feasibility of implementation procedures, more rigorous efficacy trials to assess intervention outcomes, and effectiveness and dissemination trials to examine the impact and sustainability of community-based interventions when they are taken to scale. We also illustrated how the CTC developers have followed these steps and developed and evaluated the CTC system using appropriate and rigorous research methods. During all phases of evaluation, the CTC developers used a community-based participatory research approach that allowed them to develop procedures and protocols that would best assist community members to utilize the science of prevention. As such, multiple iterations of protocol development and community feedback were required to develop a system that was easy to understand and implement. The resulting system allows community members to approach their prevention efforts as citizen scientists.

In the next section of the book, we discuss community-based prevention and the CTC system in more detail. The CTC system currently involves five phases that represent important aspects of community-based prevention, including assessing community readiness to undertake a collaborative prevention effort (which occurs in Phases 1 and 2 of the CTC system), forming coalitions (in Phase 2), conducting needs and resource assessments (in Phase 3), selecting EBIs (in Phase 4), and implementing and sustaining EBIs and coalitions (in Phase 5). We begin each chapter in section two by describing why these constructs and activities are important for achieving community-wide reductions in behavioral health problems. We also describe the challenges likely to be faced when communities engage in these activities and identify the methods that can be used to avoid or address these problems.

Throughout these chapters, we summarize findings from the larger bodies of literature on community coalitions and prevention science. We also draw upon our own work to illustrate how the five phases of CTC build community capacity to conduct community-based prevention. We continue to discuss how CTC has been refined over the years using a community-based participatory approach, in which the challenges faced by communities have led to refinements and enhancements to the CTC system, including its provision of training and technical assistance.

Additionally, we provide examples from CTC communities that have participated in the studies mentioned in this chapter, as well as examples from international sites that have adopted the CTC system. To date, the CTC system has been implemented in Australia and Canada and in some countries in Europe and South America. Many of these initiatives have involved pilot studies and/or process evaluations. The most rigorous international study to date is a quasi-experimental evaluation conducted in the Netherlands [104, 105]. As CTC is disseminated worldwide, it is even more important to understand its implementation requirements, the actions needed to ensure high-quality implementation, and the outcomes that can be achieved when CTC is fully implemented.

We believe the information provided in section two will be of value to multiple audiences. We strive to provide enough detail in these chapters so that practitioners wishing to conduct community-based prevention and/or CTC have enough information to guide their work. We also believe that scientists who are developing and testing community-based preventive interventions and/or assisting communities to implement these interventions, especially those who use a community-based participatory research approach, will find this information useful. Over the years, scientists have had many questions about how CTC is implemented, and the articles we have published in academic journals rarely allow adequate space to fully describe the ways in which the system is adopted in communities, even though such information is critical for understanding why it produces effects. Finally, we hope to convince policymakers that community-based prevention is worthy of investment, and that communities need dedicated, long-term funding to be successful in their efforts to reduce youth behavioral health problems.

SECTION TWO

Implementing CTC and Similar Community-Based Preventive Interventions

The Importance of Readiness and High-Functioning Coalitions in Community-Based Prevention

COMMUNITY-BASED PREVENTION EFFORTS seek to reduce behavioral health problems and improve health and well-being across the entire population [1, 2]. Community participation has been used as a health-promotion strategy for many decades, including efforts to improve cardiovascular health, reduce smoking, prevent alcohol and drug use, and reduce crime [3–5]. More recently, Kania and Kramer [6] recommended community participatory approaches to produce a collective impact on behavioral health problems. To achieve a collective impact requires strong support and active involvement of community stakeholders from multiple organizations and varied perspectives who work together to achieve change. Collaboration is necessary since no single group is likely to produce community-wide changes in behavioral health problems on its own, even though this is the typical method of service provision in communities [6].

Although community mobilization has the potential to create desired changes in communities, it can be difficult to achieve. Consider one of the communities implementing CTC in the Community Youth Development Study (CYDS), the efficacy trial evaluating the effectiveness of CTC. This affluent rural community, comprising five small towns all served by a single school district, had experienced a series of youth suicides just prior to the start of the study. Although they were concerned about the problem, residents were reluctant to acknowledge the factors that might have contributed to the deaths, including relatively high rates of alcohol and other drug use among teenagers and repeated episodes of bullying in the area's middle school and high school.

Law enforcement, often at the request of influential parents, tended to over-look adolescent delinquency and drug use, and service providers often worked in isolation from each other, preferring to focus on their own particular areas of concern and service populations. In early conversations about CTC, many community members reported that they were too busy to participate in a coa-lition and were wary that resources would be unequally distributed across the five towns in the region. However, the towns' leaders agreed to adopt the CTC system, and eventually, the CTC coalition had representation from residents of all five towns, and a variety of businesses and organizations provided finan-cial support for prevention activities [7].

As this example illustrates, it can be challenging to establish consensus on social problems and encourage collective action to address them, even in seemingly well-off and "organized" communities. What about "disorganized" communities? One of the first attempts to prevent juvenile crime using a community-based approach was initiated in the 1930s in socially disorgan-ized neighborhoods in Chicago—that is, in areas with high rates of juvenile crime, poverty, a lack of cohesion and trust among residents, and high res-idential turnover [8]. The (then) novel premise of the Chicago Area Project (CAP) was that delinquency prevention had to be undertaken by community members because youth problems were directly related to the social environ-ment [5]. The CAP developers acknowledged that it would be difficult to mobi-lize community members and agencies, given that many residents lacked the knowledge and skills necessary for effective prevention, and because many organizations did not have an adequate infrastructure to deliver and mon-itor services. An evaluation indicated that local residents did participate in the project [5], and the CAP still exists in many Chicago neighborhoods (www. chicagoareaproject.org/chicago-area-project-model). However, the CAP did not reduce youth crime [9]. Its failure to produce results suggests that com-munity mobilization, in and of itself, may be insufficient to produce signifi-cant reductions in behavioral health problems [10, 11].

These and other community-based preventive interventions have dem-onstrated that communities vary in their willingness to be mobilized for ac-tion and in their capacity to engage in effective prevention. At the same time, evaluations of community- and coalition-based preventive interventions have identified certain features of communities and their residents that affect the ability to reduce youth behavioral problems. To be successful, communi-ties should (1) be "ready" to undertake collaborative action; and (2) have the knowledge, skills, and infrastructure (i.e., the capacity) to engage in effective prevention actions [1, 10, 12–16]. This chapter will review these issues and pro-vide recommendations about how communities can assess and enhance their

FIGURE 4.1 The Five Phases of the Communities That Care Prevention System

readiness to engage in change efforts and to build and maintain strong, diverse coalitions. To do so, we draw upon the lessons learned from the coalition literature and our experiences with CTC, since Phases 1 (*Get Started*) and 2 (*Get Organized*) of the CTC address these two issues, as shown in Figure 4.1.

The Importance of Readiness for Community Change

To be "ready" for effective community-based prevention means that community members are willing to address behavioral health problems and believe that it is possible to prevent these negative outcomes [16, 17]. Readiness is an attitudinal construct related to the belief or perception that change is needed, will be beneficial, and is possible [18, 19]. Readiness represents the *potential* for successful community action, not whether or not actions have actually occurred or been successful. Readiness is directly related to success, however, because a new evidence-based intervention (EBI) is much more likely to be adopted, fully implemented, and sustained if readiness is present [18, 20].

Although readiness has also been conceptualized as an individual- and an organizational-level construct,[1] we consider community-level readiness in this chapter given our focus on community-based prevention. A community is ready to undertake such an initiative when community members agree that a problem is present and needs to be addressed, believe that it can be prevented, share a sense of commitment to and responsibility for the community, have effective leaders who can facilitate collaborative action, and have sufficient resources and an organizational infrastructure to support change efforts [26]. Together, these elements are also referred to as "community capacity" [19, 27–29]. Communities will vary in their readiness to engage in community-based prevention, but strategies exist to address readiness barriers and build community capacity [30].

One of the first tasks in a community-based prevention effort is to assess readiness. Readiness can be assessed by collecting qualitative data during one-on-one meetings or focus groups with community members, or by conducting quantitative surveys of key informants, the leaders and citizens who are most knowledgeable about the community and/or the problem to be addressed [18, 30]. Ruth Edwards and colleagues [16] state that readiness can be reliably assessed with information from just four or five community informants, as long as the respondents are key stakeholders who are truly concerned about the problem(s) to be addressed. Others suggest that a larger number of respondents is necessary to adequately represent the views of the entire community, including those from different racial/ethnic groups, cultural backgrounds, and economic levels [19, 31, 32]. Different groups have unique challenges and perspectives that influence their attitudes about promotion and prevention, and this diversity should be taken into account when assessing readiness.

Readiness assessments provide an opportunity for representatives from diverse groups to discuss the community climate, attitudes, infrastructure, and resources likely to affect the implementation and success of a community-based initiative. To measure these factors, readiness assessments typically ask residents to report their perceptions of the degree to which they and/or other members of the community are aware of the problem(s) to be addressed, are committed to the community, have previously participated in change efforts, and have a positive attitude regarding prevention. They may also be asked about the presence of formal and informal ties between residents and organizations, the history of collaborative efforts in the community, commitment from local leaders to address problems, leaders' ability to build consensus and collaborative relationships, and the availability of resources to address needs [19, 30–32]. The goal is to collect information on the strengths of the community that can be built upon and the deficits or obstacles that will need to be minimized prior to launching the new initiative [19]. By soliciting stakeholder input from diverse groups at the beginning of the change effort, assessments can also generate awareness of, support for, and investment in the new initiative [30, 32].

When significant barriers are identified, they must be addressed. Moving forward without doing so is likely to threaten success and demoralize residents. Furthermore, if different groups identify different issues, some reconciliation and/or prioritization of the problems may be required prior to moving forward. Some literature indicates that readiness can be built by focusing first on smaller scale, more feasible problems that do not require significant resources. For example, in the *Yes, We Can* community-based initiative in Battle Creek, Michigan, residents of seven impoverished neighborhoods agreed that educational and economic inequality were the most important problems facing their communities; however, these issues would require significant time, resources, and capacity building to address [33]. Community members decided that, in the short term, they could tackle immediate problems related to resident safety with manageable tasks such as installing streetlights and cleaning up neighborhood parks. Creating "quick" [15], "small" wins [33] like these can help to build skills, generate enthusiasm, and increase readiness and capacity, all of which will be needed to address larger scale problems. At the same time, it is important to maintain a focus on the long-term goals and not be sidetracked by less serious issues [15, 33].

Because community members will implement the prevention activities, it is important that formal and informal leaders, service providers, and the targets of intervention activities (e.g., youth and families) all agree on the problem(s) to be addressed and support the method(s) used to address the problem. For example, when a substantial proportion of adults in a community consider under-age drinking as a rite of passage and not very harmful, efforts to prevent alcohol use by teenagers using formal actions (e.g., increasing arrests) or informal mechanisms (e.g., media campaigns) will probably not be successful. Similarly, if other problems in the community (e.g., poverty or unemployment) are viewed as most important, then it may be difficult to generate community engagement in the prevention of youth behavioral health problems [34] unless these problems can be linked to other issues of concern—for example, by identifying common risk and protective factors that affect multiple problems and/or demonstrating that one issue is likely to affect the other. Readiness assessments allow communities to identify these issues early enough in the process to allow support for the initiative to be built on a common foundation.

Champions can be a very effective mechanism for generating buy-in and enhancing readiness for community-based prevention efforts [16, 20, 35]. Champions are respected, influential, and well-connected community members who enthusiastically endorse the initiative and are fully committed to putting it into practice. As early adopters [36], they seek to persuade others of the importance of the community-based intervention and to engender excitement and resources from all those in the community who need to be involved. Champions can increase visibility of the problem and identify solutions for addressing it. For example, in communities in which under-age drinking is tolerated, champions might organize town hall meetings to highlight and discuss the negative consequences of teen drinking and to describe how a community-based approach can prevent adolescent alcohol use. They might also meet individually with other key stakeholders to discuss these issues.

Even if a community is aware of and concerned about a particular behavioral health problem, there may be resistance to engaging in collaborative action to address the issue, particularly in communities with a history of failed partnerships. As a result, it is important to understand past efforts to address community problems and the degree to which community members and/or agencies trust one other and are willing to work together to solve problems. For example, Sheppard Kellam [37] noted significant challenges in creating school/community partnerships in Chicago due to preexisting tensions between school administrators and parents. In such cases, significant time and effort will be needed to foster communication and trust between groups.

Readiness for community-based prevention also requires some level of organizational infrastructure and adequate human and financial resources [6]. Unfortunately, communities with the greatest need to prevent behavioral health problems often have the lowest levels of capacity to implement and sustain change efforts [5, 38]. For example, in the 10 socially disorganized urban communities involved in the *Making Connections* project, local agencies did not typically work in unison, nonprofit groups were scarce and not well funded, and residential poverty and turnover were high [39]. Similarly, Pennie Foster-Fishman and colleagues [33] found that residents of high-poverty neighborhoods participating in the *Yes, We Can* initiative in Battle Creek struggled to collaborate and to access community resources. These types of readiness problems can undermine the success of a community-based initiative, and capacity should be built prior to seriously considering the adoption of a collaborative approach to prevention.

Assessments of prevention infrastructure must consider whether or not there is a suitable institutional home, or backbone organization [6], to support the community-based initiative. Compared to other types of EBIs like school-based programs, community-based prevention efforts are less likely to have a natural home. At the same time, since these interventions rely on participation from multiple organizations, there may be many options for the institutional home, all of which will need to be considered. In order to increase the visibility, legitimacy, and sustainability of the initiative, the lead agency should have credibility in the community and stable resources [13, 40, 41]. The PROSPER project described in chapter 1 was intentionally designed to build upon local infrastructure and embeds its community-based system in already-established educational systems: local school districts and land-grant university cooperative extension systems. These organizations are already dedicated to improving local communities and have stable funding streams, both of which should enhance local ownership and sustainability of the project [42].

Having a dedicated backbone organization is also important to support coalition staff. Community-based initiatives should have at least one paid staff person to oversee all the managerial, evaluation, and facilitation tasks required for success [6, 43]. Similar to the champion, staff should be well respected in the community, have ties to formal and informal leaders, and be viewed as credible and trustworthy [18, 44]. They will need a diverse skill set, including organizational and management skills; data collection and analysis skills; and strong interpersonal skills to help foster shared decision making, manage conflict, and delegate and oversee tasks.

To summarize, community readiness to undertake collaborative prevention is a multifaceted construct that cannot be taken for granted. The degree to which a community is ready to engage in collaborative action will affect the quality of implementation and sustainability of its prevention efforts [18, 38, 45]. For these reasons, the first steps in a community-based initiative should be to assess readiness and address all identified impediments to readiness.

How Does the CTC System Assess and Enhance Community Readiness?

Recognizing the centrality of readiness to successful community-based prevention, CTC begins with an assessment of the community's readiness to undertake a collaborative approach to the prevention of youth behavioral health problems. During Phases 1 (*Get Started*) and 2 (*Get Organized*) of the CTC system (see Figure 4.1), community leaders and stakeholders consider their community's prevention-related attitudes, resources, and history of collaboration; they determine if there are any threats to readiness; and they discuss if and how these challenges can be addressed. CTC is typically initiated by one or more community residents, or catalysts, who have a strong interest in fostering healthy youth development and believe that the system could be effective in preventing behavioral health problems of local youth. The catalyst begins the process by learning about the CTC system using the "Investing in Your Community's Youth" and "Tools for Community Leaders" guides,[2] talking to other communities that have used CTC, and/or communicating with a CTC coach. If the catalyst(s) thinks the community is ready to implement CTC, the next step is for key leaders to learn more about the system in a Key Leader Orientation. During this meeting, they conduct a comprehensive readiness assessment to determine if CTC can be successfully implemented in their community.

At this stage, CTC takes a top-down approach to community mobilization. It begins with the leadership of a community because leaders have access to the resources that will be needed to implement EBIs. Participation by the city's top government (e.g., the mayor), law enforcement (e.g., police chief or sheriff), and education (e.g., school superintendent) officials is essential because these authorities either lead or have connections to the organizations most likely to be involved in or affected by CTC activities [46, 47]. In addition, these and other leaders (e.g., administrators of human service, business, health services, public health, and United Way and other nonprofit agencies) can bring visibility and credibility to the effort and can use their influence and connections to solicit participation and support from others. They are best positioned to change local policies and practices, influence local norms, recruit stakeholders, and hold community members accountable for prevention actions. A reluctance on the part of these officials to support implementation of CTC signals problems with readiness that will have to be addressed before moving forward.

The Key Leader Orientation is designed to provide leaders with information about CTC and to generate commitment, support, and participation for its implementation. In doing so, the training workshop helps to build readiness among leaders. It familiarizes key leaders with concepts critical to the successful implementation of CTC—for example, that behavioral problems can be prevented, there are known risk and protective factors that predict youth behavioral health problems, there are proven methods for preventing these problems (i.e., EBIs), and community members can facilitate healthy youth development by creating a more supportive environment for young people, as illustrated in the Social Development Model. Key leaders are asked to pledge their commitment to CTC by participating on a Key Leader Board, the governing body that provides support and oversight for CTC initiative.

During the initial conversations between the catalyst and key leaders, as well as in the Key Leader Orientation and again in a subsequent workshop for coalition members (the Community Board Orientation), local stakeholders identify the behavioral health problems of greatest concern in their community that should be addressed by CTC. They also decide on the "community" to be involved and organized in the initiative—that is, the geographical or jurisdictional boundaries that will mark the area where CTC activities will occur. These discussions help define the scope of the initiative and set the stage for the readiness assessment.

The readiness assessment identifies features of the community expected to facilitate and impede full implementation of the CTC system. The first issue to be considered is the degree to which community members share a belief in the value of preventing behavioral health problems and if they view such behaviors as inevitable or as possible to prevent. For example, key leaders and coalition members consider local norms regarding the acceptability or tolerance of youth substance use, delinquency, and/or school drop-out. They also reflect on prior community change efforts and discuss the degree to which individuals and agencies have already demonstrated a willingness and ability to engage in collaborative actions and if collaboration will be likely to occur in CTC. Because CTC is predicated on participation by diverse and representative members of the community, they consider all the groups and individuals whose input and participation will be needed and discuss the degree to which distrust, discrimination, and competing priorities will limit participation and coordination across groups.

Next, key leaders and coalition members consider the degree to which their community has the infrastructure and resources necessary for CTC implementation, including an organization to support CTC and capable staff to oversee activities. Unlike the PROSPER system, which prescribes that coalitions are housed in local educational systems, it is up to each CTC community to determine the lead agency that is best suited to providing fiscal oversight of CTC activities, as well as meeting rooms, office space, and supervision of staff. The host organization should have credibility in the community, which will bring added visibility and legitimacy to the CTC initiative, and should be structurally and financially stable. Each coalition should have a paid, full-time staff person, the CTC coalition coordinator, who is responsible for facilitating, documenting, and evaluating coalition activities. This position requires strong administrative and interpersonal skills, as well as a willingness to work flexible hours. Key leaders must also consider whether or not the community has adequate financial resources to support the operating costs of the coalition, staff, and EBIs, or if new funding will need to be accessed or provided. They will also have to decide if their school districts will approve the administration of the CTC Youth Survey to gather data on risk, protection, and youth behavioral health problems, since information from the survey is necessary when assessing needs in Phase 3.

The final determination to be made by key leaders and coalition members is whether or not there are any "show stopper" readiness problems that are certain to threaten CTC success; for example, reluctance from schools to administer the CTC Youth Survey [48]. If challenges are considered to be insurmountable, the community should not adopt the CTC system. If threats to readiness can be addressed, then participants identify the actions that must be taken to do so, the parties responsible for these actions, and a timeline for moving forward. Even if no major concerns are identified at this stage, it is possible for readiness problems to emerge over time, and communities will have to continue to examine readiness as they move forward and take actions to solve problems as they arise. For example, an organization that initially served as the lead organization may lose its funding or experience a change in administration or mission. If it can no longer support CTC, a new host organization will have to be identified.

In our experience, threats to readiness will be present in all communities, and readiness problems can lead to a failure to adopt CTC or to poor implementation of the CTC system. Although CTC researchers have not systematically tracked the number of communities that fail to adopt CTC due to readiness issues, recall that in the Washington State pilot study discussed in chapter 3, 91% of the communities that sent leaders to a Key Leader Orientation formed coalitions [49], as did 93% of the communities participating in the Oregon pilot study [50]. In a more recent pilot evaluation of CTC in Colombia, 8 of the 10 communities (80%) had sufficient readiness to undertake CTC [51]. These data suggest that, at least among communities willing to participate in a readiness assessment and/or a Key Leader Orientation, a minority will identify "show stopper" readiness problems.

However, readiness problems that are not resolved can negatively impact CTC implementation and effectiveness. For example, in a pilot study of CTC involving three communities in the United Kingdom [52, 53], one site had a history of animosity and poor working relationships between professional service providers and grass-roots members of the community. This situation was not addressed, and over time, service providers impeded efforts by other community members to participate in the CTC coalition (e.g., by arranging meetings at inconvenient times or places), which resulted in a coalition which lacked diversity, experienced much conflict, and ultimately failed to implement EBIs at sufficient scale to achieve desired changes. In the second community, an influential key leader was instrumental in adopting CTC but left his position and the Key Leader Board shortly after CTC started. The coalition was unable to garner strong support from other key leaders, the Key Leader Board disbanded, and few funds were available to implement EBIs since key leaders were not available to solicit resources. In contrast, the third U.K. community had a strong history of collaboration and had initiated some community change efforts prior to the launch of CTC, providing much more fertile ground for CTC.

In the Community Youth Development Study, the efficacy trial evaluating CTC effectiveness, no showstopper readiness problems were identified in the 12 communities randomly assigned to implement CTC. Prior to random assignment, in all 24 communities, the project staff provided information about CTC and the study to the mayor, police chief/sheriff, and school superintendent of each community, and they all signed letters of support agreeing that their community would be randomly assigned to intervention and control conditions. In addition, all the school superintendents agreed to the administration of the CTC Youth Survey in middle and high schools. Readiness was facilitated in this study by the fact that all 24 communities had previously worked with research staff and administered the CTC Youth Survey several times as part of the Diffusion Project (see chapter 3). In addition, the efficacy trial provided each of the 12 CTC communities with funding to support a full-time CTC coordinator salary for five years and $75,000 per year for four years to implement EBIs [54].

Even with these supports, a readiness challenge reported in most communities in the randomized trial was difficulty in recruiting key leaders to serve on the Key Leader Board and to act as CTC champions [7, 55]. For example, 8 of the 12 CTC coordinators reported that it was very challenging to find champions [7]. To address this obstacle, coordinators and coalition members arranged meetings with numerous key leaders to explain CTC and the responsibilities of a CTC champion (e.g., speaking to the media, publically recognizing CTC volunteers, etc.). Eighteen months after the Key Leader Orientation, 8 of the 12 CTC communities had secured formal champions [7]. Nonetheless, some turnover of champions and members of the Key Leader Board occurred in all communities during the project, necessitating additional recruitment activities.

Securing agreement from local organizations to serve as host agencies was also challenging for some of the CTC communities. Across the 12 CTC communities, there was variation in the types of organizations serving as lead agencies and in the time required to recruit these organizations. Success was most easily achieved when key leaders used their influence and resources to secure a host organization. For example, in two communities, mayors agreed from the outset to donate office space in City Hall for coordinators and coalition meetings. Having the city serve as the lead organization brought visibility and financial security to these CTC initiatives. In both communities, administrators drew upon their relatively stable city budgets to fund the coordinators' positions when research funds ended.

In two other sites, schools served as stable lead organizations and housed coordinators throughout the first five years of the study. In other communities,

youth-serving organizations (Boys and Girls Clubs and YMCAs), health and social service agencies (including a drug treatment facility), and nonprofit organizations (e.g., the United Way organization) acted as lead agencies. Although
nonprofit organizations may strongly support CTC as a system for promoting
healthy youth development, their precarious financial stability can be problematic. The first community in the Community Youth Development Study
to fail to sustain CTC after the implementation phase had ended was unable
to find resources to support the coordinator, who was housed in a small nonprofit organization [56].

Communities in the randomized trial also experienced some challenges in
hiring and retaining skillful CTC coordinators. As discussed earlier, coalition
staff must possess a range of skills, and it can be difficult to find individuals who
are well suited to this position.[3] In the Community Youth Development Study,
communities selected coordinators with various credentials and backgrounds,
making it difficult to pinpoint the ideal coordinator. Some coordinators had
only a high school degree while several had graduate education. Some were
former educators attracted to the CTC mission of fostering healthy youth development. Because they had close connections to local school districts, these
coordinators were particularly skillful in persuading schools to adopt new EBIs
[57]. Several coordinators came from youth-serving and social service agency
backgrounds. They understood how to collaborate with community partners
and had experience making the most of scarce resources. Some coordinators
had prior experience in community mobilization and were adept at group facilitation and collaborative decision making. In one of the 12 sites, the coordinator was new to the community and had to spend more time establishing
credibility and building relationships, but the coordinator was successful in
doing so and remained in the position for the first five years of the study.

Nonetheless, some turnover in coordinators occurred. Five of the 12
coordinators who were hired at baseline resigned during the first five years of
the study. However, the reasons for their departures varied and cannot be directly tied to any particular combination or deficit of skills. Turnover in the coordinator position delayed CTC implementation to some degree and resulted
in additional strain and work for coalitions, but in no case did it lead to the
dissolution of the coalition during the first five years of the trial. In contrast, in
one of the low-implementing CTC communities in the United Kingdom, the
departure of the first coordinator led to a six-month delay in CTC activities and
significant coalition conflict about potential replacements [52]. A new coordinator was hired but left the position within the year and was never replaced,
partly due to a lack of funding and partly because of the coalition dysfunction.
In any implementation of CTC, then, coalitions must be prepared for turnover

of both key leaders and community coordinators and ensure that they have a plan in place to recruit and train new personnel.

In the Community Youth Development Study, all 12 CTC communities received extensive and proactive technical assistance during the first five years of the study to promote skillful and committed coalition coordinators. Research staff at the University of Washington conducted weekly one-on-one phone calls to the locally based CTC coalition coordinators, visited communities once or twice a year, and held monthly group trainings and a three-day in-person training each year for all coordinators.[4] During these interactions, staff and coordinators reviewed implementation progress, discussed solutions to identified implementation barriers, and celebrated successes. In addition, when coalition coordinators left, research staff helped local community members identify and train new staff and to ensure that CTC goals and activities were maintained during the interim period. Staff supervision and monitoring has been linked to better implementation of EBIs of varied types [58, 59], and the coaching provided in the randomized trial probably helped to ensure that local coordinators had the organizational, evaluation, and interpersonal skills needed for successful community-based prevention efforts [5, 60, 61].

As these examples make clear, attending to readiness at the start of a community-based intervention is essential for its long-term success. In the Pennsylvania effectiveness trial of CTC (described in chapter 3), higher scores on community readiness, as reported by key leaders in 21 CTC communities, were associated with better functioning CTC coalitions and more perceived effectiveness of the CTC initiative [62]. These findings demonstrate the linkages between the phases of CTC—namely, that a ready community is better equipped to create an effective coalition, the organizational body that is essential to achieving community-wide change, as described next.

The Importance of High-Functioning Community Coalitions

A core component of community-based preventive interventions is reliance on local stakeholders to achieve desired outcomes [e.g., 1, 31, 35, 63]. Because communities differ in behavioral health problems, and in the risk and protective factors related to these behaviors, a one-size-fits-all approach to community-wide prevention, especially a prevention effort initiated by an outsider with little community participation, is unlikely to be effective. Community members are necessary for both planning and overseeing change efforts because they are knowledgeable about their community's needs, as well as the sociopolitical context and resources that will affect the types of interventions that can be feasibly delivered to address these needs [28, 64, 65]. Compared to scientists who will eventually have to move on to other projects, residents of the community are better positioned to support the sustainability of prevention efforts [66]. Stakeholder participation also helps increase trust and communication between community members and facilitates a shared set of norms regarding acceptable and unacceptable behaviors, which should directly foster healthy youth development [67].

Although there are many benefits to mobilizing community members, community participation can be difficult to elicit. Community members may not wish to be involved in a change effort, may not know how to join the effort, or may be excluded from change efforts. Once involved, they may lose focus, disagree on the actions to be taken, and/or drift from agreed-upon goals. Community coalitions, or groups of "individuals representing diverse organizations, factions or constituencies who agree to work together in order to achieve a common goal" [15] can help minimize these problems.

Coalitions provide a structured mechanism for diverse stakeholders to participate in a community-based change effort [68]. Coalitions are important for achieving community-level changes in behavioral health problems because these behaviors are influenced by multiple risk and protective factors situated in multiple contexts. Coalitions can help coordinate a set of interventions implemented by multiple organizations to target risk and protective factors across settings [69]. In addition, coalitions provide a forum for partners to come together, discuss the issues that need to be addressed, and jointly decide on the EBIs that will be feasible to implement. They also allow for a pooling of the human and financial resources [68].

Despite their perceived utility, community coalitions are not always successful. Many coalitions have failed to significantly reduce youth behavioral health problems such as drug use, delinquency, and teen pregnancy [12, 14, 69, 70]. It is difficult to pinpoint exactly why coalition-based interventions fail, because most coalition efforts have not been rigorously evaluated. For example, efficacy trials that involve random assignment of communities to different coalition models are rare [69, 70]. Nonetheless, comprehensive reviews of the literature [10, 12–15, 43, 71] have linked coalition failure to difficulty in establishing and maintaining a diverse, high-functioning organization and to failing to implement EBIs at sufficient reach in the community. In contrast, successful coalitions tend to have the following characteristics:

- Formalized structure
- Diverse, inclusive, and representative membership
- Skilled leaders and dedicated staff
- Clearly defined, focused, and manageable goals
- Capacity to conduct needs assessments
- Reliance on EBIs to address local needs
- Adequate financial resources
- Documentation of progress toward goals

To achieve and sustain an impact on behavioral outcomes community wide, coalitions need to be durable [15]. To establish a strong base of operations, coalitions require an organizational structure that clearly defines the roles and responsibilities of leaders (e.g., chair persons, secretaries, treasurers, etc.), staff, committees or working groups, and members [60, 72]. They also need to determine how and when these parties will communicate with each other, how decisions will be made, and how conflicts will be resolved [43, 68]. These procedures may or may not be formalized in written by-laws or memorandums of understanding. In either case, organizational structure and clearly stated and agreed-upon policies help to elicit and maintain members' involvement, hold members accountable for actions, minimize disputes, and ensure the sustainability of the organization [45, 68, 72]. These elements should also facilitate the completion of prevention activities. For example, a study of youth drug-prevention coalitions in five U.S. states found that coalitions with steering groups and subcommittees were more likely to train new members and leaders, conduct needs assessments, and select EBIs compared to those without such a structure [73].

Coalitions need procedures for recruiting and training new members, and they must be prepared to spend significant time on recruitment, especially if the coalition is dedicated to diversity and representation from all sectors of the community. Coalitions will have to decide exactly which and how many individuals will need to be recruited; no ideal size or "diversity quota" has been established in the literature [73]. Nonetheless, it is important for coalitions to engage individuals and organizations who represent groups to be targeted for services, organizations likely to be responsible for delivering services, and stakeholders who can generate support and resources for the initiative [72]. Disenfranchised groups and individuals will be most difficult to recruit, and if they do participate, it will take time to build trust, foster communication, and manage tensions between members [74]. Coalitions must also realize that membership turnover is inevitable and that they will always be recruiting new members and rebuilding the organization [68].

Because members are likely to be volunteers with limited time to devote to the coalition, coalitions will require leaders and staff to ensure that tasks are completed and members are held accountable [75]. Both leaders and staff need a variety of administrative, decision-making, and interpersonal skills. Leaders, in particular, must be able to delegate tasks, generate enthusiasm and commitment from members, facilitate shared decision making, and prevent and diffuse conflict [41]. Effective leaders will help members reach consensus and maintain a focus on the goals to be achieved [68]. Describing coalitions participating in the CDC teen pregnancy prevention project, Doryn Chervin and colleagues [74] note that "the presence of strong, skilled, and dedicated leadership was the most important reason why partnerships were able to effectively engage and maintain participation by various sectors of the community." However, they also reported frequent turnover of leaders, which resulted in a loss of momentum and mission drift when new leaders established new goals [74].

This example further supports the need for coalitions to have clearly defined procedures for recruiting and training new members and leaders, as well as well-articulated missions and goals. Coalitions are almost always defined as groups working to achieve common goals, but given their diversity, members are likely to differ in their views of the organization's purpose. Members may also have competing loyalties, such as professionals who want to support the mission, clients, and/or programs of their home organization [68]. To reduce conflicts between members and foster individuals' commitment to the coalition, members must reach consensus on their mission and goals [43]. As discussed in chapter 5, conducting a needs assessment can help coalitions identify their purpose and the most significant issues to be addressed. However, members are likely to differ in their opinions about these issues, and leaders will need strong group facilitation skills to allow for input and manage conflict when prioritizing needs and identifying goals.

After they complete these planning tasks, coalitions move to an implementation phase. It is critical in this stage to use EBIs to address needs [10, 69]. As seen in the Chicago Area Project, community members may participate in a community-based prevention effort but fail to implement strategies that have been previously tested and shown to be effective [5, 76]. In the Chicago initiative, communities primarily implemented youth recreational programs and offered counseling to youth gangs or incarcerated youth. They did not, however, use interventions with proven effectiveness in changing the community conditions known to foster delinquency, and reductions in youth crime were not demonstrated [5, 76]. Similarly, an evaluation of the *Fighting Back* drug prevention initiative indicated that coalitions most frequently implemented public awareness campaigns to prevent youth substance use, rather than tested and effective preventive interventions targeting risk and protective factors [10]. Communities participating in that project did not achieve desired reductions in youth drug use [10].

Resources are also necessary. A lack of funding has been associated with a lack of long-term sustainability of both coalitions [56, 77–79] and the EBIs they implement [80–82]. The amount of funding necessary to support the coalition, and possible sources of funding, will vary across communities, and coalitions will need to spend time on resource planning and fund raising. An analysis of PROSPER coalitions' ability to generate resources indicated that higher functioning coalitions (those with clear goals, a positive culture, effective leaders, and mechanisms for integrating new members) were more successful in soliciting funds to implement EBIs compared to lower functioning coalitions [83]. These findings indicate that initial (human) investments in building a strong coalition can literally pay off in the long term.

The other factor that predicted revenue generation in PROSPER communities was the degree to which community leaders supported the PROSPER initiative [83]. Such support is unlikely to occur unless a coalition documents its activities and evaluates its progress in meeting goals. Coalitions should publicize their successes and recognize the contributions of their members and communities. Doing so should generate support from the public and could lead to financial contributions to prevention efforts [10, 12, 68]. Monitoring its efforts also allows a coalition to identify impediments to coalition functioning and address these problems before they result in a breakdown of trust, collaboration, and effectiveness [12, 35].

Communities vary in their capacity to build and maintain high-functioning coalitions. Although coalitions can do their best to recruit members with the requisite skills in community-based prevention and coalition building, they are also likely to benefit from consultation from outside experts regarding how to create and sustain healthy coalitions, assess needs, select and monitor EBIs, and evaluate the effectiveness of their activities [14, 27, 84–86]. This technical assistance can be provided by federal or state-level groups or by independent organizations [84]. For example, the Centers for Disease Control and Prevention has used its own staff to deliver technical assistance to coalitions seeking to prevent teen pregnancy [87], and it has funded university researchers to provide support to youth violence prevention coalitions [88]. In PROSPER, technical assistance is provided by cooperative extension staff from the local university [42].

To summarize, community participation is critical for preventing youth behavioral health problems, and coalitions are the preferred method for activating, organizing, and maintaining community-based collaborative action. Although there is a need for more rigorous evaluation research, certain coalition features have been linked to success, including having a defined structure and operational procedures, clear goals, skilled leadership, and reliance on EBIs to address needs. However, coalitions are difficult to establish, and community members usually need assistance to build healthy, high-functioning coalitions. As discussed in the next section, CTC provides multiple training workshops and ongoing technical assistance to build and maintain coalition capacity.

How Does the CTC Prevention System Support High-Functioning Community Coalitions?

As described in chapter 3, when CTC was originally developed, communities received limited guidance about how to form the CTC Community Board, the coalition that oversees CTC implementation. Following the Key Leader Orientation, communities had to find an existing group willing to adopt the CTC prevention system or create a new coalition to implement CTC. Very little guidance and no formal training were provided on coalition development. As a result, in the pilot study conducted in Washington State, the most frequently identified barriers to CTC implementation were the difficulty of recruiting and retaining coalition members and a lack of team direction and leadership [49]. The evaluation also indicated that new coalition members rarely received training in CTC and lacked substantive knowledge about prevention.

Based on this information, the CTC developers added a formalized training workshop for coalition members, the Community Board Orientation (CBO), held in Phase 2 following the Key Leader Orientation and the identification of local stakeholders to serve on the coalition. This training, now delivered in modules using the web-streamed CTC curriculum, is intended to provide participants with information about CTC, the Social Development Model, risk and protective factors, EBIs, and other aspects of prevention science. As in the Key Leader Orientation, coalition members also discuss readiness issues that may foster or inhibit CTC implementation in their communities. Like the key leaders, coalition members must be prepared to have candid discussions about the strengths and weaknesses of their communities that may affect CTC implementation. Consistent with community-based participatory research, the goal of the Community Board Orientation is to provide a forum in which community members can make important decisions about if and how they can implement CTC. Technical assistance from the CTC coach is provided to facilitate these conversations and help to resolve any conflicts that may arise, not to provide solutions to problems.

The Community Board Orientation includes significant attention to coalition building to build members' capacity to create high-functioning coalitions that can fully implement the CTC process. To begin this process and develop a shared commitment to the CTC process among coalition members, coalitions create a vision statement that identifies the long-term outcome(s) they would like to achieve in their community. For example, the vision statement developed in the CTC community mentioned at the beginning of the chapter was: "a compassionate, caring community of five towns where all people work together to create a safe and healthy community for all." Creating a vision statement allows all members to provide input on what is most needed for their community's youth, and it is an important first step in building trust and shared norms among community members. Although the coalition will develop more concrete goals later, the vision statement serves as the emotional foundation of the change effort. If conflicts arise, as can happen in multi-sector groups, leaders can remind coalition members that they are all working together to achieve their vision and that collaboration is the key to success.

With their vision statement in mind, participants discuss additional groups and individuals that need to be included in CTC as leaders and coalition members. The goal is to ensure that the coalition is diverse and broad based, both in demographic characteristics and in representing key sectors of the community, including elected officials, law enforcement, juvenile justice, schools, public health, health services providers, faith organizations, social services agencies, recreational organizations, businesses, media, parents, and young people [49, 64]. Working in small groups to foster input and participation, coalition members identify those who need to be recruited and the parties responsible for recruiting specific individuals or groups. As with other decisions, it is up to each community to decide on the optimal number and diversity of board members. Those facilitating the Community Board Orientation enable but do not dominate these conversations. At the same time, they challenge participants to ensure that marginalized groups are provided an opportunity to participate and that preexisting conflicts do not limit representation.

CTC recommends that coalitions have at least 10 to 15 members, but size will vary according to the size and diversity of the community. In the Community Youth Development Study, conducted in small- to medium-sized towns with a mean population of about 15,000 residents per community [54], an average of 32 individuals participated in the Community Board Orientations across the 12 CTC sites. About 1 1/2 years after CTC was initiated, the average coalition size was 37 members, with a range of 18 to 76 members. School district personnel and human service agencies together made up about 40% of all coalition members. Other sectors represented included business (7% of all coalition members), youth recreation (6%), law enforcement (6%), religious groups (6%), municipal government (6%), community members (5%), youth (4%), health agencies (4%), parent volunteers (3%), citizen advocacy organizations (3%), community coalitions (3%), juvenile justice (2%), substance-abuse-prevention organizations (2%), media (1%), and local philanthropic organizations (1%) [7]. CTC coalition members in the efficacy study appreciated the need to be diverse and recognized the benefits that diversity could produce. As noted by a coalition member in one community:[5] "We have board members from different parts of the community, different occupations, economic groups, age groups, and so forth." A member in another city reflected: "[The coalition has] been a wonderful networking experience in our community and has helped us weave together several groups."

Nonetheless, all CTC communities in the Community Youth Development Study experienced some difficulties gaining commitment from community volunteers and ensuring that coalitions included a representative group of those interested in promoting healthy youth development. As one coalition member stated: "We have a problem recruiting board members. We don't have the support from the local schools that we'd like to have." Coalitions that lacked participation from key sectors actively tried to recruit additional members, sometimes by asking champions or other influential community members already part of the coalition to personally invite a sought-after individual. For example, a coalition leader in one community, a charismatic, retired businessman, invited potential members to lunch, during which he described the coalition's mission and activities and how the targeted individual was particularly needed to achieve these goals. Most coalitions regularly presented information about CTC to community groups and organizations such as school boards, service organizations (e.g., the Kiwanis), and religious groups, then asked for representatives to participate in the coalition. Some coalitions found it helpful to hold their meetings in public settings (e.g., in restaurants or meeting rooms of local organizations) to increase their visibility and attract new members.

International replications of CTC have also identified challenges related to coalition member recruitment. In an evaluation of CTC in the Netherlands, most coalition members were professional staff from local youth-serving and human-service organizations [55, 89]. There was little participation from the broader community, such as faith communities, businesses, parents, or youth. This lack of diversity reflected the fact that in the Netherlands, citizens rely on government employees, rather than volunteers, to address social problems. Although it is important to have representation from the agencies that are most likely to implement prevention services, the professionals in the Netherlands project sometimes lacked a full commitment to the coalition and its collaborative approach to prevention. They participated on behalf of their institution rather than their own personal ideals, and when they changed jobs, their involvement typically ended. In addition, their goal was often to gain funding for their own organizations to implement EBIs. These attitudes were not well aligned with the participatory-based, data-driven decision making that guides the selection and implementation of EBIs in CTC. A comparison with coalitions in the U.S. Community Youth Development Study found that the coalitions in the Netherlands had less participation by community members, greater membership turnover, and weaker coalition cohesion [55].

One of the three communities involved in the CTC evaluation conducted in the United Kingdom could not effectively engage school representatives in the coalition, which resulted in a lack of implementation of school-based prevention programs [53]. A second community had a history of strained relationships between human service agencies and local residents, which undermined efforts to build a diverse, representative coalition. Agency representatives assumed leadership roles in the coalition and scheduled meetings at times and locations inconvenient for nonprofessional members, which blocked their participation and ultimately undermined the coalition's ability to fully implement CTC. The eight communities participating in a pilot study of CTC in Colombia had small but diverse coalitions, averaging 12 members and with representatives from health, education, local government, private business, child/family welfare, recreation/sports, law enforcement, and religious groups [51]. However, many individuals lacked commitment to the group, as evidenced by high turnover in meeting attendance, and conflict was common, even though coalitions set and enforced rules governing participation.

CTC coalitions have to be prepared to spend time building their coalitions and maintaining their diversity and functioning over time because membership turnover will occur. Volunteers will arrive or leave the community and/ or their professional positions, and their availability and desire to spend time on CTC activities is likely to wax and wane. To ensure that turnover does not threaten coalition success, CTC recommends that coalitions create a specific group, the Board Maintenance workgroup, to oversee coalition functioning [64]. The group's duties include recruiting and training new participants and ensuring that all members remain united, enthusiastic, and committed to the coalition's mission. The group may administer a regular survey of coalition members to assess coalition functioning and diversity and to take steps to correct problems when identified [90]. For example, to encourage greater participation, they may ask members to sign letters of commitment and/or to take responsibility for particular coalition activities for a certain period of time. To foster commitment and support for CTC, this group should acknowledge the contributions of individual members privately in coalition meetings and publicly at community events and in local media.

Coalition members discuss their general organizational structure and operating procedures during the Community Board Orientation. As with other decisions, it is up to the coalition to decide how it will be organized, but CTC provides recommendations based on the coalition literature. For example, coalitions are guided to have at least one formally appointed chairperson to provide leadership and oversight of CTC activities, and they may also designate a vice-chairperson, secretary, and treasurer. CTC recommends the creation of workgroups to minimize volunteer burnout, provide meaningful opportunities for coalition members to contribute to the larger organization, and ensure that needed tasks are completed. These groups include: (1) Board Maintenance, to create and maintain high-functioning coalitions; (2) Risk and Protective Factor Assessment, to conduct the needs assessment; (3) Resource Assessment, to conduct a survey of current resources available in the community to prevent youth behavioral health problems; (4) Public Relations, to promote the CTC mission and achievements; (5) Youth Involvement, to foster input and participation from youth; and (6) Funding, to solicit resources. During the Community Board Orientation, coalition members discuss the roles and responsibilities of these groups, identify potential leaders and members for each group, and set dates for subsequent workgroup meetings to further develop their membership and work plans.

Coalition members also discuss the rules and procedures that will govern coalition decision making, conflict resolution, and communication. In addition, they consider how often coalition and workgroup meetings should occur. It is the responsibility of the Board Maintenance workgroup to further develop these operating procedures and to work with coalition leaders to plan future coalition meetings.

Communities that adopt CTC may choose to use an existing coalition or to create a new coalition to implement the system. Both strategies have benefits and drawbacks. Established coalitions will have already achieved many of the tasks associated with coalition start-up. For example, they will probably have an organizational structure, leadership, staff, and operating rules and procedures. They may also have funding for coalition activities and staff salary. Their main task in Phase 2 will be to ensure that coalition members truly understand CTC and that the preexisting membership, goals, and governing procedures are well aligned with CTC. Some changes may need to occur, and members may resist altering the status quo.

Establishing new groups may or may not be desirable. CTC aims to minimize duplication of resources, not simply add to the number of coalitions in a community. Similarly, CTC tries to foster collaborative relationships and create a synergistic delivery of services across the community; therefore, CTC coalitions should avoid competing with existing groups for members and resources. If new coalitions are formed, their goals should be distinct from those of existing coalitions. New coalitions may struggle for legitimacy and will need time to a create stable, functioning organization, as well as to develop strong workgroups. Communities choosing this option must therefore be prepared for a somewhat longer timeline for CTC implementation.

In the Community Youth Development Study, most communities had coalitions or organizations with similar, but not identical, missions at the start of the study—for example, groups trying to prevent youth suicide, treat drug abuse, or promote fitness and recreation [91]. In these cases, community members considered whether or not the existing groups could expand their focus to include the youth behavioral health problems targeted by CTC. In three communities, preexisting coalitions integrated CTC into their organizations. The other nine communities created new CTC coalitions, but regularly communicated with other groups to ensure that they did not duplicate services or compete for members and resources [7].

Findings from the Community Youth Development Study indicate that the Community Board Orientation is an effective tool for educating community members about CTC and in building high-functioning coalitions. Participant surveys conducted before and after these trainings in CTC communities showed increases in knowledge of prevention science concepts (e.g., the existence of risk and protective factors associated with youth behavioral health problems), and of CTC. Attendance at the training also predicted greater CTC knowledge, attendance at coalition meetings, and participation in coalition activities, according to surveys of coalition members conducted eight months following the trainings [7].

CTC evaluations also show that CTC helps to produce high-functioning coalitions whose members engage in data-driven, science-based prevention activities. In the Pennsylvania effectiveness trial, surveys of coalition members from the first 21 CTC coalitions to receive funding to implement CTC indicated moderately high levels of functioning. For example, mean scores on constructs related to having clearly defined goals, clarity of roles, stability of leaders, and productive meetings ranged from 2.8 to 3.1 on a 4-point scale

[92]. In addition, CTC coalition functioning was related to the sustainability of coalitions and the EBIs overseen by CTC coalitions [77].

In the Community Youth Development Study, coalition members reported high levels of coalition directedness and cohesion during the first year of the study, with median ratings on both constructs of 3.7 on a 4-point scale [7]. In addition, members of coalitions in CTC communities were significantly more likely than members of coalitions in control communities not trained in CTC to report completion of tasks related to the adoption of a science-based approach to prevention, such as assessing risk and protective factors and implementing EBIs. These results were sustained four [91] and six-and-a-half years after the start of the randomized trial [56]. Moreover, greater levels of adoption of a science-based approach to prevention reported by key leaders mediated the impact of CTC on reductions in youth behavioral health problems [93], demonstrating the significant role that CTC coalitions can play in fostering healthy youth development.

Summary

Although community-based initiatives are a popular method for creating community change, they have not always produced community-wide reductions in youth behavioral health problems. Evaluations of these efforts have suggested that communities are more likely to engage in effective collaborative action when they are ready to do so—that is, when the sociopolitical context is conducive to collaboration, local organizations are at least somewhat stable and functional, and sufficient resources are available for prevention. Community success has also been associated with high-functioning coalitions: groups with an organizational structure, strong leadership, and the capacity to conduct needs assessments and implement EBIs to address local needs.

CTC is designed to address readiness issues and build coalition capacity. In the first two phases of the system, training workshops are provided to key leaders and community members to provide opportunities to discuss the facilitators and barriers that may affect full implementation of CTC in their communities, and to create plans to address perceived obstacles. Following these workshops, CTC coaches provide ongoing technical assistance and support to help communities monitor progress, address threats to readiness, and ensure high-functioning coalitions.

Although high-functioning coalitions can produce desired changes in community outcomes, dedication to a common cause does not guarantee success. To effectively prevent youth behavioral health problems, coalitions must engage in actions likely to produce changes. In the next chapters, we describe the importance of conducting needs and resource assessments (chapter 5), using EBIs to address these needs (chapter 6), and monitoring progress to ensure the quality and sustainability of prevention efforts (chapter 7).

5

Improving Community Capacity to Conduct Comprehensive Prevention Needs Assessments

ONE OF THE ADVANTAGES of community-based approaches to preventing behavioral health problems is that they allow preventive approaches to be responsive to local issues of concern [1–4]. This strength assumes that: (1) different communities have different levels of behavioral health problems and of the risk and protective factors associated with these problems, (2) communities will be able to accurately assess the prevalence of behavioral health problems and their predictors, and (3) community members will be able to agree upon the needs (i.e., behaviors, risk factors, and protective factors) to be addressed. Regarding the first issue, empirical research has demonstrated that there is community variation in levels of crime, substance use, and other behavioral health problems [5–7]. There is also some evidence that communities vary in the types and levels of risk and protective factors experienced by youth [8–10] but, until recently, little valid and reliable data have been available to estimate local levels of risk and protection [11].

Regarding the second and third issues, the coalition literature and our own experiences suggest that community members often find it difficult to accurately assess their needs and to reach consensus on the most pressing concerns to address [12, 13]. Although most communities are able to obtain data on the prevalence and frequency of behavioral health problems like teen pregnancy, school drop-out, and some types of youth crimes, it is much more difficult to access data on the degree to which local youth experience risk and protective factors that predict these problems. This lack of data is a major barrier to community-based prevention efforts. Just as a doctor performs a medical exam to pinpoint the specific cause contributing to a health problem out of the many possible causes that could be present, a community prevention needs assessment must identify the risk and protective factors that are present in the community and contributing to the behavioral health problems of concern. Even when data are available on local risk and protective factors, needs assessment can be hindered if community members disagree on which prevalent factor(s) are most important to address and/or which can reasonably be altered in the community.

Prevention science has identified community-based prevention as the key to increasing the dissemination and high-quality implementation of EBIs and has emphasized that community prevention needs assessments[1] help ensure that the right EBIs are selected to prevent behavioral health problems [18–20]. However, until recently, little practical guidance has been offered to communities to facilitate prevention needs assessments.[2] The goal of this chapter is to describe this important component of community-based prevention. We begin by identifying the advantages of conducting a community needs assessment, then describe the methods commonly used by communities to collect prevention needs assessment data and the challenges that may arise when doing so. In the second half of the chapter, we describe how the CTC system builds community capacity to assess prevention needs and provide examples from CTC communities to illustrate the barriers to and facilitators of success in completing this part of the CTC system, which is enacted in Phase 3 (*Develop a Profile*, see Figure 5.1).

FIGURE 5.1 The Five Phases of the Communities That Care Prevention System

The Importance of Comprehensive Prevention Needs Assessments

Several large-scale initiatives designed to increase the dissemination of EBIs in the United States require that local communities conduct needs assessments to be eligible to receive the funding associated with these efforts. For example, beginning in the late 1990s, the U.S. Department of Education required that local school districts conduct a needs assessment to determine levels of youth substance use in order to receive funds from the Safe and Drug Free Schools and Community Act to implement drug-prevention programs [21]. More recently, the Strategic Prevention Framework State Incentive Grants managed by the Substance Abuse and Mental Health Administration required that local coalitions conduct community prevention needs assessments to receive funds for drug prevention (see www.samhsa.gov/spf). Similarly, the Office of Adolescent Health made its funding for teen pregnancy prevention programs contingent upon a demonstration of local needs [22].

Why are needs assessments increasingly being mandated as part of publicly funded efforts to prevent behavioral health problems? Such mandates are based on the recognition that needs assessments help to generate awareness that problems exist and pinpoint the factors that contribute to these problems, which can increase the efficiency and effectiveness of prevention work. In contrast, collective action is hindered when community members do not believe that there are problems, or when they deny or cover up such issues [2, 11, 23].

Comprehensive needs assessments allow for an accurate and shared understanding of local problems and the factors responsible for these problems. Without such information, community members may overestimate or underestimate the degree to which a particular behavioral health problem exists in their community. For example, a shooting could lead to the belief that youth gangs are common in a community when they are not. Similarly, community members may have misperceptions regarding the prevalence of risk and protective factors in their community. For example, parents who have clear standards for their children's behavior may assume that all families have similar standards. Or, adolescents may think that most adults in their community think that drug use is okay, or that most youth their age are involved in substance use or delinquency, even if this is not the case.

Needs assessments involve the collection of quantifiable data on problems and their causes, rather than subjective opinions that can differ across individuals. In doing so, they can provide a more accurate picture of the problem(s) to be addressed [24]. As we will describe, to conduct a needs assessment, community members collect and analyze data, then jointly decide on the needs to be addressed. This shared decision making is meant to increase consensus regarding local needs, foster group cohesion, and provide community members with a shared mission and commitment to solving local problems, which should foster collaboration.

Another benefit of needs assessment is that it allows for a more strategic selection of EBIs to prevent behavioral health problems [18, 25]. Although untested interventions are likely to be more numerous and more widely used than EBIs, it is also true that the number of interventions developed, tested, and shown to prevent behavioral health problems has grown in recent decades [19, 26, 27]. When presented with a list of EBIs, community members often struggle to decide which intervention will be the best fit for their community. In many cases, they may select the program that is least expensive or time consuming, rather than the one that best addresses their needs [28].

Needs assessments allow communities to pinpoint their specific problem(s) and its causes (risk and protective factors) so that they can select the most appropriate EBI(s) [19]. EBIs reduce particular behavioral health problems by changing the risk and protective factors associated with those problems [29]. Thus, once communities identify the problems and risk factors that are locally prevalent, and the protective factors that are most depressed, they can select EBIs that have been demonstrated to change those factors and, in turn, to reduce the behavioral problems of interest.

To illustrate this process, consider a community with high rates of adolescent substance use. Quite a few EBIs listed on the Blueprints for Healthy Youth Development website (www.blueprintsprograms.com/) have been shown to prevent drug use. However, these programs vary in *how* they reduce this behavior—that is, they target different risk and protective factors. A community with strong anti-drug norms but high levels of family conflict would be better served implementing a family-focused intervention than a media campaign intended to change norms, even if both types of interventions have been shown to reduce drug use. In the absence of information regarding the risk and protective factors that exist in the local community, a community may select a program that has been previously shown to change the outcome(s) of interest, but not the risk and protective factors that contribute to that behavior in that community's population. Even if the EBI has a strong evidence base, if it does not address the needs that are locally prevalent, its implementation will waste resources and be less likely to reduce the behavioral problem of concern.

There is some evidence to support the premise that using data to make strategic decisions about prevention programs increases the adoption and high-quality implementation of EBIs [4, 30, 31]. For example, a national survey of U.S. middle schools found that school districts that adopted EBIs to prevent substance use were more likely to have conducted a needs assessment compared to districts that were not using EBIs [32]. Similarly, in a survey of 30 directors and chairs of coalitions receiving funds from the Centers for Disease Control to prevent teen pregnancy, two thirds reported that local needs assessments were "very important" in guiding their decision about which EBI to select [33].

Needs assessments should also enhance implementation following a community's decision to adopt an EBI [20, 34]. When stakeholders understand that an EBI will address important needs in the community, they will be more committed to implementing it. Similarly, they should be more likely to sustain the EBI in the long term [35].

A last advantage of needs assessments, described further in chapter 7, is that they can inform evaluations of the impact of prevention efforts [11, 18, 23]. To evaluate the success of their initiative, community members gather and analyze, at multiple time points after EBIs have been implemented, the same types of data used to assess needs prior to the start of the initiative. When targeted behaviors and risk factors decrease over time and targeted protective factors increase, the data indicate that EBIs are working as intended. A lack of change suggests that EBIs are not working, in which case further evaluation will be needed to determine the barriers to success. The evaluation data may also identify new problems that have arisen since the original needs assessment, in which case the community may need to implement additional EBIs.

How to Conduct a Comprehensive Prevention Needs Assessment

A comprehensive examination of prevention needs requires the collection and analysis of data on the behavioral health problems, risk factors, and protective factors that are prevalent in a community [18, 36]. This information must be specific to the community in which prevention services will be implemented and the population(s) for whom services are intended. Thus, it is important that community coalitions define the scope of their initiative early on, as part of their readiness assessment. They should identify the specific geographical region(s) that defines the "community," the behavioral problem(s) they wish to address (e.g., substance use, delinquency, teen pregnancy, or school drop-out), and the types of residents who will be targeted for services (e.g., school-aged youth and parents).

Once they define these parameters, the coalition begins to gather the information necessary to specify needs, usually starting by identifying the prevalence of behavioral health problems. Information on behavioral health problems can be obtained from several archival sources. For example, coalitions might access local crime statistics from law enforcement agencies, rates of truancy and school drop-out from school districts, statistics on teen pregnancy or violence- or drug-related injuries from local health departments, and information on drug- or alcohol-related traffic crashes and fatalities from the National Highway Traffic Safety Administration [37, 38]. The benefits of these administrative data are that they are inexpensive (though possibly time consuming) to obtain, and they tend to be regularly collected and recorded, which allows a coalition to examine changes in behaviors over time. In addition, they are often collected in multiple jurisdictions using the same method, which allows communities to compare their rates to those of similar areas (e.g., other cities in the same state).

Archival data also have disadvantages. First, it may be difficult to match the geographic region of the data provided by these sources to that of the community involved in the prevention effort. For example, law enforcement data represent crimes committed within police-defined precincts and school data are collected for particular districts or schools, but these boundaries may differ from that of the community of interest [38]. Second, official measures are likely to underestimate the occurrence and/or frequency of behavioral health problems, especially those that tend to be undetected and/or unreported to authorities, such as substance use and crime. Official data may thus lack validity, and coalitions that rely only on this type of data may not be able to accurately determine how often targeted behaviors occur or the characteristics of youth most likely to engage in them.

Archival data can also be unreliable. Whether or not behaviors are recorded often varies according to the policies and attitudes of organizations and their employees. For example, police officers have broad discretion in determining when to make an arrest, and the same act may or may not result in an arrest depending on the officer. A similar bias can exist in school records. Even with the introduction of zero tolerance policies that stipulate that certain behavioral violations are to be recorded and punished regardless of the circumstances or characteristics of the offender, the enforcement of these policies seems to disproportionately target students from minority racial/ethnic backgrounds and special education students [39, 40].

Given these limitations, coalitions should supplement archival data with information from community members, including key leaders, service providers, parents, and/or youth [41]. As discussed in chapter 4, readiness assessments involve the collection of data from key informants on the most pressing problems facing the community [42, 43], and these responses can be part of the needs assessment. However, readiness assessments are usually conducted with a small proportion of the community, and they are often based on open-ended questions and general information about problems. As a result, data from readiness assessments may not be generalizable to the entire community, and they may not provide valid and reliable estimates of the prevalence of problems.

Self-reported information collected from youth using interviews or questionnaires, such as the CTC Youth Survey, can provide more accurate, valid, and generalizable data compared to official data. To do so, surveys must be conducted with a large and/or representative proportion of the targeted population, assess behaviors using valid and reliable items, and assure participants that their responses will be confidential and anonymous. To minimize the potential that respondents may underestimate or overestimate their behavioral problems, surveys usually include multiple questions asking respondents about all acts they have engaged in, not just those which have come to the attention of authorities, directly ask respondents if they have lied on the survey, and often include follow-up items about an incident to be sure that it actually occurred [44]. To preserve confidentiality, researchers will ask respondents to use codes rather than names on surveys and provide enough physical space between participants who take surveys in a home or classroom so that responses cannot be seen or overheard by others [45].

Although some data are available to communities to measure behavioral health problems, far fewer sources of information exist to measure risk and protective factors. Official data provide limited information on risk factors and almost no coverage of protective factors because these constructs represent individual or social influences that cannot be easily observed, recorded, and quantified in public records. The U.S. Census contains information on the community risk factors of economic disadvantage and transitions and mobility, but these data are collected only every 10 years and refer to census tracts, areas which may or may not correspond to the geographic boundaries of the community involved in prevention activities. School administrative data can be used to measure commitment to school (e.g., truancy rates) and academic performance (e.g., grades and test scores), but, again, these data may or may not provide information on youth residing in the community of interest.

Given these limitations, it is best to collect data on risk and protective factors using surveys of community members. Although such information could be collected from young people, parents, and adult residents of a community, the main challenges of survey research are the time and expense involved in collecting and analyzing data. These problems are multiplied when seeking participation from multiple groups, especially if a large and representative sample of each type of population must be obtained. As discussed in chapter 3, coalitions involved in pilot studies of CTC expressed concerns about the burden of collecting data from community residents, which led to the development of the CTC Youth Survey and the guidance to rely primarily on student reports of individual, peer, family, school, and community risk and protective factors.

Some other school-based surveys have been developed and administered to collect data from students on behavioral health problems. In the United States, the Monitoring the Future (MTF) survey (www.monitoringthefuture. org/) is a nationally representative, annual survey designed to measure substance use among students in grades 8, 10, and 12. The Youth Risk Behavior Surveillance System (YRBSS; www.cdc.gov/HealthyYouth/yrbs/index.htm) is administered every two years in a representative sample of public and private high schools in all but three states in the United States and in middle schools in 18 states to assess behavioral health problems. Outside the United States, the European School Survey Project on Alcohol and Other Drugs (ESPAD) has administered school-based surveys to 15- and16-year-olds every few years to assess substance use [46], and the school-based Global Student Health Survey (GSHS; www.who.int/chp/gshs/methodology/en/) has been conducted in over 90 countries with youth aged 13 to 17 years.

Although these surveys provide information about the extent of particular behavioral health problems, none are as comprehensive as the CTC Youth Survey in assessing risk and protective factors. In addition, most of the surveys are designed to provide representative data on youth problems at a state or national level. Except in very populous cities or counties, they will include a very limited number of youth (if any) from any individual community [38]. For these reasons, we consider the CTC Youth Survey to be the optimal tool for communities to use when conducting a comprehensive prevention needs assessment. As described in the next section, the survey can be administered with large numbers of youth at minimal expense and burden, and it measures a comprehensive set of empirically derived and tested risk and protective factors.

Collecting data on behavioral health problems, risk factors, and protective factors is only the first step in a needs assessment. Communities must also analyze these data and prioritize the problems and factors they wish to address with prevention services. Only valid and reliable data should be analyzed, which means that all data should be reviewed for accuracy and consistency and questionable data should be discarded. Similarly, if using self-reports, survey response rates should be high enough to ensure that the information will reflect the intended population levels of behavioral health problems, risk factors, or protective factors.

There are also likely to be some discrepancies across the different data sources owing to differences in how and when the data were collected, the geographical regions the data represent, and the respondents providing information [38]. Coalitions will have to do their best to determine why the differences exist and to calculate rates and/or frequencies of behavioral problems and levels of risk and protective factors from the sources deemed to be most reliable and valid [37]. These determinations can be difficult, and if coalition members do not have expertise in data analysis, they may need to engage a consultant to assist with this phase of the needs assessment.

Once all the data have been analyzed, coalitions prioritize the problems and risk and protective factors of greatest concern. In most cases, priority is based on magnitude. That is, the problems reported the most frequently and/ or by the largest proportion of youth in the community would be identified as worthy of attention and action. Similarly, the risk and protective factors that are endorsed by the greatest/fewest youth would be identified as most pressing. To illustrate, Figure 5.2 shows data on the prevalence of risk factors reported by students in grades 6, 8, 10, and 12 completing the Pennsylvania Youth Survey in one county in that state [47]. The risk factors reported by the largest percentage of youth in this county, which may be good targets for prevention, include "low neighborhood attachment" (reported as elevated by 48% of the sample), "parental attitudes favorable toward antisocial behavior" (47%), and "perceived risk of drug use" (47%).

Prioritizing the highest magnitude problems and factors makes sense because the goal of community-based prevention is to reduce behavioral health problems community wide. By implementing EBIs to address the risk factors encountered by the greatest number of youth in the population, and to increase the protective factors least often experienced, prevention services have the best chance of reaching all those who are at risk for developing behavioral problems.

Other considerations besides magnitude may also be taken into account when prioritizing needs. For example, if the same data have been collected in multiple years, coalitions can consider trends over time. That is, they might prioritize the problems and factors that are consistently elevated or depressed at multiple time points, even if the magnitude is not the highest/lowest in the most recent year. Or, they may prioritize factors that have been decreasing or increasing in magnitude in recent years. For example, Figure 5.3 shows data on protective factors reported by 10th-grade students in public and charter

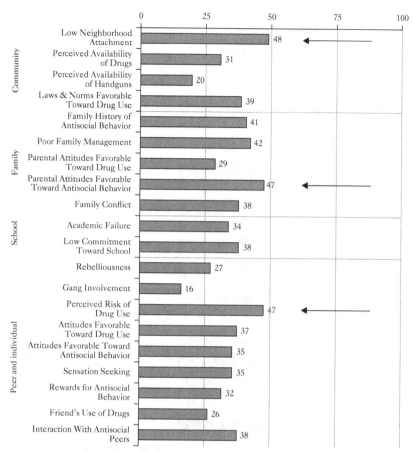

FIGURE 5.2 Percentage of 6th-, 8th-, 10th-, and 12th-Grade Students Reporting Risk Factors in One County in Pennsylvania in 2015

Source: Adapted from Pennsylvania Youth Survey [47]

schools in Arizona in 2010, 2012, and 2014 [48]. As shown, the percentage of students reporting "belief in the moral order" and "pro-social involvement" in their peer groups increased during this period, while community "rewards for pro-social involvement" and "interaction with pro-social peers" both decreased, suggesting that these protective factors should be prioritized.

Because the behavioral problems, risk factors, and protective factors will vary in occurrence and/or magnitude across development, coalitions can also analyze their data by age/developmental stage and consider if different needs should be prioritized for different groups. For example, Figure 5.4 shows the percentage of students in Washington State reporting in 2012 that they "almost always enjoy being in school" by grade level [49]. Because 10th

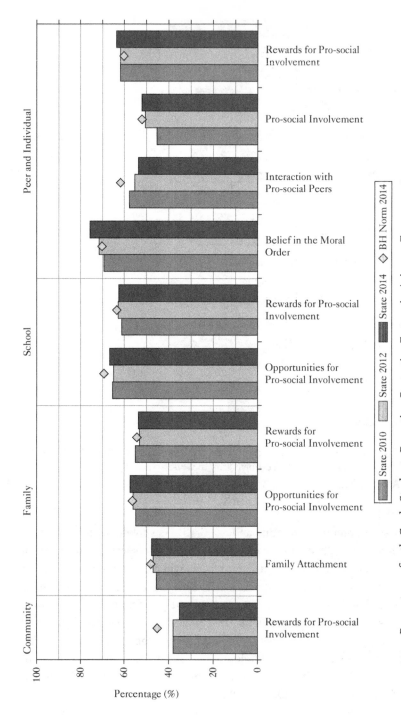

FIGURE 5.3 Percentage of 10th-Grade Students Reporting Protective Factors in Arizona, From 2010 to 2014

Source: Adapted from Arizona Youth Survey State Report [48]

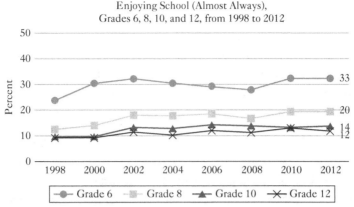

FIGURE 5.4 Percentage of Students in Washington State Reporting That They Almost Always Enjoy Being in School, by Grade

Source: Adapted from Pennsylvania Youth Survey [49]

and 12th graders report lower rates of school enjoyment than do 6th and 8th graders, it would be more important to prioritize this protective factor for the older students and to implement interventions to increase school enjoyment in high school than in middle school. For example, teachers might provide more experiential educational opportunities, such as service learning projects. Coalitions might also analyze their data according to geographical region, gender, race/ethnicity, or some other demographic group. If differences are evidenced across groups, then coalitions might prioritize different behaviors and/or factors for different groups.

Coalition members should also consider community norms and values when prioritizing needs. A community that values education, for example, might wish to see very high levels of school commitment, and if even a small proportion of students are skipping school, this risk factor may be prioritized for prevention services. Conversely, even if elevated, some risk factors may not be particularly troubling to a community. For example, a community experiencing rapid growth and development might have high rates of population turnover, but this risk factor may signify economic prosperity and may not need to be addressed. Such examples indicate the importance of involving the community in a needs assessment. Community members have the most in-depth knowledge of local issues and are in the best position to prioritize concerns.

Needs Assessments in Communities That Care

In CTC, needs assessments are considered necessary to ensure the appropriate selection of EBIs. As mentioned, many behavioral problems can be addressed by multiple EBIs, but these interventions vary in the risk and protective factors targeted for change. In the CTC system, coalitions adopt EBIs that address the risk factors that are elevated and the protective factors that are depressed in their communities, which means that they must collect comprehensive data on risk and protection experienced by young people in their communities. When stakeholders reach agreement on intervention priorities, they should be more likely to select and implement EBIs, support these interventions, and deliver them widely across the community. In turn, these actions should help them achieve community-wide prevention of behavioral health problems.

Phase 3 (*Develop a Profile*) of CTC is designed to build a community's capacity to conduct a comprehensive needs assessment (see Figure 5.1). Both the emphasis on needs assessment and the methods used to promote it differentiate CTC from many other community-based prevention approaches.[3] For example, PROSPER coalitions do not assess or prioritize needs. All PROSPER communities prioritize substance use as the main behavioral health problem of concern, and they target middle school students and their families for prevention services. PROSPER assumes that all adolescents experience peer and family risk factors and therefore guides communities to implement family-focused and school-based prevention programs. Given these assumptions, there is no need for PROSPER coalitions to identify particular risk and protective factors to be addressed by EBIs [50, 51]. In other prevention coalition models, community members have not been guided to clearly define their needs and prevention goals, which can lead to a diffusion of efforts and a lack of impact on behavioral health problems [52].

The tools and guidance provided in the CTC system to build community capacity to conduct needs assessments have been developed over time using a community-based participatory research approach that has taken into account feedback from community members. As described in chapter 3, when CTC was first developed, coalitions received a three-day training workshop to introduce them to the risk and protective factors that have been shown in research studies to be associated with behavioral health problems and to learn methods to identify levels of risk and protection in their own community.[4] Coalitions were guided to prioritize risk and protective factors from their preexisting knowledge of their youth and local communities. However, feedback from coalitions indicated that this process was too subjective and tended to result in coalition members from particular sectors of the community advocating the prioritization of risk and protective factors from the same sectors that they represented. For example, coalition members representing schools would advocate the prioritization of academic failure and low commitment to school, while those from family-based agencies would consider family management and other family factors as most important. Coalitions asked for more objective measures to help them assess and prioritize needs.

The next phase of CTC development advised coalitions to collect archival data and administrative records from local schools, police departments, and health departments to measure risk and protective factors. Coalitions were also encouraged to survey key informants and local youth and/or families and were provided with sample questions that could be asked of such respondents. However, they did not receive specific guidance on how to conduct such interviews or interpret the data that were collected in order to prioritize needs [53, 54].

The pilot study of CTC implemented in 36 Oregon communities demonstrated that this early version of CTC was somewhat effective in building coalition capacity to conduct needs assessments. All 35 communities whose coalition members attended the CTC training workshop on risk and protective factor assessment subsequently identified and prioritized local behavioral problems, risk factors, and protective factors. The evaluation showed that 100% relied on archival data to do so, 66% on key informant data, and 57% on household or school surveys [53]. A separate study indicated that CTC coalitions in Oregon were much more likely to assess needs using quantitative data than prevention coalitions in Washington that did not use CTC. In Washington, 51% of coalitions relied on archival data to assess and prioritize needs, and 21% used data from household and/or youth surveys [55].

Nonetheless, feedback from CTC coalitions indicated that the process was burdensome, and the archival data and surveys did not typically cover the full range of risk and protective factors associated with behavioral health problems. Recognizing these limitations, CTC developers determined that the optimal method of needs assessment would be a youth survey that could be efficiently administered in local schools, measure a comprehensive set of risk and protective factors using valid and reliable indicators, and provide an accurate and easy-to-interpret community-level assessment of risk and protection.

As described in chapter 3, the CTC Youth Survey[5] was developed in the Six State Consortium and was first tested with students in Oregon public schools. After several rounds of testing and revision, the survey instrument included 121 items and could be completed in a single classroom period (i.e., in about 45 minutes). Based on data from the Oregon students, the survey was shown to provide valid and reliable indicators of 29 risk and protective factors in the community, family, school, peer, and individual domains. Additional analyses based on the collection of data from a larger and more diverse sample of students in U.S. middle and high schools showed that the survey provided valid and reliable estimates of risk and protective factors across age/grade, gender, and racial/ethnic groups (i.e., African American, Asian/Pacific Islander, Caucasian, Hispanic, and Native American) [56, 57]. The survey has since been used around the world, in Australia, the United Kingdom, the Netherlands, Austria, Croatia, Cyprus, Germany, Sweden, Malaysia, Thailand, Iran, Colombia, Chile, Trinidad and Tobago, and South Africa [58–68].

In addition to creating a survey methodology that could assess risk and protective factors accurately and efficiently, the CTC developers wanted to be able to provide survey results in an easy-to-understand format that would aid in the prioritization of needs. The risk and protective factors included on the survey are measured using multiple items that are combined into scales. When the survey was first used in communities participating in the Six State Consortium, results were reported as mean scores on each risk and protective factor, using standardized scores which indicated if the community averages were lower or higher than the statewide average [69]. Feedback from communities indicated that these results were confusing to interpret and that state comparisons were not always desired.

The CTC developers decided that dichotomous indicators of risk and protective factors that could indicate the percentage of students in a community considered most at risk for behavioral health problems would provide communities with the most meaningful and user-friendly data. After trying several methods for creating dichotomous indicators, an optimal "cut point" was developed that could be applied to all risk and protective factors [69, also see 70]. This particular metric (which calls for the risk/protective factor score to be split at the median score, plus 0.15 times the mean absolute deviation statistic) could best identify, with reasonable accuracy, the percentage of students completing the survey considered most likely to engage in behavioral health problems based on their exposure to risk and protective factors.[6] Figure 5.5 provides an example of how these indicators are reported to communities and are based on results from students in a community participating in the Community Youth Development Study. Each bar in the chart identifies the percentage of youth considered to be at risk for engaging in behavioral health problems, based on their responses to items asking if they had experienced risk factors in the community, family, school, peer, and individual contexts.

The administration of the CTC Youth Survey and interpretation of data from this survey are now required elements of Phase 3 of the CTC system. To be sure they can implement this part of the system, in Phase 1, communities

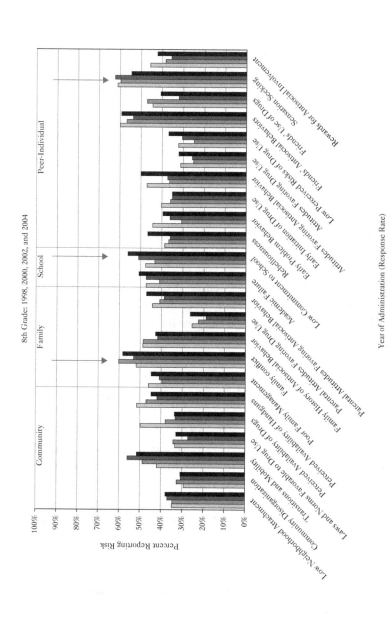

8th Grade: 1998, 2000, 2002, and 2004

Year of Administration (Response Rate)

■ 1998 (88%) ■ 2000 (71.1%) ■ 2002 (81.3%) ■ 2004 (74.3%)

FIGURE 5.5 Risk Factor Profile for 8th-Grade Students in a CTC Community in the Community Youth Development Study

must assess their readiness to administer the survey in their local middle and high schools. It can be challenging to secure such approval. School administrators and/or parents may object to the survey content, and concerns about the time and difficulty needed to administer the survey can generate resistance to its administration, especially if schools are already implementing other student surveys. Such reluctance is not specific to the United States. In the Netherlands, soliciting school board support for the survey was one of the biggest challenges reported by coalition members when implementing CTC [64, 71].

If the survey cannot be conducted, the community should not implement CTC. To avoid or overcome resistance to survey administration, coalitions should begin early with efforts to educate schools and the larger community about the importance of the survey. In trainings held during Phase 2, key leaders and coalition members learn about risk and protective factors, as well as the development and importance of the CTC Youth Survey, and communities should ensure that school officials participate in these workshops. To engender continued support from school officials, it is useful for coalition members to publicize both positive and challenging findings from the survey and to clearly indicate that information from the survey is being used to guide the choice of EBIs and promote healthy youth development. If schools are concerned about the number of surveys students must complete, they can use interleaving strategies to combine information across surveys, or alternate the administration of the CTC Youth Survey and other surveys across classrooms.

In the United States, the biggest facilitator of needs assessment has been state-level endorsement and administration of the CTC Youth Survey. As of 2017, seven states (Arizona, Kansas, Louisiana, Montana, Oklahoma, Pennsylvania, and Utah) have approved and cover the costs of statewide administration of the CTC Youth Survey. In most cases, this means that the survey is administered to a large and representative sample of students every two years in middle and high schools, usually with students in grades 6, 8, 10, and 12. It does not mean that the state has mandated that every school in the state must administer the survey. Rather, if districts or schools are not already included in the sample selected by the state, they can typically apply to have the survey administered at no charge. These states also provide written reports to participating schools to summarize the survey results, which greatly reduces the burden on community coalitions to analyze their own data. In addition to these states, many other states administer behavioral health-related surveys that include at least a partial set of the risk and protective factors the CTC Youth Survey.[7] Some states also allow local school districts to add items on risk and protective factors to such surveys, which can facilitate a comprehensive needs assessment.

In the CTC system, the Risk and Protective Factor Assessment workgroup is responsible for conducting the needs assessment in Phase 3. It is useful for the workgroup to include: (1) school district representatives, given that the CTC Youth Survey is administered in schools; (2) youth, whose perspective is needed to accurately interpret survey responses; and (3) individuals with data collection and analysis skills. The workgroup is charged with collecting data, analyzing the results, and making a recommendation to the full coalition regarding the behaviors and factors that should be prioritized. This structure allows all members of the coalition to participate in the process and reach consensus on the needs to be addressed.

The Risk and Protective Factor Assessment workgroup members receive guidance in how to conduct the needs assessment during the Community Assessment Training workshop. This workshop includes a description of the CTC Youth Survey, the risk and protective factors it measures, and the steps taken during survey development to ensure the validity and reliability of the data. It is important for workgroup members to understand these issues so that they can educate other members of the coalition and community about the survey and its results. The workshop also includes guidance on how coalitions can collect and analyze archival data on behavioral health problems (e.g., arrests, teen pregnancy, and school dropout rates) and the few risk and protective factors not included on the CTC Youth Survey (e.g., community poverty). Members discuss if and how they will collect such data and who will be responsible for doing so.

The group also learns how to interpret the results of the CTC Youth Survey and prioritize needs. In the Community Youth Development Study, CTC trainers provided workgroups with reports indicating the percentage of students reporting each behavioral problem assessed on the survey,[8] as well as the percentage reporting elevated levels of each risk factor and low levels of each protective factor, using the dichotomized indicators described previously. Results were presented separately for each grade. For example, the data shown in Figure 5.4 indicate the percentage of 8th-grade students reporting elevated risk factors in one of the CTC communities in the randomized study; results were also reported for 6th-, 10th-, and 12th-grade students. Similar reports are provided in the states administering the CTC Youth Survey.[9] If CTC coalitions are not located in these states, they are encouraged to hire a consultant to analyze the data and prepare similar reports.[10]

The last part of the workshop reviews methods for prioritizing needs. The workgroup's task is to identify two to five behavioral health problems and two to five risk and protective factors to be recommended for prioritization to the rest for the coalition. To do so, they consider the degree to which behaviors and risk and protective factors are elevated or depressed, not only in absolute terms, but also taking into account trends over time and state or national comparisons if such data are available. Coalition members also consider their ability to affect each risk and protective factor given the political, economic, and social conditions of the community. They may also consider whether or not to prioritize a different set of risk and protective factors for different geographic regions or demographic groups.

After the workgroup completes its assessment, it presents its recommendations to the full coalition. Once the entire coalition reaches consensus on the community's priorities, the Risk and Protective Factor Assessment workgroup writes a report summarizing the results of the survey and the priorities to be addressed. The report also highlights community strengths in terms of the behavioral health problems that are not elevated, depressed risk factors, and elevated protective factors. The report, or abbreviated versions of it, can be distributed across the community to help generate awareness, support, and funding for CTC. However, coalition members should be aware that publicity can sometimes generate fear or backlash [72]. To avoid such repercussions, coalitions should have school district approval to share the data, present the information in a user-friendly format, avoid blaming and stigmatizing individuals or groups, and identify the steps that they plan to take to address prioritized needs.

In the Community Youth Development Study, all 12 communities that implemented CTC completed needs assessments during the first year of the trial. This work was facilitated by the fact that these communities had administered the CTC Youth Survey in 1998, 2000, and 2002 as part of their involvement in the Diffusion Project. In 2003, the Community Assessment Training was provided to members of the Risk Assessment workgroups and CTC coalition coordinators to assist these groups to understand the survey results and prioritize needs [24].

Following the Community Assessment Training, each CTC coalition prioritized between two and seven risk and protective factors to target with prevention activities, and each identified a unique set of factors. Priorities were determined based on the levels of risk and protection reported by students, as well as coalition members' assessment of community norms and resources. For example, the community whose data are shown in Figure 5.4 prioritized three elevated risk factors for action: "family conflict," "low commitment to school," and "friends who engage in problem behaviors."

Coalition members in this community considered two other elevated risk factors but did not prioritize them. Although youth reported high rates of "transitions and mobility" (a risk factor), the coalition did not view the results as problematic given the town's growing population and the recent opening of several new schools. The coalition decided not to prioritize another elevated risk factor, "sensation seeking," because no EBI had yet been identified that, when rigorously tested, demonstrated effectiveness in reducing sensation seeking or problem behaviors specifically among sensation seekers. In addition, some coalition members did not perceive sensation seeking to be particularly problematic, as it could result in pro-social activities (e.g., skiing or rock climbing) as well as problem behaviors. As another example, in communities in which hunting was common and gun ownership customary, coalition members often did not consider elevated levels of the risk factor "availability of firearms" to be problematic and in need of preventive action [24].

These examples illustrate the community-based participatory research approach taken in CTC. Although the CTC system specifies that communities collect data on risk and protective factors and prioritize a set of factors that will be addressed by EBIs, it is up to community members to identify the factors that they consider to be most problematic. These decisions are informed primarily by data collected from the community's own youth. The survey results provide objective and quantifiable information on needs, but coalition members also rely on their firsthand knowledge of the community to prioritize prevention needs. Thus, while adhering to one of the foundations of the CTC system—grounding prevention activities in objective, epidemiologic data—coalitions tailor their efforts to the specific needs of their own young people by conducting youth surveys locally and prioritizing factors that local stakeholders agree are of greatest concern.

Evaluations of CTC in countries other than the United States have demonstrated that CTC builds coalition capacity to conduct needs assessments. All five CTC coalitions participating in a quasi-experimental evaluation of CTC in the Netherlands administered the CTC Youth Survey in local schools and prioritized risk factors [64]. Interviews with coalitions in the United Kingdom indicated that the comprehensive data generated by the CTC Youth Survey was a primary incentive for agencies to become involved in CTC coalitions because agency administrators saw the value of having access to information on community needs [73]. Focus groups held with members of seven CTC coalitions in Chile and Colombia generated positive responses regarding the needs assessment process [72]. Most participants indicated that the data accurately reflected local conditions while also specifying the degree to which problems existed. For example, one member noted: "We already knew there was [substance] use. But the report lets us see the levels, the quantities, that we are exceeding the national percentages; nobody believed that we are so high!" Other members observed that the data helped to generate support for CTC activities, both within the coalition and in the larger community: "when we observe and understand the risk factors, the graphics, [we think] what can I do to collaborate?"

Challenges with needs assessment have also been encountered. When the CTC Youth Survey is used with populations outside of the United States, the reliability and validity of the measures should be carefully reviewed, ideally in focus groups or small pilot efforts that precede a larger scale administration of the survey and well before Phase 3 of CTC. When tested with students in Trinidad and Tobago, researchers found that certain items and/or entire risk or protective factor scales on the original CTC Youth Survey could not be reliably measured [60]. Similar findings have been demonstrated in the Netherlands [74]. When such results are obtained, the survey should be revised and re-administered, or the invalid information excluded from the needs assessment, so that coalition members base their decisions on valid and reliable data.

Even in English-speaking countries, researchers may need to change survey items to ensure that the content is suitable for the local context—for example, deleting items that are irrelevant or inappropriate for the population, changing the wording of items to ensure participant understanding, and/or adding items to assess local concerns not already covered on the survey [63]. In Australia, for example, some items have been revised to ensure better cultural relevance, based on feedback from local adolescents, and additional behavioral outcomes of concern to that population (e.g., self-harm, victimization, and physical activity) have been added to the survey [75]. In non-English-speaking countries, the survey must be translated and all content reviewed for cultural relevance. In Malaysia, for example, a question was added to ask about completion of homework based on the importance placed on schoolwork in this country [59]. In countries with strict laws limiting the availability of firearms, questions related to gun carrying and gun use have been modified to ask about weapons other than guns [59, 76].

Although the CTC system provides a methodology and tools for coalition members to prioritize risk and protective factors, it can still be difficult for coalitions to conduct the needs assessment. In the Community Youth Development Study, conducting the needs assessment was rated as one of the most challenging tasks to complete [77]. When data are collected from multiple sources, time periods, and age groups, it can be hard to identify the most elevated risk factors and depressed protective factors. Similarly, differences in stakeholders' perceptions and organizational missions can lead to disagreement regarding the needs that are of greatest concern [63]. Discussions may become heated, dominated by the most vocal participants, and/or subject to political or organizational pressures to address certain areas. Coalition leaders must have strong facilitation skills to manage these conversations and help members reach agreement.

Some CTC coalitions have expressed concern that the needs assessment relies almost exclusively on data reported by middle and high school students on a school-based survey. As such, the results do not measure risk and protective factors experienced by younger children, and they may not represent the highest risk youth, those who skip school or who have dropped out [63, 72]. These challenges can be overcome by surveying younger children in schools and/or by implementing community surveys of youth and/or adults [63]. Although CTC communities can use these methods, they have not been incorporated into CTC protocols due to the additional human and financial resources they entail.

The Future of Comprehensive, Community-Based Prevention Needs Assessments

Needs assessment is an important component of community-based prevention. As posited in social disorganization theory and demonstrated in research, communities vary in their levels of behavioral health problems, as well as in the risk and protective factors that give rise to these outcomes. This variation means that communities require locally specific prevention strategies, they do not all need to worry about the same behavioral problems, and they will have to take different actions to address the problems that are most elevated in their communities.

Conducting a comprehensive needs assessment allows a community to better articulate its unique problems, needs, and solutions. Assessments are also likely to increase the efficiency and effectiveness of preventive actions. However, most communities have limited access to locally specific information on youth behavioral problems, risk factors, and protective factors, and they may not know how to interpret such data and prioritize needs even if they have the relevant information. The CTC system helps build community capacity to reliably and efficiently identify and prioritize needs. The primary method for doing so, developed over time and with feedback from communities, is the administration of the CTC Youth Survey. The survey is conducted with middle and high school students to collect accurate and valid data on community, school, family, peer, and individual risk and protective factors. During Phase 3 of CTC, training and technical assistance from CTC coaches helps coalitions to interpret data from the survey and prioritize the factors they will address using EBIs.

The main challenge faced during this phase of CTC is gaining school approval to administer the survey. Although school-based surveys have become increasingly common in the United States and in some other nations to collect information on risky behaviors like substance use, sexual activity, and delinquency, few surveys systematically ask students to report on a comprehensive set of risk and protective factors [26]. Without such information, communities are ill equipped to select the EBIs that can address their specific needs. The solution, in our opinion, is for communities to ask their state and federal governments to play a more active role in collecting surveillance data on risk and protective factors [18, 19, 23].

To date, a small number of U.S. states have endorsed the CTC Youth Survey and provide for its administration in middle and high schools throughout their regions. When more states provide resources and standardized procedures to conduct the CTC Youth Survey and provide the results in user-friendly reports to communities, needs assessment will be much more feasible. Describing the importance of local needs assessment for violence prevention, Corinne David-Ferdon and Rodney Hammond [2] state: "Linking community surveillance systems to community mobilization may be the next break-through in preventing youth violence and in promoting the safety of communities." We agree and would broaden this statement to include behavioral health problems of all types.

Increasing the Use of Evidence-Based Interventions to Reduce Youth Behavioral Health Problems

THE LACK OF dissemination of EBIs in communities is probably the greatest challenge to achieving large-scale reductions in behavioral health problems [1–4]. Although many interventions have been developed, tested, and shown to reduce behavioral health problems, EBIs are not currently being utilized at a scale or quality sufficient to produce widespread change [5]. Faced with this knowledge, and the desire to increase dissemination—the active distribution of EBIs to specific audiences using planned strategies [6, 7]—research has increasingly focused on identifying barriers to EBI implementation and strategies to overcome these impediments [5, 7, 8].

In order to increase dissemination, community-based prevention systems should build community capacity to adopt and implement EBIs. In this chapter, we discuss the importance of EBI adoption and implementation. We begin by reviewing how decisions are made regarding intervention effectiveness—that is, how interventions are defined as "evidence-based" and "effective." This issue is central to the challenge of dissemination. If interventions with strong evidence of effectiveness are promoted for widespread use, the prevention of youth behavioral problems becomes more likely. We also discuss how, once interventions are classified as effective, information about EBIs is communicated to and used by community members, as well as other factors affecting local decisions to adopt or not adopt EBIs. The chapter concludes with a review of the methods used in CTC during Phase 4 (*Create a Plan*, see Figure 6.1) to foster coalitions' capacity to select EBIs that are appropriate for the local community. These are EBIs that do not duplicate but, rather, fill in gaps in

FIGURE 6.1 The Five Phases of the Communities That Care Prevention System

current services, and that are a good fit to the community's prioritized needs, resources, and context.

Methods for Determining "What Works" to Reduce Behavioral Health Problems

The past decade has seen increasing calls for the use of evidence-based and/or effective programs and policies to improve public health and prevent problems [1–3, 9]. For example, the U.S. National Research Council and Institute of Medicine [1] have recommended that, in order to prevent mental, emotional, and behavioral disorders, "federal and state agencies should prioritize the use of evidence-based programs and promote the rigorous evaluation of prevention and promotion programs." Similarly, the World Health Organization [10] has called for more evaluation of the effectiveness of violence prevention programs worldwide and greater use of prevention programs that are "informed by evidence."

Although these recommendations can help to increase the use of EBIs, they sidestep the significant challenge of how to determine if particular programs and policies do, in fact, reduce behavioral health problems. In medicine, there are clearly defined requirements for ensuring that medical procedures and treatments that are made publically available have been tested and shown to be effective and safe, and there are regulatory bodies (e.g., the Food and Drug Administration in the United States) to ensure that ineffective and harmful treatments are not disseminated. Similarly, medical scientists are expected to conform to a standardized reporting protocol when publishing their evaluation findings [i.e., the CONSORT guidelines; see 11].

The field of prevention science has less consensus on the standards necessary to produce high-quality evidence of intervention effectiveness, and there are no regulatory agencies to enforce such standards. Intervention developers have historically been free to determine whether or not and how to evaluate prevention strategies, and whether or not and how to make their findings and products available to the public. The result is that some interventions that are currently being implemented have been evaluated in numerous, rigorous experiments and shown to reduce youth behavioral health problems, some have been well evaluated and shown to increase or have no effect on their intended outcomes, and many have never been subject to rigorous evaluation.

The number of interventions now available for implementation, and the significant variation in the degree and quality of evaluation of these interventions, has increased the need for standards and protocols to guide prevention research. In addition, evaluation design and analysis methods have become more sophisticated in recent years, and this progress has increased the number of factors that evaluators and consumers must take into account when critically assessing evaluation outcomes. Seeking to keep pace with these innovations and emulate the rigorous standards found in medicine, the Society for Prevention Research has developed a set of standards for the evaluation of preventive interventions [12, 13]. As in medicine, the Society for Prevention Research standards considers randomized controlled trials (RCTs) to be essential for establishing the efficacy of an intervention. The RCT must demonstrate a consistent pattern of non-chance findings indicating desired improvements in an intervention versus a control group, no serious harmful effects on participants, and positive effects that are sustained beyond the end of the intervention. The guidelines also recommend that, prior to widespread dissemination, interventions should be implemented and evaluated across different contexts (i.e., in effectiveness and dissemination trials). In addition, developers must be able to provide materials, training, and assistance to support implementation in community settings [13].

Although the Society for Prevention Research guidelines were developed to generate consensus among prevention scientists regarding the level and types of evidence needed to demonstrate effectiveness, not all academics agree on these standards [14, 15]. For example, some do not consider RCTs to be the "gold standard" or most optimal evaluation design and note that they can have poor external validity and may not be feasible in all contexts [16–20]. Likewise, there are no agreed-upon stipulations regarding if or how often an intervention should be replicated prior to large-scale dissemination or how long effects must be demonstrated following the end of an intervention [13].

Reaching consensus on these standards is an important aim of prevention science, particularly since differences in opinion mean that different interventions will be promoted as effective and worthy of dissemination by different parties. A related goal is to determine the best method(s) of communicating information about "what works" to the public. Most practitioners and policymakers do not have access to the scientific journals in which research evidence is published, and many do not have the time, training, or interest to read and interpret this information [21]. They need assistance to understand the results of research studies and become persuaded to invest in interventions with strong evidence of effectiveness.

CTC developers became aware of this need when community members implementing CTC in the pilot studies asked them to translate information from scientific studies and identify the risk and protective factors targeted by specific programs so that they could make more strategic decisions about which EBIs to use in their communities. In the early 1990s, Drs. Hawkins and Catalano received funding from the Office of Juvenile Justice and Delinquency Prevention to review existing evaluation literature and identify programs that were demonstrated in high-quality research trials to reduce juvenile delinquency. The review was intended to not only inform scientists about effective strategies but also to help communities become aware of and motivated to implement EBIs.

Their review resulted in a list of 25 interventions designed to be implemented in community (not correctional) settings. Information about these programs, including the risk and protective factors they addressed, was published in the *Guide for Implementing the Comprehensive Strategy for Serious, Violent, and Chronic Juvenile Offenders* [22] and shared with communities implementing the OJJDP's Comprehensive Strategy. The guide categorized interventions as "effective" and as "promising," with the former having stronger research evidence compared to the latter. The compendium was written in a user-friendly format, without overly detailed descriptions of the scientific methods used to demonstrate effectiveness. As CTC developed, information about effective preventive interventions was updated, expanded, and published in the CTC *Prevention Strategies Guide* [23].

Concurrent with the development of CTC, other organizations recognized the need to provide policymakers and practitioners with user-friendly information about effective interventions. Both private and public agencies began to critically review findings from evaluation research, synthesize the information, and identify EBIs in monographs and websites. Examples of registries devoted to identifying "what works" to reduce youth behavioral health problems include the Office of Juvenile Justice and Delinquency Program's Model

Programs Guide, which relies on ratings from the Office of Justice Program's Crime Solutions database (www.crimesolutions.gov/); the National Registry of Effective Programs and Policies (NREPP)[1] (www.nrepp. sa.gov/Index.aspx), managed by the Substance Abuse and Mental Health Services Administration (SAMHSA); and the Blueprints for Healthy Youth Development website (www.blueprintsprograms.com) developed at the University of Colorado.[2]

All the aforementioned registries seek to promote the dissemination of EBIs, but they differ markedly in the types of interventions reviewed and the criteria used to judge intervention effectiveness. The Model Programs Guide is restricted to interventions intended to prevent youth delinquency and re-cidivism, and NREPP focuses on interventions that are intended to reduce substance use/abuse and mental health problems. Blueprints is more com-prehensive, as it reviews interventions intended to prevent youth behavioral health problems including delinquency and drug use and promote pro-social behaviors such as academic achievement, mental and emotional well-being, and physical health.

A detailed comparison of the standards used to evaluate intervention effec-tiveness in these and other registries is beyond the scope of this chapter,[3] but the Blueprints registry is generally considered to have the most rigorous re-view process and standards [26–28]. Blueprints uses a systematic review pro-cess [29, 30] to search and review *all* evaluations of a particular intervention. NREPP reviews evaluations identified by program developers and conducts a comprehensive literature search to find studies. The Model Programs Guide reviews are based on the three evaluations considered to have the most rig-orous research design.

All three databases rely on multiple raters with knowledge in evaluation and/or implementation, train these reviewers in how to assess the rigor of the evaluation research using similar criteria, and require consensus on ratings across reviewers. The Model Programs Guide and NREPP sites rely on pairs of raters and staff persons to review this work and make final decisions regarding intervention effectiveness. The Blueprints review process is more extensive, as all interventions must pass an internal review conducted by staff at the University of Colorado and an external review conducted by a seven-person Advisory Board of scientific experts who must all agree on interventions' ratings.

All three registries base their determinations of effectiveness on the quality of the research evaluation(s), but Blueprints applies the most stringent cri-teria to make this determination. For example, although all three registries require interventions to be evaluated in randomized controlled trials or quasi-experimental designs with comparison groups, only Blueprints restricts its highest ratings of effectiveness (i.e., Model and Model + programs) to interventions evaluated in at least one RCT. Randomization warrants a higher score on only one indicator of evaluation quality in the Model Programs Guide, and NREPP prioritizes evaluations that best ensure the equivalence of intervention and comparison groups. In addition, Blueprints requires a replication study in order for interventions to be rated as a Model program, and a replication and evaluation by someone other than the program developer (to reduce potential bias) to be rated as a Model + program. The other two databases do not require replication for an intervention to be considered effective.

All three registries rate the quality and rigor of the evaluation (especially its ability to ensure internal validity) using multiple criteria, but all such criteria must be met in order for Blueprints to identify an intervention as effective. The other two databases rely on numerical scores on each criterion, which are averaged across these indicators, such that interventions with some research design flaws (e.g., lack of baseline equivalence between intervention and control groups, high attrition, differential attrition from conditions, or poor validity of measurement instruments) may still be rated as effective [26].

A last difference between the registries is that only Blueprints requires that programs listed on its site be ready for dissemination; that is, the program developers or other certified parties must have the capacity to provide potential implementers with program manuals and other materials, training, and technical assistance. This criterion is necessary to foster dissemination; a program can only be replicated if tools for doing so exist. As we discuss in chapter 7, practitioners often fail to implement EBIs with quality, and implementation problems tend to reduce program effectiveness [31–34]. Conversely, training and technical assistance from program developers have been demonstrated to improve implementation quality and participant outcomes [4, 31–33], making the provision of such services necessary for interventions recommended for dissemination.

It is also important that registries update their findings based on the new research evidence emerging in prevention science. Although many effective interventions are available, there are still gaps in our understanding of how to reduce certain risk factors, how to improve certain protective factors, and how to reduce health disparities of underserved populations. When new interventions are demonstrated to address these issues, they need to be promoted for replication. In addition, interventions that are shown to be effective in one study sometimes fail to show consistent results in a second research trial and may even demonstrate harmful effects on participants [35, 36]. Failure to update registries with these types of findings risks promoting ineffective programs for replication.

To summarize, because policymakers and practitioners do not usually have the time or required training to critically evaluate findings from research studies, "what works" registries play an important role in the dissemination of EBIs. However, the degree to which these registries can assist communities to reduce behavioral health problems depends on the methods and standards used to make determinations of intervention effectiveness. Registries vary in their methods and criteria for rating interventions and some do not employ sufficiently rigorous criteria, such that programs identified as effective may not be able to demonstrate significant changes when widely replicated [26, 37].

The Society for Prevention Research is helping prevention scientists to reach consensus on the most appropriate criteria for evaluation research [12, 13], and some registries are beginning to employ these criteria. In the future, it will be important to reconcile differences in the standards used across registries, not only to ensure that they all promote effective interventions but also to reduce confusion among users as to which registry to consult when selecting EBIs. As we will discuss, CTC advocates that communities use the Blueprints registry because it uses rigorous criteria to identify programs that target the prevention of numerous behavioral health problems. Another solution is to create or nominate a federal agency to be responsible for maintaining one database of interventions targeting all types of behavioral health problems [2, 38]. This agency could function like the FDA in certifying public health interventions for use in communities.

Outside the United States, the challenge is somewhat different. Many countries do not yet have "what works" registries or have very limited lists of effective interventions because rigorous evaluations are still relatively uncommon [2, 39–41]. In these countries, scientists and policymakers will have to work together to increase the development and testing of preventive interventions using the most rigorous evaluation methods possible.

Methods for Increasing the Dissemination of EBIs in Communities

Although "what works" registries are important in increasing public awareness of EBIs, their mere existence is unlikely to foster widespread use of EBIs [32, 42, 43]. Trisha Greenhalgh and her colleagues [44] characterize dissemination efforts as occurring on a continuum, from actions that "let it happen" to those that "make it happen." The former include the use of impersonal channels to communicate scientific findings, such as the "what works" registries and academic journals. Efforts to *make it happen* include more active and planned actions that involve direct contact with practitioners to support their prevention planning and implementation [44, 45]. These more purposeful actions are considered to be more effective in increasing dissemination. Similarly, in the Diffusion of Innovations theory [46] discussed in chapter 2, passive actions are considered insufficient to move individuals and organizations through the stages of adoption, from gaining knowledge of EBIs to being persuaded to use them and actually implementing the new innovation.

The widespread adoption and use of EBIs are unlikely to occur in the absence of dedicated and systematic efforts to foster dissemination. In fact, research indicates that EBIs are rarely disseminated at scale, to a large enough percentage of the population to significantly reduce behavioral health problems [7, 9, 10, 47, 48]. For example, surveys of school administrators in the United States indicate that only 8 to 10% report using EBIs to prevent adolescent substance use and delinquency [49, 50]. Moreover, schools are much more likely to use nontested and/or ineffective prevention programs than EBIs [33, 49, 51]. Internationally, a survey of 133 countries conducted by the World Health Organization [10] indicated that fewer than half the nations reported implementing effective violence-prevention strategies like home visitation, bullying prevention, and mentoring at scale. Although data on the specific interventions used to prevent violence were not collected by this organization, the report speculated that most violence-prevention efforts occurring in communities probably have insufficient evidence of effectiveness [10].

More active approaches to dissemination include federal mandates and/ or incentive programs that stipulate the use of EBIs. In the United States, the Department of Education has mandated that school districts implement research-based drug prevention programs; if they do not, they risk losing federal funding [52, 53]. The federal Maternal, Infant, and Early Childhood Home Visiting Program (MIECHV) provides funds to states and communities to implement home visitation programs that have been evaluated and shown to be effective. In addition, the Office of Adolescent Health Teen Pregnancy Prevention (TPP) initiative (www.hhs.gov/ash/oah/oah-initiatives/tpp_program/) funds communities to implement programs identified as effective in preventing teen pregnancy. These evidence-based policies stipulate that agencies will only receive funds if they implement interventions identified as effective by the sponsoring agency. However, the criteria for making such determinations vary across initiatives, and some of the initiatives promote interventions that have been evaluated using less rigorous research designs than those recommended by the Society for Prevention Research [13].

Putting aside the question of how, exactly, EBIs are defined in these initiatives, these policies can create a sociopolitical culture that supports EBIs, increase funding for EBI implementation, and foster dissemination [54]. Nonetheless, significant barriers to dissemination are still likely to exist at the local level, and without changing these factors, adoption of EBIs may not occur [52, 55]. These impediments are typically categorized as characteristics associated with the organization(s) charged with implementation, the staff who deliver EBIs, and EBI(s) itself [44, 46, 56, 57].

At the organizational level, agencies must be *ready* [58, 59] and have sufficient *capacity* [56, 60–62] to adopt new EBIs. As discussed in chapter 4, these constructs refer to awareness that a problem exists, belief that it must be addressed, and a willingness to change the status quo and embrace new innovations in order to solve the problem [55, 58]. It is important that leaders endorse these views and act as champions who can engender enthusiasm for the EBI(s) among other stakeholders in the organization and generate resources for implementation [31, 56, 63]. Staff support is also necessary. If staff are not convinced of the need for a new EBI, they can actively resist and/or block its implementation [64]. Like administrators, those charged with implementing a new EBI must also be willing to change current practices and view new methods as better than the status quo [65]. In organizations lacking strong administrative support, staff can also serve as champions and convince others to adopt EBIs [66].

EBI characteristics also affect dissemination, and EBIs that are perceived as a good "fit" are most likely to be adopted [61, 67, 68]. These determinations are best made after an organization learns as much as possible about the range of EBIs that may exist to address a particular problem, risk factor, and/or protective factor [32, 56, 69]. Adoption is most likely when EBIs are viewed as having a distinct advantage over current services, especially in terms of their effectiveness, cost effectiveness, and ability to reduce the current workload [2, 54, 70, 71].

EBIs should only be adopted if they are feasible to implement. Agency administrators and staff must understand all of the components that must be implemented as part of the EBI and the human and financial costs associated with these elements. If these requirements cannot be met, or if resources are insufficient, then the EBI should not be selected. Adoption is also fostered when the intervention(s) is viewed as culturally relevant and compatible with the norms, values, and needs of the organization and the broader community [57, 64, 71]. For example, staff must view implementation practices as consistent with their professional identity [71]. In addition, program content must be considered culturally relevant for the local population [68, 72]. For example, the Strong African American Families program is designed for African American families living in the rural South and includes training for parents on how to help their children overcome racism [73]. This program will not be relevant for white families living in urban, northern regions of the United States nor for families living outside the United States.

Although some of the research on factors affecting EBI dissemination has been based on a particular EBI or intervention type (e.g., school-based programs), most of the factors identified as important generalize across EBIs and different types of organizations. This universality means that multiple organizations in a community are likely to face the same challenges when considering how to best address an issue of concern. Community coalitions are well positioned, then, to foster EBI dissemination across service providers, to the extent that a coalition includes organizations and stakeholders from all sectors of the community, as advocated in the CTC system.

How Does CTC Promote the Dissemination of EBIs in Communities?

Dissemination research recognizes that local organizations require external supports to build their capacity to adopt EBIs and to select interventions that best address their needs [2, 21, 68]. Importantly, some community-based prevention initiatives have not included technical assistance to help local communities or agencies decide which EBI, if any, is necessary, appropriate, and feasible to implement in the local context. In contrast, all phases of the CTC system are designed to facilitate the adoption and implementation of EBIs across community agencies, and consultation and coaching are provided to assist communities throughout the process.

Phase 1 of CTC is intended to generate awareness and agreement in the community that youth behavioral health problems are preventable, if stakeholders are willing to work together to address them using EBIs. Communities that are not ready to engage in collaborative, evidence-based prevention should not adopt the CTC system until they can address the barriers that hinder the adoption and implementation of EBIs. If readiness challenges are minimal, in Phase 2, community key leaders and coalition members receive information in training workshops about interventions that have been developed, tested, and shown to be effective in preventing behavioral health problems. Support is also provided in this phase to help communities build diverse and representative coalitions that include members from all agencies and organizations likely to implement EBIs.

In Phase 3, coalitions begin to engage in the strategic selection of EBIs. The first step is to identify their specific needs, using epidemiologic data on the behavioral health problems that exist in the local community, as well as levels of risk factors and protective factors that predict these problems. Taking these data and the local context into account, coalition members prioritize their needs and identify the risk and protective factors that need to be addressed by EBIs in order to prevent or reduce behavioral health problems. Needs assessments are the essential first step in determining the fit of EBIs with the local context. As discussed in chapter 5, rather than select *any* intervention shown to be effective, CTC communities are guided to adopt the EBI(s) that has been demonstrated to address their particular needs; that is, EBIs are selected that have evidence of reducing locally elevated risk factors and increasing the protective factors reported as depressed by local youth.

With the growing number of EBIs, it can still be difficult to select the right EBI. For example, there could be multiple EBIs that address the risk and protective factors of concern to a community. How, then, do coalitions proceed to determine the best-fitting EBI for their community? In the CTC system, the next step, which is conducted during Phase 3, is to conduct a resource assessment.

The Importance of Community Resource Assessments

CTC coalitions learn how to conduct a local resource assessment in Phase 3 after completing their needs assessment. Resource assessments investigate the extent to which the prioritized risk and protective factors are currently being addressed by local services. Coalitions might initially assume that there are no prevention services targeting their priorities; if there were, then youth would not be reporting their prioritized risk factors as elevated and protective factors as depressed. There are several reasons why this assumption may be incorrect. First, local agencies may be attempting to address prioritized risk and protective factors using ineffective strategies rather than EBIs. Second, it could be that EBI implementation has just begun and it is too early for the program(s) to affect the targeted risk and/or protective factors. Third, there may be problems with the reach or quality of the EBI implementation that dilute its effectiveness. CTC provides guidance to coalitions in how to examine these possibilities, identify gaps and problems in service delivery, and determine whether or not new EBIs should be implemented or current EBIs should be expanded or implemented in a different way to address needs.

When CTC was first developed, coalitions received a three-day training workshop that covered methods for conducting both needs and resource assessments. Although the pilot evaluations indicated that this training facilitated the completion of both tasks [74, 75], attendance was difficult to ensure because the three-day time commitment was difficult for volunteer members of a coalition. In addition, as the CTC system was refined, the processes for conducting both needs and resource assessments became more clearly specified, and the work was assigned to workgroups rather than the full coalition. These changes led to splitting the single workshop into two separate workshops, with the second being the Community Resources Assessment Training.

When first developed, the Community Resources Assessment Training was delivered as a one-day, in-person training for members of the Resources Assessment and Evaluation workgroup.[4] This workgroup is charged with creating an inventory of current community resources that address prioritized needs. Thus, the Resources Assessment and Evaluation workgroup should include individuals with preexisting knowledge of community resources, as well as people who are comfortable interviewing service providers. They must also understand the community's prioritized risk and protective factors if they are to determine if a service addresses these issues. In the Community Resources Assessment Training, the workshop members begin by reviewing their coalition's prioritized factors, and they practice explaining them to each other. They also learn what it means for an intervention to be "evidence-based," since the main goal of the resource assessment is to assess the degree to which prioritized needs are being addressed by EBIs already present in the community.

To facilitate the resource assessment, the CTC coordinator or a workgroup member should gather all preexisting community directories that list resources for local youth and families, such as municipal or county resource directories, activity pages of local newspapers, school resource guides, and so on. Workgroup members review these resources and identify specific programs or policies that appear to address prioritized risk and protective factors. They volunteer to gather information about these programs from the organizations delivering these services.

The workshop then trains members on methods to collect and analyze this information. Workgroups review sample surveys they can use with service providers and decide if they will collect data in person or by phone, or if they will ask providers to independently complete surveys. Regardless of the method used, the survey should gather data on whether or not the program(s) delivered addresses any of the coalition's prioritized risk and protective factors. They should also identify the population(s) targeted by the intervention (i.e., whether or not the program is for a universal, selective, or indicated population and the demographic characteristics of participants) and determine if the program has ever been evaluated. To assess potential gaps in services and/ or implementation problems, providers should be asked to report where in the community the service is provided, funding sources and their expected duration, if the intervention is delivered in languages other than English, and if services are delivered as designed. Workgroup members ask any other questions that they think will be helpful in understanding the scope and implementation fidelity of services in their community.

After all the data are gathered, workgroup members meet to analyze the results and identify resource gaps. The Community Resources Assessment Training workshop provides guidance on how to complete this work. Members discuss their findings and learn how to determine which, if any, of their prioritized risk and protective factors are currently being addressed. If EBIs are being used to address priorities, they discuss whether or not all targeted population groups are being served, if funding challenges exist, and if programs are being delivered as designed. The goal is for the workgroup to identify problems in service delivery and provide recommendations to correct these problems, such as the need to adopt new EBIs to target prioritized needs, expand the delivery of particular services (if they are evidence based), and/or improve the implementation of existing EBIs. When the work is complete, the workgroup prepares a written report summarizing its findings and recommendations and shares the report at the next full meeting of the CTC coalition.

The step-by-step procedures, tools, and technical support provided in this phase of CTC have been demonstrated to increase coalitions' capacity to conduct resource assessments. In the Community Youth Development Study, self-reports by coalition coordinators, trainers, and technical assistance providers indicated that all 12 CTC coalitions completed a resource assessment in the first year of the study [76]. As recommended, they also periodically updated the resource assessment [77]. According to surveys of coalition leaders in the 24 communities participating in the efficacy trial, coalitions in CTC communities were significantly more likely than those in control communities to report completion of a resource assessment in the initial phase of the study [78]. In addition, in 2009, about two years following the end of implementation phase, 100% of the 11 still functioning CTC coalitions reported having completed a resource assessment in the year prior to the survey, compared to 48% of the 23 prevention coalitions operating in control communities [79].

Although CTC coalitions have successfully conducted resource assessments, some have reported that the process is challenging [80]. Especially in larger communities, it can be difficult to determine the particular interventions being offered to youth and families, and surveying service providers is time intensive. In addition, both the workgroup members and service providers may struggle with how to determine if a program is "evidence based." Indeed, even scientists disagree as to what constitutes a rigorous evaluation and demonstration of desirable results. In the Community Youth Development Study, workgroup members found it easiest to ask services providers if they implemented any of the programs identified as effective in the CTC *Prevention Strategies Guide* [23], rather than to ask them to demonstrate that their programs had been evaluated and shown to be effective. Since CTC currently guides communities to use the Blueprints registry to select EBIs, coalitions can ask services providers to identify their use of programs found on the Blueprints website.

No matter how they frame the question, coalition members must be prepared for some sensitivity to the issue of "evidence-based" interventions. If service providers are delivering programs that have not undergone a rigorous evaluation, as is often the case, they may worry that the Resource Assessment workgroup will recommend that their programs be discontinued. They may also perceive their work to be undervalued and marginalized in the CTC process. Workgroup members have to respond carefully to these concerns. During the Resources Assessment workshops, workgroup members practice negotiating such interactions and conveying the message that service providers play an important role in positive youth development. They also want to communicate that the goal is not to discontinue unevaluated programs, but to rigorously evaluate them to ensure they are achieving their intended goals.

A less sensitive but still difficult task is to determine if an intervention addresses a particular risk or protective factor. Although workgroup members practice defining the prioritized factors, matching this information to the content of local prevention programs is not always straightforward. Historically, workgroup members have used the program descriptions in the CTC *Prevention Strategies Guide* [23] to determine which factor(s) is addressed by the EBI. The Blueprints for Healthy Youth Development website also lists the risk and protective factors targeted and actually changed by EBIs,[5] which facilitates the resource assessments currently conducted by CTC coalitions.

Resource assessments are vital to the CTC process and important in fostering the adoption of well-fitting EBIs. Again, the goal of the CTC system is not to discontinue existing services but, rather, to take stock of community resources, avoid duplication of services, and fill gaps in services with high-quality implementation of EBIs. Given progress in the development and availability of EBIs, it is not uncommon for local communities to be implementing *some* effective prevention services. However, it could be that EBIs are not being well implemented or that most of the community is not aware that EBIs are available. Likewise, EBIs may have limited funding and may serve relatively few participants.

Resource assessments allow these problems to be identified. They highlight efforts already in place to target prioritized needs, which help to avoid duplication of services, and illuminate problems with implementation that need to be addressed to ensure outcomes are achieved. They can also help publicize the CTC initiative [85]. As workgroup members contact all agencies that seek to improve healthy youth development, they can invite new parties to the CTC coalition, update current members on their progress, and communicate the importance of targeting local needs with EBIs across the community.

Selecting the Best-Fitting EBI(s) to Address Prioritized Needs

The explicit goal of Phase 4 (*Create a Plan*) of CTC is to increase the adoption of EBIs that are a good fit for the community (see Figure 6.1). All members of the CTC coalition receive guidance in this topic in the Community Planning Training workshop.[6] To begin the process, coalition members review their prioritized needs and write goal statements that specify the degree to which they would like prioritized risk factors, protective factors, and problem behaviors to change as a result of the CTC initiative. These objectives are based on data from the CTC Youth Survey and are typically written as an expected reduction or increase in the percentage of youth reporting each priority in a particular time period (e.g., three to five years from the current year). Stating specific prevention objectives helps to concretize the community's vision of healthy youth development created in Phase 2. Doing so also helps to establish baseline levels that will be tracked in Phase 5 (*Implement and Evaluate*) through repeated administration of the CTC Youth Survey to evaluate the success of the CTC initiative. These goals are written into the community's action plan (see later) and can be shared with the entire community as part of the coalition's efforts to publicize and gain support for CTC [86, 87].

Next, coalition members review the resource assessment report and recommendations. The goal is to reach consensus regarding the new EBIs the coalition will select and/or the EBIs currently delivered that they will expand or improve upon to fill resource gaps. To facilitate the selection of new EBIs, CTC provides communities with a list of EBIs to select from based on the best available information about "what works." When first developed, CTC provided information about EBIs in the *Comprehensive Strategy Guide* [22] and the CTC *Prevention Strategies Guide* [23]. Given the pace of evaluation research and the need to provide communities with the most up-to-date information possible, the CTC system now has coalitions use the Blueprints for Healthy Youth Development registry (www.blueprintsprograms.com/) to select new EBIs. As mentioned, this registry was selected because it reviews interventions targeting a comprehensive set of behavioral health problems; uses a systematic review process and rigorous criteria to determine effectiveness; promotes only those EBIs that provide manuals, training, and technical assistance to new users; and regularly updates its findings. In addition, its website is user-friendly and informative. It provides detailed information about each program, including the risk and protective factors targeted and demonstrated in research trials to be altered by the intervention, appropriate population targets, intervention costs and cost effectiveness, and potential funding mechanisms. In addition, users can search the database and compare programs based on their targeted risk and protective factors, effects, costs, and other intervention features.

In the CTC Community Planning Training, coalition members learn about Blueprints and use the database to create a list of EBIs that are available to address their needs. For some risk and protective factors, Blueprints may list only one EBI, while for other factors, it may promote multiple EBIs. In either case, coalition members conduct their fit assessment by considering the degree to which potential EBIs will be well received by community members and well aligned with the local context. For each EBI, they identify the program's targeted population, requirements (e.g., length of programming, methods of delivery, implementer/client ratio, staff credentials, etc.), financial costs (including costs related to staffing, training and technical assistance, supplies, equipment, administration, transportation, etc.), and necessary human resources (e.g., the number of required volunteers, implementers, and supervisors and/or coordinators). If the coalition does not think that the community can recruit a sufficient number of participants to make the program cost effective, ensure that all components can be delivered, and provide all the resources needed for implementation, the program is not likely to be a good fit and should probably not be selected.

The community fit assessment also involves consideration of the local sociopolitical factors that can facilitate or undermine support for the intervention. Coalitions consider the degree to which the program content and methods align with community/agency norms, the demographic and cultural characteristics of the community, competing programs or initiatives, and any current or expected budget crises. Taking all these factors into account, coalition members identify the EBIs that they determine can be fully implemented, are affordable, and will be supported by program providers, participants, and the broader community [86]. Consistent with its community-based participatory research approach, CTC recognizes that only the members of the community will be able to adequately assess program fit because they are the experts on community norms, values, and resources. Presented with a menu of interventions that all have been tested and found to address prioritized risk and protective factors, coalitions choose the EBI that is best for them. Local choice and decision making helps build community members' commitment to the CTC process, increases local ownership of new EBIs, and promotes the high-quality implementation and sustainability of EBIs [87].

To engender community support for the new interventions, it is essential that all relevant stakeholders are involved in the selection process and agree on the EBIs to be adopted. If important sectors or groups are not yet involved in the coalition or are unable to participate in the Community Planning Training, additional discussions will be needed to reach consensus on the new EBIs to be adopted. By increasing collaboration among multiple and diverse stakeholders, CTC communities will be better able to produce a collective impact on problems than if organizations were to select and implement prevention efforts in an isolated and uncoordinated fashion. As John Kania and Mark Kramer [88] indicate: "The power of collective action comes not from the sheer number of participants or the uniformity of their efforts, but from the coordination of their differentiated activities through a mutually reinforcing plan of action."

CTC guides agencies to consider how a group of programs will complement rather than compete with one another and provide the best use of resources. Coalition members are encouraged to select multiple EBIs that will address elevated risk factors and depressed protective factors and be implemented across multiple contexts (e.g., in communities, families, schools, and peer groups). This comprehensive scope is based on the life-course developmental theories that guide CTC (see chapter 2). These theories indicate that behavioral problems are influenced by multiple risk and protective factors, and that the accumulation of multiple risks and few protective factors produces the most detrimental outcomes [89, 90]. Implementing a coordinated set of EBIs allows communities to simultaneously and synergistically target multiple risk and protective factors, which should enhance the potential to achieve community-wide changes [87]. As the coalition coordinator in one of the CTC communities involved in the randomized evaluation stated: "Programs are not isolated. They should be working in tandem to create a new environment in the community."

CTC also recognizes that community-wide changes require a broad scope of services. Not only is it important to implement multiple EBIs but also to ensure that the EBIs reach as many participants as possible with services.

Doing so means delivering *universal* interventions that target individuals and groups (e.g., families, schools, or communities) regardless of whether or not they have been identified as at risk for behavioral health problems, as well as *selective* EBIs designed for individuals known to have high risk or low protection, and *indicated* EBIs targeting individuals who have already developed early indicators of behavioral health problems (see Figure 6.2 for an illustration of this scope of services).

Community members are often motivated to focus services on those perceived to have the greatest need for EBIs. However, according to the prevention paradox [91], the majority of behavioral health problems can be attributed to individuals who have a relatively low risk of developing such problems because they are a much larger group within the total population than are people at high risk. Universal interventions that are delivered across the population can reach lower and higher risk populations, including those not typically involved in formal health and social services [3]. Because the goal of CTC is to reduce behavioral health problems community wide, fully saturating the community with effective prevention actions and messages should provide the best possible means of achieving population-level changes [92].

Once the coalition has agreed on a set of EBIs to support, it drafts its action plan. This document identifies the prioritized risk and protective factors, the outcomes of the resource assessment, the specific prevention objectives to be achieved, and the EBIs that will be implemented to address each prioritized risk and protective factor. Having a formal plan provides a "roadmap" for all coalition members and helps to ensure that coalition members have a shared understanding of and commitment to prevention activities [93]. The plan, or

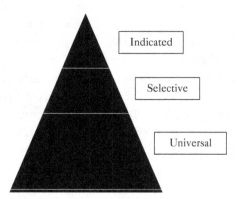

FIGURE 6.2 CTC Emphasizes the Delivery of Evidence-Based Interventions (EBIs) to Universal, Selective, and Indicated Populations

shorter versions of it, can also be shared with the community to highlight CTC activities.

To further illustrate how the selection of EBIs in CTC is consistent with community-based participatory research, it is useful to consider the experiences of the 12 communities that were randomly assigned to implement CTC in the Community Youth Development Study. These communities were each provided $75,000 annually for four years during the implementation phase of the trial to use EBIs that targeted families and children in grades 5 through 9, the developmental focus of the study [94; also see Figure 1.3 to review the study's research design and timeline]. At the time of the study, the CTC *Community Strategies Guide* identified 39 EBIs that were appropriate for this age group, including school-based, family-focused, and after-school programs. Using this menu of options, the 12 CTC communities selected 13 different EBIs during the first Community Planning Training.

Although some communities selected the same program, each CTC coalition selected a different combination of one to four EBIs based on their unique profile of risk and protective factors and local context. For example, to address the risk factor, "friends who engage in problem behavior," a community having strong support from its school district decided to implement the Life Skills Training program, which teaches middle school students to resist peer influences to use drugs. Coalitions in two other communities also prioritized this risk factor but did not think their local schools would support the adoption of a new prevention curriculum. These coalitions chose to address this risk factor with an after-school skills-based program (Stay SMART) and a parent training program (Guiding Good Choices), respectively.

The specific combination of EBIs selected depended on local context and resources. For example, one community decided to implement four EBIs: Life Skills Training, tutoring, Big Brothers/Big Sisters, and Stay SMART. The resource assessment in this community indicated that Life Skills Training was currently being taught in only one of its elementary and middle schools. With input from school representatives and endorsement from all the school principals and the superintendent, the coalition voted to expand this program to all four middle schools. The coalition and schools also agreed to create tutoring programs in two of the elementary schools. Schools appreciated the opportunity to provide students with additional educational services, and a nearby university provided low-cost tutors in the form of students who were earning their education degrees. The resource assessment had identified a regional Big Brothers/Big Sisters agency serving few youth in the CTC coalition's community. The coalition decided to supplement the salary of the coordinator in exchange for increased recruiting efforts in its community.

Last, the coalition decided to adopt the Stay SMART after-school program, to be run by the Boys and Girls Club located in an area of the community populated mostly by Native Americans. The coalition's decision was based on the desire to forge a stronger partnership with the club, which was geographically isolated and not always included in prevention efforts. In addition, the group hoped to increase interaction between Native and non-Native children, who would later meet in high school, thereby enhancing communication and friendships prior to the high school transition [86].

Successes and Challenges in Adopting EBIs in CTC Communities

CTC communities have reported both success and difficulties in completing Phase 4 of the system. In the first CTC pilot study conducted in Washington, only 30% of the coalition coordinators reported that their community had developed a written action plan, and they stated that plan development was hindered by a lack of engagement in the process by key leaders and community members [75]. In addition, most of the prevention activities specified in the plans and/or implemented by coalitions focused on raising awareness or planning drug-free events in schools or the community. These actions are not considered to be effective prevention strategies according to most registries, although at the time the Washington initiative was conducted, very few interventions had strong evidence of effectiveness.

In the CTC pilot evaluation conducted in Oregon, after additional training and support had been added to the CTC system to increase coalition functioning and provide more information about EBIs, 31 of the 36 CTC coalitions created action plans in the first year of the project and 28 completed plans in the following year [74]. Prevention services were much more likely to be evidence based, with 71% of the coalitions implementing effective interventions [74]. In the Title V project, 45 sites implemented a total of 277 delinquency prevention activities, 90% of which were rated as promising approaches in the *Comprehensive Strategies Guide* [22, 95]

According to baseline interviews conducted in all 24 communities participating in the Community Youth Development Study, only 22% of the prevention-oriented coalitions that existed in CTC communities reported having action plans to guide their prevention activities, as did 32% of the prevention-oriented coalitions in the control communities [78]. However, after they had adopted the CTC system and participated in the Community Planning Training during the first year of the study, all 12 CTC coalitions completed a written action plan [76]. In the third year of the study (2007), 92% of CTC coalitions compared to 19% of prevention coalitions in control communities reported having an action plan [78]. In 2009, one and a half years into the sustainability phase of the efficacy trial, after the technical assistance provided to CTC coalitions had stopped, significantly more coalitions in CTC communities (55%) reported having a current action plan compared to those in the control communities (22%) [79].

Particularly when considering findings from the randomized trial, these results indicate that the CTC system is effective in building coalition capacity to create a comprehensive action plan that identifies a set of EBIs to be implemented to address risk and protective factors. Yet, even in the randomized study, 10 of the 12 CTC coalitions rated completion of the initial action plan as one of their most challenging tasks [76]. Like those participating in the first evaluation in Washington, coalition members stated that it was very difficult to engage all important stakeholders in the process and to reach consensus about which EBIs to adopt. Difficult conversations tended to emerge when coalition members considered the differences between the programs defined as "evidence-based" in the *Prevention Strategies Guide* and the unevaluated programs identified in their community resource assessments. The latter were often supported by local practitioners even in the absence of strong evaluation evidence [96].

Even though the action plan presented some challenges, all 12 CTC coalitions in the Community Youth Development Study were successful in identifying a set of EBIs to be implemented as part of the CTC process. Each community initially selected 1 to 4 programs, for a total of 13 different EBIs across the 12 CTC communities [97]. These included four school-based programs, five after-school programs, and four parent-training programs. School-based EBIs were particularly challenging to reach consensus on. Ten of the 12 CTC identified a school-based EBI as a good fit for their needs during their first Community Planning Trainings, but only five were able to convince local schools to adopt the program [66, 76, 96]. Some administrators and staff expressed concern that implementing prevention programs would divert classroom time from the educational programming that had to be conducted [76]. In addition, most schools were already implementing some type of health-related curriculum, and administrators and staff often did not want to discontinue their current programs even if they had no rigorous evidence of effectiveness [66, 76, 96].

When schools and other organizations cannot be persuaded to adopt particular EBIs, coalitions have to select other types of EBIs to address their prioritized needs. This was the strategy used by the five coalitions that initially could not gain support to adopt a school-based program in the efficacy trial. Nonetheless, these CTC coalitions continued to have conversations with school administrators, teachers, and/or counselors about the importance of using EBIs to address prioritized needs. They reminded school representatives that CTC was a community-wide initiative that relied on multiple organizations to implement EBIs to address needs prioritized as important by the entire community. In some cases, coalitions eventually found a teacher or school willing to adopt the new program, then worked over time to expand the EBI to other teachers and schools, using the positive results from the initial implementation to persuade others to adopt the EBI. Using some combination of these strategies, all 12 communities in the Community Youth Development Study were ultimately successful in implementing at least one school-based prevention program [66].

When implemented outside of the U.S., CTC coalitions have been somewhat less successful in adopting EBIs during Phase 4, largely due to the lack of availability of EBIs in these countries [98]. It has taken time to develop and test preventive interventions and accumulate evidence of their effectiveness in the United States and in some other high-income countries. In many other nations, progress has been slower and fewer interventions typically exist that have been evaluated in rigorous trials and shown to decrease youth behavioral health problems [2, 10]. For example, only 15 prevention programs existed when CTC was first begun in Colombia in 2011, and only one of these programs had been rigorously evaluated [41]. Similarly, no rigorous evaluation of prevention programs had been conducted when CTC was first implemented in the Netherlands in 1999 [39]. By 2013, only 13 prevention programs had been well evaluated and shown to be effective in addressing youth behavioral health problems in the Netherlands [99].

The lack of EBIs in European countries has threatened CTC success, especially when CTC coalitions have had to rely on untested strategies to target risk and protective factors. For example, a quasi-experimental evaluation of CTC in 10 communities in the Netherlands found no intervention effects on youth substance use or delinquency, which the evaluators attributed to the limited availability and implementation of EBIs [99]. However, CTC's focus on EBIs has spurred intervention development and replication in Europe. For example, the lack of EBIs in Croatia led CTC trainers to work more closely with local program developers to help them further develop and evaluate their interventions [98]. In addition, CTC coalitions were instrumental in promoting the adoption of the U.S.-based PATHS program in Croatia.

In any country, a shortage of funds can certainly impede the adoption of EBIs. The evaluation of CTC in the Netherlands highlighted a lack of resources as another reason why Dutch communities failed to achieve the same reductions in youth behavioral health problems as coalitions participating in the randomized trial in the United States (which had received funding for EBIs) [99]. Similarly, when CTC was implemented in three communities in the United Kingdom, one was considered an implementation failure in part because key leaders did not support the initiative enough to generate resources for EBIs [96]. In contrast, the most successful coalition in this project implemented seven programs that had promising evidence of effectiveness. This community had a supportive and influential champion who helped find resources for EBIs, and all important stakeholders (except schools) participated in the selection and implementation of EBIs [96].

The Importance of EBIs in Reducing Youth Behavioral Health Problems

As emphasized throughout this chapter, CTC considers the adoption of EBIs to be necessary in order to achieve significant reductions in youth behavioral health problems. This view is not unique to CTC; it is a key tenet of prevention science [2, 3, 100]. Similarly, the failure to use EBIs has been identified as contributing to the lack of success of other community-based prevention efforts [101, 102]. For example, in the well-funded *Fighting Back* coalition initiative [102], most coalitions implemented untested and/or ineffective strategies to prevent youth and adult substance use, and no significant differences in adolescent drug use were found between the intervention and comparison communities.

CTC not only requires the use of EBIs but also provides structured guidance, training, and technical assistance/coaching to communities to increase their knowledge of EBIs and assist them to select EBIs that match their needs. CTC also emphasizes the implementation of a coordinated set of EBIs that address risk and protective factors across domains of influence. We are not aware of any other community-based system that provides such a comprehensive approach to prevention. The PROSPER initiative is most similar, in that it promotes the implementation of multiple EBIs across contexts and provides training and technical support to ensure the adoption of EBIs [103]. However, PROSPER communities do not conduct needs or resource assessments, and they select and implement only two types of EBIs (a parent training program and a school-based drug prevention program) from a much more limited menu of options compared to CTC. PROSPER has been demonstrated in a randomized controlled trial to increase knowledge about EBIs [104] and to successfully reduce adolescent substance use and delinquency [105–107].

Another similar strategy is the Strategic Prevention Framework (SPF), developed by the U.S. Substance Abuse and Mental Health Services Administration (SAMHSA). Largely modeled after the CTC system, the SPF advocates that coalitions try to reduce community levels of youth substance use by conducting needs assessments and implementing and evaluating multiple evidence-based strategies to address locally specific target risk and protective factors (see www.samhsa.gov/spf). However, the SPF defines an "evidence-based" program using much less rigorous criteria than CTC [108]. In addition, although coalitions receive some training and technical assistance through the Center for the Application of Prevention Technologies (CAPT), this support is less frequent and systematized than in CTC and is often provided using more passive technologies such as webinars and written guides rather than workshops and individualized support. Although some preliminary studies have been published regarding the effectiveness of the SPF [e.g., 109, 110], results from the more rigorous national evaluation of coalitions involved in the State Incentive Grants initiative have not yet been reported, so it is difficult to determine if adoption of the SPF can produce community-wide reductions in adolescent substance use.

Another similar approach to prevention whose effectiveness remains to be evaluated is the Center for Disease Control's (CDC) National Centers of Excellence in Youth Violence Prevention. Begun in 2000, the project has funded academic institutions to partner with local coalitions to help them conduct needs assessments, prioritize local risk and protective factors associated with youth violence, select a set of violence prevention strategies to address these needs, and implement these strategies with fidelity and at a scale large enough to impact community rates of violence [111]. The initiative has employed a less rigorous minimum criterion to identify evidence-based interventions compared to CTC. Interventions which have been evaluated in only one rigorous randomized controlled trial or one quasi-experimental evaluation can be implemented by communities participating in the project [111]. However, specific sites may adopt a more rigorous standard to select EBIs.[7]

These examples provide further evidence that standards used to determine "what works" vary across organizations and initiatives. By endorsing the Blueprints criteria and methods, CTC recommends interventions for dissemination that have the most credible evidence of effectiveness. Although this approach may reduce the number of options available to communities [37] and can create tension among local stakeholders about what it means to be "evidence-based," it minimizes the risk of endorsing interventions that may not change community levels of behavioral health problems. Furthermore, as described in chapter 8, the CTC system has been demonstrated to reduce adolescent substance use and delinquency in a well-conducted randomized trial [112–114] and is itself identified as a promising intervention by Blueprints. We hope that other coalition-based prevention systems will also be rigorously evaluated for effectiveness, as doing so will advance our understanding of the best ways to determine intervention effectiveness and improve coalition capacity to adopt these interventions.

Research now demonstrates that even when EBIs are adopted by communities, if they are not well implemented, they are unlikely to produce desired outcomes [31, 32]. Ensuring the high-quality implementation of EBIs is yet another significant challenge facing community-based prevention efforts. We discuss this challenge in chapter 7, as well as methods for ensuring the sustainability of EBIs and coalitions, using examples from CTC to illustrate these issues.

Ensuring High-Quality Implementation and Sustainability of Evidence-Based Interventions and Coalitions

COALITIONS MUST HAVE the capacity to engage in collaborative prevention efforts if they are to succeed in a community-based approach to reducing youth behavioral health problems. In chapters 4, 5, and 6, we discussed the steps and conditions needed to increase capacity *prior to* the implementation of EBIs—that is, before communities actually use new interventions, deliver them with quality, and provide an appropriate and sufficient number of participants with services [1, 2]. Building a strong foundation for prevention (i.e., ensuring readiness, engaging key leaders and community members, and forming a diverse, representative coalition of stakeholders) and engaging in comprehensive and collaborative prevention planning (i.e., conducting needs, resource, and fit assessments) are both necessary to ensure successful EBI implementation. Prevention planning also increases the likelihood that EBIs will be well integrated into systems and settings, which facilitates their long-term sustainability [3, 4].

In this chapter, we discuss additional actions that communities should take just prior to and during EBI implementation to enhance EBI effectiveness and sustainability. We review the actions and methods that coalitions can take to achieve implementation fidelity, reach a sufficient number of participants with services, and ensure that EBIs are culturally relevant. Community coalitions also need to be maintained over time, and we discuss methods for increasing the sustainability of high-functioning coalitions, including ways to maintain membership diversity and participation, monitor prevention activities,

FIGURE 7.1 The Five Phases of the Communities That Care Prevention System

and generate adequate levels of funding to support coalition functioning and EBI implementation. As in the other chapters, we illustrate these issues by drawing on the prevention science literature and describing the methods used in CTC to build coalition capacity to successfully implement and sustain EBIs, specifically the tasks to be accomplished in Phase 5 (*Implement and Evaluate*, see Figure 7.1).

The Importance of Implementation Fidelity in the Delivery of EBIs

Research indicates that community *adoption* of EBIs is necessary but insufficient to reduce behavioral health problems. To achieve desired outcomes, EBIs must also be well *implemented* [1, 5, 6]. High-quality implementation means that EBIs are replicated with fidelity, according to the specifications of intervention developers [7, 8]. Implementation fidelity includes: (1) *adherence*, which means delivering all elements of the EBI thought to produce outcomes (i.e., the EBI's core components) to the population for whom they are intended; (2) *dosage*, providing the required amount of programming; (3) *quality of delivery*, which refers to the competence and enthusiasm of program staff; and (4) *participant responsiveness*, ensuring that participants are engaged in programming and practicing new skills [8–10]. Implementation fidelity also includes the *reach* of the EBI, or the proportion of the eligible population that receives programming; greater reach helps produce population-level reductions in behavioral health problems [2].

The importance of implementation fidelity has been illustrated in a systematic review of prevention science literature that indicated that in two thirds of the 59 studies considered, greater implementation fidelity was related to better participant outcomes [1]. One of the first evaluations of a single prevention program to demonstrate this type of relationship was a randomized evaluation of the Life Skills Training drug-prevention curriculum [11]. This study indicated that students whose teachers delivered at least 60% of the required information and activities in the LST curriculum achieved significant reductions in smoking, drinking, and marijuana use compared to students in the control group. Students whose teachers did not implement the program with at least this level of fidelity (i.e., adherence) had rates of substance use that were no different from those of the control group. Even more striking are findings from an evaluation of Functional Family Therapy (FFT), an indicated therapeutic intervention for families of youth offenders [12]. This study reported that youth whose families received services from therapists who research staff rated as not competent had *higher* rates of recidivism for felony offenses compared to the control group, whereas youth whose families received programming from skilled therapists committed *fewer* felony offenses compared to the control group.

As these examples indicate, implementation matters. However, research also indicates that programs are often poorly replicated in communities [13, 14]. For example, school-based programs are often implemented incorrectly, with implementers failing to deliver all lessons, content, and activities; use the required materials; employ the recommended instructional strategies; and/or target the appropriate students for services [13, 15–18]. The delivery of family-based EBIs has also been less than ideal in many replications, with implementers changing the required content or activities, failing to deliver all of the content or sessions, and/or providing lessons to different types of participants than those specified by program developers [19–21]. Similarly, evaluations of community-based interventions have indicated problems with implementation, including a lack of participation, collaboration, and/or support by community members [22, 23].

Given the relationship between implementation fidelity and participant outcomes, studies have sought to identify the factors that impede and improve the quality of implementation. Some of this research [e.g., 24] has indicated that fit assessments are important not only for increasing the adoption of EBIs, as described in chapter 6, but also for increasing implementation fidelity. That is, implementation quality is improved when stakeholders take time to learn about the requirements of an EBI, deem it to be feasible to implement, and consider its content and methods of delivery to be compatible with the norms, values, and needs of the local community [14, 25]. When these steps are not taken, or the fit is less than optimal, practitioners are more likely to make substantial changes to the EBI, altering its content, materials, or methods of delivery, and participants are likely to be less responsive to the intervention content.

Some research suggests that EBIs can never be perfectly replicated in communities and that adaptations are always necessary because programs are developed by scientists and tested in research trials that may not be similar to the conditions found in a particular community that has chosen to replicate the intervention [20, 26–29]. Changes are expected to increase an EBI's relevance to the local context and potentially improve its effectiveness. However, changes can have the unintended consequence of reducing EBI effectiveness when they involve mis-adaptations, or significant alterations to the EBI's core components that are inconsistent with the program's theoretical foundation and/or methods of delivery [1, 26, 30, 31].

An evaluation of the Nurse-Family Partnership program showed that its effectiveness was reduced when paraprofessionals rather than registered nurses implemented the intervention [32]. This alteration to staffing is a common change made in communities that lack registered nurses. However, it represents a mis-adaptation of the program, which was designed to be delivered by registered nurses because they have high levels of professional training, clinical skills, and legitimacy in communities [32].

To avoid mis-adaptations and decreased EBI effectiveness, communities should learn as much as they can about EBIs by conducting a fit assessment. They should select only those interventions that are deemed feasible to implement with fidelity. If they cannot adhere to EBI requirements, coalitions should select a different EBI or work to build their capacity so that they can eventually deliver the EBI as specified. Any adaptations made to increase the appeal and/or relevance of an EBI should be carefully planned in advance and should not alter or be in conflict with the intervention's theory, goals, and mechanisms responsible for producing outcomes [31]. For example, useful adaptations that do not fundamentally change the EBI include adding incentives (e.g., meals or small prizes) for program participation, translating materials to a new language, and using implementers who match the demographic characteristics of participants [29, 33].

Once an EBI has been selected, but before it is implemented, a detailed implementation plan should be created to specify exactly when, where, and how often the EBI will be delivered [6, 24]. The plan should also identify the number and characteristics of participants who will receive services, the staff who will deliver it, how and when staff will be trained, and how implementation procedures and outcomes will be monitored [34]. Documenting these details can help practitioners make a final determination of feasibility and fit prior to implementation and provides a blueprint to guide the delivery and evaluation of the EBI.

Each EBI should have a written plan and an implementation team, a group of at least three individuals who know the intervention and are accountable for its delivery [24, 35]. Team members should include an administrator from the organization delivering the EBI, whose support and resources are needed to carry out services, as well as an implementer with detailed knowledge of the intervention. If the EBI requires a half- or full-time coordinator, this person should also be on the implementation team.

Because EBIs must be delivered to the right population, with enough reach to achieve community-wide reductions in outcomes [2], the implementation plan should clearly identify the eligibility criteria for participants, the number of eligible participants in the community, and the proportion targeted to receive services. Recruitment strategies should be fully specified, including all the actions that will be taken to recruit participants and all the individuals and organizations in the community who can help to refer individuals to the EBI. Implementation team members should consider all of the barriers that may impede participation and identify the actions that will be taken to avoid these challenges and encourage attendance. For example, youth and families may require transportation to access services, and incentives such as child care and food can help to facilitate attendance.

High-quality implementation is contingent upon having a sufficient number of skilled and supportive staff to deliver services [1, 8, 24]. To ensure these conditions are met, the implementation plan should document the number and credentials of staff required for implementation; if, how many, and when new staff will be hired; when staff will be trained; and how staff will be supervised to ensure that they are delivering EBIs with quality. Nearly all EBIs require that implementers receive formal training, and both training and technical assistance have been demonstrated to increase implementation quality [6, 36]. When implementers receive training, they are introduced to the theoretical background, content, and methods of delivery of the intervention, which should reduce the likelihood that they will make mis-adaptations and alter the elements that make the program successful [37]. Training also provides the opportunity for staff to practice delivering the content and master new teaching techniques [38]. If provided through an in-person meeting, training can also build a sense of community and support among the implementers.

Once an agency or organization begins to deliver the EBI, the implementation team should monitor implementation procedures as outlined in the plan. Developers of some EBIs may provide sites with tools they can use to document implementation procedures, and some may require that implementers or administrators input data into a central database that the developer maintains. If such systems do not exist, then practitioners will have to design their own tools and systems to record information [39]. Typical implementation monitoring procedures include having implementers complete checklists or surveys to record their adherence to delivery requirements, relying on administrators or external evaluators to observe sessions, or audio/videotaping and coding program sessions to rate implementation fidelity. Each of these methods has strengths and limitations related to cost, feasibility, and accuracy of information, and communities will need to decide which strategy(ies) they can employ [40–43].

Collecting data on implementation is only useful if the data are reviewed, evaluated, and used to enhance implementation quality, a process sometimes referred to as continuous quality improvement (CQI) [44]. Much of CQI involves providing staff with feedback on their performance and recommending ways to improve fidelity. Ideally, this type of coaching [45, 46] will be delivered in a supportive context to maintain implementers' commitment to the EBI. It is also important to review data and engage in quality improvement efforts regularly so that challenges can be identified quickly, before they can undermine EBI effectiveness. For example, a statewide prevention initiative in Washington stipulated that data were to be reviewed and feedback provided to staff every month [47].

Research has found that regular monitoring and quality-improvement efforts improve implementation fidelity [48]. For example, Multisystemic Therapy (MST) provides weekly feedback to therapists to help them become more proficient in the MST model [49]. An evaluation of this program demonstrated that when this regular feedback was not provided to staff, there was much greater variation in implementation procedures and lower levels of fidelity compared to prior evaluations in which feedback was provided [50]. Other studies have also indicated that implementation quality is improved when implementing organizations contract with program developers or purveyors [i.e., other organizations ceritified by a program developer to provide training and technical support to implementers; 46] to provide technical assistance [48, 51–53].

Monitoring implementation can help ensure that recruitment goals have been met and that participants are sufficiently engaged. In order for any EBI to be effective, it must be provided to the targeted group. Reach is particularly important in community-based prevention systems that try to change community levels of behavioral health problems. If data indicate that participation is not occurring at desired levels, organizations will need to increase their efforts to reach the targeted population, following and adding to the procedures described in their implementation plans.

A multifaceted recruitment plan is likely to be best able to achieve results [54]. Such efforts can include passive techniques such as advertisements in local print media and in social media, and more active efforts such as presentations to local organizations. In addition, organizations should ask as many formal and informal leaders in the community as possible to communicate positive messages about the EBI to their networks of friends and family. Recruitment techniques may also need to be tailored to the racial/ethnic background of the targeted group [55].

Much of the research on implementation fidelity has been conducted during evaluations of single EBIs, and these studies often recommend procedures for individual organizations to monitor and evaluate implementation. In community-based prevention initiatives, coalitions play an important role in collecting and evaluating monitoring data. Although the EBIs selected by a coalition will have different implementation requirements, the elements of implementation fidelity (i.e., adherence, dosage, quality of delivery, participant responsiveness, and reach) and methods for ensuring high-quality implementation (e.g., staff training, supervision, and technical assistance) do not typically vary across interventions. As a result, coalitions can assist implementation efforts by creating common methods and procedures for all organizations in the community to use to document implementation and engage in quality improvement [56].

Other than PROSPER and CTC, very few coalition-based prevention systems have been designed to enhance coalition capacity to deliver EBIs with fidelity, monitor implementation quality, and engage in continuous quality improvement procedures [57, 58]. In PROSPER, coalitions are trained in methods for assessing implementation fidelity of family- and school-based programs, primarily using observations to rate adherence, quality of delivery, and participant engagement [59]. The randomized evaluation of PROSPER indicated that community members in PROSPER sites, compared to those in the control communities, gained knowledge of how to monitor implementation fidelity from baseline to four years after the start of the study [60]. PROSPER coalitions also delivered EBIs with fidelity. A process evaluation of the 14 PROSPER communities indicated that during the first two years of programming, about 90% of the required content of the selected EBIs was implemented, and the quality of delivery and participant responsiveness were both rated very highly [59].

Although research staff initially assisted PROSPER teams in gathering and evaluating these data, the long-term goal was to build local coalition capacity to do so, thereby ensuring sustainability of monitoring procedures. Follow-up data collected in the three to four years after the initial assessment, when communities were responsible for observations, indicated that this goal was mostly achieved. This study showed that 8 of the 14 PROSPER coalitions continued to monitor the implementation of their school-based programs, and 11 continued to monitor the family-based program selected in their community. The monitoring data indicated high rates of implementation fidelity, with an average of 90% of the core content being delivered, and observers reporting moderately strong quality of delivery and participant engagement [61].

Building Coalition Capacity to Implement EBIs With Fidelity in the CTC System

How does the CTC system promote high-quality implementation of EBIs? In its early development, CTC did not provide training during Phase 5 to ensure that the EBIs described in a coalition's action plan were being well implemented, monitored, and evaluated to determine their effectiveness. As prevention science increased its emphasis on the importance of implementation fidelity, the CTC system was enhanced. Phase 5 was revised to include much more attention to how coalitions can help organizations monitor EBI delivery and engage in continuous quality improvement to overcome any deficits in implementation fidelity.

The Community Plan Implementation Training (CPIT) workshop was developed to provide coalitions with information and tools to facilitate high-quality implementation and EBI monitoring. In this training, coalitions learn about the importance of delivering EBIs with fidelity—specifically, that research has indicated that implementation fidelity leads to better outcomes and that mis-adaptations can undermine program success. Considering their community action plans and prior experiences with EBI delivery, participants identify potential implementation challenges they might encounter when delivering EBIs to address prioritized needs and discuss ways to avoid or counter these barriers. They also learn about the actions they can take to increase implementation quality, such as creating detailed implementation plans, ensuring that all staff receive training from program developers or purveyors, and fostering support from key leaders and implementers. The workshop provides suggestions for how to monitor the delivery of EBIs, such as conducting regular observations to assess adherence, dosage, quality of delivery, and participant responsiveness. Coalition members discuss how they will use implementation data to identify deviations in program protocols and provide corrective feedback to organizations to overcome challenges when they are identified.

The workshop also provides instruction on how to evaluate the degree to which EBIs lead to desired changes in participants' knowledge, attitudes, and behaviors. Coalition members learn methods for administering pre- and post-surveys of participants to assess these changes. Although data are collected only from intervention participants, without a comparison or control group, which makes it difficult to rule out other possible explanations of change, coalitions learn that a failure to achieve desired changes can indicate potential implementation problems that need to be corrected. For example, if a tutoring program designed to improve students' math skills does not lead to better grades in math or performance on standardized tests, then the intervention may be lacking in its content, duration, or ability to fully engage participants. Conversely, when desired changes in participants are achieved, these results suggest that interventions are being delivered with fidelity.

Like the other CTC training workshops, the Community Plan Implementation workshop is interactive and provides ample time for discussion and planning. Participants work together to create implementation plans for each EBI specified in their community action plans. In consultation with the organizations charged with delivering these services, coalition members document where, when, and how often EBIs will be delivered, the proportion of eligible participants to be reached with services, and the participant outcomes they expect to achieve. They consider how they will monitor and evaluate implementation procedures, including whether or not this work will be conducted solely by agency staff or if and how coalition members will assist. Finally, they identify potential community members to serve on implementation teams who will continue to refine the implementation plan and oversee delivery of the EBIs. In this manner, each community creates its own unique service delivery plan, while also conforming to the implementation standards prescribed by the developers of each selected EBI.

In the Community Youth Development Study, the Community Plan Implementation Training was provided as a one-day training in the beginning of Phase 5 after all CTC coalitions selected EBIs and drafted community action plans. These plans initially did not provide much information about how EBIs would be implemented. The lack of detail caused concern among the research staff and members of the study's advisory board, which comprised representatives from each of the participating state's office of drug abuse and prevention services. To ensure that they had a full understanding of all the required elements necessary for implementation, coalitions were asked to further develop their community action plans by providing more information on implementation. The first Community Plan Implementation workshop delivered in the randomized trial helped coalitions create more detailed plans for each selected EBI.

A second one-day Community Plan Implementation workshop was held to discuss methods for monitoring and evaluating the delivery of EBIs. Members of the coalition who would be directly involved in EBI monitoring were invited to participate, along with all the service providers who would implement the EBIs. These participants received guidance on how to create a comprehensive implementation monitoring system developed for the randomized study that included the components shown in Table 7.1. Although this methodology drew from existing CTC guidelines and materials, it was more extensive.[1]

The EBI monitoring system required CTC communities to track implementation procedures using a variety of tools and reporters. Self-report surveys were completed by staff or implementers of all interventions. In addition, observations of 10 to 15% of all sessions were conducted for most of the programs. Observations were not conducted of EBIs that were self-administered or for those that involved one-on-one or small-group administration (e.g., tutoring and mentoring programs) where observations would have been overly intrusive. Observers were selected by coalitions or agency staff and included the implementers' supervisors, CTC coordinators, CTC coalition members, and, in a few cases, other members of the community. All observers were trained by the CTC coalition coordinator or the EBI coordinator, if there was one, using procedures covered in the Community Plan Implementation Training workshop. Implementers and observers provided information on all dimensions of implementation fidelity: adherence, dosage, quality of delivery, participant responsiveness, and reach.

Session-specific checklists were used to rate *adherence* and *dosage* of programs with a discrete number of sessions. These were created either by program developers or research staff and identified the content and activities to be taught each time the program met. Program implementers documented on these checklists whether or not each objective/activity of each session was covered (to rate adherence), and the times and dates of each session (to indicate dosage). When the intervention was complete, adherence and dosage scores were calculated to indicate the percentage of content delivered out of all possible content, and the percentage of required sessions taught out of all sessions, respectively. Since implementers may under- or overestimate the extent to which they adhere to program guidelines [8, 65–67], observers completed the same fidelity instrument as program implementers to rate adherence. A comparison of data from the two sources indicated that observers and implementers provided nearly identical scores on adherence [64].

Table 7.1 EBI Implementation Monitoring Procedures Used by CTC Coalitions in the Community Youth Development Study

Component	Description	Purpose	Rater	Periodicity
Implementer self-reports	Checklists listing program content/activities or core components to be delivered	Document program fidelity, primarily adherence, and dosage	Program implementers and/or coordinators	After each session (programs with discrete sessions) Or Periodically throughout implementation (unstructured programs)
Observations of Programs	Trained observers complete checklists and rating forms	Validate adherence information from self-reports *and* Rate participant responsiveness and quality of delivery	CTC coalition coordinators, program coordinators, implementer supervisors, or other community members	10–15% of all program sessions
Participant Surveys	Anonymous surveys assessing program effects	Measure desired changes in participants' knowledge, attitudes, skills, and behaviors	All program participants who agreed to participate	Before the first session and after the last session
Local Monitoring and Accountability	Program monitoring and supervision through observation, review of data, and revisions in procedures	Identify implementation barriers and propose solutions to enhance fidelity	CTC coalitions and/or local agencies	Throughout implementation
External Monitoring and Accountability	Program monitoring and supervision through on-site, telephone, and written technical assistance	Identify implementation barriers and propose solutions to enhance fidelity	Research staff	Throughout implementation

Source: Adapted from Fagan et al. [62]

For less structured programs (i.e., programs without a specified number of sessions, or for which implementers were to adhere to general guidelines rather than teach specific content), program monitoring tools identified the core components of the program. At the end of these programs, or regularly throughout implementation, implementers and/or program coordinators rated whether or not each component was delivered. The adherence rate of these programs was calculated as the percentage of all the components that were implemented.

Observer reports were used to rate the *quality of implementation* delivery, since observers were considered to be more valid raters of this aspect of implementation than implementers. Observers rated the degree to which implementers provided clear explanations, kept on time, seemed rushed or hurried, and used examples to illustrate points. They also rated the implementer's knowledge of the program, enthusiasm, poise/confidence, rapport with participants, and ability to answer questions. These nine items, and one item regarding the overall quality of the session, were each rated on a 5-point scale. Scores on these items were combined and averaged to create the overall score of the quality of delivery.

Implementers provided information about *participant responsiveness* by rating participant misbehavior, involvement in activities, and enthusiasm during sessions. In addition, observers indicated the degree to which participants understood the material and participated in the lesson. The two observers rated items were both assessed on a 5-point scale and averaged together to rate participant responsiveness.

To document *participant participation and reach* of the program, program implementers recorded attendance at each session for parent training and after-school programs. School officials reported attendance at school programs as the number and percentage of students in the targeted grade who attended school each day during the semester(s) in which the program was taught.

To evaluate changes in participant outcomes, as shown in Table 7.1, research staff provided communities with surveys used in prior evaluations of the selected EBIs. If such tools did not exist, researchers created instruments that included reliable measures of the risk or protective factors that the programs were intended to address. Program implementers or coordinators then administered these surveys prior to the start of the first program session and at the end of the last session. All surveys were anonymous, with each participant creating a unique identifying code that allowed the pre- and post-surveys to be matched without revealing his or her identity.

As part of the technical assistance provided in the Community Youth Development Study, research staff reviewed all implementation monitoring data and provided written summaries of the results to CTC coalitions several times each year. These reports acknowledged the successes achieved during program delivery and provided recommendations to assist communities in their quality assurance procedures. Implementation data and recommendations were also reviewed during weekly telephone calls and email communications between research staff and local CTC coordinators. In addition, staff made site visits at least twice annually to CTC communities to observe program sessions and discuss implementation issues with coalition members and EBI implementers and administrators.

The goal of the extensive external monitoring and technical assistance in this phase was to foster the capacity of CTC coalitions and local organizations to monitor EBI implementation to ensure high fidelity. Although the research staff reviewed all implementation data, it was up to the CTC coalitions and implementing organizations to ensure that implementers and observers were rating implementation. They also need to collect and review the data, make changes as necessary to enhance implementation, and discontinue programs if successful implementation could not be ensured. All these efforts were undertaken and overseen by community members, and research staff provided technical assistance and coaching to support the process.

At the local level, implementation monitoring was a joint effort of CTC coalitions and the organizations delivering the EBIs. Research staff provided coaching to CTC coordinators in how to effectively deliver feedback to implementers, such as using coaching techniques to reinforce positive behaviors associated with high-fidelity implementation and providing corrective feedback to improve fidelity when needed. Each coalition, in consultation with the organizations delivering programs, decided who would deliver this feedback to staff: the coalition coordinator, the EBI coordinator, a supervisor from the implementing organization, or some combination of these people. Organizations were also encouraged to hold staff meetings during or after program delivery so that implementers could discuss as a group the positive and challenging aspects of implementation and the changes in implementation that could be made to solve identified problems.

Coalition members were also involved. They reviewed implementation data at their meetings, encouraged support and participation for EBIs from other community members, and shared information about EBIs with the community. For example, some coalitions wrote articles in local newspapers describing the number of participants in each program and how the EBIs were benefiting these members of the community. Coalitions also held celebratory events once or twice a year to recognize program participants and implementers.

Data collected during the Community Youth Development Study demonstrated that coalitions successfully implemented EBIs during Phase 5 of the CTC system. Based on information collected in 2007 (three years after EBIs were begun) from prevention-oriented coalition coordinators in both intervention and control communities, all the CTC coalitions reported monitoring the implementation of their selected EBIs, compared to 62% of coalitions operating in control communities, a statistically significant difference [68]. In 2009, about two years after the implementation phase of the study, when funding for EBIs was no longer provided, 91% of coalitions in CTC communities and 48% of those in control communities reported monitoring EBIs, a statistically significant difference [69].

According to implementation data collected only in the CTC communities, adherence rates ranged from 91 to 94% when averaged across all EBIs and over the four years that CTC coalitions received funding to implement interventions. These findings indicate that implementers reported teaching nearly all of the required material and delivering the majority of core components in all programs. Dosage was also high. When information was averaged across all four years and all EBIs, 94% of the required number, length, and frequency of sessions were delivered. According to observer reports, implementers achieved a high quality of delivery of all programs, with average quality scores greater than 4.0 on a 5-point scale. Across all programs and years, scores on participant responsiveness were also high, averaging 4.34 to 4.52 on a 5-point scale [64].

The one exception to the high rates of implementation adherence occurred during delivery of a school-based program, the Program Development Evaluation (PDE) school-wide intervention delivered in one CTC community. Although the intervention was successfully launched, adherence rates dropped from 93 to 54% from the first to second years of implementation. The decline occurred in part because the small, rural community could not find a coordinator with the required level of expertise in evaluation to manage the program. The coalition decided to discontinue the intervention given the community's limited capacity to fully implement it [63].

There were both successes and challenges in achieving program reach in the CTC communities. Reach was not difficult for the school-based programs since they were all universal interventions and student participation was mandatory. The number of students participating in school-based EBIs increased from 1,432 to 5,705 over the four years in which participation was tracked, with the last figure representing 57% of all middle school students in the 12 CTC communities.

It was more difficult for the after-school and family-based EBIs to achieve adequate reach. Across all CTC communities delivering these programs, after-school programs served approximately 500 students each year, while about 400 to 600 families participated in parent training programs each year. These figures represent an annual exposure rate of 4.5 to 6.1% of the middle school population for after-school programs and 3.8 to 6.6% of families of middle school students for the parent training programs [64]. Participation in these voluntary programs was lower than hoped for and much more difficult to ensure than anticipated. In fact, reaching the designated population with EBIs was one of the only CTC benchmarks that the majority of CTC coalitions failed to achieve during the randomized efficacy trial [64].

It was especially difficult to reach parents with parent training programs. Although CTC does not specify a particular percentage of the population to be served with prevention programming, CTC guides coalitions to set high recruitment goals because the greater the reach of services, the greater the likelihood of achieving community-wide improvements in youth behavioral health problems. Most coalitions in the Community Youth Development Study attempted to serve about 20% of families in the targeted age group with parenting programs each year, but they rarely achieved these goals. Coalition members enacted multiple, varied, and repeated marketing strategies, provided multiple incentives for participation, and attempted to remove barriers to participation, but recruitment remained a challenge in the randomized trial.

Given the considerable human and financial resources needed for recruitment, and the inability to achieve recruitment goals, one CTC coalition decided to discontinue its parent training program after two years, and another stopped two of its three family-focused programs. Recruitment challenges also led three communities to discontinue their afterschool programs. Including the PDE program termination, eight programs were discontinued in five different communities during the four years in which EBIs were funded in the Community Youth Development Study. Although these instances represent implementation failure, the overall failure rate was only 6%, as 127 programs were implemented across the 12 CTC communities over the four years. In each case, the decisions to stop a specific program were made locally by CTC coalitions and the implementing organizations in accordance with the CTC principles of local implementation monitoring and oversight. In this study, programs were discontinued only after repeated attempts by coalitions to overcome obstacles associated with program delivery and reach. In all cases, communities chose to reinvest their prevention resources in EBIs they were better equipped to implement, which is consistent with the CTC system [64].

When CTC has been implemented in other contexts, without the same level of oversight and technical assistance provided in the randomized trial, implementation monitoring and fidelity have been somewhat less successful. For example, coalitions in Pennsylvania were among the first to adopt the CTC system in the United States and most received the more limited amount of training and technical assistance in EBI implementation that existed at that time. Based on interviews with 72 leaders of CTC coalitions in Pennsylvania, 40% reported using self-reported surveys to monitor implementation of EBIs and 28% used observations, while 11% used less rigorous approaches and 21% did not monitor implementation at all [70].

Another evaluation of the Pennsylvania effectiveness trial asked CTC coordinators and EBI implementers to report whether or not they made changes to EBIs and to describe the types of adaptations made. Of the 240 respondents, 44% reported making changes, including altering the dosage, content, and recommended delivery procedures. About half (53%) of these changes were considered to be problematic mis-adaptations, as implementers reported changing the core components that were likely to be associated with program effectiveness [26].

In response to these findings, Pennsylvania designed a more intensive and proactive technical assistance system to support coalitions' delivery of EBIs. As described in chapter 9, the state created the Evidence-based Prevention and Intervention Support Center (EPISCenter; see www.episcenterpsu.edu) to assist coalitions across the state to fully implement CTC and implement EBIs with high fidelity [71]. Similar to the technical assistance provided in the efficacy trial, the EPISCenter staff assist CTC coalitions to create detailed implementation plans and form implementation teams prior to the start of EBI delivery, collect and analyze data on implementation practices, and use these data to improve implementation fidelity and reach as needed.

The Sustainability of Coalitions and EBIs

Given the financial and human resources needed to establish diverse and well-functioning coalitions and to adopt and implement EBIs with quality, it is important to sustain both the coalitions and the EBIs they support. Indeed, sustaining the use of EBIs in communities is a major goal of prevention science [72]. Sustainability is often viewed as even more important than the initial adoption of EBIs [73] because it is the long-term use of EBIs that will produce long-term changes in behavioral health problems. This relationship is explicitly referred to in Mary Ann Scheirer and James Dearing's [74] definition of sustainability: "the continued use of program components and activities for the continued achievement of desirable program and population outcomes."

In community-based prevention, coalition sustainability is also necessary to produce long-term changes in community-level outcomes [75, 76]. In the coalition literature, sustainability has been defined as the "extent to which a collaborative continues to be operational, cohesive, and growing" [77]. In community-based participatory research models, sustainability has been conceptualized as "the infrastructure that remains in a community after a research project ends" [73]. This definition refers to the gains in knowledge and skills (i.e., capacity) realized by community residents who partner with scientists in an effort to reduce behavioral health problems.

Although sustainability is an essential element of prevention science, relatively little research has investigated the factors that affect the sustainability of EBIs, and even fewer rigorous studies have examined coalition sustainability [78, 79]. Considering EBIs, a lack of funding is the most frequently identified factor affecting sustainability [80–84]. In a survey of 944 public health practitioners in 34 U.S. states, termination of funds and diversion of funding to another source were the most commonly reported reasons for the discontinuation of EBIs; these factors were cited by 85% and 61% of respondents, respectively [85]. Both the amount of funding and the diversity of funding sources appear to be important for sustainability [82]. In addition, proactive planning, especially the consideration of how the EBI will be integrated into existing services and funding streams, has been related to greater sustainability [83, 86].

Research indicates that the organization that delivers the EBI and characteristics of the EBI(s) delivered also influence EBI sustainability [75, 80, 82, 87]. At the organizational level, strong administrator and staff support for the EBI have been associated with ongoing service delivery, whereas turnover in champions has been linked to the discontinuation of EBIs [6, 75, 80, 82, 84, 85, 88]. EBIs that are selected after a careful planning process, including a fit assessment to determine if the intervention addresses local needs and is consistent with the organization's goals and service delivery mechanisms, are more likely to be sustained [78, 81, 88, 89]. Similarly, monitoring and evaluating EBI implementation have been related to greater sustainability, particularly when these data indicate that EBIs are being well implemented and addressing local needs [6, 81, 82, 84, 90].

Considering factors related to EBI delivery, a lack of participant engagement and/or participation in programs have been associated with the discontinuation of programs [83]. The provision of training and technical assistance by EBI developers and/or purveyors has also been associated with increased sustainability [75]. For example, in a study of EBIs implemented by CTC coalitions in Pennsylvania, having regular communication with program developers and trainers was related to increased longevity of classroom-based, mentoring, and family therapeutic interventions, although it was unrelated to the sustainability of universal family-focused prevention programs [83].

The body of research describing the sustainability of community coalitions is much less developed than that devoted to EBI sustainability, and most knowledge is based on anecdotal evidence and/or speculation. There have been few rigorous, long-term evaluations of the sustainability of coalitions. Descriptive research on coalitions tends to characterize these groups as having a definite life cycle, with coalitions progressing from an organizational phase, typically lasting less than a year, to an operations phase, lasting about two years, and culminating in a sustainability phase [76, 91, 92]. In the first phase, coalitions must build their membership and decide on their organizational structure. In the second phase, they implement their agreed-upon tasks. In the sustainability phase, coalitions continue to engage in preventive actions, but they also have to retain an active and diverse membership and find funding to ensure the sustainability of their group and its activities.

This literature suggests that many of the same characteristics that affect the early stages of coalition formation, described in chapter 4, also affect coalition sustainability. For example, coalitions with clear mission statements, well-defined goals, and formalized roles and procedures tend to have greater longevity [76]. Having mutually agreed-upon objectives and a clear process for achieving them helps reduce mission drift over time and increase members' commitment to achieving their goals. Ensuring a sufficient number, diversity, and commitment of members is also important for coalition sustainability [93]. Because members are volunteers, turnover is likely to occur. Moreover, most coalitions do not expect members to commit to the group for an indefinite period of time, and they typically establish membership terms to reduce burnout and ensure varied participation from the community. Given this reality, coalitions need to develop methods and protocols for ongoing recruitment and training of new members.

At the same time, coalitions want to minimize the premature loss of their members. To retain their membership, coalitions should try to increase the perceived benefits of participation for members, as this factor is related to participation [76, 91, 92]. The more that members perceive benefits like having opportunities to network with other stakeholders, share resources, and learn new skills, the more likely they will be to continue to participate in the group. Conversely, if they think the coalition lacks direction, that their actions are not appreciated, or that they have no role in decision making, members will be more likely to leave [76]. To maximize perceived benefits and minimize costs, leaders must provide periodic training for members, facilitate shared decision making, address members' concerns, manage conflicts, and delegate responsibilities to individual members and/or working groups [94].

Support from the larger community is also important for coalition sustainability. Coalition efforts that are well aligned to the needs, values, and culture of a community are most likely to be sustained, as are those that are perceived as effective in addressing local needs [95]. To this end, coalitions should be sure to publicize their goals and achievements throughout their communities. Generating strong community support for the coalition's activities and successes should also help to generate the financial resources necessary for longevity [76, 86, 95].

Both the diversity of funding streams and the total amount of funds raised have been linked to coalition sustainability [86, 96], which indicates that coalitions need to be creative and active in seeking resources. Building links to other organizations in the community can help increase the number of potential funding sources and minimize competition for scarce resources [76]. Generally, the earlier in their life span that coalitions consider how they will ensure long-term funding for their own maintenance and those of the EBIs they support, the better [96]. It is also useful for coalitions to create a specific plan for sustainability and to designate a workgroup to enact this plan [78, 82, 86].

Although many of the factors identified as important in affecting coalition sustainability are based on anecdotal evidence, a somewhat more rigorous examination of sustainability has been conducted in the PROSPER study. When the 14 PROSPER coalitions were assessed six years after the start of a randomized evaluation of this community-based system, and three years after the study funding for EBIs was discontinued, all 14 coalitions were still operating [96]. At the eight-year follow-up, two coalitions had disbanded after their coordinators had left the community and suitable replacements could not be found.

The PROSPER evaluation identified two factors as important for coalition longevity. First, in many of the communities, the state land-grant university's Cooperative Extension Systems offices created permanent positions for coalition staff which provided both the human and financial resources needed for sustainability [97]. Second, all PROSPER coalitions received technical assistance to help them create high-functioning coalitions and to plan for sustainability. Beginning in their first year of operations, coalitions were encouraged to actively promote their activities and successes in their communities, strengthen their partnerships with other organizations, monitor their teams' functioning, and take actions to improve coalition functioning when needed [56, 96].

How Does the CTC System Promote the Sustainability of Coalitions and EBIs?

Like PROSPER, the CTC system was designed to ensure the sustainability of both coalitions and the EBIs they support. In the first two phases of CTC, when CTC readiness is assessed, key leaders and coalition members are cautioned that community-based prevention is a long-term undertaking. They are advised that it will take 2 to 5 years of CTC implementation before community-level changes in risk and protective factors are demonstrated and 5 to 10 years to realize an impact on behavioral health problems [98]. Coalitions will therefore need to maintain their functionality and support the implementation of EBIs for many years. Phases 1 through 5 are designed to prepare communities for this work by helping them build strong coalitions and providing members with the skills needed to engage in comprehensive, effective community-based prevention planning and implementation.

In Phase 5 (*Implement and Evaluate*), sustainability becomes the explicit focus. The Community Plan Implementation workshop, typically held just prior to the start of Phase 5, includes information on how coalitions can ensure their long-term sustainability. Coalition members are reminded that CTC is a cyclical process, and that the activities they have engaged in during earlier phases will need to be repeated over time. For example, they will need to continue to take action to retain current members and engage new community partners, promote CTC to the larger community, and garner financial resources to support prevention activities.

In Phase 5, coalition members consider their overall functioning and how the activities of each workgroup need to be continued, revised, and/or recharged. As shown in Table 7.2, in Phase 5, the main activity of the Board Maintenance workgroup is to maintain a diverse and well-functioning coalition. Whereas its previous work primarily entailed recruiting new members, in the sustainability phase, the group considers how to engender ongoing support and commitment from current members, as well as recruit and train new members. CTC encourages planned turnover of coalition leaders and members, with suggested terms of two to five years and staggered start and end dates to maintain continuity.

Recruitment efforts should continue to focus on ensuring a diverse and representative membership, including having a mix of professionals and grass-roots members from multiple sectors of the community. The Board Maintenance workgroup must recruit new key leaders and coalition members, particularly those who can help promote the reach, high-quality implementation, and funding of EBIs. They also need to ensure that all new members receive the web-streamed training curriculum so that they fully understand

Table 7.2 CTC Workgroup Goals and Tasks in Phase 5

Workgroup	Goals and Tasks
Board Maintenance	• Recruit and train key leaders and coalition members • Ensure that new members understand the CTC system • Maintain members' commitment and participation • Recognize members' contributions • Encourage use of the Social Development Strategy throughout the community
Risk and Protective Factor Assessment	• Update the comprehensive prevention needs assessment: ensure the biennial administration of the CTC Youth Survey, collect and analyze new data from archival sources and survey participants, and revise priorities as needed • Recommend changes to EBI service delivery as needed
Resource Assessment	• Update the resource assessment: collect information from service providers about the adoption and implementation of EBIs • Collect and analyze data on the delivery of coalition-sponsored EBIs • Recommend changes to EBI service delivery as needed
Public Relations	• Create a comprehensive communications plan to inform the community about CTC • Conduct presentations to local organizations • Publicize positive outcomes
Youth Involvement	• Recruit and train youth • Inform other youth about CTC and EBIs • Celebrate youth participation
Funding/ Sustainability	• Identify potential funding sources for coalition activities and EBIs • Seek funding • Consider how to integrate EBIs into local agencies and systems

the CTC system. As membership changes, the Board Maintenance group will want to find ways to build trust and communication between members, such as ensuring that the Key Leader Board and the CTC coalition meet regularly, that meetings provide opportunities for networking and team building, and that all participants are kept updated on coalition activities between meetings.

As discussed in chapter 2, the Social Development Model [99] provides one of the theoretical frameworks for the CTC system. According to this perspective, individuals who are provided opportunities to contribute to a group, taught skills to complete needed actions, and recognized for their skilled performance will have greater bonding to the group. The Social Development Model is salient during Phase 5 because members who are bonded to the coalition will help ensure the long-term viability of the group and its activities [100]. It is therefore important that the Board Maintenance workgroup and coalition leaders regularly provide opportunities for members to participate in CTC activities, continue to bolster their skills, and promote their members' contributions. For example, during Phase 5, coalition members can help recruit participants to EBIs and assist with implementation monitoring by observing program sessions. They can participate in EBI trainings to learn more about the programs selected by their coalition and be recognized for their efforts at coalition meetings and when EBIs are publicized at community events and in local media.

Another way that CTC coalitions can maintain an active, committed membership is by asking members to enact the Social Development Strategy (see Figure 2.1) in their personal lives and to encourage other adults to do so. The CTC trainings include a workshop that explains the Social Development Strategy and asks coalition members to identify ways that they and other adults could personally help youth become more bonded to the community. Participants consider the actions they can take to provide local youth with meaningful opportunities to participate in prosocial roles in the community, help them learn the skills needed to fulfill these roles, and recognize their achievements [101]. For example, employers could give youth employees responsibilities that would allow them to contribute to the organization's success, or an adult might ask a young neighbor to help with dog sitting or lawn mowing.

The goal is for CTC coalition members to model ways to provide youth with skills, opportunities, and recognition and encourage other adults in their social networks to also do so. The more that the Social Development Strategy is used in the community, the greater the potential to increase the number of protective factors experienced by youth, promote bonding between youth and pro-social individuals and organizations, and increase the likelihood that youth will follow the norms and standards promoted by adults. Moreover, when coalition members lead these efforts, they should also experience greater bonding to their community and enhanced commitment to the CTC system. Because much of the emphasis in Phase 5 is on the EBIs delivered by service providers, having coalition members enact these strategies provides additional meaningful ways for members to contribute to the CTC mission.

CTC has other ways to keep coalition members involved and engaged during Phase 5, as shown in Table 6.2. The Risk and Protective Factor Assessment workgroup, which was responsible for conducting the needs assessment in Phase 3 (*Develop a Profile*), now ensures that the CTC Youth Survey is administered every two years to students in grades 6, 8, 10, and 12. Coalitions use the data from these surveys to track their progress in changing the risk factors, protective factors, and behavioral health problems prioritized for preventive action, as described in their community action plans. Along with the data collected on EBI implementation fidelity and reach, the survey results provide the information necessary for coalitions to evaluate whether or not EBIs are having their intended results and if they need to make changes in service provision. For example, if fewer youth report exposure to prioritized risk factors and more report protective factors in subsequent administrations of the CTC Youth Survey, the results suggest that EBIs are working as intended. If the findings do not indicate adequate progress in changing priorities, then EBIs may need to be altered (e.g., increased in intensity or delivered with greater fidelity), supplemented by additional EBIs, or replaced by different interventions.

In Phase 5, the Risk and Protective Factor Assessment workgroup is responsible for analyzing the new data collected from youth, as well as collecting and evaluating updated information from any archival data sources that had been used to identify needs. The group considers the degree to which the prioritized risk and protective factors and behavioral outcomes have changed in the past two years, the extent to which the coalition's goals (i.e., statements regarding the degree to which risk and protective factors and behaviors should change) are being met, and if any new priority areas are emerging. As before, the group summarizes its findings and communicates results to the full coalition, along with recommendations to retain or revise the current priorities and/or add new priorities.

The Resource Assessment also repeats its work in Phase 5. Because this group is charged with surveying service providers about EBIs targeting prioritized needs, many CTC coalitions assign members of this workgroup to the EBI implementation teams. The workgroup and other members of the EBI teams ensure that implementation data are being collected, reviewed to identify implementation successes and challenges, and used for continuous quality improvement. Implementation findings are summarized in written reports that can be reviewed by the full coalition and are used in conjunction with the results of the CTC Youth Survey to revise the community action plan and make changes to EBIs as needed.

During Phase 5, three other workgroups have important roles: the Public Relations, Youth Involvement, and Funding workgroups. The Public Relations group promotes the CTC mission and achievements in the community. Members develop and implement a comprehensive communication plan that identifies ways to inform key leaders, collaborating organizations and stakeholders, and the general public about CTC. They may make presentations to local groups and at community events to educate the community about the local risk and protective factors that are predictive of youth behavioral health problems and the EBIs being used to address prioritized needs. They can also identify ways that community residents can participate in CTC and EBIs, enact the Social Development Strategy, and promote norms that do not support youth substance use, delinquency, or other unhealthy behaviors [100]. The workgroup is encouraged to use social and written media and create substantive products and materials (e.g., signs, brochures, t-shirts, etc.) to publicize CTC.

The goal of the Youth Involvement workgroup is to foster youth input and participation in CTC activities. Young people can be involved in all of the CTC workgroups, but having a specific group dedicated to youth and comprised mostly of young people communicates the message that youth are important and legitimate members of the coalition. Similarly, it avoids token representation and ensures that youth have real opportunities for participation and decision making. Youth participation should also increase youth ownership of CTC and foster their empowerment by providing them with new skills and opportunities to improve their community [102].

The Youth Involvement workgroup can engage in a variety of activities. Youth members may work with the Public Relations workgroup to create messages about CTC that will be appealing to young people and to identify the best communication channels to reach youth in the community. For example, Youth Involvement workgroup members have developed videos about CTC, presented information during community events attended by youth, and promoted CTC and EBIs on the social media forums most frequently used by youth. They have also helped recruit youth to participate in EBIs, either directly through face-to-face contacts or indirectly by helping to create and distribute promotional materials. Some EBIs (e.g., Life Skills Training and the Strengthening Families Program [10–14]) allow adolescents to deliver programming, so youth in communities with these EBIs can attend trainings and serve as program implementers. As a last example, youth can assist the Board Maintenance workgroup to plan social events or activities (e.g., "icebreakers") that can be conducted during coalition meetings to facilitate positive social interactions between members. To retain youth members, it is important that CTC coalitions recognize the contributions of youth participants at their meetings and in the larger community.

The main tasks of the Funding (or Sustainability) workgroup are to identify and help generate resources to sustain the CTC coalition and its EBIs. The Community Plan Implementation Training workshop reviews fund-raising strategies to help guide this group's work. They are encouraged to document all of the initial and ongoing financial costs required for coalition maintenance and EBI implementation. They should also identify all resources that have been or could be drawn upon to conduct these activities, particularly stable and flexible funding streams that are aligned with the goals of the coalition and EBIs.

Potential funding sources can include grants from local, state, or federal agencies (see chapter 10), and/or donations from philanthropic foundations whose missions include the prevention of youth behavioral health problems. For example, in the United States, the Drug Free Communities Support Program and the Strategic Prevention Framework State Incentive Grants provide funds for coalitions focused on preventing substance use. In addition, the Centers for Disease Control has provided funding to coalitions to reduce violence via the Centers for Excellence grants. As another example, Massachusetts created a Prevention and Wellness Trust Fund in 2012 that provides community-based partnerships with funds to reduce behavioral health problems, including tobacco use and substance use/abuse (www.mass. gov/eohhs/gov/departments/dph/programs/community-health/prevention-and-wellness-fund/). This type of initiative could be replicated in other states to encourage the local adoption and implementation of EBIs to prevent problems and promote healthy behaviors.

Many of these sources provide funding only in the short term, and the optimal method for ensuring financial sustainability is to institutionalize the CTC coalition and EBIs in local organizations and systems. For example, some CTC coalitions have become independent nonprofit organizations, while others have identified existing agencies in the community that are best suited to house the coalition, either those already serving as host agencies or new organizations. The host agency should be a well-respected organization with stable funding, including resources that can be used to pay the coalition coordinator's salary. Perhaps the most stable home for the CTC coalition is the city or town government itself. In the Community Youth Development Study, two coalitions were sponsored by city government, and the coordinator's salary was written in to these cities' budget.

The Funding workgroup should seek stable funding streams for EBIs, as well as the coalition. To do so, they may work with the Public Relations workgroup to present information about an EBI to a local organization with the goal of persuading administrators to provide long-term funding for its implementation. The best strategy is to highlight the benefits of the EBI and demonstrate how its content and impact are aligned with the goals of the organization. For example, for school-based programs, the Funding workgroup could attend a school board meeting and demonstrate how one of the school-based EBIs could be implemented to prevent youth behavioral health problems and meet educational standards [103].

As these examples illustrate, much work occurs during Phase 5 of CTC. For optimal performance, all the workgroups must be aware of each other's activities and coordinate their efforts. Communication should be fostered by regular workgroup and coalition meetings, including a longer meeting every year or two to revise the community action plan. Regular meetings of the key leader board also need to occur.

How well have CTC coalitions fared during Phase 5? Most of our knowledge of CTC sustainability comes from the Community Youth Development Study and the quasi-experimental effectiveness trial conducted in Pennsylvania, as these efforts have tracked CTC coalitions over the longest time period. In the efficacy trial, implementation of all of the phases of the CTC system was assessed in CTC communities using an online survey rating the completion of the CTC milestones and benchmarks, which are the critical goals to be achieved and actions that must occur during the five phases of CTC[2] [64]. Both the coalition coordinators and the research staff who provided coalitions with technical assistance rated the extent to which each coalition completed each benchmark at four time points during Years 2 through 5 of the study. When ratings were averaged across the two groups, the results indicated a very high level of implementation of the CTC system in the early and later years of the coalitions' life spans. Approximately 90% of the benchmarks were rated as completed across all communities at each time point, with a small increase from Year 1.5 (93%) to Year 3 (96%), followed by small decreases at Year 4 (89%) and Year 5 (87%) [64].

Although the findings demonstrated that CTC coalitions could ensure successful sustainability of CTC activities and coalitions, the data also indicated that some benchmarks were difficult to achieve in Phase 5. In addition to the previously discussed problem of the limited reach of family-focused programs, the other benchmarks that were less frequently completed were repeating the CTC training workshops to orient new key leaders and coalition members, creating a specific plan for youth involvement, distributing the coalition's action plan to the community, and ensuring adoption of the Social Development Strategy by all members of the community.

Interactions between research staff and coalition coordinators revealed that training of new members was typically conducted informally, as they were recruited, rather than using formal meetings or training workshops. Feedback from coalition coordinators indicated that it was difficult to ensure attendance at training workshops that lasted one to two days. Moreover, because workshops in the randomized trial were provided by CTC trainers, it was somewhat burdensome to arrange trainings and only cost effective if a large group could attend. As described in chapter 3, the CTC training system was changed based on this feedback. Training is now facilitated locally by CTC coordinators using a web-streamed system (CTC PLUS), which allows the content to be divided into shorter modules and accessed at any time without the need for a visit from a CTC trainer.

Regarding youth participation, although youth participated in CTC coalitions, few groups had fully developed plans for how to involve youth and some did not have active Youth Involvement workgroups. Although CTC provides coalitions with specific guidelines on how to plan for and implement EBIs, methods for actively engaging youth are not as fully delineated. It is largely up to the coalitions to decide how to integrate youth into their organizations, and some struggled to recruit youth and determine how to provide meaningful opportunities for their participation.

The lack of full implementation of the Social Development Strategy may also be related to its flexible method of delivery. Unlike most of the EBIs, which have designated staff and structured protocols, community members decide if and how to increase their interactions with youth, and adults may be too busy with other activities to make this a priority. Because the Social Development Strategy is an integral part of the CTC system, the CTC developers have since revised their guidance to communities to ensure broader use of its principles. Additional materials and coaching are now provided to coalition members through the Social Development Strategy training workshop to increase their capacity to promote and model its use throughout the community. Malmo, Sweden, provides an example of how this part of the CTC system has become more concretized. CTC coalitions in Malmo are particularly interested in promoting widespread use of the Social Development Strategy as a means of fostering youth attachment to their neighborhoods because the city has seen a large influx of immigrants from other countries. CTC coalitions write detailed plans for how they will encourage use of the Strategy in their communities, and technical assistance providers (i.e., CTC coaches) follow up to ensure that these plans are followed.

Despite challenges implementing certain CTC benchmarks, CTC communities participating in the Community Youth Development Study were generally successful in sustaining their coalitions and selected EBIs. All 12 CTC coalitions formed in the first year of the study remained active during the five-year implementation phase in which training, technical assistance, and financial resources were provided [64]. In 2009, about seven years after initiation of CTC and one and a half years into the sustainability phase, 11 of the 12 CTC coalitions continued to function. One community was unable to provide funding for the CTC coordinator's salary, and that CTC coalition disbanded [69].

Most of the EBIs selected by the 12 CTC communities were sustained during the implementation phase of the study. In addition, most coalitions added new EBIs as they became more familiar with the CTC process, engaged new partners, and evaluated their success in targeting prioritized risk and protective factors. The average number of study-funded EBIs per community increased from two to three during the implementation phase [64].

When the number of EBIs was assessed in both CTC and control communities using reports from service providers, 78% of the EBIs delivered in CTC communities in 2007 (after three years of EBI implementation) were sustained in 2010 (one year into the sustainability phase of the study), compared to 43% of EBIs implemented in control communities, a statistically significant difference. Information from teachers also showed greater sustainability of school-based EBIs in CTC communities, with 48% of these EBIs sustained from 2007 to 2010, compared to 18% of school-based EBIs in the control communities; however, this difference was not statistically significant [104].

The effectiveness study conducted in Pennsylvania provides some of the only long-term information on coalition and EBI sustainability available in prevention science. This project involves a larger number of coalitions followed for a longer period of time than in most other studies. The findings indicated that 81 of the 110 coalitions (74%) that initiated CTC from 1995 to 2000 and received state funding for four years were still operating in 2006 [86]. About 11% of coalitions failed in the first year after their funding ended, and 3 to 5% disbanded each year thereafter. Predictors of increased sustainability included the amount of funding generated by coalitions, having a sustainability plan that stipulated actions for generating resources and implementing EBIs in the long term, and greater adherence to the CTC benchmarks and milestones [86]. These results support the findings reviewed earlier that factors such as funding, planning for sustainability, having formalized coalition processes and procedures, and aligning prevention efforts with community needs and values increase coalition longevity. The Pennsylvania evaluation also indicted that co-alition functioning, including the degree to which groups had clear objectives, strong leaders, stable membership, regular staff member communication, and strong cohesion, was associated with coalition sustainability [86].

Coalitions in Pennsylvania were also effective in sustaining EBIs, even after the state funding to support their delivery had ended. According to coordinators of 62 coalitions surveyed in 2007, 91% were delivering EBIs, with an average of three programs per site [86]. In a separate study involving reports from service providers whose agencies received funding to implement 77 EBIs in CTC communities, 69% of the EBIs were sustained past their in-itial two years of funding [83]. Predictors of sustainability included the level of CTC coalition functioning, planning for EBI sustainability, promoting the programs in the community, and having skilled implementers. These findings indicate that CTC coalitions can successfully sustain themselves and their selected EBIs.

Conclusion

A few decades ago, the idea that community members should work together to prevent youth behavioral health problems was appealing, but the ability of coalitions to achieve change was based almost entirely on speculation and rarely on scientific evidence. Likewise, few EBIs had been developed and tested, and there was almost no information on how to persuade communi-ties to adopt these interventions, reach consensus on which EBIs to imple-ment, deliver EBIs with quality and reach, and sustain them over time. The last decade has seen progress in all of these areas, but challenges remain in achieving effective community-based prevention and few methods for doing so have been rigorously evaluated.

CTC is one of few community-based systems created, tested, and shown to be effective in building local capacity for prevention. As we have described, CTC draws on emerging scientific evidence about "what works" to provide communities with step-by-step instructions, training, and tech-nical assistance to engage in prevention activities. Success requires sus-tained effort, and different communities face different challenges and need to enact different prevention strategies given their unique needs, resources, and context. Yet, as shown in pilot studies, a randomized efficacy trial, and effectiveness trials conducted in the United States and other countries, communities that adopt the CTC system can successfully build strong coalitions, adopt and implement EBIs, and achieve long-term sustainability of their prevention efforts. Of course, the ultimate test of a community-based prevention system is whether or not it produces community-wide reductions in behavioral health problems. The next two chapters describe the degree to which CTC has been demonstrated as effective in achieving these results.

SECTION THREE

Evaluating CTC

8

Findings From the Community Youth Development Study

THE ULTIMATE GOAL of community-based prevention is to reduce youth behavioral health problems. However, it is challenging to evaluate whether or not community-based systems produce community-wide changes in their targeted outcomes, because these interventions are comprehensive in scope, involve the recruitment and activation of many stakeholders, seek to produce change at multiple levels, and often allow for variation in prevention activities across communities. In addition, to determine effects of community-based prevention initiatives, observed changes over time need to be considered in the context of national and regional trends in behavioral health outcomes and compared with outcomes in similar communities without such initiatives. Given their complexity, relatively few community-based approaches have been developed, tested, and demonstrated to affect targeted behavioral health outcomes. CTC is a notable exception, as its impact has been evaluated in a randomized controlled trial. In this chapter, we describe in detail the results of this efficacy trial, the Community Youth Development Study,[1] which represents the most rigorous test of the CTC system to date and one of the most rigorous evaluations to be conducted of a community-based preventive intervention.

The Community Youth Development Study took place in 24 communities in seven U.S. states. The goal was to evaluate the effectiveness of the CTC system and the logic model shown in Figure 1.1. According to its logic model, CTC is expected to prevent youth behavioral health outcomes by activating broad-based and well-functioning community coalitions to facilitate positive interactions between community residents and between adults and youth, as well as increase the use of EBIs by local organizations. The logic model posits that when community members adopt and support CTC's scientific, data-driven approach to prevention, collaborate more often in prevention activities, promote norms favorable to positive youth behaviors, and employ the Social Development Strategy with youth, the community environment will be more supportive of healthy youth development. Likewise, when service providers increase their delivery and high-quality implementation of EBIs that target community needs, communities are more likely to experience changes in risk and protective factors and reduction in behavioral health problems among youth. In this chapter, we describe in detail the degree to which use of the CTC system led to reductions in behavioral health outcomes among young people in CTC communities compared to control communities. But first, we review the research design of the Community Youth Development Study and summarize changes in the community-level processes shown in the middle section of the CTC logic model.

Research Design of the Community Youth Development Study

The Community Youth Development Study involved a subset of the communities that participated in the preceding Diffusion Project (see chapter 3) conducted in 1997–2002. To recruit communities for the Diffusion Project, administrators from the primary state drug- and alcohol-prevention agencies in the seven states of Colorado, Illinois, Kansas, Maine, Oregon, Utah, and Washington identified 20 small- and medium-sized incorporated towns they thought were using an science-based approach to prevent youth behavioral health problems. These towns were then matched within state on population size, racial/ethnic diversity, economic indicators, and crime rates to 21 comparison communities (one town was matched with two comparison sites) thought to be lacking a scientific approach to prevention [1, 2].

Data collected in 1998–99 from key leaders in the 41 Diffusion communities indicated that there were 13 pairs of communities (26 in total), located across all seven states, in which neither community in the pair had adopted a science-based approach to prevention [1]. That is, key leaders did not report that their communities were routinely collecting local data to conduct needs assessments, adopting EBIs to address these needs, or monitoring the implementation of EBIs. Given that these activities are central components of the CTC system, it did not appear that any of the 26 communities were implementing CTC, making it feasible to conduct a randomized evaluation in these communities to test the effectiveness of CTC.

The 13 pairs (26 communities) were approached to participate in the Community Youth Development Study. Community leaders were informed that the research project would take five years, involved random assignment to implementation (i.e., CTC) and control conditions, and required collection of data from key leaders and service providers and administration of the CTC Youth Survey every two years with the community's 6th-, 8th-, 10th-, and 12th-grade public school students [3]. To participate in the study, each community's school superintendent, primary law enforcement administrator (i.e., the county sheriff or city police chief), and mayor or city manager were required to sign letters agreeing to these conditions.

Twelve pairs, or 24 of the 26 eligible communities (92%), agreed to participate in the study [2]. This high participation rate is important for several reasons. As stated in chapter 3, it is not easy to convince community members to agree to participate in research studies of any type, especially those lasting multiple years and requiring randomization to intervention and control conditions [e.g., 4]. It can be especially difficult to recruit communities to evaluation studies, given the scope and duration of these types of initiatives and the need to obtain consent from multiple key leaders. Yet, the ability to detect significant intervention effects in randomized controlled trials is related to the number of units assigned to intervention and control conditions, and larger sample sizes generally have greater statistical power to detect significant effects [5]. In community-based evaluations, the unit of analysis is the community, and the number of communities involved in the study must be adequate to detect effects [6, 7]. Prior to the start of the Community Youth Development Study, the research team determined that a minimum of 12 pairs of communities was required to detect significant effects on youth behavioral health problems [8].

The successful recruitment of communities in the Community Youth Development Study may be due, in part, to the fact that the CTC developers and their research team had been working with these communities for five years during the Diffusion Project and had built trust with key leaders, service providers, and school officials. The researchers shared with community members the results of the CTC Youth Surveys conducted in 1998 and 2000, which helped demonstrate their commitment to a collaborative research approach. Having community-specific information on youth behavioral problems, risk factors, and protective factors provided local leaders with evidence that their communities would likely benefit from a prevention effort such as CTC if they were randomized into the intervention condition. State administrators also helped with recruitment, as they had personal relationships with some of the local key leaders and could help to alleviate concerns and identify the benefits of the study.

Following agreement from key leaders, the 12 community pairs were randomly assigned in 2002 using a coin toss to implement CTC or to serve as control communities conducting prevention services as usual. All 24 communities were incorporated towns that were geographically distinct, and they had separate governmental, educational, and law enforcement agencies, which helped to reduce the potential for contamination and facilitated service provision. Based on data from the 2000 U.S. Census, study communities had an average population of 14,646 residents (with a range of 1,578 to 40,787 residents per community), 89% of the population was white (range: 64 to 98% per community), 3% was African American (range: 0 to 21%), and 10% was of Hispanic origin (range: 1 to 65%). In addition, 12% of the total population was aged 10 to 17 years (range: 9 to 16%), and 37% of students (range: 21 to 66%) were eligible for free or reduced-price school lunch according to the National Center for Educational Statistics. None of these characteristics differed significantly between CTC and control communities at the start of the study [3, 9].

The research design, timeline, and instruments used to collect data on community processes and youth outcomes are shown in Figure 8.1. Communities assigned to implement CTC spent the first year of the study (2003) implementing the first four phases of the CTC system. They received CTC trainings at no financial cost and $50,000 to employ a full-time coalition coordinator. In Years 2 through 5, the implementation phase of the study, CTC communities received funding for the coordinator's salary and up to $75,000 annually to implement EBIs. Throughout the implementation phase, CTC trainers and research staff at the University of Washington provided individualized technical assistance to each of the 12 CTC sites at no cost. This assistance included regular phone calls (1 to 4 times per month) and one to two site visits each year to meet with coalition coordinators and observe coalition meetings and prevention program activities. Each month, all 12 coalition coordinators participated in a one-hour group conference call that focused on CTC implementation, and coordinators attended a three-day workshop each year to discuss CTC implementation and goals for the upcoming year. The sustainability phase of the project, in which intervention communities received minimal technical assistance and no funding for CTC activities, began in 2009 (Year 6).

Throughout the study, control communities received no training or technical assistance in the CTC system and no monetary assistance except small financial incentives to participate in data collection activities. These communities conducted prevention services as usual. Data were collected from

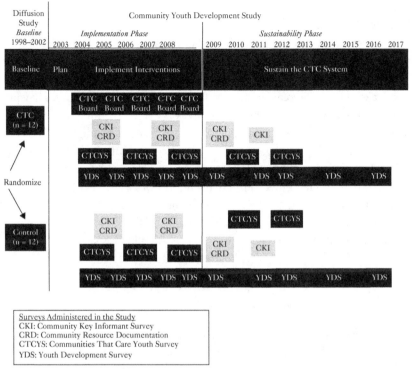

FIGURE 8.1 Research Design, Timeline, and Surveys Administered in the Community Youth Development Study

community leaders, service providers, and leaders of prevention-oriented coalitions that existed in these areas to assess the degree to which the control communities may have been implementing the CTC system since it was publically available. These surveys provided little evidence of contamination; that is, control communities did not appear to have adopted the CTC system during the Community Youth Development Study.

The research design of the Community Youth Development Study depicted in Figure 8.1 reflects optimal methods of research evaluation and takes into account CTC's theoretical frameworks and logic model. A randomized controlled trial was utilized because this type of research design is considered the best methodology for ensuring valid outcome comparisons, due to experimental internal validity, and for ruling out alternative explanations of observed intervention effects [10, 11]. Effects on youth behavioral health outcomes were assessed primarily using self-report information (collected via the Youth Development Survey shown in Figure 8.1) from a longitudinal panel of young people in intervention and control communities because longitudinal data are preferred for examining causal effects [12].[2]

Because life-course developmental theories suggest that the onset of most behavioral health problems occurs in early adolescence [13, 14], the longitudinal panel was constituted when youth were in grade 5. Since CTC posits that it will take at least five years to demonstrate community-level changes in youth behavioral health outcomes [15], the study was originally intended to last five years and to follow the longitudinal panel from grades 5 through 9. CTC communities were asked to target prevention services to youth in these age groups as much as possible. Again, based on life-course theory, it was hypothesized that, if widely implemented, EBIs delivered during the transition from early to late adolescence would produce measurable community-wide effects on behavioral outcomes [3]. The sustainability phase of the trial evaluated whether or not the initial effects were maintained over time [16].

The Impact of CTC on Community-Level Processes

The research design of the Community Youth Development Study was carefully constructed to ensure measurement and evaluation of the community attitudes and actions posited to lead to positive youth behaviors and to prevent behavioral health problems. As shown in Figure 8.1, multiple survey instruments were administered throughout the study and assessed changes using multiple informants, which is another hallmark of high-quality evaluation research. In chapter 3, we discussed the development of most of these measurement instruments, which include the CTC Board Interview, Community Key Informant Survey (CKI), and the Community Resource Documentation (CRD). Data collected from these instruments indicated that CTC communities experienced desired changes in all the community prevention-related attitudes, norms, and service provider practices depicted in the CTC logic model, in one or both periods of the efficacy trial (i.e., in the implementation and/or sustainability phases), as summarized in the following section and in Table 8.1.[3]

The CTC Board Interview assessed the functioning of coalitions operating in the CTC communities and was conducted annually in the implementation phase in the CTC communities only. Research staff conducted 40-minute telephone interviews with 20 randomly selected members of each CTC coalition in the first year of the study (2004) and with 10 members in Years 2 through 5. Each coalition's response rate was at least 90% at each year [17, 18].

Table 8.1 Desired Changes in Community-Level Processes Demonstrated in the Community Youth Development Study

Construct	Instrument Used to Assess Changes	Respondents Reporting on Changes	Desired Changes in Community Processes (citation)
Coalition Functioning	Community Board Interview (CBI)	CTC coalition members (CTC sites only)	• 2004: CTC coalition members had favorable attitudes about CTC; gained new skills by participating in the coalition; and perceived coalitions to be effective [18] • 2004–2009: CTC coalition members reported high coalition cohesion and efficiency, clear coalition goals, and opportunities for members' participation [17]
	Community Resource Documentation (CRD) Coalition Surveys	Prevention coalition leaders in CTC and control sites	• 2007, 2009: Greater use of a science-based approach to prevention by coalitions in CTC vs. control sites [19, 20]
Adoption of Science-Based Prevention	Community Key Informant Interview (CKI)	Positional and prevention leaders in CTC and control sites	• 2005, 2007, 2009, and 2011: Greater adoption of a science-based prevention framework in CTC vs. control sites [21, 23, 24, 25]
Community Collaboration for Prevention			• 2001 to 2004: Greater increase in prevention collaboration and sector collaboration in CTC vs. control sites [23]

(continued)

Table 8.1 Continued

Construct	Instrument Used to Assess Changes	Respondents Reporting on Changes	Desired Changes in Community Processes (citation)
Community Support for Prevention			• 2007, 2009: Higher desired prevention funding in CTC vs. control sites [24–25]
Community Norms Against Adolescent Substance Use			• 2007: Stronger norms against adolescent substance use in CTC communities with greater poverty vs. control sites with greater poverty [24]
			• 2001 to 2009: Greater increase in norms in CTV vs. control communities [25])
Use of the Social Development Strategy			• 2007: Greater use of the Social Development Strategy in CTC communities with more non-White youth vs. control communities with more non-white youth [24]
Appropriate Selection and Implementation of Evidence-Based Interventions (EBIs)	Community Resource Documentation (CRD) Agency Interviews	Prevention service agency administrators and implementers/ teachers in CTC and control sites	• 2007: Greater number of EBIs in CTC vs. control sites [29]
			• 2007: Greater reach of EBIs in CTC vs. control sites in 2007 [29]
			• 2011: Greater sustainability of EBIs in CTC vs. control sites [28]

According to information from the CTC Board Interviews, coalition members in all 12 CTC communities reported high levels of CTC coalition functioning, including having clear goals and working efficiently to achieve them and partnering with other organizations in the community [17, 18].

Information on prevention coalitions operating in both CTC and control communities was collected as part of the Community Resource Documentation. Coalitions included the CTC coalitions that were established in the intervention sites, as well as prevention-focused coalitions that had not adopted the CTC system in both CTC and control communities. Phone interviews were conducted with coalition leaders to ask about goals and actions typically associated with Phases 2 through 5 of CTC; for example, whether or not coalition members had been trained in methods for conducting needs assessments and had conducted a resource assessment, developed a comprehensive prevention action plan, and sponsored the implementation of EBIs [19]. Information from these surveys indicated that, in 2007, coalitions in CTC communities were more likely than those in control communities to engage in science-based prevention activities [19]. For example, CTC coalitions were more likely than prevention coalitions in control communities to report that their members had been trained in methods for conducting needs assessments, conducted a resource assessment, and developed a comprehensive prevention action plan. They were also significantly more likely to have implemented at least two EBIs and to monitor the impact of these programs on participants. Similar intervention effects were demonstrated in 2009 during the sustainability phase of the randomized trial [20].

The Community Key Informant (CKI) survey was administered in intervention and control communities in 2001 (at baseline, as part of the Diffusion Study) and in 2004, 2007, 2009, and 2011, to examine effects of the CTC system on multiple community-level processes. To capture the views of a diverse and representative sample of the community, the Community Key Informant survey involved semi-structured, 60-minute phone interviews with the lead administrators of 10 to 11 service sectors (e.g., the mayor or city manager, school superintendent, police chief or sheriff, juvenile court judge, directors of public health and recreation services, and business and faith leaders). In addition, each positional leader was asked to nominate two individuals considered to be most knowledgeable about community-based prevention services. The five prevention leaders nominated most often were interviewed, resulting in 15 key leader interviews per community. Response rates for these interviews were high, with about 90% of eligible leaders interviewed at each time point (from 2004 to 2011) in both the CTC and control communities [21].

The first community-level construct assessed using the Community Key Informant survey was the *stages of adoption of a science-based approach to prevention*. This construct was developed to operationalize the Diffusion of Innovations theory [22] and to measure the degree to which communities were engaging in actions consistent with the five phases of CTC. It was based on 21 open- and closed-ended responses from key leaders to items asking about their community's understanding of risk and protective factors, collection of data to conduct needs assessments, implementation of EBIs to address local needs, and monitoring of EBIs and levels of risk and protection over time. Responses from all leaders in each community were coded, combined, and categorized into six discrete stages to indicate the community's stage of adoption as follows: Stage 0 —little or no awareness of prevention science; Stage 1—basic awareness of prevention science concepts (e.g., risk and protective factors); Stage 2—consideration of risk and protective factors when planning prevention services; Stage 3—collection of data on risk and protective factor to guide prevention planning; Stage 4—use of EBIs to target prioritized risk and protective factors; Stage 5—monitoring of EBIs and continued collection of data on risk and protective factors to assess the impact of EBIs [1, 23].

Consistent and positive results showing a greater level of adoption of a science-based approach to prevention in CTC compared to control communities were found at multiple time points during the randomized trial. Intervention and control communities did not differ in levels of adoption in 2001, at the start of the study [23]. However, key leaders in CTC communities reported significantly greater levels of adoption compared to control communities during both the implementation phase of the study, when measured in 2004 and 2007 [23, 24], and in the sustainability phase, when measured in 2009 and 2011 [21, 25]. For example, in both 2004 and 2007, about 50% of key leaders in CTC communities reported being at Stage 4 or 5, the highest stages of adoption of a science-based approach to prevention representing the use and monitoring of EBIs, compared to about 26% of those in control communities [24].

The Community Key Informant Survey also provided data on *prevention collaboration*. This construct was developed based on leaders' ratings of agreement with nine statements indicating aspects of successful community collaboration, such as "organizations in the community share information with each other about prevention issues" and "organizations participate in joint planning and decision making about prevention issues." A second indicator of community collaboration, *sector collaboration*, reflected the degree to which leaders stated that the agency they worked for collaborated with seven other types of service providers and organizations (civic, business, school, law enforcement, coalitions, human services, and religious) [26].[4] According to reports from key leaders, CTC communities experienced small increases in prevention collaboration and sector collaboration from 2001 to 2004, while control communities experienced small decreases in collaboration; group differences in changes in both constructs were statistically significant [23]. However, significant intervention effects on each measure of collaboration were not demonstrated in later years [24, 25].

The Community Key Informant survey also assessed *community support for prevention* in both intervention and control communities. Support was represented by two constructs. First, a measure of *general support for prevention* was based on seven items in which leaders rated their agreement that community members and key leaders: are committed to reducing drug abuse and promoting positive youth development, are knowledgeable about local drug-abuse-prevention efforts, and believe that drug-abuse-prevention efforts are cost effective [24, 25]. These seven items were combined to operationalize general support for prevention. Key leaders were also asked to report the percentage of funding (out of 100%) they would hypothetically allocate to prevention, treatment, and law enforcement to reduce substance abuse. The *percentage of funds allocated to prevention* was the second measure of community support [24, 25]. No intervention effects were found from 2004 to 2011 when assessing general support for prevention. However, leaders in CTC communities were more likely than those in control communities to support the use of funds to prevent substance use in 2007 [24] and 2011 [25].

To measure perceptions of *community norms against adolescent drug use*, key leaders rated how wrong most adults in their communities think it is for adolescents to drink, smoke, and use marijuana (three items) and how much they agreed that adults in their communities think that using alcohol, tobacco, and marijuana is a normal part of growing up (three items) [24, 27]. These six items were combined in a latent factor. Based on key leaders reports, there was a greater increase in community norms discouraging youth substance use from 2001 to 2009 in intervention compared to control communities [25].

Beginning in 2007, key leaders rated *use of the Social Development Strategy*. They were asked how much they agreed that key leaders in the community work to: (1) increase opportunities for youth involvement in pro-social activities; (2) help adolescents learn new skills; (3) recognize and compliment youths for positive effort, improvement, and accomplishments; (4) promote bonding between youths and pro-social members of the community; and (5) ensure clear standards for youth behavior. The five items were combined in a latent variable [24, 25]. Key leaders in CTC versus control communities indicated significantly more use of the Social Development Strategy in 2007 [24], but only when comparing communities with greater numbers of minority youth. No intervention effects in use of the Social Development Strategy were identified in 2009 [25].

The Community Resource Documentation (CRD) was administered in 2001 (as part of the Diffusion Study) and in 2005, 2007, and 2009 in CTC and control communities to evaluate whether or not use of the CTC system increased the adoption, high-quality implementation, and reach of EBIs. The Community Resource Documentation involved a three-stage snowball sampling approach to obtain information from prevention-service agency administrators and providers. The first stage was conducted during the Community Key Informant survey, when respondents were asked to identify all agencies and coalitions providing prevention programming in the community. In the second stage, referred administrators of these groups were interviewed by phone about their implementation of prevention services. These individuals were asked to identify the main staff persons who delivered services, and these individuals were surveyed in the third stage. In addition, teachers reported on the delivery of school-based programs via web-based surveys beginning in 2005. Participation in all components of the Community Resource Documentation was high. Over 80% of eligible agency leaders and service providers and over 70% of all eligible teachers in both intervention and control communities completed surveys at each time point [28, 29].

To assess the adoption and reach of EBIs, respondents were presented with a list of programs identified as effective in the CTC *Prevention Strategies Guide.*[5] Respondents were asked to report if each EBI was provided in the past year to at least one community resident. Open-ended follow-up questions asked about the number of participants served by the program. To assess the quality of implementation, respondents reported the extent to which they delivered the core components of each program, monitored program delivery, and assessed changes in participant attitudes or behaviors. Based on data from the Community Resource Documentation, CTC and control communities did not differ in the number or reach of EBIs at the start of the study in 2001, but by 2007, service providers in CTC sites reported delivering a greater number of EBIs to a greater number of participants compared to those in control communities [29]. Similar findings were reported in 2011 [28], indicating sustainability in the effects on EBI adoption and participation between CTC and control communities.

The Impact of CTC on Youth Behavioral Health Problems
Findings From the Longitudinal Panel of Youth

We now describe the impact of CTC on youth exposure to risk and protective factors and involvement in behavioral health problems. These findings draw on data from young people participating in a longitudinal panel who completed the Youth Development Survey (YDS) on a mostly annual basis beginning in spring 2004 when they were in grade 5 (see Figure 8.1). This survey was based on the CTC Youth Survey and was designed to be completed in about 50 minutes [9]. The survey asked youth to report on risk and protective factors across the community, school, family, peer, and individual domains. Each factor comprised one to six items. Youth also reported their lifetime and past-month use of alcohol, marijuana, cigarette, and other drugs; binge drinking in the past two weeks (i.e., having five or more drinks in a row); and perpetration of delinquent and violent acts in the past year.

To capture developmental differences in involvement in crime (i.e., that the perpetration of minor offenses precede more serious offenses) items asking about past-year perpetration of delinquency were added to the Youth Development Survey as the panel aged. Starting in grade 5, youth reported on four delinquent acts (stealing, property damage, shoplifting, and attacking someone with the intent to cause physical harm). Five questions asking about serious delinquency (carrying a gun to school, beating someone up, stealing a vehicle, selling drugs, and being arrested) were added to the survey in later years as developmentally appropriate. A subset of these acts represents violent offenses. One violent act (attacking someone with the intent to cause harm) was included in the grade 5 survey, and two additional acts (carrying a gun to school and beating someone up) were included beginning in grade 6. The effects of CTC on other behavioral health problems that typically have their onset in early adulthood, such as alcohol and drug abuse/dependence, depression, suicidality, and risky sexual behaviors, as well as rates of high school graduation, were added to the YDS at the age 19 survey[6] [16].

Recruitment for the longitudinal panel began in fall, 2003. Since participants were to be surveyed in school, research staff sent information and made phone calls and visits to school district superintendents and principals in all sites. Despite the signed letters supporting the project signed by all school superintendents at the start of the study, one of the 29 eligible school districts did not agree to the administration of the Youth Development Survey in schools, and youth in this community had to complete surveys in community settings rather than in school. In the other participating schools, classroom teachers distributed consent forms to students, who were instructed to deliver them to parents.

To ensure confidentiality, no names or identifying information were included on surveys, but identification numbers were printed on the survey booklets so that participants could be tracked over time. In grade 5, trained interviewers read the survey questions aloud to youth, and they provided written responses in booklets. Beginning in grade 6 and continuing while respondents were still in school (i.e., through grade 12), youth read and completed surveys on their own [9]. After they left or graduated from high school, most completed surveys online, but a small percentage completed paper questionnaires [16].

In Year 1, parents of 63% of eligible students ($n = 3,682$) agreed to their children's participation in the longitudinal panel and surveys. This percentage was lower than desired, so research staff conducted a second recruitment and consent effort in Year 2. This effort resulted in consents from parents of another 1,146 students. However, 11% ($n = 404$) of the original panel was not eligible to continue in the study at grade 6 because they had moved out of the school district or targeted grade, were in foster care, or had severe learning disabilities. In total, 3,585 students completed surveys in grade 5, and 4,390 participated in grade 6. The baseline sample consisted of 4,407 students (76% of the eligible population, 76.1% in CTC communities and 76.7% in control communities), who completed a survey in either grade 5 or grade 6. The participants were evenly split by gender (50% male, 50% female); 70% were white, 9% were Native American, 4% were African American, and 20% were of Hispanic origin. The mean number of students per community was 184 (range: 20–454 students per community) [for a more detailed discussion of the recruitment and retention of the longitudinal sample, see 9]. According to youth responses, no significant differences were found at baseline between CTC and control communities in levels of the risk and protective factors or in the behavioral health problems of substance use and delinquency[7] [9].

Youth participants were asked to sign assent forms and complete surveys each year they were administered. Those who left the study communities after grade 6 were still eligible to participate. Participation rates were high across all waves of data collection and in no year was the attrition rate greater than 9% of the sample. Attrition rates did not significantly differ by intervention condition in any year except when respondents were, on average, age 21 (three years after completion of high school for most participants). At this time, 91% of the total active sample remained in the study, 92% in CTC communities and 90% in control communities [30].

Intervention effects on community levels of youth-reported risk and protective factors and behavioral health outcomes are summarized in Table 8.2. Intervention effects on levels of risk factors were first analyzed when students

Table 8.2 Significant Effects of the Communities That Care Prevention System on Youth Substance Use, Delinquency, and Violence, Based on Data From the Longitudinal Panel of 4,407 Youth Surveyed From Grade 5 to Age 21

Study Year	2006	2007	2009	2011	2012	2014
Grade/Age of the Panel	Grade 7	Grade 8	Grade 10	Grade 12	Age 19	Age 21
Citation	[2]	[15, 33]	[31, 34]	[32]	[16]	[30]
Risk Factors	Lower levels of risk factors (ES = .15)	n/a	Lower levels of risk factors (ES = .12) Smaller increases in risk factors from Grades 5 to 10	ns	n/a	n/a
Protective Factors	ns	Higher levels of protective factors	ns	n/a	n/a	n/a

(continued)

Table 8.2 Continued

Study Year	2006	2007	2009	2011	2012	2014
Grade/Age of the Panel	Grade 7	Grade 8	Grade 10	Grade 12	Age 19	Age 21
Citation	[2]	[15, 33]	[31, 34]	[32]	[16]	[30]
Initiation of Substance Use	ns	Lower incidence of: Alcohol use (AOR = 0.68) Cigarette use (AOR = 0.67) Smokeless tobacco (AOR = 0.67)	Lower incidence of: Alcohol use (AOR = 0.62) Cigarette use (AOR = 0.54)	Greater abstinence from: Any substance (ARR = 1.32) Gateway drug use (ARR = 1.31) Alcohol (ARR = 1.31) Cigarettes (ARR = 1.13)	ns	Greater abstinence from Gateway substance use (ARR = 1.49)
Prevalence of Substance Use	n/a	Less past month: Alcohol use (AOR = 0.80) Binge drinking (AOR = 0.71) Smokeless tobacco use (AOR = 0.56)	Less past month Tobacco use (AOR = 0.79)	Greater past month Ecstasy use (ARR = 1.89)	ns	ns

	Initiation of Delinquency and Violence	Prevalence of Delinquency and Violence
	Lower incidence of Delinquency (AOR = 0.79)	n/a
	Lower incidence of Delinquency (AOR = 0.71)	Fewer delinquent acts (AOR = 0.75)
	Lower incidence of Delinquency (AOR = 0.79)	Less past year: Delinquency (AOR = 0.83) Violence (AOR = 0.75)
	Greater abstinence from Delinquency (ARR = 1.18) Lower incidence of Violence (ARR = 0.86)	ns
	Greater abstinence from Delinquency (ARR = 1.16)	ns
	Greater abstinence from Delinquency (ARR = 1.18) Lower incidence of Violence (AOR = 0.89)	ns

Note: effect sizes and adjusted odds ratios (AORs) and adjusted risk ratios (ARRs) indicate changes in CTC compared to control communities; n/a=outcome not assessed; ns = outcome was not statistically significant ($p < .05$)

were in grade 7. As described in chapter 5, CTC coalitions conducted a comprehensive prevention needs assessments during the first year of the study, and each coalition prioritized a unique set of two to five risk factors to be addressed by EBIs. To assess intervention effects on risk factors, the average score on the set of targeted risk factors prioritized in each CTC community was compared to the average score on the same set of risk factors in its matched control community. These analyses controlled for both student- and community-level covariates and used statistical procedures that accounted for the clustering of students within communities.

Controlling for grade 5 levels of risk factors, grade 7 risk factor scores were significantly lower in CTC communities than in control communities, with the difference corresponding to a standardized effect size of 0.15 [2]. In grade 10, mean scores on targeted risk factors were again significantly lower in CTC compared to control communities. In addition, the increase from grade 5 to grade 10 in mean levels of risk factors was smaller for students in CTC versus control communities [31]. At grade 12, no significant differences in targeted risk factors were found between CTC and control conditions, which suggested that the impact of CTC was on risk exposure earlier in adolescence [32].

Most CTC coalitions did not prioritize specific protective factors but, rather, tried to increase the overall level of protection in the community. Therefore, changes in protective factors were assessed using a different procedure from that used to measure changes in risk factors. Specifically, a global test statistic compared mean scores on the 15 protective factors reported by the longitudinal panel on the Youth Development Survey. Controlling for protective factor scores at grade 5, the overall level of protection was significantly higher for grade 8 students in CTC compared to control communities [33]. However, when assessed again at grade 10, students in CTC and control communities in the longitudinal panel did not significantly differ in overall levels of protection [34]. Similar to the risk factor results, these findings suggest that, in this study, the CTC impact was on levels of protection during early adolescence, the developmental period targeted by the EBIs implemented in the CTC communities.

Intervention effects on behavioral health problems examined the incidence of first use of substances and first perpetration of a delinquent/violent act (i.e., initiation), as well as the prevalence of recent substance use, delinquency, and violence. Multi-level regression analyses were used to examine these outcomes, and the statistical models took into account the clustering of students in communities and of the communities in matched pairs (i.e., intervention and control conditions). All analyses included student- and community-level covariates and were performed using an intent-to-treat design, meaning that they examined intervention effects among all panel participants regardless of whether they remained in their CTC and control communities during the study period.

Effects on substance-use incidence were based on students' annual reports of lifetime use of tobacco, smokeless tobacco, alcohol, binge drinking, marijuana, inhalants, and beginning in grade 8, prescription drugs and other drugs (psychedelics, Ecstasy, stimulants, and cocaine). Only students who had not yet initiated substance use prior to the start of the study and CTC adoption were included in these analyses; that is, those who reported any lifetime substance use at grade 5 were not included in such models since they had already initiated substance use. Intervention effects on the prevalence of substance use were assessed using information from all students. Similar to the drug-use outcomes, analyses examining intervention effects on the incidence or initiation of delinquency/violence excluded any youth who reported past-year perpetration of these acts at grade 5. To assess prevalence, analyses considered involvement in any delinquency/violence, as well as the number of different acts (i.e., the variety) committed.

Effects on behavioral health problems were examined beginning in grade 7 (see Table 8.2). Statistically significant intervention effects showing reductions in the initiation of delinquency, but not in substance use, for youth in intervention versus control communities were demonstrated in grade 7. The adjusted odds ratio (AOR) for the effect of CTC on the initiation of delinquency by grade 7 was 0.79, indicating that students in CTC communities had 21% lower odds of initiation compared to those in the control communities [2]. In grade 8, students in CTC communities were significantly less likely to have initiated any substance use compared to those in control communities [15]. When effects on specific substances were analyzed, students in CTC communities were significantly less likely than those in control communities to have begun to use alcohol (AOR = 0.68), cigarettes (AOR = 0.67), and smokeless tobacco (AOR = 0.67). At this time, 25% of youth in CTC communities reported having ever used alcohol, compared to 17% of those in control communities; 12% reported ever smoking cigarettes, compared to 8% in control communities; and 6% reported ever using smokeless tobacco, compared to 4% in control communities. In grade 8, those in the CTC communities were also less likely to have initiated delinquency (AOR = 0.71), with 21% reporting having ever committed a delinquent act, compared to 16% of youth in the control communities [15].

Significant intervention effects in preventing and delaying the initiation of alcohol, cigarettes, and delinquency among youth in CTC compared to control communities were found again in grade 10 [31] and in grade 12 [32], as shown in

Table 8.2. For example, at grade 10, the odds of reporting any lifetime alcohol use were 38% lower in CTC compared to control communities (AOR = 0.62), and the odds of lifetime cigarette use were 46% lower (AOR = 0.54). In grade 12, students in CTC communities were significantly more likely to report abstinence from (i.e., never having used) any substance (ARR = 1.32), any gateway drug use (i.e., tobacco, alcohol, or marijuana; ARR = 1.31), any alcohol use (ARR = 1.31), and any cigarette smoking (ARR = 1.13) [32]. By grade 12, there were also desired intervention effects indicating greater lifetime abstinence of any delinquent behavior (ARR = 1.18) and lower rates of initiation of any violent behavior (ARR = 0.86) for CTC compared to control community youth. By grade 12, 42% of those in the CTC communities reporting never engaging in delinquency, compared to 33% of those in control communities, and 34% of those in the CTC communities reported having ever committed a violent act, compared to 41% of those in the control communities [32].

Desired intervention effects in delaying the initiation of substance use and/or delinquency continued to be evidenced after students left high school. At age 19, those in CTC communities were significantly more likely to report abstaining from delinquent behaviors (ARR = 1.16) [16]. When the longitudinal panel was age 21, desired and statistically significant intervention effects were found for the initiation of gateway drugs (i.e., tobacco, alcohol, and marijuana), delinquency, and violence [30]. For example, 10.1% of those in CTC communities reported never using any gateway drugs, compared to 6.7% of those in control communities, and 33.9% of those in CTC communities reported abstaining from delinquent behaviors compared to 28.8% of those in control communities The adjusted risk ratios (ARRs) for these outcomes were 1.49 and 1.18, respectively (see Table 8.2).

Intervention effects on the prevalence of recent substance use, delinquency, and violence were first assessed when students were in grade 8, given that rates of substance use and delinquency were very low at grades 6 and 7 (as indicated in Table 8.3). When in grade 8, youth in CTC communities reported less substance use of any type compared to those in control communities [15]. When examining specific substances, statistically significant differences favoring the CTC communities were found for the prevalence of past-month alcohol use (AOR = 0.80), binge drinking in the past two weeks (AOR = 0.71), and past-month smokeless tobacco (AOR = 0.56) (see Table 8.2). Prevalence did not significantly differ by condition for other substances. In terms of their delinquent behaviors, 8th-grade students in CTC reported a lower average number of delinquent acts in the past year (0.78 delinquent acts) compared to youth in the control communities (1.13 delinquent acts) [15].

In grade 10, significant intervention effects favoring CTC youth were found for the prevalence of past-month cigarette use (AOR = 0.79), but not for the

Table 8.3 Prevalence of Any Past-Month Substance Use and Any Past-Year Delinquency and Violence, by Intervention Condition, Based on the Longitudinal Panel of 4,407 Participants Surveyed From Grade 5 to Age 21

Study Year	2006		2007		2009		2011		2012		2014	
Grade/Age of the Panel	Grade 5		Grade 8		Grade 10		Grade 12		Age 19		Age 21	
Citation	[9]		[15]		[31]		[32]		[16]		[30][1]	
Outcome	CTC	Control	CTC	Control	CTC	Control	CTC	Control	CTC	Control	CTC	Control
Alcohol	3.0	3.4	16.4	21.4*	28.7	29.5	35.7	36.1	51.2	48.0	74.6	74.5
Cigarettes	0.7	1.0	6.1	8.0	13.4	16.3*	22.7	24.3	28.8	30.7	39.2	41.6
Smokeless Tobacco	1.9	2.7	2.2	4.3*	6.3	7.5	8.8	10.8	14.7	14.8	17.4	20.1
Inhalants	2.5	3.0	4.8	5.0	3.1	2.0	1.5	1.1	0.6	0.7	0.6	0.7
Marijuana	0.4	0.1	4.7	6.0	14.5	15.0	21.9	19.7	25.4	25.0	37.3	37.7
Binge drinking (past 2 weeks)	1.0	1.3	5.7	9.0*	11.0	13.6	17.3	19.7	34.1	34.9	63.8	65.4
Delinquency	n/a	n/a	n/a	n/a	36.1	42.6*	28.7	29.8	25.9	25.6	17.7	19.2
Violence	n/a	n/a	n/a	n/a	13.2	17.7*	10.4	11.6	9.3	9.3	6.9	7.8

Notes: Results indicate the percentage of the sample that reported any substance use, delinquency, or violence.

[1]Substance use outcomes at age 21 are based on reported use in the past year, not the past month as in earlier waves.

*statistically significant ($p < .05$) difference between CTC and control communities.

n/a = outcome not assessed

current prevalence of any other substances. With regard to crime, the odds of reporting any delinquent act in the past year were 17% lower (AOR = 0.83), and the odds of reporting any violent act were 25% lower (AOR = 0.75) among 10th-grade respondents from CTC communities versus control communities [31]. With one exception, intervention effects on the prevalence of recent substance use, delinquency, and violence were not found at grade 12. Counter to the study hypotheses, at grade 12, those in CTC communities were more likely to report any Ecstasy use in the past month (2.6% of respondents) compared to those in control communities (1.4%) [32]. No intervention effects on the prevalence of any behavior were found when the panel was age 19 [16] or 21 [30].

Because intervention effects may differ across different types of participants, responses from the longitudinal panel were investigated to determine if intervention effects shown at grade 8 [35] and grade 10 [36] were moderated by participant baseline risk status and gender. The risk level measured whether or not students had initiated substance use or delinquency prior to grade 5 and had higher levels of the targeted risk factors at baseline. These analyses indicated that the intervention effects favoring CTC communities on the prevalence of substance use and delinquency shown at grade 8 did not differ according to the risk level of students. However, some effects were moderated by gender. Eighth-grade boys in the CTC communities had a significantly lower prevalence of past-month alcohol use and smokeless tobacco use, as well as a lower prevalence of binge drinking, compared to boys in the control communities. Significant intervention effect on these outcomes were not found for girls [35]. Interaction terms that assessed gender differences in the size of these relationships were all marginally significant ($p < .10$) and indicated that all three of the intervention effects were somewhat stronger for boys than girls. In addition, the prevalence of past-month marijuana use was lower for boys in CTC versus control communities at grade 8. Although this difference was not statistically significant, the difference between CTC and control communities was significantly greater for boys compared to girls (i.e., the interaction term between gender and intervention status was significant).

Similar analyses conducted at grade 10 again indicated that the impact of the CTC intervention on behavioral health outcomes was not moderated by participants' risk status at the start of the study [36]. One interaction between gender and intervention status was marginally significant ($p < .10$). This finding indicated a somewhat stronger reduction in delinquency in CTC versus control communities for boys compared to girls, although the intervention effect was not statistically significant for either sex.

Given some evidence that gender moderated some intervention effects when the cohort was in middle and high school, all outcomes at age 19 were analyzed separately for males and females, and interaction terms tested if any intervention effects differed by gender [16]. With a few exceptions, the findings largely demonstrated gender invariance in outcomes. For males but not females, there were significant intervention effects showing greater abstinence from delinquency and cigarette use in the CTC versus control conditions. However, these gender differences were not large enough to be statistically significant. Only one interaction term was statistically significant, and it indicated that for females, but not males, those in CTC communities were more likely than those in control communities to report any past-month Ecstasy use.

Similar analyses were conducted when the longitudinal panel was age 21 [30]. As at the prior time point, few gender differences were found and none of the interaction terms were statistically significant. However, when results were analyzed separately by sex, statistically significant and desired intervention effects were found among males for three outcomes examining the initiation of substances. Males in the CTC communities were significantly more likely than those in the control communities to report never having smoked cigarettes or marijuana, and they had a lower lifetime incidence of inhalants. When prevalence was examined, no significant intervention effects were found among males; for females, those in the CTC communities reported *more* past-year use of Ecstasy compared to those in the control communities [30].

Data from the longitudinal panel were also examined to explore a possible "dose-response effect" of the intervention; specifically, whether or not youth who resided for a longer period of time in CTC communities benefitted the most from the intervention. All of the findings described to this point were based on an intent-to-treat design, meaning that the analyses examined intervention effects among all participants regardless of whether or not they remained in CTC or control communities during the study period. However, some youth who lived in CTC communities when the longitudinal panel was constituted (in grades 5 and 6) moved out of their towns in later years and did not receive full exposure to the CTC intervention. The hypothesis was that the positive intervention effects found in the intent-to-treat sample would be stronger among the "stayers," since youth who remained in the CTC communities would have had a longer exposure to a more supportive community context and a greater potential to participate in CTC-sponsored EBIs [37].

Isaac Rhew and colleagues [37] examined this hypothesis by assessing the impact of CTC on participants in the longitudinal panel who remained in their original intervention or control condition community through grade 8 (85% of the total sample). Because moving status was a post-baseline variable that was not subject to randomization, an inverse probability weighting approach was utilized to improve causal inference. Based on comparisons of the "stayers" in CTC and control communities, youth from CTC communities had a significantly lower likelihood of reporting any past-month alcohol or smoke-less tobacco use, any binge drinking, and any past-year delinquency. These same intervention effects were found when assessing outcomes among the full sample (using the intent-to-treat analyses), but the effects were stronger for all outcomes when examining those who remained in their original communities [37], consistent with the dose-response hypothesis.

One last study that investigated the potential for variation in the effectiveness of CTC was conducted by Kate Monahan and colleagues [38]. This evaluation investigated the potential for intervention effects to vary across the CTC communities to determine if some CTC communities experienced greater benefits from CTC implementation (versus their matched control community) compared to other communities. Although each CTC community received the same guidance, training, and technical assistance to implement CTC, variation in effectiveness could have occurred given differences across CTC sites in coalition functioning, the number and reach of EBIs, use of the Social Development Strategy, and so on.

To investigate this hypothesis, Monahan and colleagues [38] used meta-analysis to estimate intervention effects within each matched pair of study communities, as well as the overall intervention effect across all matched pairs and the variance of intervention effects across matched pairs. Effect sizes for each pair were calculated based on the number of delinquent behaviors reported by members of the longitudinal panel in all 24 communities in grade 8. Across all 12 pairs of study communities, the average effect size was 0.31. This effect was statistically significant and indicated that youth in CTC communities engaged in fewer delinquent acts compared to those in control communities, a finding similar to that shown in the intent-to-treat analysis [15]. The analyses also showed that there was significant variation in the effect size across the 12 matched pairs of communities, with 8th graders in most, but not all, CTC communities reporting less delinquency than youth in the control communities [38]. Reasons for this variation were not explored in the analysis.

The Society for Prevention Research recommends that evaluations include tests of mediation to examine if EBIs are working as intended, consistent with their underlying theories of change [10]. In the Community Youth Development Study, Ric Brown and colleagues [39] conducted mediation analyses to determine if changes in youth behavioral outcomes could be attributed to positive changes in the community context, consistent with the logic model shown in Figure 1.1. These analyses relied on data from the Community Key Leader Informant surveys conducted in all 24 study communities in 2004. Four potential mediators of intervention effects were tested: adoption of a science-based approach to prevention, community collaboration, community support for prevention, and community norms discouraging adolescent substance use. Youth outcomes were assessed using reports from the longitudinal panel at grade 8 on the four prevalence outcomes identified to be positively affected by the intervention at that grade: past-month alcohol use and smokeless tobacco use, binge drinking, and the variety of past-year delinquency [15]. These items were combined in a single latent construct representing youth behavioral health problems.

To assess mediation, the outcome was first regressed on each of the mediators, controlling for student demographic characteristics, then each mediator and outcome was regressed simultaneously on the intervention condition. Evidence of mediation was demonstrated for one of the four community-level constructs, the adoption of a science-based approach to prevention. The results indicated that the level of adoption was significantly associated with the four youth behavioral outcomes included in the latent construct, with higher adoption related to fewer problems. The impact of CTC on this outcome was fully mediated by the adoption measure, which accounted for 86% of the CTC effect on the outcome. Significant indirect effects of intervention condition on outcomes were not found for the other three constructs measuring collaboration, support for prevention, or community norms discouraging adolescent substance use [39].

Findings from the Repeated, Cross-Sectional Cohort Surveys

Results of the Community Youth Development Study on youth behavioral health problems were also analyzed using information from the CTC Youth Survey[8] administered in repeated cross-sectional surveys of students in middle and high schools in all 24 study communities. Students in grades 6, 8, 10, and 12 completed the survey three times during the Diffusion Study, in 1998, 2000, and 2002, and these data provided baseline information for the randomized trial [8]. Repeated cross-sectional surveys of students in the same grades (6, 8, 10, and 12) were conducted in the Community Youth Development Study every two years, from 2004 to 2012.[9] Sample sizes varied across the years of administration and ranged from 4,000 to 6,000 participants in each grade in the 24 communities. Participation rates varied by grade and year of data collection and ranged from approximately 70 to 90% of all eligible students [40].

The CTC Youth Survey administered in the randomized trial included items measuring risk factors and protective factors across community, school, family, peer, and individual domains. It also asked students to report on their past-month and lifetime use of tobacco, alcohol, marijuana, and other drugs, as well as their perpetration of delinquent and violent behaviors in the year prior to the survey [40]. Students completed paper questionnaires in schools, during a classroom period, using standardized procedures to ensure student anonymity and confidentiality of responses. Multiple screening criteria were used to guard against dishonest and biased answers, including student reports of how honest they were in completing the survey, use of a fictitious drug, and inconsistencies in patterns of reported substance use and delinquency (e.g., reporting past-month but not lifetime use of substances) [8].

Isaac Rhew and colleagues [40] assessed the degree to which the prevalence of substance use and delinquency changed in CTC compared to control communities from baseline through the end of the implementation phase of the randomized trial. Two-stage ANCOVA analyses compared changes in prevalence from baseline (based on combined data collected in 2000 and 2002) to post-intervention (based on combined data collected in 2006 and 2008) among students in grades 6, 8, and 10. Since these were repeated, cross-sectional surveys, this means that data were collected from students in the same grade (i.e., grades 6, 8, and 10) at each of these different years, reflecting a different approach than the longitudinal panel that collected data from the same individuals over time.

The overall pattern of outcomes from the repeated cross-sectional data showed no intervention effects on community levels of substance use, delinquency, or targeted risk factors. Only one statistically significant difference was found out of the 36 tests performed [40]. This difference showed a statistically significant *increase* in the prevalence of delinquency from baseline to post-intervention among 6th graders in CTC compared to control communities, an effect that was in the opposite direction than expected.

A second set of analyses examined intervention effects on youth outcomes using reports from 6th-grade students in 2004 (representing baseline in this analysis) and 10th-grade students in 2008 (representing the end of the implementation phase). This approach was intended to mirror, to the extent possible, the longitudinal panel design. It created a "pseudo-cohort," as most of the 6th-grade students completing the CTC Youth Survey in 2004 were expected to be in 10th grade in 2008, with the exception of those who moved out of the communities and those who moved into the communities during these four years. However, because these surveys were anonymous, the data cannot be linked to the same individuals over time, and the number or proportion of students who completed the survey in both grade 6 and grade 10 cannot be determined.

These analyses also relied on two-stage ANCOVAs to assess change. No overall intervention effects were found when examining the global test statistic for the past-month or lifetime substance use outcomes. None of the individual substance use or delinquency outcomes showed significant intervention effects except for one, which indicated a lower prevalence of lifetime smokeless tobacco use in CTC compared to control communities [40].

A final post hoc analysis using information from this pseudo-cohort was conducted to explore a possible dose-response effect of the intervention, based on youth exposure to EBIs implemented by the CTC coalitions [40]. To assess this possibility, CTC communities were dichotomized into high- and low-exposure groups based on the proportion of youth in the pseudo-cohort who participated in EBIs supported by study funds.[10] Changes in the prevalence of outcomes in the two CTC groups were compared to changes in the control communities. The analyses indicated some support for a dose-response effect. The omnibus test for lifetime substance use was statistically significant and indicated that the high EBI exposure group in CTC communities had a greater reduction in lifetime substance use compared to those in the control communities. A significant reduction was also found for lifetime marijuana use when comparing the high EBI exposure group to students in the control communities. No overall global effect was observed for the low-exposure group versus youth in the control communities. However, when individual outcomes were assessed, the low-exposure group had a greater reduction in lifetime smokeless tobacco use compared to those in the control communities [40].

Lee Van Horn and colleagues [41] used a different analysis strategy and a different classification of students from the cross-sectional data to assess intervention effects. This analysis drew on CTC Youth Survey data collected in 2010 from 8th- and 10th-grade cohorts in all intervention and control communities. Rather than assessing outcomes separately as Rhew and colleagues [40] did, this study relied on multi-level latent class analyses to assess whether or not students could be classified into different groups based on differing patterns of substance use and delinquency. The study also examined whether or not the proportion of students comprising these different groups varied across CTC and control communities.

The first set of analyses indicated that students did have differing patterns of substance use and delinquency. Eighth-graders could be differentiated into four groups: *abstainers*, those with a low probability of engaging in any substance use (tobacco, alcohol, and marijuana use and binge drinking) or any delinquent behaviors; *experimenters*, who were likely to report some lifetime substance use but little recent use and little delinquency; *drug users*, who were very likely to report current drug use but less likely to report delinquency; and *problem students*, who had a high probability of substance use and delinquency. These same groups were found when examining data from 10th-grade students. In addition, a fifth group of 10th-grade students was identified. These students had a high probability of reporting past-month *alcohol use* but no other types of substance use or delinquency.

The second set of analyses found that the proportion of students in each group did not vary across CTC and control communities at study baseline (2004 in this analysis). However, in 2010, a smaller proportion of youth in CTC communities than in control communities were likely to be in the *alcohol use* class compared to the *abstainer* group [41]. These findings suggest that use of the CTC system reduced adolescent alcohol use and promoted abstinence from alcohol, similar to the results shown in analyses of data from the longitudinal panel.

Cost-Benefit Analyses

Standards for evaluating the effectiveness of EBIs recommend analysis of the cost benefits of prevention services [10]. In the Community Youth Development Study, these analyses were conducted using data collected from the longitudinal panel at grade 8 [42] and grade 12 [43]. At both time points, the costs of CTC were estimated based on information from research staff and community members and included expenses related to coalition maintenance (primarily the annual salary of the full-time coalition coordinator), implementation of EBIs, and the training and technical assistance provided to CTC coalitions. Benefits were estimated using procedures outlined by the Washington State Institute of Public Policy [44] and took into account the tangible benefits evidenced when participants refrained from substance use and delinquency, such as increased earnings, as well as tangible avoided costs (e.g., decreased health-care and criminal justice expenses), and intangible costs (e.g., pain and suffering of victims).

For the grade 8 analyses, benefits were estimated for two of the positive intervention outcomes shown in the intent-to-treat analysis: the delayed initiation of tobacco use and delinquency in the CTC versus control communities [15]. The cost-benefit analyses indicated a positive return on investment in CTC. The average cost of CTC per youth was estimated to be $991 and the average benefit to be $5,250 per youth. The benefit-cost ratio indicated a monetary return of $5.30 for every dollar invested in the CTC system [42].

The grade 12 analyses were estimated based on the significant intervention effects indicating a sustained effect on the delayed initiation of tobacco use, alcohol use, and delinquency shown among youth in CTC versus control communities [32]. The benefit-to-cost ratio was even higher in this analysis. The average cost of CTC per youth was estimated to be $556, and the average benefit was $4,477 per youth, resulting in a return of $8.22 for every dollar invested [43]. A sensitivity analysis of the grade 12 data was performed following guidance by the Washington State Institute for Public Policy [44]. The Institute recommends reducing intervention effect sizes by half prior to estimating a benefit-to-cost ratio whenever program developers have been involved in an evaluation, as they were in the Community Youth Development Study. Doing so reduces the potential that the developer's involvement will result in better implementation of the intervention and stronger effects than if the intervention was replicated in a community without developer involvement. Using this conservative approach, CTC was found to return $4.23 for every dollar invested [43].

The Washington State Institute for Public Policy [45] also conducted a benefit-cost analysis of CTC, based on CTC effects shown when the longitudinal cohort was in grade 12. These analyses drew upon information regarding intervention costs provided by Margaret Kuklinski and colleagues [43] in the study just described, as well as the Institute's own estimations of tangible and intangible benefits. The results indicated that CTC had a benefit-to-cost ratio of $5.31, a similar estimate to that reported in the sensitivity analyses reported by Kuklinski and colleagues [43].

Summary and Interpretation of Intervention Effects

This chapter described the research design, measures, and outcomes of the Community Youth Development Study, the most rigorous and comprehensive evaluation of the effectiveness of the CTC system to date. The challenges associated with the evaluation of community-based prevention systems, especially the difficulty recruiting a sufficient number of communities and obtaining their agreement to be randomly assigned to intervention and control conditions, have been enumerated by many scholars [46–52]. Findings from the Community Youth Development Study demonstrate that it is possible to evaluate such interventions using a high-quality research design.

The study followed most of the most recent evaluation standards promoted by the Society of Prevention Research [10]. It utilized a randomized experimental design to maximize internal validity; evaluated outcomes using multiple data collection instruments and sources, with measures developed and tested to ensure reliability and validity; and assessed a range of outcomes at multiple time points to evaluate the immediate and sustained impact of CTC on community-level processes and behavioral health problems. In addition, tests of mediation investigated whether or not effects were consistent with the theories and logic model underlying the CTC system, and tests of moderation evaluated the degree to which findings were generalizable across different groups of young people. Cost-benefit analyses were also performed to provide important and practical information to policy makers and community members.

The study was not only well planned but also well executed, which further strengthens the validity of the results. Analyses indicated that randomization of communities to intervention and control conditions was successful;

that is, communities did not significantly vary in community-level processes, risk factors, protective factors, or youth behavioral health problems at the start of the study. Standardized data collection procedures and careful tracking of participants over time produced high response rates and minimal attrition of the longitudinal panel. Consistent with the CTC logic model, proactive and structured training and technical assistance were provided to intervention communities to ensure that they were fully implementing the CTC system, and a comprehensive process evaluation indicated that implementation fidelity was achieved in all CTC communities (as described in section two of this book).

Furthermore, most outcomes were consistent with the CTC logic model, increasing confidence that results can be attributed to implementation of the CTC system rather than other factors. All 12 CTC communities were demonstrated to have created diverse, well-functioning coalitions that implemented the CTC system with fidelity [17, 18]. In addition, CTC communities were more likely than the control communities to adopt a science-based approach to prevention, findings reported by leaders of prevention-oriented coalitions [19, 20], as well as key leaders of communities during the intervention and sustainability phases of the trial [21, 23–25]. Desirable changes in prevention collaboration were found early in the study when comparing CTC and control communities [23], and at other points in time, CTC communities had greater support for prevention and stronger norms against adolescent substance use compared to control communities [24, 25]. Finally, service providers in CTC communities reported a greater adoption and reach of EBIs compared to those in the control communities [28, 29]. All of these outcomes are consistent with the CTC logic model, as is the finding that reductions in youth behavioral health problems were mediated by an increased adoption of a science-based approach to prevention in CTC versus control communities [39].

Data on behavioral health outcomes were collected using a longitudinal panel of youth, the most rigorous methodology for assessing intervention effects given the ability of longitudinal data to allow analysis of changes in the same individuals over time. Results from the longitudinal panel of 4,407 youth supported the hypotheses that adoption of CTC would lead to community-wide reductions in risk factors, increases in protective factors, and reduced rates of behavioral health problems. These findings showed that youth in CTC communities delayed the initiation of substance use and delinquency and had a lower prevalence of these behaviors compared to youth in control communities at some of the follow-up time points. The CTC system was also demonstrated to be cost beneficial and to provide a fiscal return on investment for communities [42, 43, 45].

Although use of the CTC system resulted in many desired outcomes for intervention communities, not all of the hypothesized effects on youth behavioral health problems were found in the randomized study. Effects on substance use were largely confined to tobacco and alcohol use, and no main intervention effects were demonstrated for marijuana use, prescription drugs, or hard drugs. As students grew older, some effects were diminished, and sustained impacts through grade 12 were found only on the incidence or abstinence of behaviors, not on the current prevalence of substance use, delinquency or violence. In addition, at age 19, effects were not demonstrated for other types of behavioral health problems, such as depression, drug abuse/dependency, or risky sexual behavior.

There are several possible reasons why some outcomes may not have changed or been sustained over time. First, CTC communities in this study were empowered to decide for themselves the number and types of EBIs to be implemented, the populations to be targeted by these services, and the reach of their services. Communities were required to deliver study-funded EBIs to youth in grades 5–9, but they were not required to target for services the specific youth participating in the longitudinal panel or those in the cross-sectional cohorts. Process data indicated that the reach of EBIs varied substantially across communities, and many youth were not reached by EBIs, which probably limited the intervention effects observed in this study. Second, ensuring widespread participation in universal parent training programs was very challenging for the CTC communities that selected these EBIs [53], and the limited reach of these interventions may have reduced their ability to produce community-wide changes in risk and protective factors in the family domain, as shown in one of the analyses of the longitudinal panel data [33]. Third, almost no EBIs were delivered in high schools, which may have restricted the study's ability to show intervention effects on the older youth and/or to demonstrate sustained effects on the targeted behavioral health problems.

The fact that intervention effects were found when analyzing data from the longitudinal panel but not in most of the analyses of data from the repeated, cross-sectional cohorts also warrants some discussion. As Rhew and colleagues [40] acknowledge, the longitudinal panel design has greater statistical power to detect effects compared to the repeated cross-sectional surveys, given that the same youth are followed over time. Cross-sectional surveys are more likely to be biased by unmeasured characteristics (e.g., specific socioeconomic indicators, changes to school or community policies that can affect a particular grade of students, etc.) compared to longitudinal panels. Cross-sectional surveys are also subject to cohort effects, such as the secular trends that indicated decreases in adolescent substance use during the time of the randomized trial [8]. Analyses conducted prior to the start of the study indicated that, because of these secular trends, the intervention would need to produce strong effect sizes in order to demonstrate statistically significant intervention differences using the cross-sectional panel data [8]. The ability to detect such effects could have been reduced because many students participating in the cross-sectional panels in CTC communities did not receive EBIs [40]. In addition, these cohorts included individuals who moved into the community after the trial had started, thus limiting their exposure to CTC activities [40]. Similarly, some youth who participated in EBIs in the early years of the study moved out of CTC communities but were not followed over time, which may have attenuated observed intervention effects in the cross-sectional cohorts compared to the longitudinal panel.

Despite these caveats, findings from the Community Youth Development Study indicate that communities that adopt the CTC system can positively transform their communities and prevent youth behavioral health outcomes. Communities' ability to delay the initiation of substance use, delinquency, and violence is especially important given research indicating, for example, that the early initiation of alcohol is associated with a later diagnosis of alcohol abuse and dependence [54–56]. This evidence indicates that early, preventive interventions will have long-term payoffs.

The positive effects of CTC on community contexts and youth behavioral health outcomes are also notable given the failure of some other community-based prevention systems to produce community-wide benefits for youth [57]. According to the Blueprints for Healthy Youth Development website (www.blueprintsprograms.com/), only CTC and PROSPER can be considered effective coalition-based prevention systems based on having well-defined logic models, well-conducted evaluations, positive impacts on youth outcomes, and the capacity to provide training and technical assistance to communities. Many other community-change efforts have noted significant implementation challenges, especially in regards to mobilizing and maintaining engagement from diverse stakeholders [58–60]. Findings from the Community Youth Development Study indicate that communities can be effectively mobilized to engage in a science-based approach to prevention. To ensure positive outcomes, they must be ready to contribute substantial human and financial resources to prevention over an extended period of time. With the provision of systematic and ongoing training and technical assistance, as is built into the CTC system, communities can increase their capacity to initiate and sustain a comprehensive prevention approach that addresses their local needs.

9

A State-Wide Effectiveness Trial of CTC in Pennsylvania

AS REVIEWED IN chapter 3, in the typical sequence of evaluation research, an intervention is usually first evaluated in a small-scale pilot study to assess its feasibility, then in an efficacy trial to determine if the intervention can produce changes in targeted outcomes when replicated under highly controlled conditions.[1] Assuming positive results from the efficacy trial, an effectiveness trial may be conducted to assess intervention impact when the EBI is implemented under more naturalistic conditions, and a dissemination trial may investigate how to scale up the intervention while maintaining its effectiveness [1, 2]. The development and evaluation of CTC did not proceed in exactly this manner. CTC was first evaluated in pilot studies conducted in Washington and Oregon (see chapter 3). Then, the CTC system was implemented at scale in counties across the Commonwealth of Pennsylvania in a multi-year initiative that was initiated prior to the efficacy trial (the Community Youth Development Study) described in chapter 8.

In this chapter, we describe the CTC effectiveness trial conducted in Pennsylvania. Since the mid-1990s, the Commonwealth of Pennsylvania has provided interested communities[2] with financial support and technical assistance to adopt the CTC system and implement EBIs, which has to date resulted in the creation of over 120 CTC coalitions across the state. Participation in this initiative has been voluntary, and communities have adopted the CTC system at different times over the last two decades.

The large number of communities using CTC to prevent youth behavioral problems has created a naturalistic experiment in which rates of youth behavioral health problems and levels of risk and protective factors can be compared in CTC and non-CTC communities [4, 5]. These conditions have allowed researchers to conduct an effectiveness trial to examine the outcomes achieved when CTC is implemented by communities as part of their routine approach to community-based prevention, as well as a dissemination trial to understand the conditions that foster widespread use of the CTC system. As we will describe, Pennsylvania, particularly the state's Commission on Crime and Delinquency (PCCD), has invested significant financial and human resources to support the adoption, high-quality implementation, and sustainability of CTC in communities across the state. This multi-year initiative has examined the factors affecting the functioning and sustainability of CTC coalitions, as well as the adoption, implementation, and sustainability of EBIs supported by these coalitions. The project has also provided insight into the types and amount of training and technical assistance needed to build local capacity to engage in effective community-based prevention [6].

This chapter describes the history, implementation, and outcomes of the Pennsylvania initiative to increase knowledge of how to scale up effective community-based prevention. Although the strengths of coalition-based prevention models have been well articulated, the same literature indicates that local communities often face difficulties when trying to form and sustain broad-based, high-functioning coalitions [7, 8], and more research is needed on the factors associated with coalition success. Similarly, achieving significant reductions in youth behavioral health problems is contingent upon the dissemination and high-quality implementation of EBIs [9–11], yet more research is needed on how to increase the use of EBIs in communities. Finally, although the importance of providing local agencies with training and technical assistance to increase their capacity to engage in community-based prevention is recognized [12, 13], very few studies have examined how to provide such assistance, particularly at scale [14]. The state-wide dissemination of CTC in Pennsylvania provides an opportunity to examine these important aspects of community-based prevention.

History of the State-Wide Adoption of CTC in Pennsylvania

As outlined in the Diffusion of Innovations theory developed by Everett Rogers [15], the dissemination of a new innovation like CTC (or any other EBI) occurs slowly and usually proceeds in stages. Individuals or organizations must first learn about a new intervention, then be persuaded to use it, then try it out before confirming their decision to adopt and sustain the intervention. Decisions to adopt the innovation will be affected by perceptions of the need for the intervention and its utility in addressing a local problem; that is, potential users must believe that a problem exists and that the innovation can effectively solve this problem [16, 17]. Diffusion is also facilitated by the presence of a champion, particularly an influential leader who endorses the new intervention, persuades others to use it, and generates necessary resources for implementation [18–20]. Given the human and financial costs associated with preventive interventions, and the fact that social service agencies have limited funds, adequate resources and high-quality staffing are essential for the adoption and sustainability of the innovation [21, 22].

CTC's adoption by Pennsylvania communities has been enabled by all these factors. The recognition that crime was a social problem was facilitated by high crime rates [23] and public concern about juvenile offenders [i.e., "super-predators," as articulated by 24] when the Pennsylvania initiative began in the early- to mid-1990s. However, solutions to the crime problem were also proposed. In 1992, Title V of the reauthorization of the Juvenile Justice and Delinquency Prevention Act provided states with funding to address local crime problems and emphasized the utility of preventive rather than reactive strategies to do so. The federal Office of Juvenile Justice and Delinquency, charged with enforcing the Act and administering the Title V funds, identified CTC as the best strategy to prevent delinquency "because of its strong empirical basis and systematic approach to community-based, collaborative assessment and planning" [25]. Convinced of both the problem and the solution to address it, as well as a recently launched effort to reduce juvenile drug use (the PENNFREE initiative), Pennsylvania policymakers endorsed the use of CTC. Beginning in 1994, the Commonwealth began to supplement Title V funds to support adoption of the CTC system throughout the state [26].

Although he was not responsible for the initial launch of the CTC effort, Governor Tom Ridge was a CTC champion whose support enabled its expansion across the state. When he took office in 1995, Governor Ridge asked the Pennsylvania Commission on Crime and Delinquency, as well as the Juvenile Court Judges Commission (JCJC) and the Pennsylvania Council of Chief Juvenile Probation Officers, to contribute resources to help disseminate CTC. Governor Ridge also created a cabinet-level advisory commission, the Governor's Community Partnership for Safe Children (i.e., the "Children's Partnership"), whose mission was directly aligned with the CTC initiative. The Children's Partnership pledged to "assist local communities in establishing effective programs and services to reduce violence by and against children and youth" (www.oa.pa.gov/Policies/eo/Documents/1995_6.pdf). It was led by First Lady Michele Ridge and overseen by a 34-member board of directors that included top administrators in the state agencies related to criminal justice, education, health, and public welfare. In this manner, Governor Ridge not only increased the visibility and credibility of CTC but also helped spread the use of a science-based prevention approach to other agencies in the state. As noted by the Office of Juvenile Justice and Delinquency [25] in its report to Congress on the Title V initiative, "Pennsylvania has done as much as any state and more to use the training and risk-focused planning approach provided by [CTC] to reconstitute its statewide approach to delinquency."

In the initiative's first three years, the Pennsylvania Commission on Crime and Delinquency funded 21 counties to adopt the CTC system. All sites received a one-year $15,000 grant to cover costs related to CTC training and prevention planning [3]. They also received technical assistance from staff at the Center for Juvenile Justice Training and Research (CJJT&R) at Shippensburg University, the training arm of the Juvenile Court Judges Commission. Consistent with the CTC training system at the time, sites received three multi-day training workshops: one to familiarize key leaders with the CTC system and prevention science concepts, the second to assist coalition members to conduct needs assessments, and the third to identify promising approaches (i.e., interventions) communities could use to address prioritized needs. Between trainings, with the support of technical assistance providers from the Center for Juvenile Justice Training and Research, counties created coalitions, conducted prevention needs assessments, and developed action plans describing the prevention programs they would implement to address local needs. After their initial planning year, counties could apply for three-year implementation grants to cover costs associated with maintaining the CTC prevention system. Between 1994 and 2002, state funds facilitated the adoption of CTC in about 120 communities, and new coalitions have been funded since that time.

Consistent with the state's emphasis on evidence-based prevention, the Pennsylvania Commission on Crime and Delinquency asked the Prevention Research Center at the Pennsylvania State University to conduct a process evaluation of the CTC initiative. The evaluation, described in this chapter, focused on the first 21 communities that had implemented CTC [27]. Feedback from technical assistance providers, coalition members, and key leaders was largely positive, but several implementation challenges were identified. In particular, coalitions did not always provide sufficient training for new staff or coalition members, some implemented interventions that had not been well evaluated, and most did not plan in advance for the long-term sustainability of their coalitions and EBIs [27]. The evaluation team recommended the expansion of implementation support to communities to help solve these problems. Following this advice, the number of technical assistance providers supported by the state increased from one centrally located staff person to five regionally dispersed full-time staff.

The evaluators also recommended that Pennsylvania policymakers create a dedicated funding stream to support the EBIs selected for adoption by CTC coalitions. The Commonwealth agreed to do so and launched the Evidence-based Programs Initiative in 1998. From 1998 to 2008, this initiative provided about 60 million dollars to community organizations to implement one of 12 EBIs [28]. Most of these interventions had been identified as effective (i.e., Model) by the (then) Blueprints for Violence Prevention initiative [29], an effort financially supported by the Pennsylvania Commission on Crime and Delinquency.

When the Evidence-based Programs Initiative began, information from CTC coalitions indicated that EBIs were not always selected based on a comprehensive local needs assessment and were not always implemented with fidelity [30]. In response to these findings, the state revised its funding requirements to help ensure that EBIs were connected to a prevention-oriented coalition and that these coalitions had completed a risk and resource assessment in the two years prior to receipt of funding [6]. To facilitate needs assessments, and with funding from the Pennsylvania Commission on Crime and Delinquency, in 2001 the state began to administer the Pennsylvania Youth Survey (PAYS). The survey is a slightly modified version of the CTC Youth Survey and is conducted every two years in public middle and high schools across the state.

Although a biennial school survey had previously collected data on student substance use in Pennsylvania, it did not contain information on risk and protective factors, which hindered CTC coalitions' ability to conduct needs assessments. Similar to CTC coalitions participating in the early pilot evaluations conducted in Washington [31] and Oregon [32], coalitions in Pennsylvania initially had to rely on archival data or collect their own data to measure risk and protective factors as best they could. The administration of the Pennsylvania Youth Survey greatly reduced the burden of conducting a needs assessment and provided communities with information on a more comprehensive set of risk and protective factors than was possible using other methodologies. The survey is currently administered statewide at no cost to participating schools, and districts receive reports summarizing the findings so they can use this information to prioritize needs for prevention planning (see www.pccd.pa.gov/Juvenile-Justice/Pages/Pennsylvania-Youth-Survey-%28PAYS%29.aspx).

Recognizing that, even with funding, communities are often challenged to adopt, implement with quality, and sustain EBIs, in 2008, the Pennsylvania Commission on Crime and Delinquency once again bolstered its provision of technical support to CTC coalitions. With support and funding from the (then) Department of Public Welfare, the Pennsylvania Commission on Crime and Delinquency established the Evidence-based Prevention and Intervention Support Center (EPISCenter) through a competitive grant awarded to the Prevention Research Center at Pennsylvania State University. In 2010, primarily due to budget constraints, the responsibility for providing training and technical assistance to CTC coalitions was transferred from the Center for Juvenile Justice Training and Research to the EPISCenter. The EPISCenter then began to provide support for both community coalitions and the EBIs they were adopting.

The EPISCenter's mission is to promote the dissemination of EBIs by providing proactive training and technical assistance to CTC coalitions (and other prevention-oriented coalitions) and EBI providers. To foster this research–state partnership, the center is overseen by a state-level steering committee that includes representatives from the Commission on Crime and Delinquency, as well as the Departments of Human Services (formerly Public Welfare), Drug and Alcohol Programs, Education, and Health, and the Juvenile Court Judges Commission [33]. Figure 9.1 illustrates the operations of the EPISCenter.

As this short history makes clear, Pennsylvania has created a strong infrastructure to build the capacity of local communities to engage in collaborative, science-based prevention of youth behavioral problems. State leaders have recognized that large-scale reductions in youth behavioral health problems require significant financial resources provided over an extended period, and they have called upon multiple agencies with a stake in ensuring healthy youth development to contribute to this mission. They have also understood that communities will face challenges when engaging in collaborative prevention. They have attempted to minimize this problem by supporting the delivery of proactive, structured, and ongoing training and technical assistance to ensure high-functioning coalitions and well-implemented EBIs. Have these investments paid off? We describe the impact of the CTC initiative on community and youth outcomes in the next section.

Impact of the Pennsylvania Initiative on CTC Coalition Functioning and EBI Implementation
CTC Coalition Functioning and Sustainability

The Pennsylvania initiative has collected extensive data on CTC implementation, especially coalition functioning and sustainability. As described in chapter 3, researchers in Pennsylvania developed a survey to provide reliable

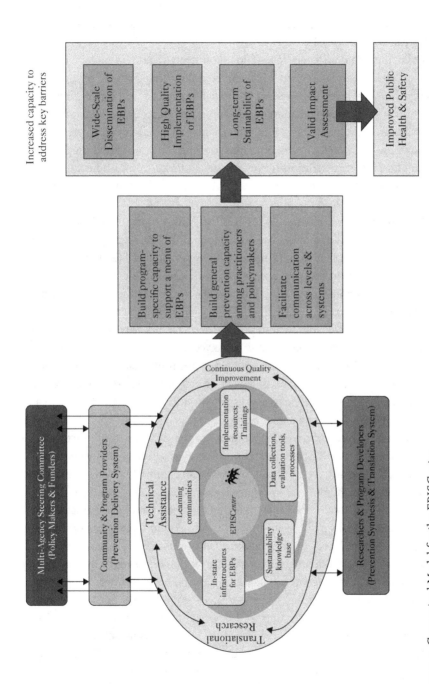

FIGURE 9.1 Conceptual Model for the EPISCenter
Source: Adapted from Bumbarger [45]

and accurate information on coalition functioning [3, 34]. Items and constructs for the survey included previously established measures, as well as new measures created by the research team.

These include constructs related to community readiness for prevention, coalition structure (e.g., clarity of roles), coalition directedness (e.g., having clear goals and objectives), member participation, and the amount of financial and human resources available to the group. The perceived effectiveness of the coalition, including how well coalition leaders have elicited support for the initiative and promoted prevention in the community, is also rated. In its early administrations, this coalition survey involved a three- to four-hour interview with the director or chairperson of the coalition, as well as shorter, one-hour interviews with key leaders in the community.

The first process evaluation of CTC in the Pennsylvania effectiveness trial was based on coalition survey data collected two to three years after the first 21 coalitions had received state funding to implement CTC. At that point, coalitions and technical assistance providers reported moderately high levels of coalition functioning. Mean scores on the various dimensions of functioning ranged from 2.7 to 3.8 on a 4-point scale across the 21 sites [34]. The evaluation also showed significant, positive associations between community readiness, coalition functioning, and perceived effectiveness of the coalition. A mediation analyses indicated that greater community readiness was associated with better coalition functioning, better functioning was related to greater perceived coalition effectiveness, and coalition functioning mediated the relationship between readiness and effectiveness [3].

When asked to report barriers that undermined CTC coalition functioning and effectiveness, participants most commonly cited a lack of resources, a lack of participation by members of the community, and conflict between members [3]. Less frequently mentioned were problems related to membership diversity and leadership. Most respondents endorsed the need for additional technical assistance across all areas listed on surveys, including leadership development, coalition building, diversity/cultural awareness, fund-raising, effective prevention approaches, program evaluation and monitoring, and program implementation [35]. However, coalitions that reported greater community readiness, better functioning, more perceived effectiveness, and more supportive attitudes about prevention, and who had more members attend CTC trainings, were less likely to report a need for technical assistance.

Although these findings generally demonstrated that new CTC communities could establish well-functioning coalitions, they also suggested that local community members would be receptive to and benefit from increased technical assistance [27]. As mentioned, based on these findings, technical

assistance was increased and changed to a regional system of provision to ensure regular contacts between CTC trainers and coalition members.

The evaluators also recognized that technical assistance would be most
useful if it were based on timely and accurate information about coalitions.
To accommodate this need, following the first implementation study, the research team changed the coalition survey from a phone interview to a web-
based survey and began to collect data from coalition members, as well as
directors. All members of smaller coalitions (those with less than 25 members)
and the most active 25 members of larger coalitions, as identified by coalition
staff, were considered eligible to complete the survey, which required about 20
minutes. These changes reduced the cost and labor of survey administration
and the time needed to complete the survey, but maintained the reliability and
validity of the measures. The new format produced response rates of about 50
to 60% at the member level and 70 to 80% at the coalition level [36, 37].

Another advantage of changing the survey administration was that the
web-based system allowed information about coalition functioning to be tab-
ulated more efficiently. In turn, technical assistance providers could more
quickly generate individual coalition reports and share them with coalition
members during in-person visits. These reports provided coalitions with average scores on each area assessed by the survey, with comparisons to all other
coalitions, as well as a summary of the coalition's strengths and weaknesses.
Coalitions are encouraged to use this information to address problematic issues identified in the surveys [36].

The extent to which the provision of technical assistance improved coalition functioning in CTC communities in Pennsylvania was examined using
data from the web-based survey as well as ratings from technical assistance
providers. Drawing on information from 95 CTC coalitions that had been operating for one to six years, given the staggered implementation of CTC, no relationship was found between the provision of technical support and coalition
functioning when all coalitions were assessed [38]. However, a greater amount
of technical assistance was related to better functioning among younger CTC
coalitions, while no relationship existed in older sites. The authors' interpretation of this finding was that coalition activities are likely to become more
established and routinized over time and therefore less responsive to outside
consultation.

Researchers in Pennsylvania have also examined the ability of CTC
coalitions to sustain themselves over time [39, 40]. The longest study of coalition sustainability, conducted in 2006, included 110 sites that had received CTC
planning and implementation grants from 1994 to 2000 [40]. Sustainability
was defined according to whether or not coalitions were still meeting regularly

and using the CTC framework to conduct needs assessments, promote the implementation of EBIs, and receive technical assistance from EBI developers. The findings indicated that 81 of the 110 coalitions (74%) were still in existence in 2006. In the year following the end of their state funding, 11% of sites terminated, and about 3 to 5% of coalitions failed to sustain each year thereafter. Coalitions had varying levels of success in generating funds after the state grants had ended. The median amount of annual funds reported by sites was about $61,000, and amounts ranged from $500 to about $455,000 per site [40].

Predictors of sustainability were examined using the annual surveys of coalition members and technical assistance providers [40]. These analyses indicated that coalitions were more likely to be sustained when coalition members and technical assistance providers reported better coalition functioning, better adherence to the CTC system, and more planning for sustainability. These factors also predicted a greater amount of funding and diversity of funding sources generated after state funds had ended. The findings support the provision of training and technical assistance to CTC coalitions as they indicate that such actions should promote both their functioning and stability.

The Adoption, Implementation, and Sustainability of EBIs

CTC promotes the adoption and high-quality implementation of EBIs, and the Commonwealth of Pennsylvania advocated for dissemination of CTC because the system emphasized the use of EBIs to prevent juvenile delinquency. In addition, the state provided resources to the Blueprints initiative to identify EBIs, offered multi-year grants to local agencies to implement EBIs, and created the EPISCenter to provide support to coalitions and organizations to successfully replicate EBIs. Given this interest in EBI dissemination, the Pennsylvania evaluation has included an assessment of whether or not CTC coalitions have addressed local needs using EBIs, implemented these interventions with fidelity, and sustained them over time.

To investigate the adoption and monitoring of EBIs by CTC coalitions, coalition chairpersons were asked during the annual coalition surveys to identify interventions that their coalitions sponsored, co-sponsored, or provided consultation for. Interventions were considered to be EBIs if they were listed as effective on registries maintained by the Substance Abuse and Mental Health Services Administration (SAMHSA),[3] Blueprints, and the National Institute of Justice, or if research staff determined that an intervention had been shown to reduce delinquency or substance use in at least one high-quality quasi-experimental evaluation [41, 42]. According to information from 62 coalitions, 85% of the interventions reported in 2007 were EBIs [41]. In 2008, 76% of the interventions identified by 60 coalitions were EBIs [42]. These results indicate that most but not all CTC coalitions were using EBIs to address their prevention needs.

The findings showed variation in the degree to which coalitions followed CTC guidelines to ensure that EBIs were delivered with fidelity and monitored to assess implementation quality. Based on data from 2007 and 2008, coalition leaders reported that implementers received training from program developers for 62% of the selected EBIs, 20% of the sites received informal trainings (e.g., workshops provided by someone familiar with the program who was not a certified trainer), and 18% had no training [42]. Technical assistance from program developers was less common and was reported for only about half (46%) of the replications. Coalition leaders reported that fidelity monitoring occurred for 79% of the EBIs and primarily relied on self-reported information from implementers (40%) and outside observers (28%); however, 21% of the EBIs were not monitored to assess implementation delivery [42].

Reports from coalition leaders, members, and research staff were used to examine the factors associated with coalitions' support of EBIs in two studies [41, 42]. Both studies measured implementation support as a composite variable based on the number of EBIs affiliated with the coalition, the coalition's level of oversight/funding (i.e., whether it was uninvolved with EBI implementation, provided consultation to implementing agencies, was a cosponsor, or was the primary sponsor/funder of the EBI), and the coalition's efforts to ensure/monitor fidelity (i.e., ensuring training and technical assistance from developers and monitoring implementation procedures). In both studies, coalition functioning was associated with greater levels of implementation support [41, 42]. More specifically, coalition members' and researchers' ratings of coalitions' cohesion, efficiency, and leadership were each related to greater EBI support [41]. In addition, coalition members' knowledge of the CTC system was related to greater implementation support [42]. In one of the studies [41], coalition age was negatively associated with implementation support, suggesting that older coalitions may experience "mission drift" and fail to implement some aspects of the CTC system such as EBI adoption and monitoring. In both studies, community poverty was negatively related to implementation support, such that coalitions in lower income communities were less likely to adopt and monitor EBIs [41, 42].

Considered as a whole, the findings indicated that coalitions in Pennsylvania differed in the degree to which they fully implemented Phase 5 of the CTC system. These results reinforce the value of providing coalitions

with ongoing training and technical assistance to ensure that members understand the CTC system and its methods for adopting and monitoring EBIs.
As described in chapter 7, it is expected that coalition members will rotate in
and out of coalitions. However, if new coalition members do not participate
in CTC training workshops, their ability to implement CTC with fidelity may
be compromised. The findings from the Pennsylvania trial also suggest that
training and technical support may be particularly valuable in communities
with structural challenges (e.g., poverty) to community-based prevention.

To provide a more detailed analysis of EBI implementation fidelity, the
Pennsylvania research team created the Annual Survey of Evidence-based
Programs (ASEP) to be completed by service providers in organizations
that had received state funding to implement EBIs [6]. This survey was first
administered in 2001 in paper-and-pencil format and focused on assessing
EBI providers' technical assistance needs. In 2005, the survey was changed
to a web-based format and was expanded to collect information on the sustainability, coalition involvement, implementation processes, and effects on
participants of the 10 EBIs funded by the state at that time.

One item on the survey asked service providers to report whether or not
their agency had "adapted" or "improved" EBIs to meet local needs [30]. Almost
half (44%) of the 240 respondents reported making adaptations, most often
changing the program's dosage (identified in 42% of the follow-up responses
about adaptations) or content (38% of responses). Participants reported that
most adaptations were made in response to logistical challenges, such as
having a lack of time to deliver the program, a shortage of resources, or difficulty recruiting and/or retaining participants. Half the changes were considered by the research team to be mis-adaptations—that is, changes which
deviated from the programs' theoretical basis, goals, and/or logic models [30].

To guard against mis-adaptations, which are likely to undermine program
effectiveness [18], EPISCenter staff have developed a proactive and comprehensive approach to deliver technical assistance to EBI providers. To reduce
the likelihood that providers will deviate from the interventions' protocols, the
EPISCenter staff have created written manuals for each of the EBIs supported
by the state. These manuals identify each EBI's implementation requirements,
common implementation challenges, and logic models (see www.episcenter.
psu.edu/ebp).

To ensure that EBIs are successfully launched, technical assistance
providers and staff from the Pennsylvania Commission on Crime and
Delinquency arrange for an orientation for all grantees shortly after they
have received funding. Following the orientation, EPISCenter staff assist

implementers to develop detailed implementation plans using the EBI manuals. These plans guide program delivery and also include attention to how the EBI will be integrated into the agency/community and funded in the long term. To facilitate the collection and analysis of EBI data, EPISCenter staff, in collaboration with the Pennsylvania Commission on Crime and Delinquency and EBI providers, have created performance measures and tools to assess implementation fidelity (e.g., adherence, dosage, and participant engagement) and outcomes (e.g., changes in participant attitudes and behaviors) for each state-supported EBI. Technical assistance is available to help agencies interpret these data and use the information to improve implementation procedures as needed [6, 43].

Building communities' capacity to implement and evaluate EBIs is expected to not only reduce mis-adaptations but also enhance sustainability. To assess this possibility, the Annual Survey of Evidence-based Programs asks respondents to indicate the extent to which their program is still operating at the time of the survey administration. Response items include "not operating," "operating at a reduced level," "operating at the same level as in its final year of funding," and "operating at a higher level as in its final year of funding" [43].

Based on responses to this survey collected from 2005 to 2009, 69% of all EBIs that had received EBI grants were still operating after state funding had ended; however, 60% of the sustained EBIs were operating at a lower level of functioning. Compared to programs that had ended, sustained EBIs were affiliated with better functioning coalitions (as reported by EBI staff), had more contact with program developers, had staff with more knowledge of the EBI's logic model, and had planned better for sustainability. EBIs that were not maintained, compared to those that were sustained, had more problems with participant recruitment, less administrator support, and weaker implementation fidelity [43]

These findings indicate that communities using the CTC system in Pennsylvania have successfully adopted, implemented, and sustained EBIs, and that EBIs connected to high-functioning coalitions have a greater likelihood of being implemented with quality and sustained over time. Although positive findings were not evidenced in all sites, the generally favorable results are notable given that CTC and EBI implementation were conducted under naturalistic conditions. However, in Pennsylvania, this means that local communities received considerable financial support and proactive training and technical assistance to promote high-functioning coalitions, which no doubt contributes to these positive findings.

Impact of the Pennsylvania Initiative on Youth Behavioral Health Problems

Communities that adopt the CTC system are expected to experience reductions in youth behavioral health problems. The degree to which such findings were shown in Pennsylvania has been evaluated in a quasi-experimental evaluation [4, 5]. Two studies have compared data from 6th-, 8th-, 10th-, and 12th-grade students completing the Pennsylvania Youth Survey in school districts affiliated with a CTC coalition and responses from students in school districts not affiliated with a CTC coalition.

The first study examined differences in risk factors, substance use, and delinquency in 2001 and 2003 among students in CTC and non-CTC affiliated school districts. In 2001, 92 school districts participated in the survey, 50 CTC-affiliated districts and 42 non-CTC districts. On average, CTC sites had been implementing the CTC system for 16.8 months. In 2003, 159 districts participated (102 CTC districts and 57 non-CTC districts),[4] and CTC sites had been operating for a mean of 43 months. Averaged across all districts and both years, 6% of households in participating districts were below the poverty line, 6% of the population was non-white, and 2% were Hispanic. Districts were mostly in rural regions of the state and had an average of 28,706 students per district. After excluding districts and/or students with missing data and/or outliers, the 2001 dataset included information from 79 districts and 38,107 students, and the 2003 dataset included 146 districts and 96,875 students [4].

Analyses were conducted separately by year of survey administration, grade level, risk factor scores, and outcomes. They also controlled for the percentage of families in the district who were below the poverty level and accounted for clustering of students in school districts. The results indicated that CTC districts had lower levels of some risk factors, substance use, and delinquency compared to non-CTC districts. More specifically, four comparisons in 2001 and 16 comparisons in 2003 were statistically significant and favored CTC-affiliated districts. This pattern of effects provides some evidence of a dose-response impact, as the average time implementing CTC in 2001 was less than a year and a half, while in 2003 it was about three and a half years. In terms of the behavioral health outcomes, significant findings favoring CTC sites were found in 2003 for reductions in past month alcohol use (as reported by 6th and 12th graders), past month cigarette use (6th graders), binge drinking (12th graders), and delinquency (6th and 10th graders) [4].

Because CTC communities varied in the age groups they targeted for prevention services, a dose-response analysis was conducted to determine if intervention effects would be stronger when restricting the analyses to data from districts in which CTC coalitions reported implementing EBIs with students in the participating grades (about half of the full CTC sample). This hypothesis was generally supported. The results indicated significant effects favoring CTC-affiliated districts for most of the risk factors and behaviors reported by 6th-grade students and for some of the comparisons in each of the other grades. In all cases, results indicated higher levels of risk factors and behavioral problems in non-CTC compared to CTC districts, with odds-ratios ranging from 1.12 to 1.36 [4].

The second study utilized student data from the Pennsylvania Youth Survey administered in 2001, 2003, and 2005. Similar to the methods used in Rhew and colleagues' [44] analysis of the CTC Youth Survey data from the randomized trial (see chapter 8), the Pennsylvania study compared results in CTC and non-CTC districts using pseudo-cohorts. For example, responses from 6th graders in 2001 were linked to responses from 8th graders in 2003 and from 10th graders in 2005. Four pseudo-cohorts, including just over 59,000 students, were created by linking cohorts with data collected in at least two of the three data time points. Separate analyses were conducted to examine differences in each of the seven risk and protective factor indices (i.e., factor scores comprising multiple risk and/or protective factor scales) and six behavioral outcomes. Multi-level models took into account clustering by school district and controlled for school district poverty rates [5].

The main analyses indicated no significant differences between CTC and non-CTC districts in risk and protective factor indices or substance use. However, students in CTC districts were significantly less likely than those in non-CTC districts to report increases in delinquency across the survey years. Secondary dose-response analyses compared data from students in (1) the CTC districts reporting the delivery of universal EBIs to the pseudo-cohorts to (2) the non-CTC districts combined with the CTC districts that did not provide EBIs to the pseudo-cohorts. These analyses showed significant effects favoring the higher dosage CTC sites for all of the risk and protective factor indices, with small to medium effect sizes ranging from 0.09 to 0.35. Similar reductions were found for delinquency (the effect size was 0.19). Increases in students' self-reported grades were also demonstrated (the effect size was 0.32), but no significant differences were found for substance use [5].

Findings from the Pennsylvania initiative support the CTC logic model and provide some evidence that the adoption of the CTC system can alter the developmental trajectories of risk and protective factors and problem behaviors as youth progress through the risky period of adolescence. Although differences between CTC and non-CTC communities were not as large as those demonstrated in the Community Youth Development Study efficacy trial, and not all risk and protective factors and outcomes had significant effects favoring CTC communities, it is important to remember that these findings are based solely on repeated cross-sectional surveys of students, which have less statistical power to detect significant changes compared to longitudinal surveys [44]. In addition, CTC coalitions in Pennsylvania did not target every possible risk and protective factor but, rather, focused on a few priorities, consistent with the CTC system, and they did not provide EBIs to all youth in CTC communities. The Pennsylvania initiative was more naturalistic than the efficacy trial, in that CTC was not implemented with the same level of oversight. Training and technical assistance was provided, but coalitions adopting the CTC system early in the Pennsylvania study received a more abbreviated set of trainings and less intensive technical assistance compared to those adopting the CTC system in the latter years of the study.

Although the results described thus far were based on information reported by students in middle and high schools, official crime statistics also suggest that CTC implementation can reduce adolescent involvement in the juvenile justice system [45]. According to data from the Uniform Crime Reports (UCR), the juvenile arrest rate for violent crimes has decreased 29% from 2007 to 2013 in Pennsylvania, from 408 to 288 arrests per 100,000 juveniles. In addition, the number of juvenile delinquency dispositions for new illegal offenses decreased by 44% from 2007 to 2014 in Pennsylvania, from 45,573 to 25,567, and the number of youth placed in secure detention facilities during this period decreased by 48%, from 19,294 to 10,120. The drop in placements has resulted in the closing of nine of Pennsylvania's 24 juvenile residential facilities (38%), saving the state over 85 million dollars annually.

Although these declines cannot be definitively attributed to use of the CTC system, the fact that CTC has been adopted widely in the state suggests a relationship between CTC adoption and reduced juvenile crime. In addition, one analysis of criminal justice data in Pennsylvania found that counties that implemented EBIs had greater reductions in juvenile residential placement compared to counties which did not implement EBIs [46].

Conclusion

As we have described in this chapter, Pennsylvania's approach to community-based prevention has been comprehensive and innovative. Pennsylvania was an early adopter of CTC, supplementing Title V funds to communities and extending financial support long after the Title V funding had ended. Pennsylvania was among the first states to make possible a state-wide administration of a school-based survey based on the CTC Youth Survey in order to collect information on risk factors, protective factors, and behaviors. These data allow communities to conduct local needs assessments and engage in data-driven and community-specific prevention planning. Pennsylvania recognized early on the value of promoting the widespread adoption and high-quality implementation of EBIs to prevent youth behavioral health problems. State agencies not only provided initial funding to the Blueprints initiative to facilitate its identification of EBIs, but also offered multi-year grants to local agencies to implement the EBIs designated as effective by Blueprints. Pennsylvania leaders also had the foresight to build local capacity and infrastructure for prevention by ensuring the delivery of training and technical assistance to communities, services now provided by the EPISCenter.

The Commonwealth's efforts have paid off. Communities adopting the CTC system in Pennsylvania built well-functioning coalitions and the majority have sustained them over time. Following CTC's principles, coalitions have primarily selected EBIs to prevent youth behavioral problems and have worked with local service providers to oversee implementation procedures. The evidence shows that EBIs have generally been implemented with fidelity and sustained over time, and high-quality implementation and sustainability are even more likely to occur in communities with high-functioning coalitions that support EBIs. Consistent with the CTC logic model, communities establishing high-functioning CTC coalitions and delivering EBIs have shown greater reductions in risk factors and behavioral health problems compared to communities that have not adopted the CTC system.

The Pennsylvania initiative can inform the efforts of other states and communities to foster community-based prevention. In particular, findings from this study provide guidance for how to build effective, stable coalitions and how to increase the use and high-quality implementation of EBIs. In addition, while the need to provide communities with training and technical assistance to increase their capacity to engage in successful community-based prevention has been articulated, the optimal methods for delivering such supports are still unclear [47]. The services provided by the EPISCenter can be a model for other states.

The contributions of the Pennsylvania initiative to prevention science are beginning to be recognized. The EPISCenter's model of training and technical provision has been promoted by many government and nonprofit agencies, incorporated into various preventive initiatives, and referenced in numerous research publications. For example, the EPISCenter has been identified as a Center of Excellence by the Annie E. Casey Foundation and as an outstanding criminal justice program by the National Criminal Justice Association. The EPISCenter has also been referenced by the Institute of Medicine, the

Pew-MacArthur Results First Initiative, and the Trust for America's Health (for a list of sources promoting the EPISCenter, see http://episcenter.psu.edu/about/recognitions-and-features).

Based largely on the experiences of Pennsylvania, Greenwood and Welsh [48] provide a set of state actions recommended to reduce juvenile crime. These steps include facilitating the collection of data on local levels of risk and protective factors, recommending at least a small number of EBIs for state-wide dissemination, establishing funding streams to support these EBIs, ensuring that EBIs are well implemented, creating state-wide resource centers to increase community capacity to prevent youth behavioral health problems, fostering champions to support these efforts, and engaging all relevant stakeholders in community-based prevention, especially organizations that control resources. As described by the authors, it is important that states emulate these practices because "state governments are a vital component to advancing evidence-based practice and to ensuring that efforts at the local level can flourish" [48].

As other states move forward in their efforts to facilitate effective community-based prevention, what does the future hold for Pennsylvania? The continuation of funds to support CTC coalitions and EBIs seems likely. In 2015, the Pennsylvania Commission on Crime and Delinquency provided funding for 15 new CTC coalitions, and the Evidence-based Programs Initiative continued to provide funds to support EBIs as of 2018. Communities have also been able to draw on funding through Medical Assistance (MA) to deliver intensive therapeutic EBIs like Functional Family Therapy, Multisystemic Therapy, and Treatment Foster Care Oregon, which allows a more diversified portfolio of funding options.

The Pennsylvania Commission on Crime and Delinquency continues to financially support the EPISCenter, and the EPISCenter staff continue to provide high-quality training and technical assistance to coalitions and agencies via individualized in-person, web-based, and telephone contacts, as well as group calls and meetings to foster learning communities among those implementing CTC and EBIs. They provide coalitions with training and technical assistance to help members complete the milestones and benchmarks associated with each of the five phases of CTC, including how to interpret data from the Pennsylvania Youth Survey and conduct needs assessments, select EBIs to match local needs, and monitor the implementation of these EBIs. Each month, coalition coordinators complete a written summary of the CTC milestones and benchmarks they have achieved, their accomplishments, and the challenges they have experienced. This information is reviewed during monthly phone calls with EPISCenter staff, and staff make site visits as needed to facilitate problem solving. Every quarter, in-person meetings are held in each of the five regions of the state to update CTC coalition coordinators and members on new resources available to coalitions and to provide training and technical support on issues of concern to coalitions. The EPISCenter also provides support directly to agencies implementing the EBIs affiliated with CTC coalitions, including descriptions and logic models of the set of EBIs they support, as well as tools for collecting, analyzing, and reporting data on implementation procedures and outcomes [6, 43].

According to its 2014 annual report (www.episcenter.psu.edu/ annualreport2014), the EPISCenter provided 63 coalitions with technical assistance in 2013–2014 and sponsored 44 CTC trainings for 872 attendees. In addition, 70 agencies received technical assistance to implement the 11 EBIs supported by the EPISCenter. In 2015, the Pennsylvania Commission on Crime and Delinquency contracted with the Center for Communities That Care at the University of Washington for EPISCenter staff to become certified as coaches for the web-streamed CTC training curriculum. The EPISCenter then begin working with 16 newly established and older CTC coalitions to use this web-streamed training system.

We anticipate that the technical assistance provided by the EPISCenter, along with the considerable infrastructure and support for prevention that has been built in Pennsylvania over the last two decades, will allow new CTC coalitions to be established, new EBIs to be implemented, and current prevention efforts to be maintained well into the future. We hope that other states will take seriously the lessons learned in Pennsylvania and follow the steps recommended by Greenwood and Welsh [48]. We are confident that if other states replicated the model used in Pennsylvania to promote CTC and EBI implementation and dissemination, they could reduce behavioral health problems at scale.

Moving Forward

What Is Needed to Successfully Implement CTC and Other Community-Based Prevention Systems?

The Future of CTC and Community-Based Prevention*

Our job across America is to create communities of choice, not of destiny, and create conditions for neighborhoods where the odds are not stacked against the people who live there.

PRESIDENT BARACK OBAMA, SPEAKING ABOUT
THE PROMISE NEIGHBORHOODS INITIATIVE

SCIENTISTS ARE INCREASINGLY calling for a more preventive approach to youth behavioral health problems, one that relies on EBIs to reduce the risk factors and increase the protective factors associated with these outcomes [1, 2]. Rather than responding to problems after they develop, prevention is recognized as a smarter, more efficient, and more cost effective solution, and one likely to have public support in an age of fiscal accountability [3–5]. At the same time, it is recognized that, to have a public health impact, EBIs must not only be disseminated at scale, but also implemented with quality [6, 7]. Further, EBIs must be a good fit for the local context, address relevant needs, be implemented with fidelity and sufficient reach, and be sustained over time [8, 9]. As CTC evaluations have shown, these aims can be achieved via a community-based prevention approach in which local stakeholders select and oversee the implementation of a coordinated set of EBIs that target risk and protective factors of concern to the community.

Community-based prevention is not yet the norm, but there is growing recognition of its potential to reduce behavioral health problems [4, 9–11]. In the last decade, multiple federal initiatives in the United States have supported community-based prevention efforts to reduce youth behavioral health problems. These include, for example, the Promise Neighborhoods initiative to promote youth educational outcomes (www2.ed.gov/programs/ promiseneighborhoods/index.html), the Centers for Disease Control's Communitywide Teen Pregnancy initiatives (www.cdc.gov/teenpregnancy/ prevent-teen-pregnancy/), the Strategic Prevention Framework to prevent youth substance use (www.samhsa.gov/capt/applying-strategic-prevention-framework), and the Department of Justice's support for community-oriented policing to reduce crime (www.cops.usdoj.gov/Default.asp?Item=65). Philanthropic institutions and businesses have also begun to endorse this approach and to partner with social and human service agencies, political leaders, and community stakeholders in a variety of collective impact initiatives aimed at solving diverse social problems [12].

Despite calls for increased community-based prevention, there are currently few well-developed, rigorously tested, effective community-based prevention systems available to communities. This book describes a model that is available, the Communities That Care prevention system, and demonstrates that it is possible to produce community-wide improvements in youth behavioral health problems using this community-based prevention system. As described in chapters 8 and 9, CTC's ability to positively transform community norms and services and reduce behavioral health problems have been demonstrated in a high-quality randomized controlled trial, the Community Youth Development Study (CYDS), and in a state-wide effectiveness trial in Pennsylvania.

Findings from the randomized study indicated that CTC communities experienced desired changes in community-level processes consistent with the CTC logic model (shown in Figure 1.2). All 12 communities that implemented CTC were able to establish representative and well-functioning coalitions during the first study year [13, 14]. Compared to members of prevention-oriented coalitions in the control communities, CTC coalition members reported engaging in more activities indicative of effective prevention planning and implementation, such as measuring risk and protective factors in their communities and implementing EBIs to address elevated risk factors [15, 16].

CTC communities also realized improvements in prevention-related attitudes, norms, and service delivery systems. According to interviews with key leaders and local prevention experts, CTC compared to control communities reported significantly greater levels of adoption of a science-based approach to prevention in both the implementation and sustainability phases of the randomized trial [17–20]. These findings indicated that CTC communities had a greater awareness of prevention science, conducted needs assessments, implemented EBIs to address prioritized risk and protective factors, and monitored their prevention activities. There were also greater increases in collaboration between individuals and organizations in CTC versus control communities in the first two years of the study [20], although this effect was not maintained in later years [17, 18]. Leaders in CTC communities were more likely than those in control communities to support the use of funds to prevent substance use and abuse, based on interviews conducted in 2007 [17] and 2011 [18]. They also reported a greater increase in community norms discouraging youth substance use from the start of the study through 2009 [18].

Also consistent with the CTC logic model, CTC communities were more likely than control communities to select, implement, and sustain EBIs. A process evaluation conducted in the 12 CTC communities during the implementation phase indicated that all coalitions selected EBIs to target their prioritized risk and protective factors, with an average of three programs implemented per community [21]. Different sets of interventions were selected by different communities, including school-based, after-school, and parent training interventions. These programs sought to change an array of the most prevalent risk factors identified in the CTC communities, including individual characteristics, as well as peer, family, school, and community factors. Reports from service providers in CTC sites indicated that the selected EBIs were well implemented and delivered in accordance with the models' specifications [21–23]. Furthermore, compared to control communities, CTC communities delivered a greater number of EBIs to greater numbers of participants and were more likely to sustain their programs after study funding had ended [24, 25].

The evaluation also indicated that use of the CTC system led to reductions in risk factors, improvements in protective factors, and the prevention of behavioral health problems among youth. According to data from a longitudinal panel of 4,407 youth surveyed in all 24 communities beginning in grade 5, those in the CTC communities reported significantly lower levels of the risk factors targeted by EBIs compared to those in control communities when in grade 7 [26] and grade 10 [27]. Youth in CTC communities also reported greater increases in protective factors in grade 8 compared to those in control communities [28], although these differences were not sustained through grade 10 [29]. CTC also had positive short- and long-term effects on the initiation of substance use, delinquency, and violence, beginning in grade 7 and continuing through age 21 [26, 27, 30–33]. Significant reductions in the current prevalence of illegal substances, delinquency, and violence for CTC compared to control group youth were found when students in the longitudinal panel were in middle school [33] and in grade 10 [27], but these outcomes were not maintained at later years.

Based on these results, as well as findings from the large-scale trial in Pennsylvania that support the feasibility and effectiveness of the CTC system (see chapter 9), CTC has received national recognition for its potential to help communities prevent youth behavioral health problems. The Blueprints for Healthy Youth Development initiative rates CTC as a "Promising" intervention (www.blueprintsprograms.com/), a designation reserved for interventions that have been well evaluated in at least one randomized trial or two quasi-experimental evaluations and demonstrated to show reductions in youth behavioral health problems. In addition, the Washington State Institute for Public Policy [34] has indicated that CTC produces statistically significant reductions in substance use and crime, and that it is has a positive benefit-to-cost ratio, returning $5.31 for every dollar spent. CTC has also been recognized as an evidence-based intervention by the Centers for Disease Control [2], Institute of Medicine [1], National Institute of Justice (www.crimesolutions. gov/ProgramDetails.aspx?ID=94), Substance Abuse and Mental Health Services Administration (www.nrepp.samhsa.gov/landing.aspx),[1] and U.S. Surgeon General [9].

Our hope is that this book will generate more knowledge and use of community-based prevention, particularly the Communities That Care prevention system. To that end, in the preceding chapters, we described the evolution, implementation, and evaluation of the CTC prevention system. The goal was to show that it is feasible to: (1) mobilize diverse community stakeholders; (2) increase the use and high-quality implementation of EBIs; (3) reduce youth behavioral health problems via community mobilization, EBI implementation, and the use of the Social Development Strategy; and (4) evaluate the effectiveness of a community-based prevention system using a rigorous randomized controlled research design and a community-based participatory research approach. Over the years, policymakers, practitioners, and scientists have all expressed enthusiasm about the CTC system, and they have asked many questions about why and how it works, as well as how this community-based system differs from other systems. We are pleased that this book has provided us with the opportunity to speak to these audiences, and we hope that readers will find the information useful in their own work with communities.

To help inspire such work, in this final chapter, we summarize what we consider to be the core components of CTC—that is, the elements which, together, are likely to produce community-wide reductions in youth behavioral health problems. As we described in previous chapters, these components have been part of other community-based prevention initiatives. However, many other community-based prevention systems have involved only a subset of the components, have not provided the proactive training and assistance needed to build community capacity to take these preventive actions that CTC provides, and/or have not evaluated the effectiveness of their models in rigorous research trials.

CTC is unique in having created, using community-based participatory research methods, a five-phase approach to community-based prevention that builds in training and technical assistance to communities. Furthermore, it has been demonstrated as effective in well-conducted studies. Because it is not easy to implement CTC or other community-based prevention systems, we summarize in this chapter the challenges most likely to be faced by communities when engaging in community-based prevention. We also provide recommendations for overcoming these difficulties. We conclude this chapter and the book by describing the recent developments in the implementation, evaluation, and dissemination of the CTC system.

Core Components of the CTC Prevention System

What accounts for CTC's desirable effects and makes CTC a worthwhile investment for communities? In our estimation, the CTC system has been able to impact youth behavioral health problems, and should be used widely by communities to achieve such outcomes, because:

- It is based on theories that specify the causes and development of youth behavioral health problems, particularly the Social Development Model, which states that youth development is affected by multiple risk and protective factors and that increasing youth bonds to positive social groups and environments by enhancing opportunities, skills, and recognition for pro-social involvement will foster positive development.
- It has been developed, evaluated, and refined over many years using a community-based participatory research approach that ensures that its principles and procedures can be implemented in communities and will be supported by local stakeholders.
- It brings together cross-sector community stakeholders to make prevention decisions and coordinate community prevention efforts.
- It builds community capacity to conduct needs assessments, by providing tools and coaching for community members in how to assess and prioritize risk factors, protective factors, and youth behavioral problems through epidemiological surveys of middle and high school youth.
- It builds community capacity to select, monitor, and evaluate EBIs—that is, interventions that target for change locally prioritized risk and protective

factors and that have been well evaluated and shown to reduce behavioral health problems.

- It has been evaluated and shown to reduce youth substance use, delinquency, and violence community-wide using rigorous methods, including a randomized controlled trial in 24 U.S. communities.

Theoretical Foundations

In order to be effective in reducing behavioral health problems, preventive interventions must be guided by theories of human development [35–37]. CTC has been developed following this principle, as described in chapter 2. Its focus on preventing the development of youth behavioral health problems draws from life-course developmental theories that describe human development as a sequenced set of events [38–40]. As individuals develop, they encounter new social contexts, each of which includes risk and protective factors that increase or decrease the likelihood of behavioral health problems. Life-course theories indicate that what happens at one stage of life has consequences for the next stage, and when risky contexts experienced early in life produce an early onset of behavioral health problems, the potential for subsequent problems is increased. Drawing from this theoretical perspective, CTC advocates that communities implement EBIs in multiple contexts to reduce risk factors and increase protective factors, and that they provide these interventions to children and adolescents to reduce the onset and escalation of problem behaviors.

The Social Development Model also recognizes that multiple risk and protective factors exist in children's lives [41]. The theory states that healthy development is most likely when youth are bonded to primary social groups (e.g., peers, teachers, parents, and community members) and when these groups promote healthy beliefs and clear standards for behavior. Drawing from this perspective, CTC recommends the implementation of EBIs that promote bonding, particularly interventions that provide opportunities for youth to be involved in social groups, that teach them the individual and social, emotional, and cognitive skills required to contribute to these groups, and that recognize young people for their skillful contributions.

Social disorganization theory has also guided the development of CTC [42]. This perspective recognizes that crime and related behavioral health problems are not evenly distributed across social areas but, rather, cluster in highly disorganized communities, such as communities in which residents do not have strong pro-social norms and lack collective efficacy [i.e., mutual trust and a willingness to use informal social control to prevent local problems; 42]. CTC helps to create more socially integrated and organized communities by encouraging all residents to provide pro-social opportunities, strengthen youth skills, recognize youth efforts, and communicate healthy standards for behavior. CTC also fosters broad-based, well-functioning coalitions that allow residents to work together to identify the problems that need to be addressed and to learn how to reduce these problems using EBIs.

Community-Based Participatory Research and Community Mobilization

As explained in chapter 2, community-based participatory research involves partnerships between scientists and communities [43–45]. A major goal of community-based participatory research is to build community capacity and empower community members to address their own needs, rather than relying on an outside "expert" to "fix" a community's "problem" [46, 47]. In this approach, the community is not an object of research inquiry but is, instead, an active and equitable collaborator [45]. Similarly, researchers and community members recognize and respect the knowledge, strengths, and resources of one another [43, 48].

In accordance with this approach, CTC recognizes that efforts to change communities should be owned and operated by community members. In the CTC system, community representation is guaranteed because all activities are planned and overseen by key leaders and broad-based coalitions. CTC provides coalitions with tools, guidance, and coaching to help coalitions enact all five phases of the CTC system. Following the Social Development Model, CTC creates opportunities and provides skills for all stakeholders to be involved in the initiative. By participating in the CTC coalition, community members learn organizational skills to conduct meetings, set and accomplish goals, make sound decisions based on evidence, and recognize accomplishments. Stakeholders' involvement in the CTC coalition should not only build community members' skills but also help them become more attached to their communities and more invested in the prevention of youth behavioral health problems. Also following the Social Development Model, CTC encourages all adults in the community to directly encourage youth bonding by employing the Social Development Strategy. In doing so, they promote norms that discourage problem behaviors and encourage positive behaviors, and in their daily activities, they provide youth with the opportunities, skills, and recognition necessary to foster bonding.

Although the CTC system provides community members with a structured process to enable community-based prevention, coalitions are empowered to decide how, exactly, they will implement each phase of the system. For example, communities decide on the number and representation of individuals and groups that will make up their coalitions, who will fill leadership positions, and how the coalitions will operate. In addition, coalitions use epidemiological data to prioritize the needs that they consider to be most important, determine which EBIs will be implemented to address these needs, and decide how these services will be delivered. The CTC system is built on the premise that different communities will have different needs and that different EBIs will be selected in different communities depending on these needs. It also recognizes that the social and political context, and the human and financial resources of a community, will affect the number and types of EBIs to be implemented. Coalitions are guided to adopt EBIs that are the best fit for their community.

As described in chapter 3, CTC has been developed in collaboration and consultation with community, state, and federal stakeholders. The CTC developers collected extensive process data in early pilot studies to determine CTC's implementation feasibility, and CTC was refined based on this information. For example, when communities asked for more guidance on how to implement CTC, the developers expanded the number of training workshops and created separate trainings to discuss how to create well-functioning coalitions, assess needs and resources, and select and implement EBIs. In addition, the CTC Youth Survey was developed when community members reported difficulty in collecting and analyzing local data on risk and protective factors. More recently, the CTC training and technical support system has been again revised. Recognizing the human and financial costs of multi-day training workshops delivered by CTC training staff, the CTC developers created web-streamed workshops that are facilitated by local coalition coordinators in multiple, shorter sessions.

The feedback from communities has been invaluable in creating a system that can be understood and supported by local communities. Implementation research has indicated that interventions are more likely to be adopted and sustained if they are a good fit for the organization or community [49–51]. The evidence to date suggests that CTC is appealing to communities. It has been replicated in small towns and large urban areas in the United States, across the state of Pennsylvania, and in countries across the world.

Emphasis on the Adoption, High-Fidelity Implementation, and Sustainability of EBIs

Following the public health approach to disease prevention, prevention science stipulates that the best way to reduce youth behavioral health problems is to implement EBIs that reduce risk factors and increase protective factors [35, 52]. In the last few decades, many interventions have been developed, tested, and shown to reduce behavioral health problems, but these EBIs are not currently being utilized at a scale or quality sufficient to produce widespread change [53]. The lack of dissemination of EBIs in communities has been identified as the greatest challenge to achieving large-scale reductions in behavioral health problems [1, 4, 11, 54]. However, a solution has also been proposed, which is to build the capacity of local communities to learn about EBIs, be persuaded to use them, and sustain their use over time.

The CTC system does that. Drawing from Everett Rogers's [55] Diffusion of Innovations theory (see chapter 2), CTC outlines a five-phase approach to prevention that begins by raising community awareness of the existence and importance of EBIs and culminates in the adoption and sustained use of EBIs by coalitions. As shown in Figure 1.1 and described in section two, the five phases include: (1) *Get Started*: assessing and enhancing readiness for community-based prevention, (2) *Get Organized*: engaging key community leaders and forming a prevention-oriented coalition, (3) *Develop a Profile*: assessing community needs and resources, (4) *Create a Plan*: selecting EBIs which address needs and fill gaps in resources, and (5) *Implement and Evaluate*: implementing EBIs and monitoring their delivery to ensure fidelity and reach.

The emphasis on selecting EBIs that target prioritized risk and protective factors and on implementing these interventions with fidelity and sustaining them over time distinguishes CTC from some other community-based approaches and likely contributes to its ability to reduce youth behavioral health problems. For example, some coalition-based prevention systems, like the *Fighting Back* initiative [56] have not required coalitions to use EBIs to reduce targeted behavioral problems. Coalitions that rely on untested and/or ineffective strategies to prevent youth and adult substance use have not been demonstrated to achieve significant impacts on youth behavioral problems [57]. Similarly, when CTC has been implemented in countries with few EBIs, substantial reductions in youth behavioral outcomes have not been realized [58]. In the Community Youth Development Study, the randomized efficacy trial, CTC communities adopted and sustained a greater number of EBIs than did control communities [15, 16, 24, 25]. In addition, the greater adoption of a science-based approach to prevention, including the use of EBIs, mediated the impact of CTC implementation on youth behavioral health problems [59].

Building Community Capacity to Prevent Youth Behavioral Health Problems via the Provision of Training and Technical Assistance

Community-based prevention efforts are, by design, intended to be implemented by community members. However, many local stakeholders do not have extensive knowledge of prevention science, including how to create and sustain healthy coalitions, conduct needs assessments, select and monitor EBIs, and evaluate the effectiveness of their activities. Training and technical assistance are recommended to provide community members with these skills and increase the likelihood that coalitions will reduce behavioral health problems [60–62].

The CTC system provides a structured process, multiple training workshops, and technical assistance to build coalitions' capacity to engage in effective community-based prevention. The CTC system breaks down a challenging and long-term goal (i.e., the reduction of youth behavioral health problems) into a series of more manageable goals by outlining a five-phased approach to prevention with specific milestones and benchmarks that should be achieved in each phase. This structure allows coalitions to achieve "small wins" [63] as they work toward their final goal.

The provision of training and coaching also help to ensure that coalitions can successfully implement the CTC system. As noted in other studies [6, 53], when implementation challenges are not identified or addressed, intervention effectiveness can be compromised [64, 65]. In the efficacy trial of CTC, technical assistance providers (i.e., CTC coaches) worked closely with coalition coordinators to help them solve challenges that arose during CTC implementation, and all 12 communities successfully enacted all five phases of the system [13, 21]. Similarly, in the Pennsylvania effectiveness trial, members of the first cohorts to receive state funding to adopt CTC identified the need for technical support to help them implement the CTC system with fidelity [66]. In response, Pennsylvania built a comprehensive and innovative system for technical assistance, and CTC coalitions in this state have been relatively successful in sustaining their coalitions [67] and their EBIs [68].

Rigorous Research Evaluation

Chapter 3 summarized the stages of research evaluation, which progress from early pilot studies to assess implementation feasibility, to efficacy trials to determine effectiveness, to effectiveness trials to examine outcomes when interventions are implemented in more naturalistic conditions, and culminating in dissemination trials to identify the factors that impede or facilitate widespread use of an intervention. Prevention science standards of evidence advocate that interventions only be widely disseminated after all of these types of research have been conducted [69]. Multiple evaluations allow interventions to be tested under different conditions and with different populations, which helps establish the generalizability of their effects. Moreover, when effects are replicated across studies, there is more evidence that the intervention produced the effects and that they are not due to chance.

The CTC developers have ensured that the CTC prevention system has been well evaluated. CTC was developed and first tested for feasibility in small pilot studies. Once its basic components were established, it was evaluated in a large-scale study conducted in Pennsylvania. The fact that CTC has also been evaluated in a randomized controlled trial (the Community Youth Development described in chapter 8), is especially notable. Few community-based prevention systems have been evaluated in a randomized experiment, despite the fact that randomized trials are recommended by the Society for Prevention Research's Standards of Evidence [69] because they are one of the most rigorous methods for establishing intervention effectiveness. CTC has a large and well-developed research base, and its rigorous evaluation history and ability to produce community-wide reductions in youth behavioral problems make it a strong candidate for scaling up in communities.

Challenges of Community-Based Prevention and Recommendations for Addressing Them

Assisting communities to implement the CTC system has increased our appreciation for the challenges associated with community-based prevention. Although the challenges we discuss in this section have been reported by others, what is notable is that many of the barriers faced by coalitions participating in the randomized efficacy trial were overcome. We suspect that success is due to the training and technical assistance provided by CTC coaches, which helped coalitions to identify problems early on and to take action to address these problems. Nonetheless, some challenges, such as increasing the reach of universal parent training programs, were less amenable to change [13, 21]. In this section, we identify the challenges we view as most likely to arise when implementing CTC and similar community-based prevention systems, and we provide recommendations for local, state, and federal practitioners and policymakers to reduce these barriers and enhance the high-quality implementation and effectiveness of community-based prevention.

Generating and Sustaining Support From Stakeholders

Engaging stakeholders in community-based prevention efforts is a necessary but often difficult task [70], and in the CTC efficacy trial, recruiting key leaders and building a diverse coalition were some of the most challenging tasks faced in the first year of CTC adoption [13]. Preexisting political or personal conflicts can impede efforts to recruit community members from all necessary sectors, and individuals will have competing interests and time constraints that can limit their involvement and jeopardize their ongoing participation [71–73].

There is no easy solution to this problem, and coalitions must be prepared to spend time and exert effort to create and maintain a diverse, active membership. Coalition leaders and other influential community members (i.e., champions) will need to draw upon and/or build new relationships when recruiting the stakeholders they deem necessary for success. The mission and goals of the coalition must be clear and mutually agreed upon so that new and continuing members support the vision and understand how they can contribute to it [72, 74]. Feedback from CTC communities has also indicated that it is important that coalitions create workgroups that are responsible for completing the milestones and benchmarks. This structure holds all members accountable for prevention activities and helps reduce the burden on coalition staff or particular coalition members.

The CTC system considers a full-time coalition coordinator to be necessary for coalition effectiveness. Without a dedicated staff person, prevention tasks may not be completed and mission drift may occur. It may take time to find the right individual to fulfill this role, given that coalition coordinators must possess a range of skills, especially interpersonal skills that will allow them to recruit members and delegate tasks. Coalitions also benefit from having clearly identified leaders (i.e., chairs and co-chairs). They will need to seek out individuals who have credibility in the community, as well as those who can defuse conflicts, ensure democratic decision making, provide meaningful opportunities for members to participate, and recognize members' contributions [75, 76]. All these practices help to build group cohesion and reduce turnover [77].

Conducting Comprehensive Prevention Needs Assessments

CTC and some other community-based prevention systems require that coalitions conduct needs assessments in order to select EBIs that will address the particular needs of the community. Needs assessments are usually based on information recorded in administrative records or reported by local youth and/or adults. In addition to the challenges and costs associated with collecting such data, the data can be difficult to analyze, particularly when the data sources provide discrepant information due to differences in how, when, and where the information was collected [78]. Coalition members may also disagree on how to interpret the findings and on the needs to be prioritized [60, 62].

In our experience, the administration of the CTC Youth Survey is the optimal way to facilitate local needs assessments. The CTC Youth Survey is a school-based survey designed to collect reliable and valid data on youth behaviors, as well as a comprehensive set of risk and protective factors shown to predict multiple behavioral health problems. The survey can be administered in school classrooms in about 50 minutes, making it a quick and inexpensive way of gathering data, especially compared to household-based surveys. In the CTC system, the survey is conducted every two years with a large proportion of middle and high school students. It is the main source of data used by coalitions to prioritize their needs and to assess the impact of their efforts over time.

Developed with input from state policymakers and local community members, the survey provides an easy-to-understand comparison of risk and protective factors reported by youth across multiple grades (e.g., see Figure 5.5). A common metric was created to identify the percentage of youth considered most at risk for problem behaviors and least protected. This methodology allows coalition members to more easily scan their data, identify the risk factors that are most elevated and the protective factors that are most depressed, and prioritize the factors that should be addressed by EBIs.

Feedback from communities has indicated that it can be difficult for coalitions to obtain school district permission to administer the survey. To address this challenge, coalitions have found it helpful to enlist the help of their champions, key leaders, and coalition members. They should ask those who have relationships with school leaders to communicate the importance of the survey and request that it be administered in local schools. Another approach for coalitions in the United States is to lobby state administrators to regularly implement the CTC Youth Survey in schools across the state. Several U.S. state governments currently administer portions or all of the CTC Youth Survey to measure state and local levels of risk, protection and behavioral health outcomes (see chapter 5). Some of these states provide data and reports to participating schools summarizing the responses of their students, often with comparisons to statewide data. States that provide for survey administration, as well as the analysis and reporting of local school survey data, greatly increase the ability of community coalitions to conduct comprehensive prevention needs assessments.

Increasing the Adoption and Implementation Fidelity of EBIs

EBI implementation is a core component of CTC, but the use of EBIs is not the norm in communities [53]. Even when they adopt EBIs, they often do not implement them with fidelity, but may instead make changes to an intervention's content, length, method of delivery, or targeted participants [79, 80]. Further, communities often fail to deliver programs to a large enough proportion of the eligible population to achieve community-wide reductions in behavioral health problems. Community members often wish to target the youth and families considered to have the greatest need. As a result, it can be difficult to convince stakeholders to provide universal services to a large segment of the population. Although reaching higher risk populations is important, the prevention paradox also makes clear that the majority of behavioral health problems are found among moderate- and lower risk populations, meaning that these groups must also receive prevention services to achieve population-level reductions in behavioral health problems [81, 82].

CTC was designed to increase the adoption, reach, and high-quality implementation of EBIs in communities. Although evaluations have indicated that CTC increases the use of well-implemented EBIs, it is not easy for communities to achieve this goal. Some of the international evaluations of CTC have found coalitions unable to adopt EBIs because they are not available in the particular country in which CTC is being implemented [83–85]. It has taken time to develop and test preventive interventions and accumulate evidence of their effectiveness in the United States. There has been less progress in the development and testing of interventions in other countries, especially low-income nations, and fewer programs typically exist which have been evaluated in rigorous trials and shown to decrease youth behavioral health problems [11, 86]. The scientific training and financial resources required to develop and test interventions may be lacking in these nations, and the prevention infrastructure needs to be built to allow for the dissemination of EBIs [87].

Nonetheless, Gregor Burkhart [85] reports that the adoption of the CTC system has helped advance the development and testing of EBIs in European nations. In Croatia, for example, CTC trainers have added a "pre-Phase 1" training to the CTC system to educate community key leaders and stakeholders about the importance of evaluation and the existence of EBIs, and they have assisted prevention program developers to further develop and evaluate their interventions. Demand for EBIs by CTC coalitions has also led researchers to develop national registries of EBIs in Germany and the Netherlands [85].

In terms of implementation fidelity, the main challenge faced in CTC communities participating in the Community Youth Development Study was meeting their recruitment goals when implementing universal parent training interventions. The lack of participation is a problem because it can undermine coalition efforts to produce a community-wide impact on risk and protective factors in the family domain. Recruitment problems are not specific to CTC. Other research has noted that it can be difficult to engage families in parent training programs [88–91]. Parents may not perceive a need for services, especially if their children are not currently having problems. They may avoid programs for fear of being labeled or stigmatized. They may lack the time or financial means to attend sessions. Or, they may not have confidence in the organizations providing parenting workshops to advise them on how to raise their children [88, 89, 91].

In the randomized efficacy trial of CTC, communities tried a variety of strategies to overcome parental resistance to participation. They created recruitment materials that emphasized the positive benefits of participation for all families, minimized common barriers to participation by providing child care and food at sessions, and asked previous participants to recruit others via word-of-mouth [21]. These strategies had limited effectiveness, however, and none of the 11 coalitions that implemented parent training programs was able to fully achieve its recruitment goals.

To increase participation in parent training programs, program developers might use community-based participatory research strategies to gather information from parents about their needs and preferences and then create intervention recruitment and delivery approaches that address these concerns [90]. Some have designed interventions that can be self-administered using phone or web-based technology, which can reduce some of the physical barriers to participation (e.g., transportation to services), provide more flexibility in use, and reduce costs to participants. The eHealth Familias Unidas parenting program is an example currently being tested in an experimental trial in primary health care [92, 93]. Community coalitions can also help organizations consider how to combine the delivery of parent training interventions with other services that are more commonly used by parents, and/or to implement programs in settings that are regularly accessed by families, such as pediatric primary health care and family medicine settings [91]. Laurel Leslie and colleagues [91] have argued that low parental recruitment rates caused by problems of stigma and lack of confidence in providers of parenting programs could be overcome by providing these EBIs through pediatric primary healthcare settings [see also 94].

To guard against implementation challenges, CTC and some other community-based prevention systems advocate that coalitions create data monitoring systems—that is, tools and systems which allow them to regularly collect data to determine if EBIs are being delivered with fidelity and at sufficient scale to the intended population [54]. These systems can be challenging to set up and utilize. CTC coalitions typically support a variety of EBIs, each with its own requirements, and it can be difficult to create a comprehensive surveillance system that can be applied to all EBIs.

The EPISCenter in Pennsylvania provides useful guidance and support to help CTC coalitions determine how they will monitor an array of EBIs and engage in continuous quality improvement to ensure the high-quality implementation of these interventions. As described in chapter 9 [and in 95], research staff at the EPISCenter have created specific tools (e.g., short guides, logic models) to ensure that community members understand the requirements of all EBIs that are eligible for state funding. Staff provide individualized and group-based technical assistance to coalitions and service providers to help them set up monitoring systems, to regularly collect data on implementation processes, and to analyze these data and make changes to EBI delivery to address implementation challenges. This type of assistance facilitates EBI delivery and effective community-based prevention.

Ensuring Adequate Financial Support for Coalitions and EBIs

Another challenge typically faced by communities is a lack of funding to support prevention coalitions and EBIs. It is possible for coalitions to raise funds to support community-based prevention [e.g., see findings from the PROSPER intiative: 96, 97], but doing so requires significant time and effort. Without more funding dedicated to prevention, coalition [67, 98, 99] and EBI sustainability are challenging [100–103].

In the United States, some federal funding is available to support community-based coalitions with the broad mission of preventing youth behavioral health problems. For example, the Drug Free Communities Support Program and the Strategic Prevention Framework provide funds for coalitions focused on preventing substance use. The Centers for Disease Control has provided funding to coalitions to reduce violence via the Centers for Excellence grants.

Federal agencies have also provided funds to support EBIs. For example, federal initiatives have supported the delivery of mentoring (e.g., large-scale funding from the Office of Juvenile Justice and Delinquency Prevention), nurse-home visitation (e.g., the U.S. Department of Health and Human Service's Maternal, Infant, and Early Childhood Home Visiting program), and early childhood education (e.g., Head Start programs administered by the Office of the Administration for Children and Families and the U.S. Department of Education's early learning initiative) programs. In addition, the Office of Adolescent Health has provided funds to implement teen pregnancy prevention programs. Although these funds are not provided directly to coalitions, if a community-based coalition is broad based, it should include organizations that are eligible to draw upon these funding sources.

The Results First initiative (www.pewtrusts.org/en/projects/pew-macarthur-results-first-initiative) is also helping to promote and find funds for EBI implementation in the United States. This project provides assistance to administrators of state systems (e.g., criminal justice, education, health, etc.) to evaluate their current spending on publicly funded programs, reduce implementation of programs that lack evidence of effectiveness, and increase the use of EBIs to improve a range of public health problems. This effort does not require the use of local coalitions to guide EBI adoption and implementation. However, coalitions located in states that have participated in the Results First initiative should benefit from the increased awareness of the importance of EBIs among their state administrators, and the organizations involved in these groups may have greater access to state funds to implement EBIs.

In addition to these funding sources, what other stable funding streams can be used to support community-based prevention? In the randomized evaluation of CTC, two coalitions were able to draw upon city funds to support their prevention coalitions and to provide for the salary of the CTC coordinator. Local government funds tend to be fairly stable, and if the coordinator's position can be written into the annual city or county budget, the coalition has a much better chance of sustaining itself. In terms of EBI funding, many CTC coalitions were able to convince their school districts to support the delivery of school-based EBIs once the research funds had ended. This funding stream is a logical one, especially since schools are required to teach health-related curricula.

As described in chapter 9, Pennsylvania provides a promising model for how state systems can provide long-term funding of coalitions as well as EBIs. Influential champions in this state were able to elicit collaboration and funding to support CTC adoption from multiple state agencies, including those responsible for juvenile justice (i.e., the Commission on Crime and Delinquency and the Juvenile Court Judges' Commission), health (i.e., the Department of Human Services) and education. Funding from these agencies allowed local communities to receive training and technical assistance in the CTC system. In addition, they made possible a separate funding stream to support EBI adoption and implementation.

Utah, Michigan, and Colorado are also providing state resources to support CTC coalition formation and to build CTC coaching and technical assistance infrastructures within their states. If these types of approach are replicated in other states, community-based prevention will be greatly enhanced.

A different approach has been used in Massachusetts to support community-based prevention efforts. In 2012, the state created a Prevention and Wellness Trust Fund that provides community-based partnerships with funds to reduce behavioral health problems, including tobacco use and substance use/abuse (www.mass.gov/eohhs/gov/departments/dph/programs/community-health/prevention-and-wellness-fund/). This type of initiative could be replicated in other states to encourage the local adoption and implementation of EBIs to prevent problems and promote healthy behaviors.

Some prevention coalitions have found funding for EBIs through the Prevention and Public Health Fund included in the Affordable Care Act. This fund included Community Transformation grants to local and state governments to improve public health [9]. Another potential source of support is the "community benefit requirement" that nonprofit hospitals conduct community health needs assessments at least every three years, involve community representatives served by the hospital in the needs assessment, and demonstrate that they are addressing identified needs with health services. Partnerships with prevention coalitions can fulfill these requirements. For example, the Franklin County CTC coalition in Massachusetts received a three-year grant from the community benefit program of its local hospital to support CTC coalition staffing and the delivery of the Life Skills Training drug prevention program in middle schools.

Community-Based Prevention in Disorganized and Under-Resourced Communities

Community-based prevention is especially challenging in under-resourced communities, those with limited financial and human capital, unstable populations, and multiple public health problems that need to be addressed [104,105]. These communities are often the least ready to undertake community-based prevention because they may have a history of failed collaborations, there may be a lack of trust between residents and/or leaders, and there may be few well-resourced organizations available to implement EBIs.

We know no easy solutions to these problems, but their presence does not mean that CTC and other community-based prevention systems cannot or should not be implemented. In the CTC system, communities spend significant time in Phases 1 and 2 assessing their readiness to undertake a collaborative approach to prevention that requires community support, needs assessments, and the implementation of EBIs. All communities must spend adequate time identifying readiness issues, and if significant readiness challenges are apparent, they should delay the adoption of the CTC system until these obstacles can be at least partially overcome. For example, community leaders and stakeholders may need to improve their relationships and build trust before moving ahead. Other research suggests that communities may want to start with small, manageable tasks that can be feasibly achieved in order to build capacity and generate enthusiasm prior to launching a larger community-based prevention effort like CTC [63].

Although the majority of the examples of CTC implementation we have cited in this book are drawn from the experiences of relatively stable communities, CTC has been successfully implemented in more disenfranchised and under-resourced communities. For example, CTC was adopted in Montbello, Colorado, in 2011 to support positive youth development and prevent youth violence (www.stepstosuccessmontbello.com/what-we-do/). Montbello is an urban section of Denver of about 30,000 residents with high rates of poverty and crime. The population is predominantly African American and Latino. Readiness problems were identified in Montbello and included limited financial resources, few existing EBIs, and some distrust of the researchers from the University of Colorado who were planning to provide the community with training and consultation in the CTC system. Yet, there was some support for CTC in the community, and University of Colorado staff were able to obtain funds from the Centers for Disease Control (via its Centers for Excellence grants) to launch CTC. Researchers and community members spent about

18 months in Phases 1 and 2 of the CTC system to nurture their relationship, build coalition capacity, and enhance community readiness prior to moving to undertaking the next phases.

These efforts have helped to ensure successful implementation of the CTC system in Montbello. The community established an advisory board of key leaders and a diverse coalition of community stakeholders. The coalition conducted a needs assessment by conducting household surveys of local youth and parents and implementing the CTC Youth Survey in schools. The coalition selected several school- and community-based EBIs to address their prioritized needs using the Blueprints for Healthy Youth Development website [106].

CTC has also been implemented in the Hazel Park neighborhood of East St. Paul, Minneapolis. The Hazel Park CTC effort has focused its efforts on youth attending one K–8 school with mostly low-income students from diverse racial/ethnic groups (primarily African American, Asian, and Latino youth), as well as youth attending a local Boys & Girls Club. The school principal serves as the CTC champion and works in partnership with researchers at the University of Minnesota. Consistent with the CTC system, a full-time coordinator has helped the coalition to implement all five phases of CTC [107]. However, in consultation with a CTC coach, some adjustments have been made to the system to respond to the community context. For example, faced with school resistance to implementing the full CTC Youth Survey, the coalition decided to remove some items from the survey and add some items to gather data on issues of local concern (e.g., youth experiences with discrimination). As another example, the coalition decided to rename the four risk factors prioritized during Phase 3 to use more positive language; for example, referring to "academic engagement" rather than "academic failure." They believed that doing so would avoid making community members feel shamed or judged and instead inspire more pride, investment, and involvement in the CTC coalition and imitative [107].

Similar to the Montbello, Colorado, implementation of CTC, the Hazel Park CTC effort reflects a successful model of community-based participatory research. It involves a partnership between local agencies and university researchers and efforts to ensure that the CTC system is compatible with and responsive to the unique challenge and resources of these communities. As Brady and colleagues note [107], the modifications made in Hazel Park preserved the integrity of the CTC system, but also helped ensure that the CTC activities were responsive to the local context and well received by the community, which is especially critical in "communities whose residents are experiencing historical and current inequities relative to the broader society."

The Future of CTC

A goal of this book is to promote greater use of the CTC system in communities. Over time, different approaches have been used to disseminate CTC, all of which have attempted to disseminate the system in an efficient and cost-effective manner while still providing adequate training and technical assistance to ensure CTC implementation fidelity, prevent the development of youth behavioral problems, and promote positive youth outcomes. In the first pilot study in Washington, faculty at the Washington State University Cooperative Extension offices delivered technical assistance to CTC coalitions [108]. The program developers selected these staff because they were located across the state in the same communities as the coalitions that they would advise, which provided ease of contact, familiarity with the local context, and legitimacy with stakeholders. However, staff varied in the skills needed to provide technical assistance and in their commitment to promoting the coalitions' work. Moreover, the developers had little authority to influence staff activities since they were located in a different academic institution. To remedy this problem, and to be able to work more directly with communities, CTC developers, Drs. Hawkins and Catalano, created the CTC training materials and technical assistance system and provided supports to communities through their company, Developmental Research and Programs (DRP).

As demand for CTC grew, particularly during the Title V and Pennsylvania initiatives, the CTC developers recognized that a commercial curriculum distribution company with experience in marketing, sales, and distribution could enhance distribution of the CTC system. The Channing Bete Company purchased CTC in 1999 and distributed it through 2005. At that time, the company determined that it could not disseminate CTC at scale and return an adequate profit, given the levels of training and technical assistance required to ensure full implementation of the CTC system in communities.

In 2005, the Substance Abuse and Mental Health Services Administration (SAMHSA) purchased CTC from the Channing Bete Company. This change offered great promise for CTC dissemination, as SAMHSA placed the CTC training materials in the public domain and made all of the CTC materials available on its website free of charge to communities. SAMHSA planned to provide training and technical assistance via its regional Centers for the Application of Prevention Technologies (CAPT). However, this vision was never realized. SAMHSA did not create a formal system to provide communities with ongoing support for CTC implementation. At the same time, the randomized evaluation of CTC was demonstrating positive results, and the

CTC developers received repeated requests from communities and states to provide training in the CTC system.

These requests led the CTC developers to again take responsibility for the dissemination of the CTC system. They created a new institution, the Center for Communities That Care, located at their home research institution, the Social Development Research Group at the School of Social Work at the University of Washington. In 2013, with support from the National Institute on Drug Abuse, they developed a web-streamed delivery system for CTC training workshops. As mentioned in chapter 3, this new system (CTC Plus) was designed to facilitate CTC implementation and address several problems reported by communities.

The training system used in the Community Youth Development Study required certified CTC trainers to make site visits to deliver trainings of one to three days each, for a total of nine days of training. That method was cost- and time-intensive, and it was difficult for coalitions to ensure attendance at the trainings given the time commitment required of volunteers. The web-streamed system, in contrast, relies on local coalition coordinators to facilitate the training workshops, after they receive a three-day facilitation training that introduces them to the system and builds their skills to deliver the material. The content has been broken into modules that are usually delivered in two- to four-hour workshops for the community coalition. Coalition members who miss workshops or who want to review the training content can access the materials any time via the CTC website (www.communitiesthatcare.net/). The website also provides communities interested in adopting CTC with information about the system, its effectiveness, and contact information for CTC coaches located at the Center for Communities That Care.

Also to promote CTC dissemination, CTC developers have begun working with several states to develop a state-wide CTC implementation model similar to that used in Pennsylvania. In this model, state staff persons receive the three-day facilitation training followed by a two-day coaching training from the Center for Communities That Care. Then, in tandem with a certified coach from the Center for CTC, the state staff person provides technical assistance to a local community to support all five phases of CTC. This model of co-facilitation of CTC builds the skills while providing the new coach with ongoing support. As in the standard CTC system, the state CTC coach has two to three monthly phone calls with a local CTC coordinator to review CTC implementation progress and to help the coordinator facilitate the web-streamed training system. Once the state staff person completes these steps, he or she becomes a certified CTC coach and can then deliver TA to local CTC coalitions across that state, without assistance from certified CTC coaches from the

University of Washington. This process builds prevention capacity at both state and local levels and is likely to be cost effective.

To date, Pennsylvania, Utah, and Michigan have all had state staff persons certified as CTC coaches, and these staff are now using the web-streamed CTC PLUS modules with CTC coalitions in their states. Pennsylvania has begun to implement the web-streamed workshops in 16 communities, Utah has begun implementation with 20 communities, and Michigan is supporting 15 communities in the Upper Peninsula. Following the legalization of recreational marijuana use, the Colorado Department of Public Health and Environment adopted CTC statewide and is funding 48 communities to implement CTC. The state currently provides funds to communities to use the web-streamed workshops and to support the salary of local CTC coalition coordinators, and they help CTC coalitions to find funds to support the EBI delivery. Colorado plans to have state staff persons become certified as CTC coaches.

The Evidence2Success project, funded by the Annie E. Casey Foundation (see www.aecf.org/work/evidence-based-practice/evidence2success/), is another CTC initiative that is designed to integrate local prevention efforts with state systems. Evidence2Success uses CTC as its operating system and adds components that seek to promote greater involvement of public agencies concerned with education, child welfare, and juvenile justice. In this project, leaders of these systems commit to a collaborative, evidence-based approach to promote healthy youth development and prevent youth behavioral health problems. Together with community members, they support the administration of school-based surveys, adapted from the CTC Youth Survey, and the prioritization of risk and protective factors to be targeted by EBIs. With the assistance of financial professionals, administrators analyze the types of services that are currently funded by their agencies and agree to shift some of their investments from other activities to EBIs. In this manner, existing infrastructures and funding streams are utilized for community-based prevention, which should increase the dissemination of EBIs, ensure they target local needs, and improve their sustainability. Evidence2Success is being piloted in six U.S. cities to determine its feasibility and potential impact on youth behavioral health problems.

Progress has also been made in recent years in the international dissemination of CTC, particularly in Europe (for example, see www.ctc-network.eu/nano.cms/effective-programmes). Researchers from Austria, Croatia, Cyprus, Germany, the Netherlands, Sweden, and the United Kingdom are collaborating to create materials and tools to facilitate and standardize CTC implementation across Europe [109]. This work includes the development of a CTC Implementation Guide tailored to the needs of European communities and nations. Group members are also conducting a cross-national comparison of findings from administrations of the CTC Youth Survey across their home countries [110].

The European project has also involved a review of the evaluation literature using the standards of evidence promoted by the Blueprints for Healthy Youth Development to identify EBIs available for replication in Europe [111]. As of 2017, nearly 100 programs have been identified. To facilitate use of these EBIs, the European Monitoring Centre for Drugs and Drug Addiction (EMCDDA) has developed a website similar to the Blueprints registry that provides information about the EBIs (www.emcdda.europa.eu/best-practice/xchange_en). Together, these efforts should substantially enhance the ability of coalitions in Europe to implement CTC with quality and implement EBIs to target local needs.

One European city that has benefited from the international development of CTC is Malmö, the third largest city in Sweden. The City Council of Malmö decided that the CTC system would be adopted city-wide to organize its prevention work. The city started by implementing CTC in six communities, and it plans to create new CTC coalitions every 18th month until the entire city is reached. The city is committed to implementing CTC with fidelity, including ensuring that coalitions assess each community´s local needs and implement EBIs to address these needs. To promote implementation fidelity, the city has built its own capacity to train and coach CTC facilitators, has received training from developers in a number of effective programs, and has organized a "delivery unit" within the City Office to oversee the implementation work. The CTC process is linked to the overall budget process in Malmö.

The city of Malmö is also committed to promoting the Social Development Strategy in communities, hypothesizing that doing so can address low attachment to neighborhoods, a risk factor that has become elevated due to a large migration to the city of individuals from other countries. A high-quality implementation of the Social Development Strategy, with enough saturation in the communities, is secured by asking coalitions to write action plans that detail how the Social Development Strategy will be enacted, then having coalitions and technical assistance providers monitor delivery of these actions as they do when implementing EBIs. The University of Lund will evaluate the use of the Social Development Strategy in Malmö.

Outside of Europe, Australia has probably made the most progress in its implementation and evaluation of CTC. CTC has existed in this country since 1999, when a not-for-profit company was formed [Communities That Care (CTC) Ltd] to support CTC implementation and an Australian version of the CTC Youth Survey was designed and administered. The first Australian guide to EBIs was published in 2002, and this list is regularly updated and provides data on EBIs on a searchable website (http://nest.org.au/).

John Toumbourou and colleagues [112] conducted a quasi-experimental evaluation of the effectiveness of CTC in the first four localities that completed the CTC process. They used multi-level modeling to evaluate annual trends in substance use reported by youth (N=41,328) on the CTC Youth Survey conducted between 1999 and 2015 in the four CTC sites. Compared with youth residing in 105 comparison localities that did not implement CTC, those in the CTC sites had significantly steeper annual reductions in any lifetime alcohol [Adjusted Odds Ratio (AOR) 0.93; 95% Confidence Intervals [CI] 0.92 - 0.94], tobacco (AOR=0.96; CI: 0.95 - 0.97), and marijuana use (AOR=0.96; CI: 0.94–0.98) and delinquent behavior (AOR=0.98; CI: 0.96–0.99).

In the second stage of the Australian dissemination, with funding from a Linkage grant from the Australian Research Council (ARC), 28 communities were matched based on socioeconomic disadvantage, urban/ nonurban location, and population size. The pairs were then randomly assigned to implement the CTC system (n =14) or to serve as control communities (n = 14). In 2012–2013, the CTC communities completed Phases 1 (*Get Ready*) and 2 (*Get Organized*) of the CTC system; conducted a social marketing campaign that included brief communications to parents and adolescents to encourage adolescents to abstain from drinking; and monitoring of and feedback to liquor outlets to reduce sales of alcohol to minors. An evaluation of these efforts reported a 10% relative reduction in past-month adolescent alcohol use in the CTC compared to control communities and significantly greater intentions to not use alcohol among youth in the CTC communities [113]. Based on these findings, the Australian National Health and Medical Research Council (NHMRC) has funded an extension of this evaluation, including a cost-benefit analysis. From 2016 to 2020, the 14 CTC communities will complete all five phases of CTC and scale up their alcohol prevention interventions.

Progress in disseminating CTC in other countries, particularly those lacking a well-developed menu of EBIs, has been more limited. Nonetheless, CTC developers are working with researchers in other nations to develop a set of standards that can guide CTC implementation internationally. They are also involved in some pilot studies to evaluate the implementation and effectiveness of CTC in some of these nations, including Australia, Chile, and Colombia.

In the United States, analysis of the long-term effects of CTC on youth participating in the Community Youth Development Study is ongoing. In 2016, participants in the longitudinal cohort were aged 23, on average. At this age, participation in criminal behavior tends to decline, but other behavioral health problems, such as substance use/abuse and depression, are still occurring, and information from the longitudinal cohort will be analyzed to examine whether or not respondents in CTC communities are reporting lower levels of these behaviors compared to those originally in control communities.

The Future of Community-Based Prevention

The expansion of CTC in recent years has been facilitated by advances in prevention science, as well as the support for evidence-based interventions and community-based prevention. Prohibitions of the words "evidence-based" and "science-based" in budgetary proposals to be submitted by agencies during the Trump administration (in 2018) challenge the very foundations of the idea of good government in which tax dollars are spent most efficiently to achieve desired outcomes. Now is the time to make a significant investment in healthy youth development and community-based prevention. As stated in *Unleashing the Power of Prevention* [4], "we stand at the threshold of a new age of prevention." We now have the knowledge and tools needed to make significant reductions in youth behavioral health problems. Now more than ever we require the political will to invest in sufficient prevention infrastructure to assist communities, states, and nations to engage in successful prevention.

We all have a stake in preventing youth behavioral health problems. Until very recently, we largely worked in isolation from one another to address these concerns. Achieving significant community-wide reductions in these problems requires better cross-sector collaboration, even greater support for community-based prevention, and resources redirected toward prevention.

A decade ago, Farrington and Welsh [10] called for the United States to create one federal agency responsible for crime prevention—specifically, an agency that would promote the implementation of developmental prevention programs targeting risk and protective factors. Likewise, we advocate for the development of a federal youth development council to support and oversee the promotion of youth cognitive, behavioral, and affective health and the prevention of youth behavioral health problems. This agency would increase knowledge of and support for the implementation of evidence-based, preventive interventions that target the risk and protective factors predictive of behavioral health problems; help create systems to collect and analyze data on community needs, resources, and EBI implementation; and develop stable funding streams to support community-based prevention systems. We do not have to wait for the federal government to act, as illustrated by the leadership of state governments in Pennsylvania and Colorado. Those states have already institutionalized these functions in state agencies and support multiple CTC communities within their boundaries. Through these initiatives, these states can achieve population-level reductions in these problems [114]. We know more than we ever have about the effectiveness of prevention. Now is the time to make it happen.

Notes

CHAPTER 1

1. For a summary of CTC and its effects, see: www.communitiesthatcare.net/research-results/.
2. In the crime prevention literature, efforts to change the physical environment of places, neighborhoods, or cities to make crimes more difficult to commit and easier to detect are sometimes considered community-based prevention strategies [78]. Following Farrington and Welsh [35], we classify such actions as situational crime prevention, rather than community-based prevention, since they do not typically try to alter community-level risk and protective factors.
3. For a list of the milestones and benchmarks associated with each of the five phases of CTC, see the "Tools for Community Leaders" guide [114] at: www.communitiesthatcare.net/getting-started/.

CHAPTER 3

1. Some researchers recommend against a linear approach to evaluation and instead advocate that research should *begin* with dissemination evaluation and examine implementation and effectiveness when the intervention is delivered in the real-world setting in which it is intended to be used [13, 25].
2. The CTC Youth Survey can be found at: www.communitiesthatcare.net/userfiles/files/2014CTCYS.pdf.
3. In fact, the CTC developers began planning an efficacy trial in the mid-1990s, following the early pilot evaluations in Washington and Oregon. However, they were not successful in securing the research funds necessary to rigorously evaluate the CTC system until 2002.

4. For a description of the web-streamed training workshops, see the CTC website: www.communitiesthatcare.net/.

CHAPTER 4

1. For example, individual-level readiness for change is considered essential to the success of therapeutic interventions intended to change individual behaviors [21], and organizational readiness has been shown to increase the likelihood that an agency will adopt a new EBI [20, 22–25].

2. These guides are written for a lay audience and provide information and planning tools for communities interested in the CTC system. They can be downloaded from the CTC website: www.communitiesthatcare.net/getting-started/. The website also provides information about how catalysts can contact a CTC coach to find out more about the CTC system.

3. For a sample position description listing the preferred credentials, skills, and responsibilities of a CTC community coordinator (referred to as the *mobilizer* in Pennsylvania), see www.episcenter.psu.edu/CTC/tools.

4. CTC coaches from the Center for Communities That Care at the University of Washington, or individuals certified as coaches by the Center, currently provide coalition coordinators with technical assistance. Coordinators typically receive two to three calls per month from a CTC coach to discuss CTC implementation progress.

5. These quotes are from annual surveys of CTC coalition members participating in the Community Youth Development Study.

CHAPTER 5

1. Needs assessments can be performed by an organization; for example, to determine if an agency has adequate human and financial resources to implement an EBI or to identify challenges that may impede EBI adoption [14, 15]. They can also be done at a state level, to determine statewide levels of behavioral health problems and/or risk and protective factors (e.g., as used in the Strategic Prevention Framework State Incentive Grants to assess state levels of youth substance use and abuse; see www.samhsa.gov/spf). Correctional facilities also conduct needs assessments to identify the treatment needs of individual offenders, usually by documenting individuals' prior offenses and their exposure to risk and protective factors [16, 17]. Given the focus of this book on community-based prevention, this chapter describes needs assessment conducted by communities and/or coalitions to identify levels of behavioral health problems, risk factors, and protective factors that exist in a community.

2. We note, however, that the U.S. Substance Abuse and Mental Health Services Administration (SAMHSA) website (https://www.samhsa.gov/capt/applying-strategic-prevention-framework/step1-assess-needs) provides communities with useful information and guidance on how to gather and analyze data and prioritize needs related to substance use.

3. It should be noted that the Getting To Outcomes (GTO) model includes needs assessment as a first step in its system [14], and GTO provides explicit guidance to practitioners to assess needs (see www.rand.org/health/projects/getting-to-outcomes.html). GTO is a broader model than CTC that provides community-based organizations of various types with methods and tools to plan for, implement, and evaluate programs and policies to address public health issues of concern to the implementing organization.

4. This training also included information on how to conduct an assessment of the resources (i.e., interventions) already in place in the community to address risk and protective factors [53, 54]. This information subsequently became the focus of a separate training workshop, the Community Resource Assessment Training, which is described in chapter 6.

5. A copy of the CTC Youth Survey can be found at: www.communitiesthatcare.net/userfiles/files/2014CTCYS.pdf.

6. A detailed description of how the cut point methodology was developed is provided by Arthur et al. [69] and Briney et al. [70]. The cut point was derived by examining both the levels of risk and protective factors reported by survey respondents, and the relationship between the risk and protective factors and the behavioral health problems (specifically, substance use and delinquency) reported by these respondents. In the needs assessments conducted in CTC communities, coalitions do not select the risk and protective factors shown in research literature to be most strongly correlated with behavioral health problems, which are typically the factors that are most developmentally proximate to the outcome of interest (e.g., exposure to delinquent peers is one of the strongest predictors of adolescent delinquency). If this strategy were used, communities would be likely to overlook risk and protective factors that occur earlier in development (e.g., early academic failure or a lack of parental warmth), but which nonetheless predict later behavioral problems. The cut points used to report data from the CTC Youth Survey provide an ideal methodology for needs assessments, as they identify the proportion of youth in the community considered to be at risk for problems, based on their high exposure to risk factors which have been shown to predict problems, and their low exposure to protective factors which have been shown to mitigate against behavioral health problems.

7. As best we can determine, the following states include at least some of the risk and protective factor scales in their state-wide surveys: Arkansas, Colorado, Florida, Illinois, Indiana, Iowa, Maine, Michigan, Missouri, Nebraska, Oregon,

Washington, West Virginia, and Wyoming. However, not all of the factors included on the CTC Youth Survey are represented on these surveys; interested readers should compare the items/scales included on the CTC Youth Survey www.communitiesthatcare.net/userfiles/files/2014CTCYS.pdf) with those included in these state surveys.

8. The CTC Youth Survey asks students to report on the frequency with which they committed delinquent behaviors and used illegal substances. Although they can examine the frequency data, coalitions typically base their priorities using the prevalence data (i.e., the proportion of students reporting any delinquency/substance use) because their goal is to reduce behavioral health problems among all youth in the community.

9. For an example of a report provided in Pennsylvania, see: www.pccd.pa.gov/Juvenile-Justice/Pages/PAYS-for-2013---County-Reports-.aspx#.VxfZ_3rUdMQ.

10. For example, the Bach Harrison survey research group (www.bach-harrison.com/) prepares many of the reports used by the states that administer the CTC Youth Survey, and they can also be hired to provide such services to community coalitions that are located in other states.

CHAPTER 6

1. In January 2018, the U.S. federal government issued a press release stating that it is no longer supporting the development and use of the National Registry of Evidence-based Programs and Practices (NREPP), and that the registry is likely to be taken off the SAMHSA website.

2. Many other registries of interventions intended to reduce behavioral health problems exist. For example, the What Works Clearinghouse (http://ies.ed.gov/ncee/wwc/) developed by the Institute of Education Sciences reviews educational interventions, as does the Best Evidence Encyclopedia (www.bestevidence.org/). In addition, the California Evidence-Based Clearinghouse for Child Welfare (CEBC; www.cebc4cw.org/) reviews interventions for families involved with the child welfare system. The Washington State Institute for Public Policy also maintains a database of evidence-based interventions (www.wsipp.wa.gov/). The goal of this agency is to evaluate the effectiveness of a range of programs, practices, and policies and to calculate their financial costs and benefits in order to inform the selection of interventions by public agencies in Washington State.

3. For a detailed comparison of the standards used by a comprehensive set of registries of social and behavioral interventions, see Burkhardt et al. [24] and Means et al. [25]. In addition, Fagan and Buchanan [26] review in more detail the similarities and differences of the NREPP, Model Programs Guide/Crime Solutions, and Blueprints registries. Note that the discussion in this chapter compares criteria used to rate the effectiveness of prevention *programs*. The

Model Programs Guide/Crime Solutions apply different criteria to rate prevention *practices*, and Blueprints is expanding its review procedures to include prevention *policies*.

4. With the development of the web-streamed training curriculum, this workshop does not have to be accomplished in a single day, but can be delivered in multiple, shorter sessions. It can also be facilitated by coalition coordinators.

5. A challenge facing prevention science and community-based prevention is that many EBIs have never been evaluated to determine if they change targeted risk and protective factors. Most evaluations focus on assessing the main effects of an intervention on participants' behaviors, rather than assessing changes in risk and protective factors, which typically requires statistical methods for assessing mediation [81–84]. The Society for Prevention Research guidelines [13] recommend that evaluations include mediation analysis.

6. In the early versions of CTC, training in how to match prioritized needs with effective prevention strategies was provided in the same three-day workshop that covered needs and resources assessments. Based on coalitions' request for more information on this topic, a separate two-day Community Planning Training was developed and evaluated in the Oregon TOGETHER! project [74]. The two-day workshop format was delivered in the Community Youth Development Study, and now the web-streamed curriculum covers the content and activities of this training.

7. In fact, two of the Centers of Excellence funded by the Centers for Disease Control have adopted the CTC system for use in partnering communities. Following the CTC guidelines, community coalitions use the Blueprints registry to select EBIs that have been shown in at least one randomized controlled trial or two quasi-experimental evaluations to reduce behavioral health problems.

CHAPTER 7

1. For a more detailed description of the monitoring system utilized by CTC coalitions in the randomized study, see Fagan and colleagues [62–64].

2. For a list of all the Milestones and Benchmarks, see the "Tools for Community Leaders" guide at www.communitiesthatcare.net/getting-started/ctc-training/.

CHAPTER 8

1. Funding for the Community Youth Development Study was provided by the National Institute on Drug Abuse, National Cancer Institute, National Institute of Child Health and Human Development, National Institute of Mental Health, Center for Substance Abuse Prevention, and the National Institute on Alcohol Abuse and Alcoholism. For a full list of publications from the Community Youth

Development Study, see the CTC website at: www.communitiesthatcare.net/research-results/.

2. As discussed later in the chapter, the statistical procedures analyzing outcomes on youth behavioral health problems took into account the fact that youth were nested within the 24 study communities. This approach follows recommendations to ensure that analyses are conducted at the level of randomization (the community, in this case) and appropriately model the clustering of individuals within larger units [7, 10].

3. It is also important to note that these surveys were also administered during the Diffusion Study, which provided baseline data on most of the constructs shown in the logic model. Analyses indicated that CTC and control communities did not differ in their levels of any of the community-level constructs shown in the logic model at baseline (excepting use of the Social Development Strategy, which was assessed for the first time in 2007).

4. The prevention collaboration and sector collaboration constructs were both measured as latent constructs. In some analyses [e.g., 24, 25], the two measures were combined into a second-order latent factor which represented overall levels of community collaboration.

5. These lists were mailed in advance of the phone surveys. In the web-based surveys, teachers were provided with the program name, logo if available, name of the program developer and/or distribution company, and a short description of the program.

6. For the complete list of behaviors analyzed beginning at the age 19 follow-up, see Oesterle and colleagues [16].

7. Recall that the number of participants in the cohort increased from grade 5 to grade 6. To analyze the baseline data, missing grade 5 data were imputed using 40 separate datasets. Imputation was conducted separately by intervention condition to account for within-condition mean and covariance structures, then combined for analysis [9]. Similar procedures were followed in the analysis of data from the longitudinal panel in subsequent years of the study.

8. The CTC Youth Survey can be found at www.communitiesthatcare.net/userfiles/files/2014CTCYS.pdf.

9. Recall that the CTC communities used data from these surveys as part of their needs assessments. The CTC Youth Survey was also conducted in the control communities to allow a comparison of changes in risk and protective factors and behavioral health outcomes for the intervention compared to control communities.

10. CTC communities were guided to target youth in grades 5 through 9, those participating in the longitudinal cohort, with study-funded EBIs. Although communities generally followed this advice, they also provided services to younger and older youth. The pseudo-cohort was selected for analysis because it overlapped in age with the longitudinal cohort and thus had a greater potential than the other

cohorts to receive EBIs. When EBI implementation was examined in the CTC communities, the proportion and number of youth in the pseudo-cohort who participated in EBIs varied substantially, making it possible to create two groups of intervention communities, those reaching greater and lower proportions of the pseudo-cohort with EBIs.

CHAPTER 9

1. We would like to acknowledge the contributions to this chapter made by Brian Bumbarger, Mark Greenberg, and Stephanie Bradley. They provided valuable information and feedback regarding the history of the CTC initiative in Pennsylvania and how the state is currently supporting CTC coalitions and EBIs.

2. Funds were awarded to counties, but most counties targeted smaller geographic regions to receive prevention services, such as a town within the county or the catchment area of a school district [3].

3. At the time this study was conducted, SAMHSA's National Evidence-based Programs and Practice (NREPP) registry identified interventions as being effective or not effective based on the quality and outcomes of their research studies. The site later changed to a scoring system which did not explicitly differentiate effective and non-effective interventions.

4. The increase in CTC-affiliated districts from 2001 to 2003 is the result of the influx of new counties funded to implement CTC during these two years [4].

CHAPTER 10

* We would like to acknowledge the contributions to this chapter made by Blair-Brooke-Weiss, Mats Glans, and John Toumbourou. They provided descriptions of recent implementation experiences of CTC communities nationally and internationally.

1. In January 2018, the U.S. federal government issued a press release stating that it is no longer supporting the development and use of the National Registry of Evidence-based Programs and Practices (NREPP), and that the registry is likely to be taken off the SAMHSA website.

References

CHAPTER 1

1. Hawkins, J. D., Jenson, J. M., Catalano, R. F., Fraser, M. W., Botvin, G. J., Shapiro, V., et al. (2015). *Unleashing the power of prevention.* Discussion paper. Washington, DC: Institute of Medicine and National Research Council.

2. National Research Council and Institute of Medicine. (2009). *Preventing mental, emotional, and behavioral disorders among young people: Progress and possibilities* (M. E. O'Connell, T. Boat, & K. E. Warner, Eds.). Washington, DC: National Academies Press.

3. Hale, D. R., & Viner, R. M. (2012). Policy responses to multiple risk behaviours in adolescents. *Journal of Public Health, 34,* 111–119.

4. Jessor, R. (1991). Risk behavior in adolescence: A psychosocial framework for understanding and action. *Journal of Adolescent Health, 12,* 597–605.

5. Patton, G. C., Sawyer, S. M., Santelli, J. S., Ross, D. A., Afifi, R. A., Allen, N. B., et al. (2016). Our future: A Lancet commission on adolescent health and well-being. *Lancet, 387,* 2423–2478.

6. Merikangas, K. R., He, J., Burstein, M., Swanson, S. A., Avenevoli, S., Cui, L., et al. (2010). Lifetime prevalence of mental disorders in U.S. adolescents: Results from the National Comorbidity Survey Replication–Adolescent Supplement (NCS-A). *Journal of the American Academy of Child and Adolescent Psychiatry, 49,* 980–989.

7. U.S. Department of Health and Human Services, Office of the Surgeon General. (2016, November). *Facing addiction in America: The Surgeon General's report on alcohol, drugs, and health.* Washington, DC: Author.

8. World Health Organization. (2014). *Global status report on violence prevention 2014.* Geneva, Switzerland: Author.

9. Hamilton, B. E., Martin, J. A., Osterman, M. J. K., Curtin, S. C., & Mathews, T. J. (2015). Births: Final data for 2014. *National Vital Statistics Reports, 64,* 1–64.

10. Miech, R. A., Johnston, L. D., O'Malley, P. M., Bachman, J. G., & Schulenberg, J. E. (2017). *Monitoring the Future: National survey results on drug use, 1975–2016.*

Volume 1: Secondary school students. Ann Arbor, MI: Institute for Social Research, University of Michigan.

11. Kann, L., McManus, T., Harris, W. A., Shanklin, S. L., Flint, K. H., Hawkins, J., et al. (2016). Youth risk behavior surveillance—United States, 2015. *Morbidity and Mortality Weekly Report. Surveillance Summaries, 65*, 1–174.

12. World Health Organization. (2014). *Global status report on alcohol and health 2014*. Geneva, Switzerland: Author.

13. Elliott, D. S., Huizinga, D., & Ageton, S. S. (1985). *Explaining delinquency and drug use*. Beverly Hills, CA: Sage Publications.

14. Moffitt, T. E. (1993). Adolescence-limited and life-course persistent anti-social behavior: A developmental taxonomy. *Psychological Review, 100*, 674–701.

15. Resnick, M. D., Ireland, M., & Borowsky, I. (2004). Youth violence perpetration: What protects? What predicts? Findings from the National Longitudinal Study of Adolescent Health. *Journal of Adolescent Health, 35*, 424.e1–424.e10.

16. Piquero, A. R., Hawkins, J. D., Kazemian, L., & Petechuk, D. (2013). *Bulletin 2: Criminal career patterns*. Washington, DC: National Institute of Justice.

17. Hawkins, J. D., Oesterle, S., Brown, E. C., Abbott, R. D., & Catalano, R. F. (2014). Youth problem behaviors 8 years after implementing the Communities That Care prevention system: A community randomized trial. *JAMA Pediatrics, 168*, 122–129.

18. Hawkins, J. D., & Weis, J. G. (1985). The social development model: An integrated approach to delinquency prevention. *Journal of Primary Prevention, 6*, 73–97.

19. Duncan, G. J., & Raudenbush, S. W. (1999). Assessing the effects of context in studies of child and youth development. *Educational Psychologist, 34*, 29–41.

20. Sampson, R. J. (2012). *Great American city: Chicago and the enduring neighborhood effect*. Chicago: University of Chicago Press.

21. Aneshensel, C. S., & Sucoff, C. A. (1996). The neighborhood context of adolescent mental health. *Journal of Health and Social Behavior, 37*, 293–310.

22. Peterson, D., Esbensen, F.-A., Taylor, T. J., & Freng, A. (2007). Youth violence in context: The roles of sex, race, and community in offending. *Youth Violence and Juvenile Justice, 5*, 385–410.

23. Catalano, R. F., Fagan, A. A., Gavin, L. E., Greenberg, M. T., Irwin, C. E., Ross, D. A., et al. (2012). Worldwide application of prevention science in adolescent health. *Lancet, 379*, 1653–1664.

24. Patton, G. C., Coffey, C., Currie, D., Riley, L., Gore, F., Degenhardt, L., et al. (2012). Health of the world's adolescents: A synthesis of internationally comparable data. *Lancet, 379*, 1665–1675.

25. Gore, F. M., Bloem, P. J. N., Patton, G. C., Ferguson, J., Joseph, V., Coffey, C., et al. (2011). Global burden of disease in young people aged 10–24 years: A systematic analysis. *Lancet, 377*, 2093–2102.

26. Office of Juvenile Justice and Delinquency Prevention. (2012). *Effects and consequences of underage drinking.* Washington, DC: Author.

27. Hingson, R. W., Heeren, T., & Winter, M. R. (2006). Age at drinking onset and alcohol dependence: Age at onset, duration, and severity. *Archives of Pediatrics and Adolescent Medicine, 160,* 739–746.

28. Farrington, D. P. (2003). Developmental and life-course criminology: Key theoretical and empirical issues—The 2002 Sutherland Award address. *Criminology, 41,* 221–255.

29. U.S. Department of Health and Human Services. (2001). *Youth violence: A report of the Surgeon General.* Centers for Disease Control and Prevention, National Center for Injury Prevention and Control; Substance Abuse and Mental Health Services Administration, Center for Mental Health Services; National Institutes of Health, National Institute of Mental Health. Rockville, MD: Author.

30. Farrington, D. P., Loeber, R., & Berg, M. T. (2012). Young men who kill: A prospective longitudinal examination from childhood. *Homicide Studies, 16,* 99–128.

31. McCollister, K. E., French, M. T., & Fang, H. (2010). The cost of crime to society: New crime-specific estimates for policy and program evaluation. *Drug and Alcohol Dependence, 108,* 98–109.

32. Sacks, J. J., Gonzales, K. R., Bouchery, E. E., Tomedi, L. E., & Brewer, R. D. (2015). 2010 national and state costs of excessive alcohol consumption. *American Journal of Preventive Medicine, 49,* e73–e79.

33. National Drug Intelligence Center. (2011). *National drug threat assessment.* Washington, DC: United States Department of Justice.

34. Insel, T. R. (2008). Assessing the economic costs of serious mental illness. *American Journal of Psychiatry, 165,* 663–665.

35. Farrington, D. P., & Welsh, B. C. (2007). *Saving children from a life of crime: Early risk factors and effective interventions.* New York: Oxford University Press.

36. Coie, J. D., Watt, N. F., West, S. G., Hawkins, J. D., Asarnow, J. R., Marman, H. J., et al. (1993). The science of prevention: A conceptual framework and some directions for a national research program. *American Psychologist, 48,* 1013–1022.

37. Glasgow, R. E., Vinson, C., Chambers, D., Khoury, M. J., Kaplan, R. M., & Hunter, C. (2012). National Institutes of Health approaches to dissemination and implementation science: Current and future directions. *American Journal of Public Health, 102,* 1274–1281.

38. Glasgow, R. E., & Emmons, K. (2007). How can we increase translation of research into practice? Types of evidence needed. *Annual Review of Public Health, 28,* 413–433.

39. Institute of Medicine (IOM). (2001). *Crossing the quality chasm: A new health system for the 21st century.* Washington, DC: National Academies Press.

40. U.S. Department of Education. (2011). *Prevalence and implementation fidelity of research-based prevention programs in public schools: Final report.* Office of

Planning, Evaluation and Policy Development, Policy and Program Studies Service. Washington, DC: Author.

41. Ringwalt, C., Vincus, A. A., Hanley, S., Ennett, S. T., Bowling, J. M., & Haws, S. (2011). The prevalence of evidence-based drug use prevention curricula in U.S. Middle schools in 2008. *Prevention Science, 12*, 63–69.

42. Rosenbaum, D. P. (2007). Just say no to D.A.R.E. *Criminology and Public Policy, 6*, 815–824.

43. Sloboda, Z., Stephens, R. C., Stephens, P., Grey, S. F., Teasdale, B., Hawthorne, R.D., et al. (2009). The Adolescent Substance Abuse Prevention Study: A randomized field trial of a universal substance abuse prevention program. *Drug and Alcohol Dependence, 102*, 1–10.

44. David-Ferdon, C., & Simon, T. R. (2014). *Preventing youth violence: Opportunities for action*. Atlanta, GA: National Center for Injury Prevention and Control, Centers for Disease Control and Prevention.

45. Spoth, R. L., Rohrbach, L. A., Greenberg, M. T., Leaf, P., Brown, C. H., Fagan, A., et al. (2013). Addressing core challenges for the next generation of type 2 translation research and systems: The Translation Science to Population Impact (TSCI Impact) Framework. *Prevention Science, 14*, 319–351.

46. Foster-Fishman, P. G., & Behrens, T. R. (2007). Systems change reborn: Rethinking our theories, methods, and efforts in human services reform and community-based change. *American Journal of Community Psychology, 39*, 191–196.

47. Woolf, S. H. (2008). The power of prevention and what it requires. *Journal of the American Medical Association, 299*, 2437–2439.

48. Kania, J., & Kramer, M. (2011). Collective impact. *Stanford Social Innovation Review, 9*, 36–41.

49. Hawkins, J. D., Catalano, R. F., & Arthur, M. W. (2002). Promoting science-based prevention in communities. *Addictive Behaviors, 27*, 951–976.

50. Shepherd, J. P., & Farrington, D. P. (1993). Assault as a public health problem. *Journal of the Royal Society of Medicine, 86*, 89–92.

51. Hawkins, J. D., Catalano, R. F., & Miller, J. Y. (1992). Risk and protective factors for alcohol and other drug problems in adolescence and early adulthood: Implications for substance abuse prevention. *Psychological Bulletin, 112*, 64–105.

52. Kellam, S. G., Koretz, D., & Moscicki, E. K. (1999). Core elements of developmental epidemiologically based prevention research. *American Journal of Community Psychology, 27*, 463–482.

53. Herrenkohl, T. I., Maguin, E., Hill, K. G., Hawkins, J. D., Abbott, R. D., & Catalano, R. F. (2000). Developmental risk factors for youth violence. *Journal of Adolescent Health, 26*, 176–186.

54. Lipsey, M. W., & Derzon, J. H. (1998). Predictors of violent or serious delinquency in adolescence and early adulthood: A synthesis of longitudinal research. In R. Loeber & D. P. Farrington (Eds.), *Serious and violent juvenile offenders: Risk factors and successful interventions* (pp. 86–105). Thousand Oaks, CA: Sage Publications.

55. Farrington, D. P., Gaffney, H., & Ttofi, M. M. (2017). Systematic reviews of explanatory risk factors for violence, offending, and delinquency. *Aggression and Violent Behavior, 33*, 24–36.

56. Hall, J. E., Simon, T. R., Mercy, J. A., Loeber, R., Farrington, D. P., & Lee, R. D. (2012). Centers for Disease Control and Prevention's Expert Panel on Protective Factors for Youth Violence Perpetration: Background and overview. *American Journal of Preventive Medicine, 43*(2 Suppl. 1), S1–S7.

57. Sameroff, A. (2006). Identifying risk and protective factors for health child development. In A. Clarke-Stewart & J. Dunn (Eds.), *Families count: Effects on child and adolescent development* (pp. 53–76). Cambridge: Cambridge University Press.

58. Rutter, M. (1985). Resilience in the face of adversity: Protective factors and resistance to psychiatric disorder. *British Journal of Psychiatry, 147*, 598–611.

59. Ttofi, M. M., Farrington, D. F., Piquero, A. R., & DeLisi, M. (2016). Protective factors against offending and violence: Results from prospective longitudinal studies. *Journal of Criminal Justice, 45*, 1–3.

60. Werner, E. E. (1989). High-risk children in young adulthood: A longitudinal study from birth to 32 years. *American Journal of Orthopsychiatry, 59*, 72–81.

61. Farrington, D. P. (1996). The explanation and prevention of youthful offending. In J. D. Hawkins (Ed.), *Delinquency and crime: Current theories* (pp. 68–148). Cambridge: Cambridge University Press.

62. Catalano, R. F., Hawkins, J. D., Berglund, L., Pollard, J. A., & Arthur, M. W. (2002). Prevention science and positive youth development: Competitive or cooperative frameworks? *Journal of Adolescent Health, 31*, 230–239.

63. Farrington, D. P., Ttofi, M. M., & Piquero, A. R. (2016). Risk, promotive, and protective factors in youth offending: Results from the Cambridge Study in Delinquent Development. *Journal of Criminal Justice, 45*, 63–70.

64. Jolliffe, D., Farrington, D. P., Loeber, R., & Pardini, D. A. (2016). Protective factors for violence: Results from the Pittsburgh Youth Study. *Journal of Criminal Justice, 45*, 32–40.

65. Catalano, R. F., & Hawkins, J. D. (1996). The social development model: A theory of antisocial behavior. In J. D. Hawkins (Ed.), *Delinquency and crime: Current theories* (pp. 149–197). New York: Cambridge University Press.

66. Pollard, J. A., Hawkins, J. D., & Arthur, M. W. (1999). Risk and protection: Are both necessary to understand diverse behavioral outcomes in adolescence? *Social Work Research, 23*, 145–158.

67. Jessor, R., & Jessor, S. L. (1977). *Problem behavior and psychosocial development: A longitudinal study of youth.* San Diego, CA: Academic Press.

68. Sacks, V., Beckwith, S., & Moore, K. A. (2015). *Social service programs that foster multiple positive outcomes.* Bethesda, MD: Child Trends.

69. Hale, D. R., Fitzgerald-Yau, N., & Viner, R. M. (2014). A systematic review of effective interventions for reducing multiple health risk behaviors in adolescence. *American Journal of Public Health, 104,* e19–e41.

70. Thornberry, T. P. (1987). Toward an interactional theory of delinquency. *Criminology, 25,* 863–891.

71. Kellam, S. G., Branch, J. D., Agrawal, K. C., & Ensminger, M. E. (1975). *Mental health and going to school: The Woodlawn program of assessment, early intervention, and evaluation.* Chicago: University of Chicago Press.

72. Sherman, L. W., Gottfredson, D. C., MacKenzie, D. L., Eck, J., Reuter, P., & Bushway, S. D. (1998). *Preventing crime: What works, what doesn't, what's promising.* Washington, DC: National Institute of Justice.

73. Sherman, L. W., Farrington, D. P., Welsh, B. C., & MacKenzie, D. L. (Eds.). (2006). *Evidence-based crime prevention* (2nd ed.) New York: Routledge.

74. Guldi, M. (2008). Fertility effects of abortion and birth control pill access for minors. *Demography, 45,* 817–827.

75. Wagenaar, A. C., & Toomey, T. L. (2002). Effects of minimum drinking age laws: Review and analyses of the literature from 1960 to 2000. *Journal of Studies on Alcohol, 14S,* 206–225.

76. Institute of Medicine. (1994). *Reducing risks for mental disorders: Frontiers for preventive intervention research* (P. J. Mrazek & R. J. Haggerty, Eds.). Washington, DC: National Academy Press.

77. Fagan, A. A., & Hawkins, J. D. (2012). Community-based substance use prevention. In B. C. Welsh & D. P. Farrington (Eds.), *The Oxford handbook on crime prevention* (pp. 247–268). New York: Oxford University Press.

78. Hope, T. (1995). Community crime prevention. In M. Tonry & D. P. Farrington (Eds.), *Crime and justice: Building a safer society: Strategic approaches to crime prevention* (pp. 21–89). Chicago: Chicago University Press.

79. Welsh, B. C., & Hoshi, A. (2006). Communities and crime prevention. In L. W. Sherman, D. P. Farrington, B. C. Welsh, & D. L. MacKenzie (Eds.), *Evidence-based crime prevention* (pp. 165–197). New York: Routledge.

80. Pratt, T. C., & Cullen, F. T. (2005). Assessing macro-level predictors and theories of crime: A meta-analysis. In M. Tonry (Ed.), *Crime and justice* (pp. 373–450). Chicago: University of Chicago Press.

81. Sampson, R. J., Raudenbush, S. W., & Earls, F. (1997). Neighborhoods and violent crime: A multilevel study of collective efficacy. *Science, 277,* 918–924.

82. Butterfoss, F. D., Goodman, R. M., & Wandersman, A. (1993). Community coalitions for prevention and health promotion. *Health Education Research, 8,* 315–330.

83. Foster-Fishman, P. G., Cantillon, D., Pierce, S. J., & Van Egeren, L. A. (2007). Building an active citizenry: The role of neighborhood problems, readiness, and capacity for change. *American Journal of Community Psychology, 39,* 91–106.

84. Wallerstein, N. B., & Duran, B. (2010). Community-based participatory research contributions to intervention research: The intersection of science and practice to improve health equity. *American Journal of Public Health, 100*(Suppl. 1), S40–46.

85. Reiss, D., & Price, R. H. (1996). National research agenda for prevention research: The National Institute of Mental Health report. *American Psychologist, 51,* 1109–1115.

86. Arthur, M. W., & Blitz, C. (2000). Bridging the gap between science and practice in drug abuse prevention through needs assessment and strategic community planning. *Journal of Community Psychology, 28,* 241–55.

87. Fagan, A. A., & Montes, A. (2015). Neighborhood-based prevention of juvenile delinquency. In M. D. Krohn & J. Lane (Eds.), *Handbook of juvenile delinquency and juvenile justice* (pp. 388–404). Malden, MA: John Wiley.

88. Biglan, A., Ary, D. V., & Wagenaar, A. C. (2000). The value of interrupted time-series experiments for community intervention research. *Prevention Science, 1,* 31–49.

89. Raudenbush, S. W., & Sampson, R. J. (1999). Toward a science of assessing ecological settings, with application to the systematic social observation of neighborhoods. *Sociological Methodology, 29,* 1–41.

90. Merzel, C., & D'Afflitti, J. (2003). Reconsidering community-based health promotion: Promise, performance, and potential. *American Journal of Public Health, 93,* 557–574.

91. Stith, S., Pruitt, I., Dees, J., Fronce, M., Green, N., Som, A., et al. (2006). Implementing community-based prevention programming: A review of the literature. *Journal of Primary Prevention, 27,* 599–617.

92. Wandersman, A., & Florin, P. (2003). Community intervention and effective prevention. *American Psychologist, 58,* 441–448.

93. Rosenbaum, D. P., & Schuck, A. M. (2012). Comprehensive community partnerships for preventing crime. In B. C. Welsh & D. P. Farrington (Eds.), *The Oxford handbook on crime prevention* (pp. 226–246). New York: Oxford University Press.

94. Hallfors, D., & Godette, D. (2002). Will the "Principles of Effectiveness" improve prevention practice? Early findings from a diffusion study. *Health Education Research, 17,* 461–470.

95. Bursik Jr., R. J., & Grasmick, H. G. (1993). *Neighborhoods and crime: The dimensions of effective community control.* New York: Lexington Books.

96. Schlossman, S., & Sedlak, M. (1983). The Chicago Area Project revisited. *Crime and Delinquency, 26,* 398–462.

97. Yin, R. K., Kaftarian, S. J., Yu, P., & Jansen, M. A. (1997). Outcomes from CSAP's community partnership program: Findings from the national cross-site evaluation. *Evaluation and Program Planning, 20,* 345–355.

98. Fagan, A. A., Hawkins, J. D., & Catalano, R. F. (2011). Engaging communities to prevent underaged drinking. *Alcohol Research and Health, 34,* 167–174.

99. Wandersman, A., Duffy, J., Flaspohler, P. D., Noonan, R. K., Lubell, K., Stillman, L., et al. (2008). Bridging the gap between prevention research and practice: The Interactive Systems Framework for Dissemination and Implementation. *American Journal of Community Psychology, 41,* 171–181.

100. Lab, S. P. (2010). *Crime prevention: Approaches, practices, and evaluations.* New Providence, NJ: Anderson.

101. Bennett, T., Holloway, K., & Farrington, D. P. (2008). *The effectiveness of neighborhood watch.* Oslo, Norway: Campbell Collaboration.

102. Rosenbaum, D. P. (1987). The theory and research behind Neighborhood Watch: Is it a sound fear and crime reduction strategy? *Crime and Delinquency, 33,* 103–134.

103. Braga, A. A., & Weisburd, D. L. (2012). The effects of focused deterrence strategies on crime: A systematic review and meta-analysis of the empirical evidence. *Journal of Research in Crime and Delinquency, 49,* 323–358.

104. Braga, A. A., Kennedy, D. M., Waring, E. J., & Piehl, A. M. (2001). Problem-oriented policing, deterrence, and youth violence: An evaluation of Boston's Operation Ceasefire. *Journal of Research in Crime and Delinquency, 38,* 195–225.

105. Klein, M. W. (2011). Comprehensive gang and violence reduction programs: Reinventing the square wheel. *Criminology and Public Policy, 10,* 1037–1044.

106. Wilson, J. M., & Chermak, S. (2011). Community-driven violence reduction programs: Examining Pittsburgh's One Vision One Life. *Criminology and Public Policy, 10,* 993–1027.

107. Braga, A. A., Hureau, D. M., & Papachristos, A. V. (2014). Deterring gang-involved gun violence: Measuring the impact of Boston's Ceasefire on street gang behavior. *Journal of Quantitative Criminology, 30,* 113–139.

108. Braga, A. A., & Weisburd, D. L. (2014). Must we settle for less rigorous evaluations in large area-based crime prevention programs? Lessons from a Campbell review of focused deterrence. *Journal of Experimental Criminology, 10,* 573–597.

109. Wagenaar, A. C., & Perry, C. L. (1994). Community strategies for the reduction of youth drinking: Theory and application. *Journal of Research on Adolescence, 4,* 319–345.

References277

110. Perry, C. L., Williams, C. L., Veblen-Mortenson, S., Toomey, T. L., Komro, K., Anstine, P.S., et al. (1996). Project Northland: Outcomes of a communitywide alcohol use prevention program during early adolescence. *American Journal of Public Health, 86,* 956–965.

111. Pentz, M. A., Dwyer, J. H., MacKinnon, D. P., Flay, B. R., Hansen, W. B., Wang, E. Y. I., et al. (1989). A multicommunity trial for primary prevention of adolescent drug abuse. *Journal of the American Medical Association, 261,* 3259–3266.

112. Toomey, T. L., & Lenk, K. M. (2011). A review of environmental-based community interventions. *Alcohol Research and Health, 34,* 163–166.

113. Arthur, M. W., Hawkins, J. D., Pollard, J. A., Catalano, R. F., & Baglioni, A. J. (2002). Measuring risk and protective factors for substance use, delinquency, and other adolescent problem behaviors: The Communities That Care Youth Survey. *Evaluation Review, 26,* 575–601.

114. Hawkins, J. D., & Catalano, R. F. (2002). *Tools for community leaders: A guidebook for getting started.* South Deerfield, MA: Channing Bete Company.

115. Fagan, A. A., & Hawkins, J. D. (2013). Preventing substance use, delinquency, violence, and other problem behaviors over the life-course using the Communities That Care system. In C. L. Gibson & M. D. Krohn (Eds.), *Handbook of life-course criminology* (pp. 277–296). New York: Springer.

116. Hawkins, J. D., Catalano, R. F., Arthur, M. W., Egan, E., Brown, E. C., Abbott, R. D., et al. (2008). Testing Communities That Care: The rationale, design and behavioral baseline equivalence of the Community Youth Development Study. *Prevention Science, 9,* 178–190.

117. Quinby, R., Fagan, A. A., Hanson, K., Brooke-Weiss, B., Arthur, M. W., & Hawkins, J. D. (2008). Installing the Communities That Care prevention system: Implementation progress and fidelity in a randomized controlled trial. *Journal of Community Psychology, 36,* 313–332.

118. Hawkins, J. D., Brown, E. C., Oesterle, S., Arthur, M. W., Abbott, R. D., & Catalano, R. F. (2008). Early effects of Communities That Care on targeted risks and initiation of delinquent behavior and substance use. *Journal of Adolescent Health, 43,* 15–22.

119. Hawkins, J. D., Oesterle, S., Brown, E. C., Arthur, M. W., Abbott, R. D., Fagan, A. A., et al. (2009). Results of a type 2 translational research trial to prevent adolescent drug use and delinquency: A test of Communities That Care. *Archives of Pediatric and Adolescent Medicine, 163,* 789–798.

120. Hawkins, J. D., Oesterle, S., Brown, E. C., Monahan, K. C., Abbott, R. D., Arthur, M. W., et al. (2012). Sustained decreases in risk exposure and youth problem behaviors after installation of the Communities That Care prevention system in a randomized trial. *Archives of Pediatrics and Adolescent Medicine, 166,* 141–148.

121. Oesterle, S., Hawkins, J. D., Kuklinski, M. R., Fagan, A. A., Fleming, C., Rhew, I. C., et al. (2015). Effects of Communities That Care on males' and females' drug use and delinquency 9 years after baseline in a community-randomized trial. *American Journal of Community Psychology, 56*, 217–228.

122. Oesterle, S., Kuklinski, M. R., Hawkins, J. D., Skinner, M. L., Guttmannova, K., & Rhew, I. C. (2018). Long-term effects of the Communities That Care trial on substance use, antisocial behavior, and violence through age 21 years. *American Journal of Public Health, 108*, 659–665.

123. Washington State Institute for Public Policy. (2017). *Benefit-cost results.* Olympia, WA: Author.

124. Kuklinski, M. R., Fagan, A. A., Hawkins, J. D., Briney, J. S., & Catalano, R. F. (2015). Benefit-cost analysis of a randomized evaluation of Communities That Care: Monetizing intervention effects on the initiation of delinquency and substance use through grade 12. *Journal of Experimental Criminology, 11*, 165–192.

125. Spoth, R. L., Greenberg, M. T., Bierman, K. L., & Redmond, C. (2004). Prosper community-university partnership model for public education systems: Capacity-building for evidence-based, competence-building prevention. *Prevention Science, 5*, 31–39.

126. Spoth, R., Redmond, C., Shin, C., Greenberg, M. T., Feinberg, M. E., & Schainker, L. M. (2013). PROSPER community-university partnership delivery system effects on substance misuse through 6 1/2 years past baseline from a cluster randomized controlled intervention trial. *Preventive Medicine, 56*, 190–196.

127. Spoth, R. L., Redmond, C., Clair, S., Shin, C., Greenberg, M. T., & Feinberg, M. E. (2011). Preventing substance misuse through community–university partnerships randomized controlled trial outcomes 4½ years past baseline. *American Journal of Preventive Medicine, 40*, 440–447.

128. Spoth, R. L., Trudeau, L. S., Redmond, C., Shin, C., Greenberg, M. T., Feinberg, M. E., et al. (2015). PROSPER partnership delivery system: Effects on adolescent conduct problem behavior outcomes through 6.5 years past baseline. *Journal of Adolescence, 45*, 44–55.

129. Spoth, R., Redmond, C., Shin, C., Greenberg, M. T., Feinberg, M. E., & Trudeau, L. (2017). PROSPER delivery of universal preventive interventions with young adolescents: Long-term effects on emerging adult substance misuse and associated risk behaviors. *Psychological Medicine, 47*, 2246–2259.

130. Center for Substance Abuse Prevention. (2009). *Identifying and selecting evidence-based interventions: Revised guidance document for the Strategic Prevention Framework State Incentive Grant Program.* Substance Abuse and Mental Health Services Administration. Rockville, MD: Author.

131. Anderson-Carpenter, K. D., Watson-Thompson, J., Chaney, L., & Jones, M. (2016). Reducing binge drinking in adolescents through implementation of the

Strategic Prevention Framework. *American Journal of Community Psychology,* 57, 36–46.

132. Flewelling, R. L., Austin, D., Hale, K., LaPlante, M., Liebig, M., Piasecki, L., et al. (2005). Implementing research-based substance abuse prevention in communities: Effects of a coalition-based prevention initiative in Vermont. *Journal of Community Psychology, 33,* 333–353.

133. Collins, D., Johnson, K., & Becker, B. J. (2007). A meta-analysis of direct and mediating effects of community coalitions that implemented science-based substance abuse prevention interventions. *Substance Use and Misuse, 42,* 985–1007.

134. Substance Abuse and Mental Health Services Administration. (2016). *Program evaluation for prevention: SPF sig annual report.* Report Fy2016. Rockville, MD: Author.

135. Farrington, D. P., & Welsh, B. C. (2005). Randomized experiments in criminology: What have we learned in the last two decades? *Journal of Experimental Criminology, 1,* 9–38.

136. Backer, T. E. (1995). Assessing and enhancing readiness for change: Implications for technology transfer. In T. E. Backer, S. L. David, & G. Soucy (Eds.), *Reviewing the behavioral science knowledge base on technology transfer* (pp. 21–41). Rockville, MD: National Institute on Drug Abuse.

137. Rohrbach, L. A., Grana, R., Sussman, S., & Valente, T. W. (2006). Type II translation: Transporting prevention interventions from research to real-world settings. *Evaluation and the Health Professions, 29,* 302–333.

138. Latessa, E. J., Cullen, F. T., & Gendreau, P. (2002). Beyond correctional quackery-professionalism and the possibility of effective treatment. *Federal Probation, 66,* 43–49.

139. Fagan, A. A., Brooke-Weiss, B., Cady, R., & Hawkins, J. D. (2009). If at first you don't succeed . . . keep trying: Strategies to enhance coalition/school partnerships to implement school-based prevention programming. *Australian and New Zealand Journal of Criminology, 42,* 387–405.

140. Fagan, A. A., Hanson, K., Hawkins, J. D., & Arthur, M. W. (2009). Translational research in action: Implementation of the Communities That Care prevention system in 12 communities. *Journal of Community Psychology* 37, 809–829.

CHAPTER 2

1. Coie, J. D., Watt, N. F., West, S. G., Hawkins, J. D., Asarnow, J. R., Marman, et al. (1993). The science of prevention: A conceptual framework and some directions for a national research program. *American Psychologist, 48,* 1013–1022.

2. Farrington, D. P. (2000). Explaining and preventing crime: The globalization of knowledge—The American Society of Criminology 1999 Presidential address. *Criminology, 38*, 1–24.

3. Institute of Medicine. (1994). *Reducing risks for mental disorders: Frontiers for preventive intervention research* (P. J. Mrazek & R. J. Haggerty, Eds.). Washington, DC: National Academy Press.

4. Sampson, R. J., & Laub, J. H. (1993). *Crime in the making: Pathways and turning points through life.* Cambridge, MA: Harvard University Press.

5. Elder Jr., G. H. (1998). The life course as developmental theory. *Child Development, 69*, 1–12.

6. Bowlby, J. (1969). *Attachment and loss: Vol. I. Attachment.* New York: Basic Books.

7. Steinberg, L. (2001). We know some things: Parent-adolescent relationships in retrospect and prospect. *Journal of Research on Adolescence, 11*, 1–19.

8. Arnett, J. J. (2000). Emerging adulthood: A theory of development from the late teens through the twenties. *American Psychologist, 55*, 469–480.

9. National Research Council and Institute of Medicine. (2009). *Preventing mental, emotional, and behavioral disorders among young people: Progress and possibilities* (M. E. O'Connell, T. Boat, & K. E. Warner, Eds.). Washington, DC: National Academies Press.

10. Yoshikawa, H. (1994). Prevention as cumulative protection: Effects of early family support and education on chronic delinquency and its risks. *Psychological Bulletin, 115*, 28–54.

11. Shonkoff, J. P., & Fisher, P. A. (2013). Rethinking evidence-based practice and two-generation programs to create the future of early childhood policy. *Development and Psychopathology, 25*, 1635–1653.

12. Masten, A. S., & Powell, J. L. (2003). A resilience framework for research, policy, and practice. In A. S. Masten & J. L. Powell (Eds.), *Resilience and vulnerability: Adaptation in the context of childhood adversities* (pp. 1–26). New York: Cambridge University Press.

13. Patterson, G. R., DeBaryshe, B. D., & Ramsey, E. (1989). A developmental perspective on antisocial behavior. *American Psychologist, 44*, 329–335.

14. Sampson, R. J., & Laub, J. H. (1997). A life-course theory of cumulative disadvantage and the stability of delinquency. In T. P. Thornberry (Ed.), *Developmental theories of crime and delinquency* (pp. 133–161). New Brunshwick, NJ: Transaction.

15. Catalano, R. F., Fagan, A. A., Gavin, L. E., Greenberg, M. T., Irwin, C. E., Ross, D. A., et al. (2012). Worldwide application of prevention science in adolescent health. *Lancet, 379*, 1653–1664.

16. Blumstein, A., & Cohen, J. (1987). Characterizing criminal careers. *Science, 237*, 985–991.

17. Farrington, D. P. (2003). Developmental and life-course criminology: Key theoretical and empirical issues—The 2002 Sutherland Award address. *Criminology*, 41, 221–255.

18. Hingson, R. W., Heeren, T., & Winter, M. R. (2006). Age at drinking onset and alcohol dependence: Age at onset, duration, and severity. *Archives of Pediatric Adolescent Medicine*, 160, 739–746.

19. Piquero, A. R., Hawkins, J. D., Kazemian, L., & Petechuk, D. (2013). *Bulletin 2: Criminal career patterns*. Washington, DC: National Institute of Justice.

20. Moffitt, T. E. (1993). Adolescence-limited and life-course persistent anti-social behavior: A developmental taxonomy. *Psychological Review*, 100, 674–701.

21. Grant, B. F., & Dawson, D. (1998). Age of onset of drug use and its association with DSM-IV drug abuse and dependence: Results from the National Longitudinal Alcohol Epidemiologic Survey. *Journal of Substance Abuse*, 10, 163–173.

22. Guttmannova, K., Bailey, J. A., Hill, K. G., Lee, J. O., Hawkins, J. D., Woods, M. L., et al. (2001). Sensitive periods for adolescent alcohol use initiation: Predicting the lifetime occurrence and chronicity of alcohol problems in adulthood. *Journal of Studies on Alcohol and Drugs*, 72, 221–232.

23. Elder Jr., G. H. (1995). The life course paradigm: Social change and individual development. In P. Moen, G. H. ElderJr., & K. Luscher (Eds.), *Examining lives in context: Perspectives on the ecology of human development* (pp. 101–139). Washington, DC: APA Press.

24. Bronfenbrenner, U. (2005). *Making human beings human: Bioecological perspectives on human development*. Thousand Oaks, CA: Sage Publications.

25. Catalano, R. F., & Hawkins, J. D. (1996). The social development model: A theory of antisocial behavior. In J. D. Hawkins (Ed.), *Delinquency and crime: Current theories* (pp. 149–197). New York: Cambridge University Press.

26. Thornberry, T. P. (1987). Toward an interactional theory of delinquency. *Criminology*, 25, 863–891.

27. Cleveland, M. J., Feinberg, M. E., Bontempo, D. E., & Greenberg, M. T. (2008). The role of risk and protective factors in substance use across adolescence. *Journal of Adolescent Health*, 43, 157–164.

28. Elliott, D. S., Huizinga, D., & Ageton, S. S. (1985). *Explaining delinquency and drug use*. Beverly Hills, CA: Sage Publications.

29. Gomby, D. S., Culross, P. L., & Berhman, R. E. (1999). Home visiting: Recent program evaluations—Analysis and recommendations. *The Future of Children*, 9, 4–26.

30. Olds, D. (2002). Prenatal and infancy home visiting by nurses: From randomized trials to community replication. *Prevention Science*, 3, 153–172.

31. Kim, B. K. E., Oesterle, S., Catalano, R. F., & Hawkins, J. D. (2015). Change in protective factors across adolescent development. *Journal of Applied Developmental Psychology, 40*, 26–37.

32. Herrenkohl, T. I., Maguin, E., Hill, K. G., Hawkins, J. D., Abbott, R. D., & Catalano, R. F. (2000). Developmental risk factors for youth violence. *Journal of Adolescent Health, 26*, 176–186.

33. Pollard, J. A., Hawkins, J. D., & Arthur, M. W. (1999). Risk and protection: Are both necessary to understand diverse behavioral outcomes in adolescence? *Social Work Research, 23*, 145–158.

34. Tonry, M., & Farrington, D. P. (1995). Strategic approaches to crime prevention. In M. Tonry & D. P. Farrington (Eds.), *Building a safer society: Strategic approaches to crime prevention* (pp. 1–20). Chicago: University of Chicago Press.

35. Hirschi, T. (1969). *Causes of delinquency*. Berkeley: University of California Press.

36. Sutherland, E. H. (1947). *Principles of criminology*. Philadelphia: J. B. Lippincott.

37. Akers, R. L., Krohn, M. D., Lanza-Kaduce, L., & Radosevich, M. (1979). Social learning and deviant behavior: A specific test of a general theory. *American Sociological Review, 44*, 636–655.

38. Cressey, D. R. (1953). *Other people's money*. New York: Free Press.

39. Matsueda, R. L. (1988). The current state of differential association theory. *Crime and Delinquency, 34*, 277–306.

40. Hawkins, J. D., Catalano, R. F., & Arthur, M. W. (2002). Promoting science-based prevention in communities. *Addictive Behaviors, 27*, 951–976.

41. Shaw, C. R. & McKay, H. D. (1942). *Juvenile delinquency and urban areas*. Chicago: University of Chicago Press.

42. Bursik Jr., R. J., & Grasmick, H. G. (1993). *Neighborhoods and crime: The dimensions of effective community control*. New York: Lexington Books.

43. Sampson, R. J., Raudenbush, S. W., & Earls, F. (1997). Neighborhoods and violent crime: A multilevel study of collective efficacy. *Science, 277*, 918–924.

44. Bernat, D. H., Lazovich, D., Forster, J. L., Oakes, J. M., & Chen, V. (2009). Area-level variation in adolescent smoking. *Public Health Research, Practice, and Policy, 6*, 1–8.

45. Sampson, R. J. (2012). *Great American city: Chicago and the enduring neighborhood effect*. Chicago: University of Chicago Press.

46. Hawkins, J. D., Van Horn, M. L., & Arthur, M. W. (2004). Community variation in risk and protective factors and substance use outcomes. *Prevention Science, 5*, 213–220.

47. Feinberg, M. E., Jones, D. E., Cleveland, M. J., & Greenberg, M. T. (2012). The community epidemiology of underage drinking: Variation across communities in relations of risk to alcohol use. *Prevention Science, 13*, 551–561.

48. Anderson, E. (1999). *Code of the street*. New York: W.W. Norton.

49. Pratt, T. C., & Cullen, F. T. (2005). Assessing macro-level predictors and theories of crime: A meta-analysis. In M. Tonry (Ed.), *Crime and justice* (pp. 373–450). Chicago: University of Chicago Press.

50. Elliott, D. S., Wilson, W. J., Huizinga, D., Sampson, R. J., Elliott, A., & Rankin, B. (1996). The effects of neighborhood disadvantage on adolescent development. *Journal of Research in Crime and Delinquency, 33,* 389–426.

51. Jain, S., Buka, S. L., Subramanian, S. V., & Molnar, B. E. (2010). Neighborhood predictors of dating violence victimization and perpetration in young adulthood: A multilevel study. *American Journal of Public Health, 100,* 1737–1744.

52. Molnar, B. E., Miller, M. J., Azrael, D., & Buka, S. L. (2004). Neighborhood predictors of concealed firearm carrying among children and adolescents: Results from the project on human development in Chicago neighborhoods. *Archives of Pediatric Adolescent Medicine, 158,* 657–664.

53. Simons, R. L., Gordon Simons, L., Burt, C. H., Brody, G., & Cutrona, C. (2005). Collective efficacy, authoritative parenting and delinquency: A longitudinal test of a model integrating community- and family-level processes. *Criminology, 43,* 989–1029.

54. Aisenberg, E., & Herrenkohl, T. I. (2008). Community violence in context: Risk and resilience in children and families. *Journal of Interpersonal Violence, 23,* 296–315.

55. Fagan, A. A., Wright, E. M., & Pinchevsky, G. M. (2014). The protective effects of neighborhood collective efficacy on adolescent substance use and violence following exposure to violence. *Journal of Youth and Adolescence, 43,* 1498–1512.

56. Rogers, E. M. (1995). *Diffusion of innovations* (4th ed.). New York: Free Press.

57. Hawkins, J. D., Jenson, J. M., Catalano, R. F., Fraser, M. W., Botvin, G. J., Shapiro, V., et al. (2015). *Unleashing the power of prevention.* Discussion paper. Washington, DC: Institute of Medicine and National Research Council.

58. Glasgow, R. E., & Emmons, K. (2007). How can we increase translation of research into practice? Types of evidence needed. *Annual Review of Public Health, 28,* 413–433.

59. Spoth, R. L., Rohrbach, L. A., Greenberg, M. T., Leaf, P., Brown, C. H., Fagan, A., et al. (2013). Addressing core challenges for the next generation of type 2 translation research and systems: The Translation Science to Population Impact (TSCI Impact) Framework. *Prevention Science, 14,* 319–351.

60. Fagan, A. A., Brooke-Weiss, B., Cady, R., & Hawkins, J. D. (2009). If at first you don't succeed . . . keep trying: Strategies to enhance coalition/school partnerships to implement school-based prevention programming. *Australian and New Zealand Journal of Criminology, 42,* 387–405.

61. Wandersman, A., Duffy, J., Flaspohler, P. D., Noonan, R. K., Lubell, K., Stillman, L., et al. (2008). Bridging the gap between prevention research and practice: The

interactive systems framework for dissemination and implementation. *American Journal of Community Psychology, 41*, 171–181.

62. Elliott, D. S., & Mihalic, S. (2004). Issues in disseminating and replicating effective prevention programs. *Prevention Science, 5*, 47–53.

63. Meyers, D. C., Durlak, J. A., & Wandersman, A. (2012). The quality implementation framework: A synthesis of critical steps in the implementation process. *American Journal of Community Psychology, 50*, 462–480.

64. Flaspohler, P. D., Duffy, J., Wandersman, A., Stillman, L., & Maras, M. A. (2008). Unpacking prevention capacity: An intersection of research-to-practice models and community-centered models. *American Journal of Community Psychology, 41*, 182–196.

65. Damschroder, L. J., Aron, D. C., Keith, R. E., Kirsh, S. R., Alexander, J. A., & Lowery, J. C. (2009). Fostering implementation of health services research findings into practice: A consolidated framework for advancing implementation science. *Implementation Science, 4*, 50.

66. Gottfredson, D. C., & Gottfredson, G. D. (2002). Quality of school-based prevention programs: Results from a national survey. *Journal of Research in Crime and Delinquency, 39*, 3–35.

67. Rohrbach, L. A., Grana, R., Sussman, S., & Valente, T. W. (2006). Type II translation: Transporting prevention interventions from research to real-world settings. *Evaluation and the Health Professions, 29*, 302–333.

68. Fixsen, D. L., Naoom, S. F., Blase, K. A., Friedman, R. M., & Wallace, F. (2005). *Implementation research: A synthesis of the literature.* National Implementation Research Network (FMHI Publication #231). Tampa, FL: University of South Florida, Louis de la Parte Florida Mental Health Institute.

69. Johnson, K., Hays, C., Center, H., & Daley, C. (2004). Building capacity and sustainable prevention innovations: A sustainability planning model. *Evaluation and Program Planning, 27*, 135–149.

70. Scheirer, M. A. (2005). Is sustainability possible? A review and commentary on empirical studies of program sustainability. *American Journal of Evaluation, 26*, 320–347.

71. Israel, B. A., Schultz, A. J., Parker, E. A., & Becker, A. B. (1998). Review of community-based research: Assessing partnership approaches to improve public health. *American Review of Public Health, 19*, 173–202.

72. Wallerstein, N. B., & Duran, B. (2006). Using community-based participatory research to address health disparities. *Health Promotion and Practice, 7*, 312–323.

73. Wandersman, A., & Florin, P. (2003). Community intervention and effective prevention. *American Psychologist, 58*, 441–48.

74. Wandersman, A. (2003). Community science: Bridging the gap between science and practice with community-centered models. *American Journal of Community Psychology, 31*, 227–242.

75. Holder, H. D., Saltz, R. F., Grube, J. W., Treno, A. J., Reynolds, R. I., Voas, R. B., et al. (1997). Summing up: Lessons from a comprehensive community prevention trial. *Addiction, 92*, S293–S301.

76. Fetterman, D. M. (2005). Empowerment evaluation principles in practice. In D. M. Fetterman & A. Wandersman (Eds.), *Empowerment evaluation principles* (pp. 42–72). New York: Guilford Publishers.

77. Macaulay, A. C., Commanda, L. E., Freeman, W. L., Gibson, N., McCabe, M. L., Robbins, C. M., et al. (1999). Participatory research maximises community and lay involvement. *British Medical Journal, 319*, 774–778.

78. Altman, D. G. (1995). Sustaining interventions in community systems: On the relationship between researchers and communities. *Health Psychology, 14*, 526–536.

79. Green, L. W., Ottoson, J. M., Garcia, C., & Hiatt, R. A. (2009). Diffusion theory and knowledge dissemination, utilization, and integration in public health. *Annual Review of Public Health, 30*, 151–174.

80. Morrel-Samuels, S., Bacallao, M., Brown, S., Bower, M., & Zimmerman, M. (2016). Community engagement in youth violence prevention: Crafting methods to context. *Journal of Primary Prevention, 37*, 189–207.

81. Kellam, S. G. (2000). Community and institutional partnerships for school violence prevention. In Preventing school violence: Plenary papers of the 1999 conference on criminal justice research and evaluation—enhancing policy and practice through research (pp.1–21). Washington, DC: National Institute of Justice.

82. Stevenson, J., & Mitchell, R. (2003). Community-level collaboration for substance abuse prevention. *Journal of Primary Prevention, 23*, 371–404.

83. Hyndman, B., Giesbrecht, N., Bernardi, D. R., Coston, N., Douglas, R. R., Ferrence, R.G., et al. (1992). Preventing substance abuse through multicomponent community action research projects: Lessons learned from past experiences and challenges for future initiatives. *Contemporary Drug Problems, 19*, 133–164.

84. Merzel, C., & D'Afflitti, J. (2003). Reconsidering community-based health promotion: Promise, performance, and potential. *American Journal of Public Health, 93*, 557–574.

85. Wallerstein, N. B., & Duran, B. (2010). Community-based participatory research contributions to intervention research: The intersection of science and practice to improve health equity. *American Journal of Public Health, 100*, S40–46.

86. Brownson, R. C., Fielding, J., & Maylahn, C. M. (2009). Evidence-based public health: A fundamental concept for public health practice. *Annual Review of Public Health, 30*, 175–201.

87. Goodman, R. M., Speers, M. A., McLeroy, K. R., Fawcett, S., Kegler, M. C., Parker, E. A., et al. (2000). Identifying and defining the dimensions of community

capacity to provide a basis for measurement. *Health Education & Behavior, 25,* 258–278.

88. Harachi, T. W., Abbott, R. D., Catalano, R. F., Haggerty, K. P., & Fleming, C. B. (1999). Opening the black box: Using process evaluation measures to assess implementation and theory building. *American Journal of Community Psychology, 27,* 711–731.

CHAPTER 3

1. Sussman, S., Valente, T. W., Rohrbach, L. A., Skara, S., & Pentz, M. A. (2006). Translation in the health professions: Converting science into action. *Evaluation and the Health Professions, 29,* 7–32.

2. Institute of Medicine. (1994). *Reducing risks for mental disorders: Frontiers for preventive intervention research* (P. J. Mrazek & R. J. Haggerty, Eds.). Washington, DC: National Academy Press.

3. Spoth, R. L., Rohrbach, L. A., Greenberg, M. T., Leaf, P., Brown, C. H., Fagan, A., et al. (2013). Addressing core challenges for the next generation of type 2 translation research and systems: The Translation Science to Population Impact (TSCI Impact) Framework. *Prevention Science, 14,* 319–351.

4. Rogers, E. M. (1995). *Diffusion of innovations* (4th ed.). New York: Free Press.

5. Coie, J. D., Watt, N. F., West, S. G., Hawkins, J. D., Asarnow, J. R., Marman, H. J., et al. (1993). The science of prevention: A conceptual framework and some directions for a national research program. *American Psychologist, 48,* 1013–1022.

6. Kellam, S. G., Koretz, D., & Moscicki, E. K. (1999). Core elements of developmental epidemiologically based prevention research. *American Journal of Community Psychology, 27,* 463–482.

7. Catalano, R. F., & Hawkins, J. D. (1996). The social development model: A theory of antisocial behavior. In J. D. Hawkins (Ed.), *Delinquency and crime: Current theories* (pp. 149–197). New York: Cambridge University Press.

8. Moffitt, T. E. (1993). Adolescence-limited and life-course persistent anti-social behavior: A developmental taxonomy. *Psychological Review, 100,* 674–701.

9. Thornberry, T. P. (1987). Toward an interactional theory of delinquency. *Criminology, 25,* 863–891.

10. Loeber, R., Burke, J. D., & Pardini, D. A. (2009). Development and etiology of disruptive and delinquent behavior. *Annual Review of Clinical Psychology, 5,* 291–310.

11. Patterson, G. R. (1982). *A social learning approach. Volume 3: Coercive family practices.* Eugene, OR: Castalia Publishing.

12. Webster-Stratton, C., & Taylor, T. K. (2001). Nipping early risk factors in the bud: Preventing substance abuse, delinquency, and violence in adolescence

through interventions targeted at young children (0-8 years). *Prevention Science, 2,* 165–192.

13. Damschroder, L. J., & Hagedorn, H. J. (2011). A guiding framework and approach for implementation research in substance use disorders treatment. *Psychology of Addictive Behaviors, 25,* 194–205.

14. Lipsey, M., Petrie, C., Weisburd, D., & Gottfredson, D. C. (2006). Improving evaluation of anti-crime programs: Summary of a National Research Council report. *Journal of Experimental Criminology, 2,* 271–307.

15. Sampson, R. J., Raudenbush, S. W., & Earls, F. (1997). Neighborhoods and violent crime: A multilevel study of collective efficacy. *Science, 277,* 918–924.

16. Kellam, S. G., & Langevin, D. J. (2003). A framework for understanding "evidence" in prevention research and programs. *Prevention Science, 4,* 137–153.

17. Gottfredson, D. C., Cook, T. D., Gardner, F. E. M., Gorman-Smith, D., Howe, G. W., Sandler, I. N., et al. (2015). Standards of evidence for efficacy, effectiveness and scale-up research in prevention science: Next generation. *Prevention Science, 16,* 893–926.

18. Kraemer, H. C., Wilson, T., Fairburn, C. G., & Agras, W.S. (2002). Mediators and moderators of treatment effects in randomized clinical trials. *Archives of General Psychiatry, 59,* 877–883.

19. Sherman, L. W. (2003). Misleading evidence and evidence-led policy: Making social science more experimental. *Annals of the American Academy of Political and Social Science, 589,* 6–19.

20. Weisburd, D. (2010). Justifying the use of non-experimental methods and disqualifying the use of randomized controlled trials: Challenging folklore in evaluation research in crime and justice. *Journal of Experimental Criminology, 6,* 209–227.

21. Cook, T. D., & Campbell, D. T. (1979). *Quasi-experimentation: Design and analysis issues for field settings.* Boston: Houghton Mifflin.

22. Farrington, D. P. (2003). Methodological quality standards for evaluation research. *Annals of the American Academy of Political and Social Science, 587,* 49–68.

23. Rohrbach, L. A., Gunning, M., Sun, P., & Sussman, S. (2010). The Project Towards No Drug Abuse (TND) dissemination trial: Implementation fidelity and immediate outcomes. *Prevention Science, 11,* 77–88.

24. Olds, D. (2009). In support of disciplined passion. *Journal of Experimental Criminology, 5,* 201–214.

25. Green, L. W., Ottoson, J. M., Garcia, C., & Hiatt, R. A. (2009). Diffusion theory and knowledge dissemination, utilization, and integration in public health. *Annual Review of Public Health, 30,* 151–174.

26. Gruenewald, P. J. (1997). Analysis approaches to community evaluation. *Evaluation Review, 21,* 209–230.

27. Wandersman, A., & Florin, P. (2003). Community intervention and effective prevention. *American Psychologist, 58,* 441–448.

28. Raudenbush, S. W., & Sampson, R. J. (1999). Toward a science of assessing ecological settings, with application to the systematic social observation of neighborhoods. *Sociological Methodology, 29,* 1–41.

29. Foster-Fishman, P. G., Cantillon, D., Pierce, S. J., & Van Egeren, L. A. (2007). Building an active citizenry: The role of neighborhood problems, readiness, and capacity for change. *American Journal of Community Psychology, 39,* 91–106.

30. Peterson, P. L., Hawkins, J. D., & Catalano, R. F. (1992). Evaluating comprehensive community drug risk reduction interventions: Design challenges and recommendations. *Evaluation Review, 16,* 579–602.

31. Weisburd, D., & Gill, C. (2014). Block randomized trials at places: Rethinking the limitations of small n experiments. *Journal of Quantitative Criminology, 30,* 97–112.

32. Biglan, A., Ary, D. V., & Wagenaar, A. C. (2000). The value of interrupted time-series experiments for community intervention research. *Prevention Science, 1,* 31–49.

33. Merzel, C., & D'Afflitti, J. (2003). Reconsidering community-based health promotion: Promise, performance, and potential. *American Journal of Public Health, 93,* 557–574.

34. Hawkins, J. D., Lishner, D. M., Jenson, J. M., & Catalano, R. F. (1987). Delinquents and drugs: What the evidence suggests about prevention and treatment programming. In B. S. Brown & A. R. Mills (Eds.), *Youth at high risk for substance abuse* (pp. 81–131). Rockville, MD: National Institute on Drug Abuse.

35. Jessor, R. (1991). Risk behavior in adolescence: A psychosocial framework for understanding and action. *Journal of Adolescent Health, 12,* 597–605.

36. Elliott, D. S., Huizinga, D., & Ageton, S. S. (1985). *Explaining delinquency and drug use.* Beverly Hills, CA: Sage Publications.

37. Institute of Medicine. (1994). *Reducing risks for mental disorders: Frontiers for preventive intervention research* (P. J. Mrazek & R. J. Haggerty, Eds.). Washington, DC: National Academy Press.

38. Hawkins, J. D., Arthur, M. W., & Catalano, R. F. (1995). Preventing substance abuse. In M. Tonry & D. P. Farrington (Eds.), *Crime and justice. Building a safer society: Strategic approaches to crime prevention* (pp. 343–427). Chicago: University of Chicago Press.

39. Hawkins, J. D., Catalano, R. F., & Miller, J. Y. (1992). Risk and protective factors for alcohol and other drug problems in adolescence and early adulthood: Implications for substance abuse prevention. *Psychological Bulletin, 112,* 64–105.

40. Catalano, R. F., Arthur, M. W., Hawkins, J. D., Berglund, L., & Olson, J. J. (1998). Comprehensive community and school based interventions to prevent antisocial

behavior. In R. Loeber & D. P. Farrington (Eds.), *Serious and violent juvenile offenders: Risk factors and successful interventions* (pp. 248–283). Thousand Oaks, CA: Sage Publications.

41. Brewer, D. D., Hawkins, J. D., Catalano, R. F., & Neckerman, H. J. (1995). Preventing serious, violent, and chronic juvenile offending: A review of evaluations of selected strategies in childhood, adolescence, and the community. In J. C. Howell, B. Krisberg, J. D. Hawkins, & J. J. Wilson (Eds.), *A sourcebook: Serious, violent, & chronic juvenile offenders* (pp. 61–141). Thousand Oaks, CA: Sage Publications.

42. Hawkins, J. D., Von Cleve, E., & Catalano, R. F. (1991). Reducing early childhood aggression: Results of a primary prevention program. *Journal of the American Academy of Child and Adolescent Psychiatry, 30*, 208–217.

43. Olds, D. (2002). Prenatal and infancy home visiting by nurses: From randomized trials to community replication. *Prevention Science, 3*, 153–172.

44. Hale, D. R., Fitzgerald-Yau, N., & Viner, R. M. (2014). A systematic review of effective interventions for reducing multiple health risk behaviors in adolescence. *American Journal of Public Health, 104*, e19–e41.

45. Sacks, V., Beckwith, S., & Moore, K. A. (2015). *Social service programs that foster multiple positive outcomes.* Bethesda, MD: Child Trends.

46. Office of Juvenile Justice and Delinquency Prevention. (1995). *Guide for implementing the comprehensive strategy for serious, violent, and chronic juvenile offenders.* Washington, DC: Author.

47. Developmental Research and Programs. (1996). *Communities That Care Prevention strategies: A research guide to what works.* Seattle, WA: Developmental Research and Programs.

48. Bracht, N. (Ed.). (1990). *Health promotion at the community level: New advances.* Thousand Oaks, CA: Sage Publications.

49. Wilson, J. J., & Howell, J. C. (1993). *A comprehensive strategy for serious, violent, and chronic juvenile offenders.* Washington, DC: Office of Juvenile Justice and Delinquency Prevention.

50. Manger, T. H., Hawkins, J. D., Haggerty, K. P., & Catalano, R. F. (1992). Mobilizing communities to reduce risks for drug abuse: Lessons on using research to guide prevention practice. *Journal of Primary Prevention, 13*, 3–22.

51. Harachi, T. W., Ayers, C. D., Hawkins, J. D., Catalano, R. F., & Cushing, J. (1996). Empowering communities to prevent adolescent substance abuse: Process evaluation results from a risk- and protection-focused community mobilization effort. *Journal of Primary Prevention, 16*, 233–254.

52. Arthur, M. W., Ayers, C. D., Graham, K. A., & Hawkins, J. D. (2003). Mobilizing communities to reduce risk for drug abuse: A comparison of two strategies. In W. J. Bukoski & Z. Sloboda (Eds.), *Handbook of drug abuse prevention: Theory, science and practice* (pp. 129–144). New York: Kluwer Academic/Plenum Publishers.

53. Office of Juvenile Justice and Delinquency Prevention. (1996). *Report to Congress: Title V incentive grants for local delinquency prevention programs.* Washington, DC: Author.

54. Office of Juvenile Justice and Delinquency Prevention. (1995). *Report to Congress: Title V incentive grants for local delinquency prevention programs.* Washington, DC: Author.

55. Jenson, J. M., Hartman, J. C., Smith, J. R., Draayer, D., & Schurtz, R. (1997). *An evaluation of Iowa's Juvenile Crime Prevention Community Grant Fund Program.* Iowa City: School of Social Work, University of Iowa.

56. U.S. Government Accountability Office. (1996). *Report to the Committee on the Judiciary, U.S. Senate, and the Committee on Economic and Educational Opportunity.* House of Representatives. Washington, DC: Author.

57. Hawkins, J. D., & Catalano, R. F. (1996, 2000, 2004). *Communities That Care Prevention Strategies Guide.* South Deerfield, MA: Channing Bete.

58. Arthur, M. W., Hawkins, J. D., Pollard, J. A., Catalano, R. F., & Baglioni, A. J. (2002). Measuring risk and protective factors for substance use, delinquency, and other adolescent problem behaviors: The Communities That Care Youth Survey. *Evaluation Review, 26*, 575–601.

59. Feinberg, M. E. (2012). Community epidemiology of risk and adolescent substance use: Practical questions for enhancing prevention. *American Journal of Public Health, 102*, 457–468.

60. Glaser, R. R., Van Horn, M. L., Arthur, M. W., Hawkins, J. D., & Catalano, R. F. (2005). Measurement properties of the Communities That Care Youth Survey across demographic groups. *Journal of Quantitative Criminology, 21*, 73–102.

61. Briney, J. S., Brown, E. C., Hawkins, J. D., & Arthur, M. W. (2012). Predictive validity of established cut points for risk and protective factor scales from the Communities That Care Youth Survey. *Journal of Primary Prevention, 33*, 249–258.

62. Arthur, M. W., Briney, J. S., Hawkins, J. D., Abbott, R. D., Brooke-Weiss, B., & Catalano, R. F. (2007). Measuring community risk and protection using the Communities That Care Youth Survey. *Evaluation and Program Planning, 30*, 197–211.

63. Arthur, M. W., Glaser, R. R., & Hawkins, J. D. (2005). Steps towards community-level resilience: Community adoption of science-based prevention programming. In R. D. Peters, B. Leadbeater, & R. J. McMahon (Eds.), *Resilience in children, families, and communities: Linking context to practice and policy* (pp. 177–194). New York: Kluwer Academic/Plenum Publishers.

64. Hawkins, J. D., Brown, E. C., Oesterle, S., Arthur, M. W., Abbott, R. D., & Catalano, R. F. (2008). Early effects of Communities That Care on targeted risks and initiation of delinquent behavior and substance use. *Journal of Adolescent Health, 43*, 15–22.

65. Brown, E. C., Hawkins, J. D., Arthur, M. W., Abbott, R. D., & Van Horn, M. L. (2008). Multilevel analysis of a measure of community prevention collaboration. *American Journal of Community Psychology, 41*, 115–126.

66. Brown, E. C., Hawkins, J. D., Arthur, M. W., Briney, J. S., & Fagan, A. A. (2011). Prevention service system transformation using Communities That Care. *Journal of Community Psychology, 39*, 183–201.

67. Van Horn, M. L., Hawkins, D., Arthur, M. W., & Catalano, R. F. (2007). Assessing community effects on adolescent substance use and delinquency. *Journal of Community Psychology, 35*, 925–946.

68. Fagan, A. A., Arthur, M. W., Hanson, K., Briney, J. S., & Hawkins, J. D. (2011). Effects of Communities That Care on the adoption and implementation fidelity of evidence-based prevention programs in communities: Results from a randomized controlled trial. *Prevention Science, 12*, 223–234.

69. Elliott, D. S., & Mihalic, S. (2004). Issues in disseminating and replicating effective prevention programs. *Prevention Science, 5*, 47–53.

70. Gottfredson, D. C., Kumpfer, K., Polizzi-Fox, D., Wilson, D., Puryear, V., Beatty, P., et al. (2006). The Strengthening Families Washington D.C. Families Project: A randomized effectiveness trial of family-based prevention. *Prevention Science, 7*, 57–73.

71. Hallfors, D., & Godette, D. (2002). Will the "Principles of Effectiveness" improve prevention practice? Early findings from a diffusion study. *Health Education Research, 17*, 461–470.

72. Ringwalt, C., Vincus, A. A., Hanley, S., Ennett, S. T., Bowling, J. M., & Haws, S. (2011). The prevalence of evidence-based drug use prevention curricula in U.S. middle schools in 2008. *Prevention Science, 12*, 63–69.

73. Sloboda, Z., Pyakuryal, A., Stephens, P. C., Teasdale, B., Forrest, D., Stephens, R. C., et al. (2008). Reports of substance abuse prevention programming available in schools. *Prevention Science, 9*, 276–287.

74. Feinberg, M. E., Greenberg, M. T., Osgood, D. W., Anderson, A., & Babinski, L. (2002). The effects of training community leaders in prevention science: Communities That Care in Pennsylvania. *Evaluation and Program Planning, 25*, 245–259.

75. Feinberg, M. E., Bontempo, D., & Greenberg, M. T. (2008). Predictors and level of sustainability of community prevention coalitions. *American Journal of Preventive Medicine, 34*, 495–501.

76. Feinberg, M. E., Jones, D., Greenberg, M. T., Osgood, D. W., & Bontempo, D. (2010). Effects of the Communities That Care model in Pennsylvania on change in adolescent risk and problem behaviors. *Prevention Science, 11*, 163–171.

77. Feinberg, M. E., Greenberg, M. T., Osgood, D. W., Sartorius, J., & Bontempo, D. (2007). Effects of the Communities That Care model in Pennsylvania on youth risk and problem behaviors. *Prevention Science, 8*, 261–270.

78. Feinberg, M. E., Greenberg, M. T., & Osgood, D. W. (2004). Readiness, functioning, and perceived effectiveness in community prevention coalitions: A study of Communities That Care. *American Journal of Community Psychology, 33*, 163–176.

79. Gomez, B. J., Greenberg, M. T., & Feinberg, M. E. (2005). Sustainability of community coalitions: An evaluation of Communities That Care. *Prevention Science, 6*, 199–202.

80. Brown, L. D., Feinberg, M. E., & Greenberg, M. T. (2010). Determinants of community coalition ability to support evidence-based programs. *Prevention Science, 11*, 287–297.

81. Moore, J. E., Bumbarger, B. K., & Cooper, B. R. (2013). Examining adaptations of evidence-based programs in natural contexts. *Journal of Primary Prevention, 34*, 147–161.

82. Rhoades, B. J., Bumbarger, B. K., & Moore, J. E. (2012). The role of a state-level prevention support system in promoting high-quality implementation and sustainability of evidence-based programs. *American Journal of Community Psychology, 50*, 386–401.

83. Cooper, B. R., Bumbarger, B. K., & Moore, J. E. (2015). Sustaining evidence-based prevention programs: Correlates in a large-scale dissemination initiative. *Prevention Science, 16*, 145–157.

84. Bumbarger, B. K., & Campbell, E. M. (2012). A state agency-university partnership for translational research and dissemination of evidence-based prevention and intervention. *Administration and Policy in Mental Health, 39*, 268–277.

85. Eisner, M. P. (2009). No effects in independent prevention trials: Can we reject the cynical view? *Journal of Experimental Criminology, 5*, 163–183.

86. Gorman, D. M., & Conde, E. (2007). Conflict of interest in the evaluation and dissemination of "model" school-based drug and violence prevention programs. *Evaluation and Program Planning, 30*, 422–429.

87. Petrosino, A., & Soydan, H. (2005). The impact of program developers as evaluators on criminal recidivism: Results from meta-analyses of experimental and quasi-experimental research. *Journal of Experimental Criminology, 1*, 435–450.

88. Hawkins, J. D., Catalano, R. F., Arthur, M. W., Egan, E., Brown, E. C., Abbott, R. D., et al. (2008). Testing Communities That Care: The rationale, design and behavioral baseline equivalence of the Community Youth Development Study. *Prevention Science, 9*, 178–190.

89. Quinby, R., Fagan, A. A., Hanson, K., Brooke-Weiss, B., Arthur, M. W., & Hawkins, J. D. (2008). Installing the Communities That Care prevention system: Implementation progress and fidelity in a randomized controlled trial. *Journal of Community Psychology, 36*, 313–332.

90. Fagan, A. A., Hanson, K., Hawkins, J. D., & Arthur, M. W. (2009). Translational research in action: Implementation of the Communities That Care prevention system in 12 communities. *Journal of Community Psychology, 37,* 809–829.

91. Gloppen, K. M., Arthur, M. W., Hawkins, J. D., & Shapiro, V. B. (2012). Sustainability of the Communities That Care prevention system by coalitions participating in the Community Youth Development Study. *Journal of Adolescent Health, 51,* 259–264.

92. Rhew, I. C., Brown, E. C., Hawkins, J. D., & Briney, J. S. (2013). Sustained effects of the Communities That Care system on prevention service system transformation. *American Journal of Public Health, 103,* 529–535.

93. Arthur, M. W., Hawkins, J. D., Brown, E. C., Briney, J. S., Oesterle, S., & Abbott, R. D. (2010). Implementation of the Communities That Care prevention system by coalitions in the Community Youth Development Study. *Journal of Community Psychology, 38,* 245–258.

94. Hawkins, J. D., Oesterle, S., Brown, E. C., Abbott, R. D., & Catalano, R. F. (2014). Youth problem behaviors 8 years after implementing the Communities That Care prevention system: A community randomized trial. *JAMA Pediatrics, 168,* 122–129.

95. Hawkins, J. D., Oesterle, S., Brown, E. C., Arthur, M. W., Abbott, R. D., Fagan, A. A., et al. (2009). Results of a type 2 translational research trial to prevent adolescent drug use and delinquency: A test of Communities That Care. *Archives of Pediatric and Adolescent Medicine, 163,* 789–798.

96. Hawkins, J. D., Oesterle, S., Brown, E. C., Monahan, K. C., Abbott, R. D., Arthur, M. W., et al. (2012). Sustained decreases in risk exposure and youth problem behaviors after installation of the Communities That Care prevention system in a randomized trial. *Archives of Pediatrics and Adolescent Medicine, 166,* 141–148.

97. Kim, B. K. E., Gloppen, K. M., Rhew, I. C., Oesterle, S., & Hawkins, J. D. (2015). Effects of the Communities That Care prevention system on youth reports of protective factors. *Prevention Science, 16,* 652–662.

98. Rhew, I. C., Hawkins, J. D., Murray, D. M., Fagan, A. A., Oesterle, S., Abbott, R. D., et al. (2016). Evaluation of community-level effects of Communities That Care on adolescent drug use and delinquency using repeated cross-sectional design. *Prevention Science, 17,* 177–187.

99. Oesterle, S., Hawkins, J. D., Fagan, A. A., Abbott, R. D., & Catalano, R. F. (2014). Variation in the sustained effects of the Communities That Care prevention system on adolescent smoking, delinquency, and violence. *Prevention Science, 15,* 138–145.

100. Oesterle, S., Hawkins, J. D., Kuklinski, M. R., Fagan, A. A., Fleming, C., Rhew, I. C., et al. (2015). Effects of Communities That Care on males' and females' drug use and delinquency 9 years after baseline in a community-randomized trial. *American Journal of Community Psychology, 56,* 217–228.

101. Oesterle, S., Kuklinski, M. R., Hawkins, J. D., Skinner, M. L., Guttmannova, K., & Rhew, I. C. (2018). Long-term effects of the Communities That Care trial on substance use, antisocial behavior, and violence through age 21 years. *American Journal of Public Health, 100,* 659–665.

102. Brown, E. C., Hawkins, J. D., Rhew, I. C., Shapiro, V. B., Abbott, R. D., Oesterle, S., et al. (2014). Prevention system mediation of Communities That Care: Effects on youth outcomes. *Prevention Science, 15,* 623–632.

103. Campbell, L., & Bumbarger, B. K. (2012). *Looking back, moving forward: The history & current state of evidence-based intervention in Pennsylvania.* College Station: Pennsylvania State University.

104. Jonkman, H. B., Haggerty, K. P., Steketee, M., Fagan, A., Hanson, K., & Hawkins, J. D. (2009). Communities That Care, core elements and context: Research of implementation in two countries. *Social Development Issues, 30,* 42–57.

105. Jonkman, H. B., Aussems, C., Steketee, M., Boutellier, H., & Cuijpers, P. (2015). Prevention of problem behaviours among adolescents: The impact of the Communities That Care strategy in the Netherlands (2008–2011). *International Journal of Developmental Science, 9,* 37–52.

CHAPTER 4

1. Bracht, N., & Tsouros, A. (1990). Principles and strategies of effective community participation. *Health Promotion International, 5,* 199–208.

2. Bracht, N. (Ed.). 1990. *Health promotion at the community level: New advances.* Thousand Oaks, CA: Sage Publications.

3. Carlaw, R. W., Mittlemark, M. B., Bracht, N., & Luepker, R. V. (1984). Organization for a community cardiovascular health program: Experiences from the Minnesota Heart Health program. *Health Education & Behavior, 11,* 243–252.

4. Johnson, C. A., Hansen, W. B., & Pentz, M. A. (1986). Comprehensive community programs for drug abuse prevention. *Journal of Children in Contemporary Society, 18,* 181–199.

5. Kobrin, S. (1959). The Chicago Area Project: A 25-year assessment. *Annals of the American Academy of Political and Social Science, 322,* 19–29.

6. Kania, J., & Kramer, M. (2011). Collective impact. *Stanford Social Innovation Review, 9,* 36–41.

7. Quinby, R., Fagan, A. A., Hanson, K., Brooke-Weiss, B., Arthur, M. W., & Hawkins, J. D. (2008). Installing the Communities That Care prevention system: Implementation progress and fidelity in a randomized controlled trial. *Journal of Community Psychology, 36,* 313–332.

8. Shaw, C. R., & McKay, H. D. (1942). *Juvenile delinquency and urban areas.* Chicago: University of Chicago Press.

9. Bursik Jr., R. J., & Grasmick, H. G. (1993). *Neighborhoods and crime: The dimensions of effective community control*. New York: Lexington Books.

10. Hallfors, D. D., Cho, H., Livert, D., & Kadushin, C. (2002). Fighting back against substance use: Are community coalitions winning? *American Journal of Preventive Medicine, 23*, 237–245.

11. Fagan, A. A., & Hawkins, J. D. (2012). Community-based substance use prevention. In B. C. Welsh & D. P. Farrington (Eds.), *The Oxford handbook on crime prevention* (pp. 247–268). New York: Oxford University Press.

12. Roussos, S., & Fawcett, S. (2000). A review of collaborative partnerships as a strategy for improving community health. *Annual Review of Public Health, 21*, 369–402.

13. Rosenbaum, D. P., & Schuck, A. M. (2012). Comprehensive community partnerships for preventing crime. In B. C. Welsh & D. P. Farrington (Eds.), *The Oxford handbook on crime prevention* (pp. 226–246). New York: Oxford University Press.

14. Kreuter, M. W., Lezin, N. A., & Young, L. A. (2000). Evaluating community-based collaborative mechanisms: Implications for practitioners. *Health Promotion Practice, 1*, 49–63.

15. Butterfoss, F. D., Goodman, R. M., & Wandersman, A. (1993). Community coalitions for prevention and health promotion. *Health Education Research, 8*, 315–330.

16. Edwards, R. W., Jumper-Thurman, P., Plested, B. A., Oetting, E. R., & Swanson, L. (2000). Community readiness: Research to practice. *Journal of Community Psychology, 28*, 291–307.

17. Dymnicki, A. B., Wandersman, A., Osher, D., Grigorescu, V., & Huang, L. (2014). *Willing, able, ready: Basics and policy implications of readiness as a key component for implementation of evidence-based interventions*. ASPE Research Brief. Washington, DC: Office of the Assistant Secretary for Planning and Evaluation, Office of Human Services Policy, U.S. Department of Health and Human Services.

18. Backer, T. E. (1995). Assessing and enhancing readiness for change: Implications for technology transfer. In T. E. Backer, S. L. David, & G. Soucy (Eds.), *Reviewing the behavioral science knowledge base on technology transfer* (pp. 21–41). Rockville, MD: National Institute on Drug Abuse.

19. Chilenski, S. M., Greenberg, M. T., & Feinberg, M. E. (2007). Community readiness as a multidimensional construct. *Journal of Community Psychology, 35*, 347–365.

20. Elliott, D. S., & Mihalic, S. (2004). Issues in disseminating and replicating effective prevention programs. *Prevention Science, 5*, 47–53.

21. Lundahl, B. W., Kunz, C., Brownell, C., Tollefson, D., & Burke, B. L. (2010). A meta-analysis of motivational interviewing: Twenty-five years of empirical studies. *Research on Social Work Practice, 20*, 137–160.

22. Meyers, D. C., Durlak, J. A., & Wandersman, A. (2012). The quality implementation framework: A synthesis of critical steps in the implementation process. *American Journal of Community Psychology, 50,* 462–480.

23. Flaspohler, P. D., Duffy, J., Wandersman, A., Stillman, L., & Maras, M. A. (2008). Unpacking prevention capacity: An intersection of research-to-practice models and community-centered models. *American Journal of Community Psychology, 41,* 182–196.

24. Damschroder, L. J., Aron, D. C., Keith, R. E., Kirsh, S. R., Alexander, J. A., & Lowery, J. C. (2009). Fostering implementation of health services research findings into practice: A consolidated framework for advancing implementation science. *Implementation Science, 4,* 50.

25. Weiner, B. (2009). A theory of organizational readiness for change. *Implementation Science, 4,* 67.

26. Hawkins, J. D., & Catalano, R. F. (2002). *Investing in your community's youth: An introduction to the Communities That Care system.* South Deerfield, MA, Channing Bete.

27. Chinman, M., Hannah, G., Wandersman, A., Ebener, P., Hunter, S.B., Imm, P., et al. (2005). Developing a community science research agenda for building community capacity for effective preventive interventions. *American Journal of Community Psychology, 35,* 143–157.

28. Foster-Fishman, P. G., Cantillon, D., Pierce, S. J., & Van Egeren, L. A. (2007). Building an active citizenry: The role of neighborhood problems, readiness, and capacity for change. *American Journal of Community Psychology, 39,* 91–106.

29. Goodman, R. M., Speers, M. A., McLeroy, K. R., Fawcett, S., Kegler, M. C., Parker, E.A., et al. (2000). Identifying and defining the dimensions of community capacity to provide a basis for measurement. *Health Education & Behavior, 25,* 258–278.

30. Plested, B. A., Edwards, R. W., & Jumper-Thurman, P. (2006). *Community readiness: A handbook for successful change.* Fort Collins, CO: Tri-Ethnic Center for Prevention Research.

31. Foster-Fishman, P. G., & Watson, E. R. (2012). The able change framework: A conceptual and methodological tool for promoting systems change. *American Journal of Community Psychology, 49,* 503–516.

32. Perry, C. L., Williams, C. L., Komro, K. A., Veblen-Mortension, S., Forster, J. L., Bernstein-Lachter, R., et al. (2000). Project Northland high school interventions: Community action to reduce adolescent alcohol use. *Health Education & Behavior, 27,* 29–49.

33. Foster-Fishman, P. G., Fitzgerald, K., Brandell, C., Nowell, B., Chavis, D., & Van Egeren, L. A. (2006). Mobilizing residents for action: The role of small wins and strategic supports. *American Journal of Community Psychology, 38,* 143–152.

34. Komro, K., Perry, C. L., Veblen-Mortenson, S., Farbakhsh, K., Toomey, T. L., Stigler, M.H., et al. (2008). Outcomes from a randomized controlled trial of a multi-component alcohol use preventive intervention for urban youth: Project Northland Chicago. *Addiction, 103,* 606–618.

35. Hanleybrown, F., Kania, J., & Kramer, M. (2012). Channeling change: Making collective impact work. *Stanford Social Innovation Review, 10,* 1–8.

36. Rogers, E. M. (1995). *Diffusion of innovations.* (4th ed.). New York: Free Press.

37. Kellam, S. G. (2000). Community and institutional partnerships for school violence prevention. In Sheppard Kellam, Ronald J. Prinz, & Joseph F. Sheley (Eds.), *Preventing school violence: Plenary papers of the 1999 conference on criminal justice research and evaluation—enhancing policy and practice through research* (pp. 1–21). Washington, DC: National Institute of Justice.

38. Greenberg, M. T., Feinberg, M. E., Chilenski, S. M., Spoth, R., & Redmond, C. (2007). Community and team member factors that influence the early phase functioning of community prevention teams: The PROSPER project. *Journal of Primary Prevention, 28,* 485–504.

39. The Annie E. Casey Foundation. (2013). *Lessons learned: Community change: Lessons from Making Connections.* Baltimore, MD: Author.

40. Stevenson, J., & Mitchell, R. (2003). Community-level collaboration for substance abuse prevention. *Journal of Primary Prevention, 23,* 371–404.

41. Zakocs, R. C., & Guckenburg, S. (2007). What coalition factors foster community capacity? Lessons learned from the Fighting Back initiative. *Health Education & Behavior, 34,* 354–75.

42. Spoth, R. L., Greenberg, M. T., Bierman, K. L., & Redmond, C. (2004). PROSPER community-university partnership model for public education systems: Capacity-building for evidence-based, competence-building prevention. *Prevention Science, 5,* 31–39.

43. Wolff, T. (2001). A practitioner's guide to successful coalitions. *American Journal of Community Psychology, 29,* 173–191.

44. Watson-Thompson, J., Fawcett, S. B., & Schultz, J. A. (2008). A framework for community mobilization to promote healthy youth development. *American Journal of Preventive Medicine, 34,* S72–S81.

45. Feinberg, M. E., Chilenski, S. M., Greenberg, M. T., Spoth, R. L., & Redmond, C. (2007). Community and team member factors that influence the operations phase of local prevention teams: The PROSPER project. *Prevention Science, 8,* 214–226.

46. Harachi, T. W., Abbott, R. D., Catalano, R. F., Haggerty, K. P., & Fleming, C. B. (1999). Opening the black box: Using process evaluation measures to assess implementation and theory building. *American Journal of Community Psychology, 27,* 711–31.

47. Hawkins, J. D., & Catalano, R. F. (1992). *Communities That Care: Action for drug abuse prevention.* San Francisco: Jossey-Bass.

48. Jonkman, H. B., Junger-Tas, J., & van Dijk, B. (2005). From behind dikes and dunes: Communities That Care in the Netherlands. *Children and Society, 19,* 105–116.

49. Manger, T. H., Hawkins, J. D., Haggerty, K. P., & Catalano, R. F. (1992). Mobilizing communities to reduce risks for drug abuse: Lessons on using research to guide prevention practice. *Journal of Primary Prevention, 13,* 3–22.

50. Harachi, T. W., Ayers, C. D., Hawkins, J. D., Catalano, R. F., & Cushing, J. (1996). Empowering communities to prevent adolescent substance abuse: Process evaluation results from a risk- and protection-focused community mobilization effort. *Journal of Primary Prevention, 16,* 233–254.

51. Perez-Gomez, A., Mejia-Trujillo, J., Brown, E. C., & Eisenberg, N. (2016). Adaptation and implementation of a science-based prevention system in Colombia: Challenges and achievements. *Journal of Community Psychology, 44,* 538–545.

52. Crow, I., France, A., Hacking, S., & Hart, M. (2004). *Does Communities That Care work? An evaluation of a community-based risk prevention programme in three neighbourhoods.* New York: Joseph Rowntree Foundation.

53. France, A., & Crow, I. (2005). Using the "risk factor paradigm" in prevention: Lessons from the evaluation of Communities That Care. *Children and Society, 19,* 172–184.

54. Hawkins, J. D., Catalano, R. F., Arthur, M. W., Egan, E., Brown, E. C., Abbott, R. D., et al. (2008). Testing Communities That Care: The rationale, design and behavioral baseline equivalence of the Community Youth Development Study. *Prevention Science, 9,* 178–190.

55. Jonkman, H. B., Haggerty, K. P., Steketee, M., Fagan, A., Hanson, K., & Hawkins, J. D. (2009). Communities That Care, core elements and context: Research of implementation in two countries. *Social Development Issues, 30,* 42–57.

56. Gloppen, K. M., Arthur, M. W., Hawkins, J. D., & Shapiro, V. B. (2012). Sustainability of the Communities That Care prevention system by coalitions participating in the Community Youth Development Study. *Journal of Adolescent Health, 51,* 259–264.

57. Fagan, A. A., Brooke-Weiss, B., Cady, R., & Hawkins, J. D. (2009). If at first you don't succeed . . . keep trying: Strategies to enhance coalition/school partnerships to implement school-based prevention programming. *Australian and New Zealand Journal of Criminology, 42,* 387–405.

58. Fixsen, D. L., Naoom, S. F., Blase, K. A., Friedman, R. M., & Wallace, F. (2005). *Implementation research: A synthesis of the literature.* National Implementation Research Network (FMHI Publication #231). Tampa, FL: University of South Florida, Louis de la Parte Florida Mental Health Institute.

59. Becker, K. D., Bradshaw, C. P., Domitrovich, C., & Ialongo, N. S. (2013). Coaching teachers to improve implementation of the Good Behavior Game. *Administration and Policy in Mental Health, 40,* 482–493.

60. Foster-Fishman, P. G., Berkowitz, S. L., Lounsbury, D. W., Jacobson, S., & Allen, N. A. (2001). Building collaborative capacity in community coalitions: A review and integrative framework. *American Journal of Community Psychology, 29,* 241–261.

61. Wilson, J. M., & Chermak, S. (2011). Community-driven violence reduction programs: Examining Pittsburgh's One Vision One Life. *Criminology and Public Policy, 10,* 993–1027.

62. Feinberg, M. E., Greenberg, M. T., & Osgood, D. W. (2004). Readiness, functioning, and perceived effectiveness in community prevention coalitions: A study of Communities That Care. *American Journal of Community Psychology, 33,* 163–176.

63. Wandersman, A., Imm, P., Chinman, M., & Kaftarian, S. J. (2000). Getting to Outcomes: A results-based approach to accountability. *Evaluation and Program Planning, 23,* 389–395.

64. Hawkins, J. D., Catalano, R. F., & Arthur, M. W. (2002). Promoting science-based prevention in communities. *Addictive Behaviors, 27,* 951–976.

65. Reiss, D., & Price, R. H. (1996). National research agenda for prevention research: The National Institute of Mental Health report. *American Psychologist, 51,* 1109–1115.

66. Altman, D. G. (1995). Sustaining interventions in community systems: On the relationship between researchers and communities. *Health Psychology, 14,* 526–536.

67. Sampson, R. J., Raudenbush, S. W., & Earls, F. (1997). Neighborhoods and violent crime: A multilevel study of collective efficacy. *Science, 277,* 918–924.

68. Wandersman, A., Goodman, R. M., & Butterfoss, F. D. (1997). Understanding coalitions and how they operate: An open systems framework. In M. Minkler (Ed.), *Community organizing and community building for health* (pp. 261–277). New Brunswick, NJ: Rutgers University Press.

69. Wandersman, A., & Florin, P. (2003). Community intervention and effective prevention. *American Psychologist, 58,* 441–448.

70. Zakocs, R. C., & Edwards, E. M. (2006). What explains community coalition effectiveness? A review of the literature. *American Journal of Preventive Medicine, 30,* 351–361.

71. David-Ferdon, C., & Hammond, W. R. (2008). Community mobilization to prevent youth violence and to create safer communities. *American Journal of Preventive Medicine, 34*(3 Suppl.), S1–S2.

72. Florin, P., Mitchell, R., & Stevenson, J. (1993). Identifying training and technical assistance needs in community coalitions: A developmental approach. *Health Education Research, 8,* 417–432.

73. Jasuja, G. K., Chou, C.-P., Bernstein, K., Wang, E., McClure, M., & Pentz, M. A. (2005). Using structural characteristics of community coalitions to predict progress in adopting evidence-based prevention programs. *Evaluation and Program Planning, 28,* 173–184.

74. Chervin, D. D., Philliber, S., Brindis, C. D., Chadwick, A. E., Revels, M. L., Kamin, S.L., et al. (2005). Community capacity building in CDC's Community Coalition Partnership Programs for the Prevention of Teen Pregnancy. *Journal of Adolescent Health, 37,* S11–S19.

75. Kegler, M. C., Steckler, A., McIeroy, K., & Malek, S. H. (1998). Factors that contribute to effective community health promotion coalitions: A study of 10 Project Assist coalitions in North Carolina. *Health Education & Behavior, 25,* 338–353.

76. Hope, T. (1995). Community crime prevention. In M. Tonry & D. P. Farrington (Eds.), *Crime and justice: Building a safer society: Strategic approaches to crime prevention* (pp. 21–89). Chicago: University of Chicago Press.

77. Feinberg, M. E., Bontempo, D., & Greenberg, M. T. (2008). Predictors and level of sustainability of community prevention coalitions. *American Journal of Preventive Medicine, 34,* 495–501.

78. Kramer, J. S., Philliber, S., Brindis, C. D., Kamin, S. L., Chadwick, A. E., Revels, M.L., et al. (2005). Coalition models: Lessons learned from the CDC's Community Coalition Partnership Programs for the Prevention of Teen Pregnancy. *Journal of Adolescent Health, 37,* S20–S30.

79. Rog, D., Boback, N., Barton-Villagrana, H., Marrone-Bennett, P., Cardwell, J., Hawdone, J., et al. (2004). Sustaining collaboratives: A cross-site analysis of the National Funding Collaborative on Violence Prevention. *Evaluation and Program Planning, 27,* 249–261.

80. Scheirer, M. A. (2005). Is sustainability possible? A review and commentary on empirical studies of program sustainability. *American Journal of Evaluation, 26,* 320–347.

81. Shediac-Rizkallah, M. C., & Bone, L. R. (1998). Planning for the sustainability of community-based health programs: Conceptual frameworks and future directions for research, practice, and policy. *Health Education Research, 13,* 87–108.

82. Johnson, K., Hays, C., Center, H., & Daley, C. (2004). Building capacity and sustainable prevention innovations: A sustainability planning model. *Evaluation and Program Planning, 27,* 135–149.

83. Greenberg, M. T., Feinberg, M. E., Johnson, L. E., Perkins, D. F., Welsh, J. A., & Spoth, R. L. (2015). Factors that predict financial sustainability of community coalitions: Five years of findings from the PROSPER partnership project. *Prevention Science, 16,* 158–167.

84. Mitchell, R., Florin, P., & Stevenson, J. F. (2002). Supporting community-based prevention and health promotion initiatives: Developing effective technical assistance systems. *Health Education & Behavior, 29,* 620–639.

85. Feinberg, M. E., Greenberg, M. T., & Osgood, D. W. (2004). Technical assistance in prevention programs: Correlates of perceived need in Communities That Care. *Evaluation and Program Planning, 27,* 263–274.

86. Feinberg, M. E., Ridenour, T. A., & Greenberg, M. T. (2008). The longitudinal effect of technical assistance dosage on the functioning of Communities That Care prevention boards in Pennsylvania. *Journal of Primary Prevention, 29,* 145–165.

87. Cassell, C., Santelli, J., Gilbert, B. C., Dalmat, M., Mezoff, J., & Schauer, M. (2005). Mobilizing communities: An overview of the community coalition partnership programs for the prevention of teen pregnancy. *Journal of Adolescent Health, 37,* S3–S10.

88. Backer, T. E., & Guerra, N. G. (2011). Mobilizing communities to implement evidence-based practices in youth violence prevention: The state of the art. *American Journal of Community Psychology, 48,* 31–42.

89. Steketee, M., Oesterle, S., Jonkman, H. B., Hawkins, J. D., Haggerty, K. P., & Aussems, C. (2013). Transforming prevention systems in the United States and the Netherlands using Communities That Care. *European Journal on Criminal Policy Research, 19,* 99–116.

90. Walker, S. C., Bumbarger, B. K., & Phillippi Jr., S. W. (2015). Achieving successful evidence-based practice implementation in juvenile justice: The importance of diagnostic and evaluative capacity. *Evaluation and Program Planning, 52,* 189–197.

91. Arthur, M. W., Hawkins, J. D., Brown, E. C., Briney, J. S., Oesterle, S., & Abbott, R. D. (2010). Implementation of the Communities That Care prevention system by coalitions in the Community Youth Development Study. *Journal of Community Psychology, 38,* 245–258.

92. Feinberg, M. E., Greenberg, M. T., Osgood, D. W., Anderson, A., & Babinski, L. (2002). The effects of training community leaders in prevention science: Communities That Care in Pennsylvania. *Evaluation and Program Planning, 25,* 245–259.

93. Brown, E. C., Hawkins, J. D., Rhew, I. C., Shapiro, V. B., Abbott, R. D., Oesterle, S., et al. (2014). Prevention system mediation of Communities That Care: Effects on youth outcomes. *Prevention Science, 15,* 623–632.

CHAPTER 5

1. Kreuter, M. W., Lezin, N. A., & Young, L. A. (2000). Evaluating community-based collaborative mechanisms: Implications for practitioners. *Health Promotion Practice, 1,* 49–63.

2. David-Ferdon, C., & Hammond, W. R. (2008). Community mobilization to prevent youth violence and to create safer communities. *American Journal of Preventive Medicine, 34*(3 Suppl.), S1–S2.

3. Wandersman, A., & Florin, P. (2003). Community intervention and effective prevention. *American Psychologist, 58,* 441–448.

4. Stith, S., Pruitt, I., Dees, J., Fronce, M., Green, N., Som, A., et al. (2006). Implementing community-based prevention programming: A review of the literature. *Journal of Primary Prevention, 27,* 599–617.

5. Shaw, C. R., & McKay, H. D. (1942). *Juvenile delinquency and urban areas.* Chicago: University of Chicago Press.

6. Bernat, D. H., Lazovich, D., Forster, J. L., Oakes, J. M., & Chen, V. (2009). Area-level variation in adolescent smoking. *Public Health Research, Practice, and Policy, 6,* 1–8.

7. Sampson, R. J. (2012). *Great American city: Chicago and the enduring neighborhood effect.* Chicago: University of Chicago Press.

8. Hawkins, J. D., Van Horn, M. L., & Arthur, M. W. (2004). Community variation in risk and protective factors and substance use outcomes. *Prevention Science, 5,* 213–220.

9. Feinberg, M. E., Jones, D. E., Cleveland, M. J., & Greenberg, M. T. (2012). The community epidemiology of underage drinking: Variation across communities in relations of risk to alcohol use. *Prevention Science, 13,* 551–561.

10. Hawkins, J. D., Catalano, R. F., & Arthur, M. W. (2002). Promoting science-based prevention in communities. *Addictive Behaviors, 27,* 951–976.

11. Feinberg, M. E. (2012). Community epidemiology of risk and adolescent substance use: Practical questions for enhancing prevention. *American Journal of Public Health, 102,* 457–468.

12. Chinman, M., Hannah, G., Wandersman, A., Ebener, P., Hunter, S. B., Imm, P., et al. (2005). Developing a community science research agenda for building community capacity for effective preventive interventions. *American Journal of Community Psychology, 35,* 143–157.

13. Foster-Fishman, P. G., Berkowitz, S. L., Lounsbury, D. W., Jacobson, S., & Allen, N. A. (2001). Building collaborative capacity in community coalitions: A review and integrative framework. *American Journal of Community Psychology, 29,* 241–261.

14. Wandersman, A., Imm, P., Chinman, M., & Kaftarian, S. J. (2000). Getting to Outcomes: A results-based approach to accountability. *Evaluation and Program Planning, 23,* 389–395.

15. Flaspohler, P. D., Meehan, C., Maras, M. A., & Keller, K. E. (2012). Ready, willing, and able: Developing a support system to promote implementation of school-based prevention programs. *American Journal of Community Psychology, 50,* 428–444.

16. National Research Council. (2012). *Reforming juvenile justice: A developmental approach*. Washington, DC: National Academies Press.

17. Vincent, G. M., Guy, L. S., Grisso, T., & National Youth Screening and Assessment Project. (2012). *Risk assessment in juvenile justice: A guidebook for implementation*. Chicago: MacArthur Foundation.

18. Spoth, R. L., Rohrbach, L. A., Greenberg, M. T., Leaf, P., Brown, C. H., Fagan, A., et al. (2013). Addressing core challenges for the next generation of type 2 translation research and systems: The Translation Science to Population Impact (TSCI Impact) Framework. *Prevention Science, 14*, 319–351.

19. Catalano, R. F., Fagan, A. A., Gavin, L. E., Greenberg, M. T., Irwin, C. E., Ross, D. A., et al. (2012). Worldwide application of prevention science in adolescent health. *Lancet, 379*, 1653–1664.

20. Meyers, D. C., Durlak, J. A., & Wandersman, A. (2012). The quality implementation framework: A synthesis of critical steps in the implementation process. *American Journal of Community Psychology, 50*, 462–480.

21. Hallfors, D., & Godette, D. (2002). Will the "Principles of Effectiveness" improve prevention practice? Early findings from a diffusion study. *Health Education Research, 17*, 461–470.

22. Margolis, A. L., & Roper, A. Y. (2014). Practical experience from the Office of Adolescent Health's large scale implementation of an evidence-based teen pregnancy prevention program. *Journal of Adolescent Health, 54*, S10–S14.

23. Biglan, A., Mrazek, P. J., Carnine, D., & Flay, B. R. (2003). The integration of research and practice in the prevention of youth problem behaviors. *American Psychologist, 58*, 433–440.

24. Fagan, A. A., Hawkins, J. D., & Catalano, R. F. (2008). Using community epidemiologic data to improve social settings: The Communities That Care prevention system. In M. Shinn & H. Yoshikawa (Eds.), *The power of social settings: Promoting youth development by changing schools and community programs* (pp. 292–312). New York: Oxford University Press.

25. Arthur, M. W., & Blitz, C. (2000). Bridging the gap between science and practice in drug abuse prevention through needs assessment and strategic community planning. *Journal of Community Psychology, 28*, 241–255.

26. Hawkins, J. D., Jenson, J. M., Catalano, R. F., Fraser, M. W., Botvin, G. J., Shapiro, V., et al. (2015). *Unleashing the power of prevention*. Discussion paper. Washington, DC: Institute of Medicine and National Research Council.

27. Farrington, D. P., & Welsh, B. C. (2005). Randomized experiments in criminology: What have we learned in the last two decades? *Journal of Experimental Criminology, 1*, 9–38.

28. Wandersman, A., Morrissey, E., Davino, K., Seybolt, D., Crusto, C., Nation, M., et al. (1998). Comprehensive quality programming and accountability: Eight

essential strategies for implementing successful prevention programs. *Journal of Primary Prevention, 19*, 3–30.

29. Coie, J. D., Watt, N. F., West, S. G., Hawkins, J. D., Asarnow, J. R., Marman, H. J., et al. (1993). The science of prevention: A conceptual framework and some directions for a national research program. *American Psychologist, 48*, 1013–1022.

30. Metz, A., & Albers, B. (2014). What does it take? How federal initiatives can support the implementation of evidence-based programs to improve outcomes for adolescents. *Journal of Adolescent Health, 54*(3 Suppl.), S92–S96.

31. Walker, S. C., Bumbarger, B. K., & Phillippi Jr., S. W. (2015). Achieving successful evidence-based practice implementation in juvenile justice: The importance of diagnostic and evaluative capacity. *Evaluation and Program Planning, 52*, 189–197.

32. Rohrbach, L. A., Ringwalt, C. L., Ennett, S. T., & Vincus, A. A. (2005). Factors associated with adoption of evidence-based substance use prevention curricula in US school districts. *Health Education Research, 20*, 514–526.

33. Shearer, D. L., Gyaben, S. L., Gallagher, K. M., & Klerman, L. V. (2005). Selecting, implementing, and evaluating teen pregnancy prevention interventions: Lessons from the CDC's Community Coalition Partnership Programs for the Prevention of Teen Pregnancy. *Journal of Adolescent Health, 37*, S42–S52.

34. Horner, R. H., & Blitz, C. (2014). *The importance of contextual fit when implementing evidence-based interventions.* ASPE Research Brief. Office of the Assistant Secretary for Planning and Evaluation, Office of Human Services Policy. Washington, DC: U.S. Department of Health and Human Services.

35. Johnson, K., Hays, C., Center, H., & Daley, C. (2004). Building capacity and sustainable prevention innovations: A sustainability planning model. *Evaluation and Program Planning, 27*, 135–149.

36. Supplee, L. H., & Metz, A. (2015). Opportunities and challenges in evidence-based social policy. *Social Policy Report, 28*, 1–16.

37. Imm, P., Chinman, M., Wandersman, A., Rosenbloom, D., Guckenburg, S., & Leis, R. (2007). *Preventing underage drinking: Using Getting To Outcomes with the SAMHSA Strategic Prevention Framework to achieve results.* Santa Monica, CA: RAND Corporation.

38. Masho, S., Schoeny, M., Webster, D. W., & Sigel, E. (2016). Outcomes, data, and indicators of violence at the community level. *Journal of Primary Prevention, 37*, 121–139.

39. Kang-Brown, J., Trone, J., Fratello, J., & Daftary-Kapur, T. (2013). *A generation later: What we've learned about zero tolerance in schools.* New York: Vera Institute of Justice, Center on Youth Justice.

40. Cook, P. J., Gottfredson, D. C., & Na, C. (2010). School crime control and prevention. In M. Tonry (Ed,), *Crime and justice* (pp. 313–440). Chicago: University of Chicago Press.

41. Greenwood, P., & Welsh, B. C. (2012). Promoting evidence-based practice in delinquency prevention at the state level: Principles, progress, and policy directions. *Criminology and Public Policy, 11,* 493–513.

42. Backer, T. E. (1995). Assessing and enhancing readiness for change: Implications for technology transfer. In T. E. Backer, S. L. David, & G. Soucy (Eds.), *Reviewing the behavioral science knowledge base on technology transfer* (pp. 21–41). Rockville, MD: National Institute on Drug Abuse.

43. Plested, B. A., Edwards, R. W., & Jumper-Thurman, P. (2006). *Community readiness: A handbook for successful change.* Fort Collins, CO: Tri-Ethnic Center for Prevention Research.

44. Thornberry, T. P., & Krohn, M. D. (2000). The self-report method for measuring delinquency and crime. In D. Duffee, D. McDowall, L. G. Mazerolle, & S. D. Mastrofski (Eds.), *Measurement and analysis of crime and justice* (pp. 33–83). Washington, DC: U.S. Department of Justice, Office of Justice Programs.

45. Krohn, M. D., Thornberry, T. P., Gibson, C. L., & Baldwin, J. M. (2010). The development and impact of self-report measures of crime and delinquency. *Journal of Quantitative Criminology, 26,* 509–525.

46. Hibell, B., Guttormsson, U., Ahlström, S., Balakireva, O., Bjarnason, T., Kokkevi, A., & Kraus, L. (2009). *The 2007 ESPAD report: Substance use among students in 35 European countries.* Stockholm: Swedish Council for Information on Alcohol and Other Drugs.

47. Pennsylvania Commission on Crime and Delinquency. (2015). *Pennsylvania Youth Survey.* Pennsylvania Department of Drug and Alcohol Programs, Pennsylvania Department of Education.

48. Arizona Criminal Justice Commission. (2014). *Arizona Youth Survey. State Report.*

49. Washington State Department of Health. (2012). *Healthy Youth Survey: Analytic report.* Office of the Superintendent of Public Instruction, Department of Social and Health Services, Department of Commerce, and Liquor Control Board.

50. Spoth, R. L., Greenberg, M. T., Bierman, K. L., & Redmond, C. (2004). PROSPER community-university partnership model for public education systems: Capacity-building for evidence-based, competence-building prevention. *Prevention Science, 5,* 31–39.

51. Spoth, R. L., & Greenberg, M. T. (2011). Impact challenges in community science-with-practice: Lessons from PROSPER on transformative practitioner-scientist partnerships and prevention infrastructure development. *American Journal of Community Psychology, 48,* 106–119.

52. Hallfors, D. D., Cho, H., Livert, D., & Kadushin, C. (2002). Fighting back against substance use: Are community coalitions winning? *American Journal of Preventive Medicine, 23,* 237–245.

53. Harachi, T. W., Ayers, C. D., Hawkins, J. D., Catalano, R. F., & Cushing, J. (1996). Empowering communities to prevent adolescent substance abuse: Process

evaluation results from a risk- and protection-focused community mobilization effort. *Journal of Primary Prevention, 16,* 233–254.

54. Manger, T. H., Hawkins, J. D., Haggerty, K. P., & Catalano, R. F. (1992). Mobilizing communities to reduce risks for drug abuse: Lessons on using research to guide prevention practice. *Journal of Primary Prevention, 13,* 3–22.

55. Arthur, M. W., Ayers, C. D., Graham, K. A., & Hawkins, J. D. (2003). Mobilizing communities to reduce risk for drug abuse: A comparison of two strategies. In W. J. Bukoski & Z. Sloboda (Eds.), *Handbook of drug abuse prevention: Theory, science and practice* (pp. 129–144). New York: Kluwer Academic/Plenum Publishers.

56. Arthur, M. W., Hawkins, J. D., Pollard, J. A., Catalano, R. F., & Baglioni, A. J. (2002). Measuring risk and protective factors for substance use, delinquency, and other adolescent problem behaviors: The Communities That Care Youth Survey. *Evaluation Review, 26,* 575–601.

57. Glaser, R. R., Van Horn, M. L., Arthur, M. W., Hawkins, J. D., & Catalano, R. F. (2005). Measurement properties of the Communities That Care Youth Survey across demographic groups. *Journal of Quantitative Criminology, 21,* 73–102.

58. Wongtongkam, N., Ward, P. R., Day, A., & Winefield, A. H. (2014). The influence of protective and risk factors in individual, peer and school domains on Thai adolescents' alcohol and illicit drug use: A survey. *Addictive Behaviors, 39,* 1447–1451.

59. Razali, M. M., & Kliewer, W. (2015). Validation of the Communities That Care measure adapted for use in Malaysia. *International Perspectives in Psychology: Research, Practice, Consultation, 4,* 267–280.

60. Maguire, E. R., Wells, W., & Katz, C. M. (2011). Measuring community risk and protective factors for adolescent problem behaviors: Evidence from a developing nation. *Journal of Research in Crime and Delinquency, 48,* 594–620.

61. Baheiraei, A., Soltani, F., Ebadi, A., Cheraghi, M. A., Foroushani, A. R., & Catalano, R. F. (2016). Psychometric properties of the Iranian version of 'Communities That Care Youth Survey'. *Health Promotion International, 31,* 59–72.

62. Beyers, J. M., Toumbourou, J. W., Catalano, R. F., Arthur, M. W., & Hawkins, J. D. (2004). A cross-national comparison of risk and protective factors for adolescence substance use: The United States and Australia. *Journal of Adolescent Health, 35,* 3–16.

63. Crow, I., France, A., Hacking, S., & Hart, M. (2004). *Does Communities That Care work? An evaluation of a community-based risk prevention programme in three neighbourhoods.* New York: Joseph Rowntree Foundation.

64. Jonkman, H. B., Haggerty, K. P., Steketee, M., Fagan, A., Hanson, K., & Hawkins, J. D. (2009). Communities That Care, core elements and context: Research of implementation in two countries. *Social Development Issues, 30,* 42–57.

65. Perez-Gomez, A., Mejia-Trujillo, J., Brown, E. C., & Eisenberg, N. (2016). Adaptation and implementation of a science-based prevention system in

Colombia: Challenges and achievements. *Journal of Community Psychology, 44,* 538–545.

66. Morojele, N. K., Flisher, A., Muller, M., Ziervogel, C. F., Reddy, P., & Lombard, C. J. (2002). Measurement of risk and protective factors for drug use and anti-social behavior among high school students in South Africa. *Journal of Drug Education, 32,* 25–39.

67. Hemphill, S. A., Heerde, J. A., Herrenkohl, T. I., Patton, G. C., Toumbourou, J. W., & Catalano, R. F. (2011). Risk and protective factors for adolescence substance use in Washington State, the United States and Victoria, Australia: A longitudinal study. *Journal of Adolescent Health, 49,* 312–320.

68. Groeger-Roth, F. (2016). *Communities That Care in Europe: 2016 update.* CTC International Meeting, Society for Prevention Research annual meeting. San Francisco.

69. Arthur, M. W., Briney, J. S., Hawkins, J. D., Abbott, R. D., Brooke-Weiss, B., & Catalano, R. F. (2007). Measuring community risk and protection using the Communities That Care Youth Survey. *Evaluation and Program Planning, 30,* 197–211.

70. Briney, J. S., Brown, E. C., Hawkins, J. D., & Arthur, M. W. (2012). Predictive validity of established cut points for risk and protective factor scales from the Communities That Care Youth Survey. *Journal of Primary Prevention, 33,* 249–258.

71. Jonkman, H. B., Junger-Tas, J., & van Dijk, B. (2005). From behind dikes and dunes: Communities That Care in the Netherlands. *Children and Society, 19,* 105–116.

72. Eisenberg, N., Brown, E. C., Perez, A., Mejia, J., Paredes, M., Cardozo, F., et al.. *Community utilization of risk and protective factor data: Voices from prevention coalitions in Colombia and Chile.* Unpublished manuscript.

73. Fairnington, A. (2004). Communities That Care: A case study of regeneration from Wales. *Critical Public Health, 14,* 27–36.

74. Oesterle, S., Hawkins, J. D., Steketee, M., Jonkman, H., Brown, E. C., Moll, M., et al. (2012). A cross national comparison of risk and protective factors for adolescent drug use and delinquency in the Netherlands and the United States. *Journal of Drug Issues, 42,* 337–357.

75. Toumbourou, J. W. (2000). Will crime prevention using the Communities That Care approach be relevant in Australia? In *Reducing Criminality: Partnerships and Best Practice.* Perth, Western Australia: Australian Institute of Criminology.

76. Wongtongkam, N., Ward, P. R., Day, A., & Winefield, A. H. (2013). Reliability and validity of self-reported questionnaires related to adolescent violence and consequences, Thailand. *International Journal of Social Science Studies, 1,* 82–92.

77. Quinby, R., Fagan, A. A., Hanson, K., Brooke-Weiss, B., Arthur, M. W., & Hawkins, J. D. (2008). Installing the Communities That Care prevention

system: Implementation progress and fidelity in a randomized controlled trial. *Journal of Community Psychology, 36*, 313–332.

CHAPTER 6

1. National Research Council and Institute of Medicine. (2009). *Preventing mental, emotional, and behavioral disorders among young people: Progress and possibilities* (M. E. O'Connell, T. Boat, & K. E. Warner, Eds.). Washington, DC: National Academies Press.
2. Catalano, R. F., Fagan, A. A., Gavin, L. E., Greenberg, M. T., Irwin, C. E., Ross, D. A., et al. (2012). Worldwide application of prevention science in adolescent health. *Lancet, 379*, 1653–1664.
3. Hawkins, J. D., Jenson, J. M., Catalano, R. F., Fraser, M. W., Botvin, G. J., Shapiro, V., et al. (2015). *Unleashing the power of prevention.* Discussion paper. Washington, DC: Institute of Medicine and National Research Council.
4. Spoth, R. L., Rohrbach, L. A., Greenberg, M. T., Leaf, P., Brown, C. H., Fagan, A., et al.. (2013). Addressing core challenges for the next generation of Type 2 translation research and systems: The Translation Science to Population Impact (TSci Impact) Framework. *Prevention Science, 14*, 319–351.
5. Neta, G., Glasgow, R. E., Carpenter, C. S., Grimshaw, J. M., Rabin, B. A., Fernandez, M. E., et al. (2015). A framework for enhancing the value of research for dissemination and implementation. *American Journal of Public Health, 105*, 49–57.
6. Rabin, B. A., Brownson, R. C., Haire-Joshu, D., Kreuter, M. W., & Weaver, N. L. (2008). A glossary for dissemination and implementation research in health. *Journal of Public Health Management and Practice, 14*, 117–123.
7. Glasgow, R. E., Vinson, C., Chambers, D., Khoury, M. J., Kaplan, R. M., & Hunter, C. (2012). National Institutes of Health approaches to dissemination and implementation science: Current and future directions. *American Journal of Public Health, 102*, 1274–1281.
8. Nilsen, P. (2015). Making sense of implementation theories, models and frameworks. *Implementation Science, 10*, 53.
9. U.S. Department of Health and Human Services. (2016, November). *Facing addiction in America: The Surgeon General's report on alcohol, drugs, and health.* Office of the Surgeon General. Washington, DC: Author.
10. World Health Organization. (2014). *Global status report on violence prevention.* Geneva, Switzerland: Author.
11. Altman, D., Schultz, K. F., Moher, D., Egger, M., Davidoff, F., Elbourne, D., et al. (2001). The revised CONSORT statement for reporting randomized trials: Explanation and elaboration. *Annals of Internal Medicine, 134*, 663–694.

12. Flay, B. R., Biglan, A., Boruch, R. F., Castro, F. G., Gottfredson, D. C., Kellam, S. G., et al. (2005). Standards of evidence: Criteria for efficacy, effectiveness, and dissemination. *Prevention Science, 6,* 151–175.

13. Gottfredson, D. C., Cook, T. D., Gardner, F. E. M., Gorman-Smith, D., Howe, G.W., Sandler, I. N., et al. (2015). Standards of evidence for efficacy, effectiveness and scale-up research in prevention science: Next generation. *Prevention Science, 16,* 893–926.

14. Biglan, A., Flay, B. R., & Wagenaar, A. C. (2015). Commentary on the 2015 SPR Standards of Evidence. *Prevention Science, 16,* 927–932.

15. Bickman, L. (2015). The revised quality standards: "A man's reach should exceed his grasp" or "A bridge too far": Which is the case? *Prevention Science, 16,* 933–937.

16. Sampson, R. J. (2010). Gold standard myths: Observations on the experimental turn in quantitative criminology. *Journal of Quantitative Criminology, 26,* 489–500.

17. Hough, M. (2010). Gold standard or fool's gold? The pursuit of certainty in experimental criminology. *Criminology and Criminal Justice, 10,* 11–22.

18. Mears, D. P. (2007). Towards rational and evidence-based crime policy. *Journal of Criminal Justice, 35,* 667–682.

19. Lipsey, M., Petrie, C., Weisburd, D., & Gottfredson, D. C. (2006). Improving evaluation of anti-crime programs: Summary of a National Research Council report. *Journal of Experimental Criminology, 2,* 271–307.

20. Pawson, R., & Tilley, N. (1994). What works in evaluation research. *British Journal of Criminology, 34,* 291–306.

21. Wandersman, A., Duffy, J., Flaspohler, P. D., Noonan, R. K., Lubell, K., Stillman, L., et al. (2008). Bridging the gap between prevention research and practice: The Interactive Systems Framework for Dissemination and Implementation. *American Journal of Community Psychology, 41,* 171–181.

22. Office of Juvenile Justice and Delinquency Prevention. (1995). *Guide for implementing the Comprehensive Strategy for Serious, Violent, and Chronic Juvenile Offenders.* Washington, DC: Author.

23. Hawkins, J. D., & Catalano, R. F. (1996, 2000, 2004). *Communities That Care Prevention Strategies Guide.* South Deerfield, MA: Channing Bete.

24. Burkhardt, J. T., Schroter, D. C., Magura, S., Means, S. N., & Coryn, C. L. S. (2015). An overview of evidence-based program registers (EBPRs) for behavioral health. *Evaluation and Program Planning, 48,* 92–99.

25. Means, S., Magura, S., Burkhart, B. R., Schroter, D. C., & Coryn, C. L. S. (2015). Comparing rating paradigms for evidence-based program registers in behavioral health: Evidentiary criteria and implications for assessing programs. *Evaluation and Program Planning, 48,* 100–116.

26. Fagan, A. A., & Buchanan, M. (2016). What works in crime prevention? Comparison and critical review of three crime prevention registries. *Criminology and Public Policy, 15*, 617–649.

27. Wright, B. J., Zhang, S. X., & Farabee, D. (2012). A squandered opportunity? A review of SAMHSA'S National Registry of Evidence-Based Programs and Practices for offenders. *Crime and Delinquency, 58*, 954–972.

28. Gandhi, A. G., Murphy-Graham, E., Petrosino, A., Chrismer, S. S., & Weiss, C. H. (2007). The devil is in the details: Examining the evidence for "proven" school-based drug abuse prevention programs. *Evaluation Review, 31*, 43–74.

29. Wilson, D. B. (2009). Missing a critical piece of the pie: Simple document search strategies inadequate for systematic reviews. *Journal of Experimental Criminology, 5*, 429–440.

30. Farrington, D. P., & Petrosino, A. (2001). The Campbell Collaboration Crime and Justice Group. *Annals of the American Academy of Political and Social Science, 578*, 35–49.

31. Durlak, J. A., & DuPre, E. P. (2008). Implementation matters: A review of the research on the influence of implementation on program outcomes and the factors affecting implementation. *American Journal of Community Psychology, 41*, 327–350.

32. Fixsen, D. L., Naoom, S. F., Blase, K. A., Friedman, R. M., & Wallace, F. (2005). *Implementation research: A synthesis of the literature.* National Implementation Research Network (FMHI Publication #231). Tampa, FL: University of South Florida, Louis de la Parte Florida Mental Health Institute.

33. Gottfredson, D. C., & Gottfredson, G. D. (2002). Quality of school-based prevention programs: Results from a national survey. *Journal of Research in Crime and Delinquency, 39*, 3–35.

34. Welsh, B. C., Sullivan, C. J., & Olds, D. L. (2010). When early crime prevention goes to scale: A new look at the evidence. *Prevention Science, 11*, 115–125.

35. Valentine, J. C., Biglan, A., Boruch, R. F., Castro, F. G., Collins, L. M., Flay, B.R., et al. (2011). Replication in prevention science. *Prevention Science, 12*, 103–117.

36. Aos, S., Cook, T. D., Elliott, D. S., Gottfredson, D. C., Hawkins, J. D., Lipsey, M. W., et al. (2011). Commentary on Valentine, Jeffrey, et al. *Prevention Science, 12*, 121–122.

37. Elliott, D. S. (2013). Crime prevention and intervention over the life course: Emerging trends and directions for future research. In C. L. Gibson & M. D. Krohn (Eds.), *Handbook of life-course criminology* (pp. 297–316). New York: Springer.

38. Farrington, D. P., & Welsh, B. C. (2007). *Saving children from a life of crime: Early risk factors and effective interventions.* New York: Oxford University Press.

39. Jonkman, H. B., Junger-Tas, J., & van Dijk, B. (2005). From behind dikes and dunes: Communities That Care in the Netherlands. *Children and Society*, *19*, 105–116.

40. Toumbourou, J. W. (2000). Will crime prevention using the Communities That Care approach be relevant in Australia? In *Reducing Criminality: Partnerships and Best Practice*. Perth, Western Australia: Australian Institute of Criminology.

41. Perez-Gomez, A., Mejia-Trujillo, J., Brown, E. C., & Eisenberg, N. (2016). Adaptation and implementation of a science-based prevention system in Colombia: Challenges and achievements. *Journal of Community Psychology*, *44*, 538–545.

42. National Advisory Mental Health Council. (2006). *The road ahead: Research partnerships to transform services*. Washington, DC: National Institutes of Health, National Institute of Mental Health.

43. Backer, T. E. (2000). The failure of success: Challenges of disseminating effective substance abuse prevention programs. *Journal of Community Psychology*, *28*, 363–373.

44. Greenhalgh, T., Robert, G., Macfarlane, F., Bate, P., & Kyriakidou, O. (2004). Diffusion of innovations in service organizations: Systematic review and recommendations. *Milbank Quarterly*, *82*, 581–629.

45. Fixsen, D. L., Blase, K. A., Metz, A., & Van Dyke, M. (2013). Statewide implementation of evidence-based programs. *Exceptional Children*, *79*, 213–230.

46. Rogers, E. M. (1995). *Diffusion of innovations*. (4th ed.). New York: Free Press.

47. Glasgow, R. E., & Emmons, K. (2007). How can we increase translation of research into practice? Types of evidence needed. *Annual Review of Public Health*, *28*, 413–433.

48. Institute of Medicine (IOM). (2001). *Crossing the quality chasm: A new health system for the 21st century*. Washington, DC: National Academies Press.

49. U.S. Department of Education. (2011). *Prevalence and implementation fidelity of research-based prevention programs in public schools: Final report*. Washington, DC: Office of Planning, Evaluation and Policy Development, Policy and Program Studies Service.

50. Ringwalt, C., Hanley, S., Vincus, A. A., Ennett, S. T., Rohrbach, L. A., & Bowling, J. M. (2008). The prevalence of effective substance use prevention curricula in the Nation's high schools. *Journal of Primary Prevention*, *29*, 479–488.

51. Ringwalt, C., Vincus, A. A., Hanley, S., Ennett, S. T., Bowling, J. M., & Haws, S. (2011). The prevalence of evidence-based drug use prevention curricula in U.S. middle schools in 2008. *Prevention Science*, *12*, 63–69.

52. Hallfors, D., & Godette, D. (2002). Will the "Principles of Effectiveness" improve prevention practice? Early findings from a diffusion study. *Health Education Research*, *17*, 461–470.

53. Hallfors, D., Pankratz, M., & Hartman, S. (2007). Does federal policy support the use of scientific evidence in school-based prevention programs? *Prevention Science, 8,* 75–81.

54. Glasgow, R. E., Vogt, T. M., & Boles, S. M. (1999). Evaluating the public health impact of health promotion interventions: The RE-AIM framework. *American Journal of Public Health, 89,* 1322–1327.

55. Foster-Fishman, P. G., Nowell, B., & Yang, H. (2007). Putting the system back into systems change: A framework for understanding and changing organizational and community systems. *American Journal of Community Psychology, 39,* 197–215.

56. Damschroder, L. J., Aron, D. C., Keith, R. E., Kirsh, S. R., Alexander, J. A., & Lowery, J. C. (2009). Fostering implementation of health services research findings into practice: A consolidated framework for advancing implementation science. *Implementation Science, 4,* 50.

57. Rohrbach, L. A., Grana, R., Sussman, S., & Valente, T. W. (2006). Type II Translation: Transporting prevention interventions from research to real-world settings. *Evaluation and the Health Professions, 29,* 302–333.

58. Backer, T. E. (1995). Assessing and enhancing readiness for change: Implications for technology transfer. In T. E. Backer, S. L. David, & G. Soucy (Eds.), *Reviewing the behavioral science knowledge base on technology transfer* (pp. 21–41). Rockville, MD: National Institute on Drug Abuse.

59. Edwards, R. W., Jumper-Thurman, P., Plested, B. A., Oetting, E. R., & Swanson, L. (2000). Community readiness: Research to practice. *Journal of Community Psychology, 28,* 291–307.

60. Elliott, D. S., & Mihalic, S. (2004). Issues in disseminating and replicating effective prevention programs. *Prevention Science, 5,* 47–53.

61. Meyers, D. C., Durlak, J. A., & Wandersman, A. (2012). The quality implementation framework: A synthesis of critical steps in the implementation process. *American Journal of Community Psychology, 50,* 462–480.

62. Flaspohler, P. D., Duffy, J., Wandersman, A., Stillman, L., & Maras, M. A. (2008). Unpacking prevention capacity: An intersection of research-to-practice models and community-centered models. *American Journal of Community Psychology, 41,* 182–196.

63. Dariotis, J. K., Bumbarger, B. K., Duncan, L. G., & Greenberg, M. T. (2008). How do implementation efforts relate to program adherence? Examining the role of organizational, implementer, and program factors. *Journal of Community Psychology, 36,* 744–760.

64. Brown, B. S. (1995). Reducing impediments to technology transfer in drug abuse programming. In T. E. Backer, S. L. David, & G. Soucy (Eds.), *Reviewing the behavioral science knowledge base on technology transfer* (pp. 169–185). Rockville, MD: National Institute on Drug Abuse.

65. Aarons, G. A., Hurlburt, M., & Horwitz, S. M. (2011). Advancing a conceptual model of evidence-based practice implementation in public service sectors. *Administration and Policy in Mental Health, 38*, 4–23.

66. Fagan, A. A., Brooke-Weiss, B., Cady, R., & Hawkins, J. D. (2009). If at first you don't succeed . . . keep trying: Strategies to enhance coalition/school partnerships to implement school-based prevention programming. *Australian and New Zealand Journal of Criminology, 42*, 387–405.

67. Flaspohler, P. D., Meehan, C., Maras, M. A., & Keller, K. E. (2012). Ready, willing, and able: Developing a support system to promote implementation of school-based prevention programs. *American Journal of Community Psychology, 50*, 428–444.

68. Supplee, L. H., & Metz, A. (2015). Opportunities and challenges in evidence-based social policy. *Social Policy Report, 28*, 1–16.

69. Gingiss, P. M., Roberts-Gray, C., & Boerm, M. (2006). Bridge-It: A system for predicting implementation fidelity for school-based tobacco prevention programs. *Prevention Science, 7*, 197–207.

70. Woolf, S. H. (2008). The power of prevention and what it requires. *Journal of the American Medical Association, 299*, 2437–2439.

71. Roberts-Gray, C., Gingiss, P. M., & Boerm, M. (2007). Evaluating school capacity to implement new programs. *Evaluation and Program Planning, 30*, 247–257.

72. Castro, F. G., Barrera, M., & Holleran Steiker, L. K. (2010). Issues and challenges in the design of culturally adapted evidence-based interventions. *Annual Review of Clinical Psychology, 6*, 213–239.

73. Brody, G. H., McBride Murry, V., Gerrard, M., Gibbons, F. X., Molgaard, V., McNair, L., et al. (2004). The Strong African American Families Program: Translating research into prevention programming. *Child Development, 75*, 900–917.

74. Harachi, T. W., Ayers, C. D., Hawkins, J. D., Catalano, R. F., & Cushing, J. (1996). Empowering communities to prevent adolescent substance abuse: Process evaluation results from a risk- and protection-focused community mobilization effort. *Journal of Primary Prevention, 16*, 233–254.

75. Manger, T. H., Hawkins, J. D., Haggerty, K. P., & Catalano, R. F. (1992). Mobilizing communities to reduce risks for drug abuse: Lessons on using research to guide prevention practice. *Journal of Primary Prevention, 13*, 3–22.

76. Quinby, R., Fagan, A. A., Hanson, K., Brooke-Weiss, B., Arthur, M. W., & Hawkins, J. D. (2008). Installing the Communities That Care prevention system: Implementation progress and fidelity in a randomized controlled trial. *Journal of Community Psychology, 36*, 313–332.

77. Fagan, A. A., Hanson, K., Hawkins, J. D., & Arthur, M. W. (2009). Translational research in action: Implementation of the Communities That Care prevention system in 12 communities. *Journal of Community Psychology, 37*, 809–829.

78. Arthur, M. W., Hawkins, J. D., Brown, E. C., Briney, J. S., Oesterle, S., & Abbott, R. D. (2010). Implementation of the Communities That Care prevention system by coalitions in the Community Youth Development Study. *Journal of Community Psychology, 38,* 245–258.

79. Gloppen, K. M., Arthur, M. W., Hawkins, J. D., & Shapiro, V. B. (2012). Sustainability of the Communities That Care prevention system by coalitions participating in the Community Youth Development Study. *Journal of Adolescent Health, 51,* 259–264.

80. Jonkman, H. B., Haggerty, K. P., Steketee, M., Fagan, A., Hanson, K., & Hawkins, J. D. (2009). Communities That Care, core elements and context: Research of implementation in two countries. *Social Development Issues, 30,* 42–57.

81. Kazdin, A. E. (2007). Mediators and mechanisms of change in psychotherapy research. *Annual Review of Clinical Psychology, 3,* 1–27.

82. Liddle, H. A. (2004). Family-based therapies for adolescent alcohol and drug use: Research contributions and future research needs. *Addiction, 99,* 76–92.

83. Fairchild, A. J., & MacKinnon, D. P. (2014). Using mediation and moderation analyses to enhance prevention research. In Z. Sloboda & H. Petras (Eds.), *Defining prevention science* (pp. 537–556). New York: Springer.

84. Weersing, V. R., & Weisz, J. R. (2002). Mechanisms of action in youth psychotherapy. *Journal of Child Psychology and Psychiatry, 43,* 3–29.

85. Fairnington, A. (2004). Communities That Care: A case study of regeneration from Wales. *Critical Public Health, 14,* 27–36.

86. Fagan, A. A., Hawkins, J. D., & Catalano, R. F. (2008). Using community epidemiologic data to improve social settings: The Communities That Care prevention system. In M. Shinn & H. Yoshikawa (Eds.), *The power of social settings: Promoting youth development by changing schools and community programs* (pp. 292–312). New York: Oxford University Press.

87. Hawkins, J. D., Catalano, R. F., & Arthur, M. W. (2002). Promoting science-based prevention in communities. *Addictive Behaviors, 27,* 951–976.

88. Kania, J., & Kramer, M. (2011). Collective impact. *Stanford Social Innovation Review, 9,* 36–41.

89. Hawkins, J. D., Catalano, R. F., & Miller, J. Y. (1992). Risk and protective factors for alcohol and other drug problems in adolescence and early adulthood: Implications for substance abuse prevention. *Psychological Bulletin, 112,* 64–105.

90. Farrington, D. P. (2000). Explaining and preventing crime: The globalization of knowledge—The American Society of Criminology 1999 Presidential Address. *Criminology, 38,* 1–24.

91. Rose, G. (1985). Sick individuals and sick populations. *International Journal of Epidemiology, 14,* 32–38.

92. Fagan, A. A., & Hawkins, J. D. (2013). Preventing substance use, delinquency, violence, and other problem behaviors over the life-course using the Communities That Care system. In C. L. Gibson & M. D. Krohn (Eds.), *Handbook of life-course criminology* (pp. 277–296). New York: Springer.

93. Hanleybrown, F., Kania, J., & Kramer, M. (2012). Channeling change: Making collective impact work. *Stanford Social Innovation Review*, 10, 1–8.

94. Hawkins, J. D., Catalano, R. F., Arthur, M. W., Egan, E., Brown, E. C., Abbott, R. D., et al. (2008). Testing Communities That Care: The rationale, design and behavioral baseline equivalence of the Community Youth Development Study. *Prevention Science*, 9, 178–190.

95. U.S. Government Accountability Office. (1996). *Report to the Committee on the Judiciary, U.S. Senate, and the Committee on Economic and Educational Opportunity*. House of Representatives. Washington, DC: Author.

96. France, A., & Crow, I. (2005). Using the "risk factor paradigm" in prevention: Lessons from the evaluation of Communities That Care. *Children and Society*, 19, 172–184.

97. Fagan, A. A., Hanson, K., Hawkins, J. D., & Arthur, M. W. (2008). Bridging science to practice: Achieving prevention program fidelity in the Community Youth Development Study. *American Journal of Community Psychology*, 41, 235–249.

98. Burkhart, G. (2013). *North Americans drug prevention programmes: Are they feasible in European cultures and contexts?* Lisbon, Portugal: European Monitoring Centre for Drugs and Drug Addiction.

99. Jonkman, H. B., Aussems, C., Steketee, M., Boutellier, H., & Cuijpers, P. (2015). Prevention of problem behaviours among adolescents: The impact of the Communities That Care strategy in the Netherlands (2008–2011). *International Journal of Developmental Science*, 9, 37–52.

100. Coie, J. D., Watt, N. F., West, S. G., Hawkins, J. D., Asarnow, J. R., Marman, H.J., et al. (1993). The science of prevention: A conceptual framework and some directions for a national research program. *American Psychologist*, 48, 1013–1022.

101. Fagan, A. A., & Hawkins, J. D. (2012). Community-based substance use prevention. In B. C. Welsh & D. P. Farrington (Eds.), *The Oxford handbook on crime prevention* (pp. 247–268). New York: Oxford University Press.

102. Hallfors, D. D., Cho, H., Livert, D., & Kadushin, C. (2002). Fighting back against substance use: Are community coalitions winning? *American Journal of Preventive Medicine*, 23, 237–245.

103. Spoth, R. L., & Greenberg, M. T. (2005). Toward a comprehensive strategy for effective practitioner-scientist partnerships and larger-scale community health and well-being. *American Journal of Community Psychology*, 35, 107–126.

104. Crowley, D. M., Greenberg, M. T., Feinberg, M. E., Spoth, R. L., & Redmond, C. (2012). The effect of the PROSPER partnership model on cultivating local stakeholder knowledge of evidence-based programs: A five-year longitudinal study of 28 communities. *Prevention Science, 13*, 96–105.

105. Spoth, R., Redmond, C., Shin, C., Greenberg, M. T., Feinberg, M. E., & Schainker, L. M. (2013). PROSPER Community-University Partnership delivery system effects on substance misuse through 6 1/2 years past baseline from a cluster randomized controlled intervention trial. *Preventive Medicine, 56*, 190–196.

106. Spoth, R. L., Redmond, C., Clair, S., Shin, C., Greenberg, M. T., & Feinberg, M. E. (2011). Preventing substance misuse through community–university partnerships randomized controlled trial outcomes 4½ years past baseline. *American Journal of Preventive Medicine, 40*, 440–447.

107. Spoth, R. L., Trudeau, L. S., Redmond, C., Shin, C., Greenberg, M. T., Feinberg, M. E., et al. (2015). PROSPER partnership delivery system: Effects on adolescent conduct problem behavior outcomes through 6.5 years past baseline. *Journal of Adolescence, 45*, 44–55.

108. Center for Substance Abuse Prevention. (2009). *Identifying and selecting evidence-based interventions: Revised guidance document for the Strategic Prevention Framework State Incentive Grant Program.* Substance Abuse and Mental Health Services Administration. Rockville, MD: Author.

109. Anderson-Carpenter, K. D., Watson-Thompson, J., Chaney, L., & Jones, M. (2016). Reducing binge drinking in adolescents through implementation of the Strategic Prevention Framework. *American Journal of Community Psychology, 57*, 36–46.

110. Eddy, J. J., Gideonsen, M. D., McClaflin, R. R., O'Halloran, P., Peardon, F. A., Radcliff, P. L., & Masters, L. A. (2012). Reducing alcohol use in youth aged 12-17 years using the Strategic Prevention Framework. *Journal of Community Psychology, 40*, 607–620.

111. Matjasko, J. L., Massetti, G. M., & Bacon, S. (2016). Implementing and evaluating comprehensive evidence-based approaches to prevent youth violence: Partnering to create communities where youth are safe from violence. *Journal of Primary Prevention, 37*, 109–119.

112. Hawkins, J. D., Brown, E. C., Oesterle, S., Arthur, M. W., Abbott, R. D., & Catalano, R. F. (2008). Early effects of Communities That Care on targeted risks and initiation of delinquent behavior and substance use. *Journal of Adolescent Health, 43*, 15–22.

113. Hawkins, J. D., Oesterle, S., Brown, E. C., Arthur, M. W., Abbott, R. D., Fagan, A. A., et al. (2009). Results of a type 2 translational research trial to prevent adolescent drug use and delinquency: A test of Communities That Care. *Archives of Pediatric and Adolescent Medicine, 163*, 789–798.

114. Hawkins, J. D., Oesterle, S., Brown, E. C., Abbott, R. D., & Catalano, R. F. (2014). Youth problem behaviors 8 years after implementing the Communities That Care prevention system: A community randomized trial. *JAMA Pediatrics, 168,* 122–129.

CHAPTER 7

1. Durlak, J. A., & DuPre, E. P. (2008). Implementation matters: A review of the research on the influence of implementation on program outcomes and the factors affecting implementation. *American Journal of Community Psychology, 41,* 327–350.

2. Glasgow, R. E., Vogt, T. M., & Boles, S. M. (1999). Evaluating the public health impact of health promotion interventions: The RE-AIM framework. *American Journal of Public Health, 89,* 1322–1327.

3. Rabin, B. A., Brownson, R. C., Haire-Joshu, D., Kreuter, M. W., & Weaver, N. L. (2008). A glossary for dissemination and implementation research in health. *Journal of Public Health Management and Practice 14,* 117–123.

4. Damschroder, L. J., Aron, D. C., Keith, R. E., Kirsh, S. R., Alexander, J. A., & Lowery, J. C. (2009). Fostering implementation of health services research findings into practice: A consolidated framework for advancing implementation science. *Implementation Science, 4,* 50.

5. Neta, G., Glasgow, R. E., Carpenter, C. S., Grimshaw, J. M., Rabin, B. A., Fernandez, M. E., et al. (2015). A framework for enhancing the value of research for dissemination and implementation. *American Journal of Public Health, 105,* 49–57.

6. Fixsen, D. L., Naoom, S. F., Blase, K. A., Friedman, R. M., & Wallace, F. (2005). *Implementation research: A synthesis of the literature.* National Implementation Research Network (FMHI Publication #231). Tampa, FL: University of South Florida, Louis de la Parte Florida Mental Health Institute.

7. Carroll, C., Patterson, M., Wood, S., Booth, A., Rick, J., & Balain, S. (2007). A conceptual framework for implementation fidelity. *Implementation Science, 2,* 40–49.

8. Dusenbury, L., Brannigan, R., Falco, M., & Hansen, W. B. (2003). A review of research on fidelity of implementation: Implications for drug abuse prevention in school settings. *Health Education Research, 18,* 237–256.

9. Berkel, C., Mauricio, A. M., Schoenfelder, E., & Sandler, I. N. (2011). Putting the pieces together: An integrated model of program implementation. *Prevention Science, 12,* 23–33.

10. Blase, K. A., & Fixsen, D. L. (2013). *Core intervention components: Identifying and operationalizing what makes programs work.* Washington, DC: Office of the Assistant Secretary for Planning and Evaluation, U.S. Department of Health and Human Services.

11. Botvin, G. J., Baker, E., Dusenbury, L., Botvin, E. M., & Diaz, T. (1995). Long-term follow-up results of a randomized drug abuse prevention trial in a white middle-class population. *Journal of the American Medical Association, 273,* 1106–1112.

12. Washington State Institute for Public Policy. (2002). *Washington State's implementation of Functional Family Therapy for juvenile offenders: Preliminary findings.* Olympia, WA: Author.

13. Gottfredson, D. C., & Gottfredson, G. D. (2002). Quality of school-based prevention programs: Results from a national survey. *Journal of Research in Crime and Delinquency, 39,* 3–35.

14. Rohrbach, L. A., Grana, R., Sussman, S., & Valente, T. W. (2006). Type II Translation: Transporting prevention interventions from research to real-world settings. *Evaluation and the Health Professions, 29,* 302–333.

15. Hallfors, D., & Godette, D. (2002). Will the "Principles of Effectiveness" improve prevention practice? Early findings from a diffusion study. *Health Education Research, 17,* 461–470.

16. U.S. Department of Education. (2011). *Prevalence and implementation fidelity of research-based prevention programs in public schools: Final report.* Washington, DC: Office of Planning, Evaluation and Policy Development, Policy and Program Studies Service.

17. Ringwalt, C. L., Ennett, S. T., Johnson, R., Rohrbach, L. A., Simons-Rudolph, A., Vincus, A. A., et al. (2003). Factors associated with fidelity to substance use prevention curriculum guides in the Nation's middle schools. *Health Education & Behavior, 30,* 375–391.

18. Ennett, S. T., Ringwalt, C., Thorne, J., Rohrbach, L. A., Vincus, A. A., Simons-Rudolph, A., et al. (2003). A comparison of current practice in school-based substance use prevention programs with meta-analysis findings. *Prevention Science, 4,* 1–14.

19. Gottfredson, D. C., Kumpfer, K., Polizzi-Fox, D., Wilson, D., Puryear, V., Beatty, P., et al. (2006). The Strengthening Families Washington D.C. Families Project: A randomized effectiveness trial of family-based prevention. *Prevention Science, 7,* 57–73.

20. Hoagwood, K., Burns, B. J., Kiser, L., Ringeisen, H., & Schoenwald, S. K. (2001). Evidence-based practice in child and adolescent mental health services. *Psychiatric Services, 52,* 1179–1189.

21. Hill, L. G., Maucione, K., & Hood, B. K. (2006). A focused approach to assessing program fidelity. *Prevention Science, 8,* 25–34.

22. Komro, K., Perry, C. L., Veblen-Mortenson, S., Farbakhsh, K., Toomey, T. L., Stigler, M. H., et al. (2008). Outcomes from a randomized controlled trial of a multi-component alcohol use preventive intervention for urban youth: Project Northland Chicago. *Addiction, 103,* 606–618.

23. Wandersman, A., & Florin, P. (2003). Community intervention and effective prevention. *American Psychologist, 58,* 441–448.

24. Meyers, D. C., Durlak, J. A., & Wandersman, A. (2012). The quality implementation framework: A synthesis of critical steps in the implementation process. *American Journal of Community Psychology, 50,* 462–480.

25. Brown, B. S. (1995). Reducing impediments to technology transfew in drug abuse programming. In T. E. Backer, S. L. David, & G. Soucy (Eds.), *Reviewing the behavioral science knowledge base on technology transfer* (pp. 169–185). Rockville, MD: National Institute on Drug Abuse.

26. Moore, J. E., Bumbarger, B. K., & Cooper, B. R. (2013). Examining adaptations of evidence-based programs in natural contexts. *Journal of Primary Prevention, 34,* 147–161.

27. Castro, F. G., Barrera, M., & Holleran Steiker, L. K. (2010). Issues and challenges in the design of culturally adapted evidence-based interventions. *Annual Review of Clinical Psychology, 6,* 213–239.

28. Backer, T. E. (2001). *Finding the balance: Programme fidelity in substance abuse prevention: A state-of-the-art review.* Rockville, MD: Substance Abuse and Mental Health Services Administration, Center for Substance Abuse Prevention.

29. Kumpfer, K. L., Alvarado, R., Smith, P., & Bellamy, N. (2002). Cultural sensitivity and adaptation in family-based prevention interventions. *Prevention Science, 3,* 241–246.

30. Elliott, D. S., & Mihalic, S. (2004). Issues in disseminating and replicating effective prevention programs. *Prevention Science, 5,* 47–53.

31. U.S. Department of Health and Human Services. (2016, November). *Facing addiction in America: The Surgeon General's report on alcohol, drugs, and health.* Office of the Surgeon General. Washington, DC: Author.

32. Olds, D. L., Robinson, J., O'Brien, R., Luckey, D. W., Pettitt, L. M., Henderson Jr., C., et al. (2002). Home visiting by paraprofessionals and by nurses: A randomized, controlled trial. *Pediatrics, 110,* 486–496.

33. Lau, A. S. (2006). Making the case for selective and directed cultural adaptations of evidence-based treatments: Examples from parent training. *Clinical Psychology: Science and Practice, 13,* 295–310.

34. Elliott, D.S., & Fagan, A. A. (2017). *The prevention of crime.* Hoboken, NJ: John Wiley.

35. Fixsen, D. L., Blase, K. A., Metz, A., & Van Dyke, M. (2013). Statewide implementation of evidence-based programs. *Exceptional Children, 79,* 213–230.

36. Becker, K. D., Bradshaw, C. P., Domitrovich, C., & Ialongo, N. S. (2013). Coaching teachers to improve implementation of the Good Behavior Game. *Administration and Policy in Mental Health, 40,* 482–493.

37. Bumbarger, B. K., Perkins, D. F., & Greenberg, M. T. (2010). Taking effective prevention to scale. In B. Doll, W. Pfohl, & J. Yoon (Eds.), *Handbook of youth prevention science* (pp. 433–444). New York: Routledge.

38. Kealey, K. A., Peterson, A. V. J., Gaul, M. A., & Dinh, K. T. (2000). Teacher training as a behavior change process: Principles and results from a longitudinal study. *Health Education & Behavior, 27,* 64–81.

39. Massetti, G. M., Holland, K. M., & Gorman-Smith, D. (2016). Implementation measurement for evidence-based violence prevention programs in communities. *Journal of Community Health, 41,* 881–894.

40. Hogue, A., Ozechowski, T. J., Robbins, M. S., & Waldron, H. B. (2013). Making fidelity an intramural game: Localizing quality assurance procedures to promote sustainability of evidence-based practices in usual care. *Clinical Psychology Science and Practice, 20,* 60–77.

41. Schoenwald, S. K., Garland, A. F., Chapman, J. E., Frazier, S. L., Sheidow, A. J., & Southam-Gerow, M. A. (2011). Toward the effective and efficient measurement of implementation fidelity. *Administration and Policy in Mental Health, 38,* 32–43.

42. Proctor, E. K., Silmere, H., Raghavan, R., Hovmand, P., Aarons, G. A., Bunger, A., et al. (2011). Outcomes for implementation research: Conceptual distinctions, measurement challenges, and research agenda. *Administration and Policy in Mental Health, 38,* 65–76.

43. Dusenbury, L., Brannigan, R., Hansen, W. B., Walsh, J., & Falco, M. (2005). Quality of implementation: Developing measures crucial to understanding the diffusion of preventive interventions. *Health Education Research, 20,* 308–313.

44. Wandersman, A., Imm, P., Chinman, M., & Kaftarian, S. J. (2000). Getting to Outcomes: A results-based approach to accountability. *Evaluation and Program Planning, 23,* 389–395.

45. Dusenbury, L., Hansen, W. B., Jackson-Newsom, J., Pittman, D. S., Wilson, C. V., Nelson-Smiley, K., et al. (2010). Coaching to enhance quality of implementation in prevention. *Health Education, 110,* 43–60.

46. Fixsen, D. L., Blase, K. A., Naoom, S. F., & Wallace, F. (2009). Core implementation components. *Research on Social Work Practice, 19,* 531–540.

47. Sedlar, G., Bruns, E. J., Walker, S. C., Kerns, S., & Negrete, A. (2017). Developing a quality assurance system for multiple evidence based practices in a statewide service improvement initiative. *Administration and Policy in Mental Health, 44,* 29–41.

48. Fagan, A. A., & Mihalic, S. (2003). Strategies for enhancing the adoption of school-based prevention programs: Lessons learned from the Blueprints for Violence Prevention replications of the Life Skills Training Program. *Journal of Community Psychology, 31,* 235–254.

49. Schoenwald, S. K., Sheidow, A. J., & Letourneau, E. J. (2004). Toward effective quality assurance in evidence-based practice: Links between expert consultation,

therapist fidelity, and child outcomes. *Journal of Clinical Child and Adolescent Psychology, 33,* 94–104.

50. Henggeler, S. W., Melton, G. B., Brondino, M. J., Scherer, D. G., & Hanley, J. H. (1997). Multisystemic Therapy with violent and chronic juvenile offenders and their families: The role of treatment fidelity in successful dissemination. *Journal of Consulting and Clinical Psychology, 65,* 821–833.

51. Dumas, J. E., Lynch, A. M., Laughlin, J. E., Smith, E. P., & Printz, R. J. (2001). Promoting intervention fidelity: Conceptual issues, methods, and preliminary results from the Early Alliance Prevention Trial. *American Journal of Preventive Medicine, 20,* 38–47.

52. Spoth, R. L., & Redmond, C. (2002). Project Family prevention trials based in community-university partnerships: Toward scaled-up preventive interventions. *Prevention Science, 3,* 203–222.

53. Roth, D., Panzano, P. C., Crane-Ross, D., Massatti, R., Carstens, C., Seffrin, B., et al. (2005). The innovation diffusion and adoption research project (IDARP): Moving from the diffusion of research results to promoting the adoption of evidence-based innovations in the Ohio mental health system. In D. Roth & W. J. Lutz (Eds.), *New research in mental health, Vol 16* (pp. 78–89). Columbus: Ohio Department of Mental Health.

54. Catalano, R. F., Kosterman, R., Haggerty, K. P., Hawkins, J. D., & Spoth, R. L. (1998). A universal intervention for the prevention of substance abuse: Preparing for the Drug Free Years. In R. S. Ashery, E. B. Robertson, & K. L. Kumpfer (Eds.), NIDA Research Monograph No. 177: *Drug abuse prevention through family interventions* (pp. 130–159). Rockville, MD: National Institute on Drug Abuse.

55. Harachi, T. W., Catalano, R. F., & Hawkins, J. D. (1997). Effective recruitment for parenting programs within ethnic minority communities. *Child and Adolescent Social Work Journal, 14,* 23–39.

56. Spoth, R. L., & Greenberg, M. T. (2011). Impact challenges in community science-with-practice: Lessons from PROSPER on transformative practitioner-scientist partnerships and prevention infrastructure development. *American Journal of Community Psychology, 48,* 106–119.

57. Chinman, M., Hannah, G., Wandersman, A., Ebener, P., Hunter, S. B., Imm, P., et al. (2005). Developing a community science research agenda for building community capacity for effective preventive interventions. *American Journal of Community Psychology, 35,* 143–157.

58. Mitchell, R., Florin, P., & Stevenson, J.F. (2002). Supporting community-based prevention and health promotion initiatives: Developing effective technical assistance systems. *Health Education & Behavior, 29,* 620–639.

59. Spoth, R. L., Guyll, M., Lillehoj, C. J., Redmond, C., & Greenberg, M. T. (2007). PROSPER study of evidence-based intervention implementation quality by community-university partnerships. *Journal of Community Psychology, 35,* 981–999.

60. Crowley, D. M., Greenberg, M. T., Feinberg, M. E., Spoth, R. L., & Redmond, C. (2012). The effect of the PROSPER partnership model on cultivating local stakeholder knowledge of evidence-based programs: A five-year longitudinal study of 28 communities. *Prevention Science, 13*, 96–105.

61. Spoth, R. L., Guyll, M., Redmond, C., Greenberg, M. T., & Feinberg, M. E. (2011). Six-year sustainability of evidence-based intervention implementation quality by community-university partnerships: The PROSPER study. *American Journal of Community Psychology, 48*, 412–425.

62. Fagan, A. A., Hanson, K., Hawkins, J. D., & Arthur, M. W. (2008). Bridging science to practice: Achieving prevention program fidelity in the Community Youth Development Study. *American Journal of Community Psychology, 41*, 235–249.

63. Fagan, A. A., Hanson, K., Hawkins, J. D., & Arthur, M. W. (2008). Implementing effective community-based prevention programs in the Community Youth Development Study. *Youth Violence and Juvenile Justice, 6*, 256–278.

64. Fagan, A. A., Hanson, K., Hawkins, J. D., & Arthur, M. W. (2009). Translational research in action: Implementation of the Communities That Care prevention system in 12 communities. *Journal of Community Psychology, 37*, 809–829.

65. Bodisch Lynch, K., Geller, S. R., Hunt, D. R., Galano, J., & Semon Dubas, J. (1998). Successful program development using implementation evaluation. *Journal of Prevention and Intervention in the Community, 17*, 51–64.

66. Mowbray, C. T., Holter, M. C., Teague, G. B., & Bybee, D. (2003). Fidelity criteria: Development, measurement and validation. *American Journal of Evaluation, 24*, 315–340.

67. Rohrbach, L. A., Graham, J. W., & Hansen, W. B. (1993). Diffusion of a school-based substance abuse prevention program: Predictors of program implementation. *Preventive Medicine, 22*, 237–260.

68. Arthur, M. W., Hawkins, J. D., Brown, E. C., Briney, J. S., Oesterle, S., & Abbott, R. D. (2010). Implementation of the Communities That Care prevention system by coalitions in the Community Youth Development Study. *Journal of Community Psychology, 38*, 245–258.

69. Gloppen, K. M., Arthur, M. W., Hawkins, J. D., & Shapiro, V. B. (2012). Sustainability of the Communities That Care prevention system by coalitions participating in the Community Youth Development Study. *Journal of Adolescent Health, 51*, 259–264.

70. Brown, L. D., Feinberg, M. E., Shapiro, V. B., & Greenberg, M. T. (2015). Reciprocal relations between coalition functioning and the provision of implementation support. *Prevention Science, 16*, 101–109.

71. Bumbarger, B. K., & Campbell, E. M. (2012). A state agency-university partnership for translational research and dissemination of evidence-based prevention and intervention. *Administration and Policy in Mental Health, 39*, 268–277.

72. Spoth, R. L., Rohrbach, L. A., Greenberg, M. T., Leaf, P., Brown, C. H., Fagan, A., et al. (2013). Addressing core challenges for the next generation of Type 2 translation research and systems: The Translation Science to Population Impact (TSci Impact) Framework. *Prevention Science, 14,* 319–351.

73. Altman, D. G. (1995). Sustaining interventions in community systems: On the relationship between researchers and communities. *Health Psychology, 14,* 526–536.

74. Scheirer, M. A., & Dearing, J. W. (2011). An agenda for research on the sustainability of public health programs. *American Journal of Public Health, 101,* 2059–2067.

75. Shediac-Rizkallah, M. C., & Bone, L. R. (1998). Planning for the sustainability of community-based health programs: Conceptual frameworks and future directions for research, practice, and policy. *Health Education Research, 13,* 87–108.

76. Butterfoss, F. D., Goodman, R. M., & Wandersman, A. (1993). Community coalitions for prevention and health promotion. *Health Education Research, 8,* 315–330.

77. Rog, D., Boback, N., Barton-Villagrana, H., Marrone-Bennett, P., Cardwell, J., Hawdone, J., et al. (2004). Sustaining collaboratives: A cross-site analysis of the National Funding Collaborative on Violence Prevention. *Evaluation and Program Planning, 27,* 249–261.

78. Johnson, K., Collins, D., & Wandersman, A. (2013). Sustaining innovations in community prevention systems: A data-informed sustainability strategy. *Journal of Community Psychology, 41,* 322–340.

79. Aarons, G. A., Hurlburt, M., & Horwitz, S. M. (2011). Advancing a conceptual model of evidence-based practice implementation in public service sectors. *Administration and Policy in Mental Health, 38,* 4–23.

80. Stirman, S. W., Kimberly, J., Cook, N., Calloway, A., Castro, F., & Charns, M. (2012). The sustainability of new programs and innovations: A review of the empirical literature and recommendations for future research. *Implementation Science, 7,* 17.

81. Scheirer, M. A. (2005). Is sustainability possible? A review and commentary on empirical studies of program sustainability. *American Journal of Evaluation, 26,* 320–347.

82. Johnson, K., Hays, C., Center, H., & Daley, C. (2004). Building capacity and sustainable prevention innovations: A sustainability planning model. *Evaluation and Program Planning, 27,* 135–149.

83. Cooper, B. R., Bumbarger, B. K., & Moore, J. E. (2015). Sustaining evidence-based prevention programs: Correlates in a large-scale dissemination initiative. *Prevention Science, 16,* 145–157.

84. Greenhalgh, T., Robert, G., Macfarlane, F., Bate, P., & Kyriakidou, O. (2004). Diffusion of innovations in service organizations: Systematic review and recommendations. *Milbank Quarterly, 82,* 581–629.

85. Brownson, R. C., Allen, P., Jacob, R., Harris, J. K., Duggan, K., Hipp, P. R., et al. (2015). Understanding mis-implementation in public health practice. *American Journal of Public Health, 48,* 543–551.

86. Feinberg, M. E., Bontempo, D., & Greenberg, M. T. (2008). Predictors and level of sustainability of community prevention coalitions. *American Journal of Preventive Medicine, 34,* 495–501.

87. Gruen, R. L., Elliott, J. H., Nolan, M. L., Lawton, P. D., Parkhill, A., McLaren, C. J., et al. (2008). Sustainability science: An integrated approach for health-programme planning. *Lancet, 372,* 1579–1589.

88. Proctor, E. K., Luke, D., Calhoun, A., McMillen, C. J., Brownson, R. C., McCrary, S., et al. (2015). Sustainability of evidence-based healthcare: Research agenda, methodological advances, and infrastructure support. *Implementation Science, 10,* 88.

89. August, G. J., Bloomquist, M. L., Lee, S. S., Realmuto, G. M., & Hektner, J. M. (2006). Can evidence-based prevention programs be sustained in community practice settings? The Early Risers' advanced-stage effectiveness trial. *Prevention Science, 7,* 151–165.

90. Tibbits, M. K., Bumbarger, B., Kyler, S., & Perkins, D. F. (2010). Sustaining evidence-based interventions under real-world conditions: Results from a large-scale diffusion project. *Prevention Science, 11,* 252–262.

91. Feinberg, M. E., Chilenski, S. M., Greenberg, M. T., Spoth, R. L., & Redmond, C. (2007). Community and team member factors that influence the operations phase of local prevention teams: The PROSPER project. *Prevention Science, 8,* 214–226.

92. Kreuter, M. W., Lezin, N. A., & Young, L. A. (2000). Evaluating community-based collaborative mechanisms: Implications for practitioners. *Health Promotion Practice, 1,* 49–63.

93. Leviton, L. C., Herrera, C., Pepper, S. K., Fishman, N., & Racine, D. P. (2006). Faith in Action: Capacity and sustainability of volunteer organizations. *Evaluation and Program Planning, 29,* 201–207.

94. Shapiro, V. B., Oesterle, S., & Hawkins, J. D. (2015). Relating coalition capacity to the adoption of science-based prevention in communities: Evidence from a randomized trial of Communities That Care. *American Journal of Community Psychology, 55,* 1–12.

95. Holder, H. D., & Moore, R. S. (2000). Institutionalization of community action projects to reduce alcohol-use related problems: Systematic facilitators. *Substance Use and Misuse, 35,* 75–86.

96. Greenberg, M. T., Feinberg, M. E., Johnson, L. E., Perkins, D. F., Welsh, J. A., & Spoth, R. L. (2015). Factors that predict financial sustainability of community coalitions: Five years of findings from the PROSPER partnership project. *Prevention Science, 16*, 158–167.

97. Welsh, J. A., Chilenski, S. M., Johnson, L. E., Greenberg, M. T., & Spoth, R. L. (2016). Pathways to sustainability: 8-year follow-up from the PROSPER project. *Journal of Primary Prevention, 37*, 263–286.

98. Hawkins, J. D., Brown, E. C., Oesterle, S., Arthur, M. W., Abbott, R. D., & Catalano, R. F. (2008). Early effects of Communities That Care on targeted risks and initiation of delinquent behavior and substance use. *Journal of Adolescent Health, 43*, 15–22.

99. Catalano, R. F., & Hawkins, J. D. (1996). The Social Development Model: A theory of antisocial behavior. In J. D. Hawkins (Ed.), *Delinquency and crime: Current theories* (pp. 149–197). New York: Cambridge University Press.

100. Hawkins, J. D., Catalano, R. F., & Arthur, M. W. (2002). Promoting science-based prevention in communities. *Addictive Behaviors, 27*, 951–976.

101. Brown, E. C., Hawkins, J. D., Arthur, M. W., Briney, J. S., & Fagan, A. A. (2011). Prevention service system transformation using Communities That Care. *Journal of Community Psychology, 39*, 183–201.

102. Watson-Thompson, J., Fawcett, S. B., & Schultz, J. A. (2008). A framework for community mobilization to promote healthy youth development. *American Journal of Preventive Medicine, 34*, S72–S81.

103. Fagan, A. A., Brooke-Weiss, B., Cady, R., & Hawkins, J. D. (2009). If at first you don't succeed . . . keep trying: Strategies to enhance coalition/school partnerships to implement school-based prevention programming. *Australian and New Zealand Journal of Criminology, 42*, 387–405.

104. Fagan, A. A., Hanson, K., Briney, J. S., & Hawkins, J. D. (2012). Sustaining the utilization and high quality implementation of tested and effective prevention programs using the Communities That Care prevention system. *American Journal of Community Psychology, 49*, 365–377.

CHAPTER 8

1. Arthur, M. W., Glaser, R. R., & Hawkins, J. D. (2005). Steps towards community-level resilience: Community adoption of science-based prevention programming. In R. D. Peters, B. Leadbeater, & R. J. McMahon (Eds.), *Resilience in children, families, and communities: Linking context to practice and policy* (pp. 177–194). New York: Kluwer Academic/Plenum Publishers.

2. Hawkins, J. D., Brown, E. C., Oesterle, S., Arthur, M. W., Abbott, R. D., & Catalano, R. F. (2008). Early effects of Communities That Care on targeted risks

and initiation of delinquent behavior and substance use. *Journal of Adolescent Health, 43,* 15–22.

3. Hawkins, J. D., Catalano, R. F., Arthur, M. W., Egan, E., Brown, E. C., Abbott, R. D., et al. (2008). Testing Communities That Care: The rationale, design and behavioral baseline equivalence of the Community Youth Development Study. *Prevention Science, 9,* 178–190.

4. Weisburd, D. (2010). Justifying the use of non-experimental methods and disqualifying the use of randomized controlled trials: Challenging folklore in evaluation research in crime and justice. *Journal of Experimental Criminology, 6,* 209–227.

5. Brown, C. H., & Liao, J. (1999). Principles for designing randomized preventive trials in mental health: An emerging developmental epidemiology paradigm. *American Journal of Community Psychology, 27,* 673–710.

6. Weisburd, D., & Gill, C. (2014). Block randomized trials at places: Rethinking the limitations of small N experiments. *Journal of Quantitative Criminology, 30,* 97–112.

7. Murray, D. M. (1998). *Design and analysis of group-randomized trials.* Monographs in Epidemiology and Biostatistics (Vol. 27). New York: Oxford University Press.

8. Murray, D. M., Van Horn, M. L., Hawkins, J. D., & Arthur, M. W. (2006). Analysis strategies for a community trial to reduce adolescent ATOD use: A comparison of random coefficient and ANOVA/ANCOVA models. *Contemporary Clinical Trials, 27,* 188–206.

9. Brown, E. C., Graham, J. W., Hawkins, J. D., Arthur, M. W., Baldwin, M. M., Oesterle, S., et al. (2009). Design and analysis of the Community Youth Development Study longitudinal cohort sample. *Evaluation Review, 33,* 311–334.

10. Gottfredson, D. C., Cook, T. D., Gardner, F. E. M., Gorman-Smith, D., Howe, G. W., Sandler, I. N., et al. (2015). Standards of evidence for efficacy, effectiveness and scale-up research in prevention science: Next generation. *Prevention Science, 16,* 893–926.

11. Shadish, W. R., Cook, T. D., & Campbell, D. T. (2002). *Experimental and quasi-experimental designs for generalized causal inference.* Boston: Houghton-Mifflin.

12. Blumstein, A., Cohen, J., Roth, J. A., & Visher, C. A. (Eds.). 1986. *Criminal careers and "career criminals." Vol. I: Report of the Panel on Research on Criminal Careers.* National Research Council. Washington, DC: National Academy Press.

13. Catalano, R. F., & Hawkins, J. D. (1996). The Social Development Model: A theory of antisocial behavior. In J. D. Hawkins (Ed.), *Delinquency and crime: Current theories* (pp. 149–197). New York: Cambridge University Press.

14. Farrington, D. P. (2003). Developmental and life-course criminology: Key theoretical and empirical issues—The 2002 Sutherland Award address. *Criminology, 41,* 221–255.

15. Hawkins, J. D., Oesterle, S., Brown, E. C., Arthur, M. W., Abbott, R. D., Fagan, A. A., et al. (2009). Results of a type 2 translational research trial to prevent adolescent drug use and delinquency: A test of Communities That Care. *Archives of Pediatric and Adolescent Medicine, 163,* 789–798.

16. Oesterle, S., Hawkins, J. D., Kuklinski, M. R., Fagan, A. A., Fleming, C., Rhew, I.C., et al. (2015). Effects of Communities That Care on males' and females' drug use and delinquency 9 years after baseline in a community-randomized trial. *American Journal of Community Psychology, 56,* 217–228.

17. Shapiro, V. B., Oesterle, S., Abbott, R. D., Arthur, M. W., & Hawkins, J. D. (2013). Measuring dimensions of coalition functioning for effective and participatory community practice. *Social Work Research, 37,* 349–359.

18. Shapiro, V. B., Oesterle, S., & Hawkins, J. D. (2015). Relating coalition capacity to the adoption of science-based prevention in communities: Evidence from a randomized trial of Communities That Care. *American Journal of Community Psychology, 55,* 1–12.

19. Arthur, M. W., Hawkins, J. D., Brown, E. C., Briney, J. S., Oesterle, S., & Abbott, R. D. (2010). Implementation of the Communities That Care prevention system by coalitions in the Community Youth Development Study. *Journal of Community Psychology, 38,* 245–258.

20. Gloppen, K. M., Arthur, M. W., Hawkins, J. D., & Shapiro, V. B. (2012). Sustainability of the Communities That Care prevention system by coalitions participating in the Community Youth Development Study. *Journal of Adolescent Health, 51,* 259–264.

21. Gloppen, K. M., Brown, E. C., Wagenaar, B. H., Hawkins, J. D., Rhew, I. C., & Oesterle, S. (2016). Sustaining adoption of science-based prevention through Communities That Care. *Journal of Community Psychology, 44,* 78–89.

22. Rogers, E. M. (1995). *Diffusion of innovations.* (4th ed.). New York: Free Press.

23. Brown, E. C., Hawkins, J. D., Arthur, M. W., Briney, J. S., & Abbott, R. D. (2007). Effects of Communities That Care on prevention services systems: Findings from the Community Youth Development Study at 1.5 years. *Prevention Science, 8,* 180–191.

24. Brown, E. C., Hawkins, J. D., Arthur, M. W., Briney, J. S., & Fagan, A. A. (2011). Prevention service system transformation using Communities That Care. *Journal of Community Psychology, 39,* 183–201.

25. Rhew, I. C., Brown, E. C., Hawkins, J. D., & Briney, J. S. (2013). Sustained effects of the Communities That Care system on prevention service system transformation. *American Journal of Public Health, 103,* 529–535.

26. Brown, E. C., Hawkins, J. D., Arthur, M. W., Abbott, R. D., & Van Horn, M. L. (2008). Multilevel analysis of a measure of community prevention collaboration. *American Journal of Community Psychology, 41,* 115–126.

27. Van Horn, M. L., Hawkins, D., Arthur, M. W., & Catalano, R. F. (2007). Assessing community effects on adolescent substance use and delinquency. *Journal of Community Psychology, 35*, 925–946.

28. Fagan, A. A., Hanson, K., Briney, J. S., & Hawkins, J. D. (2012). Sustaining the utilization and high quality implementation of tested and effective prevention programs using the Communities That Care prevention system. *American Journal of Community Psychology, 49*, 365–377.

29. Fagan, A. A., Arthur, M. W., Hanson, K., Briney, J. S., & Hawkins, J. D. (2011). Effects of Communities That Care on the adoption and implementation fidelity of evidence-based prevention programs in communities: Results from a randomized controlled trial. *Prevention Science, 12*, 223–234.

30. Oesterle, S., Kuklinski, M. R., Hawkins, J. D., Skinner, M. L., Guttmannova, K., & Rhew, I. C. (2018). Long-term effects of the Communities That Care trial on substance use, antisocial behavior, and violence through age 21 years. *American Journal of Public Health, 108*, 659–666.

31. Hawkins, J. D., Oesterle, S., Brown, E. C., Monahan, K. C., Abbott, R. D., Arthur, M. W., et al. (2012). Sustained decreases in risk exposure and youth problem behaviors after installation of the Communities That Care prevention system in a randomized trial. *Archives of Pediatrics and Adolescent Medicine, 166*, 141–148.

32. Hawkins, J. D., Oesterle, S., Brown, E. C., Abbott, R. D., & Catalano, R. F. (2014). Youth problem behaviors 8 years after implementing the Communities That Care prevention system: A community randomized trial. *JAMA Pediatrics, 168*, 122–129.

33. Kim, B. K. E., Gloppen, K. M., Rhew, I. C., Oesterle, S., & Hawkins, J. D. (2015). Effects of the Communities That Care prevention system on youth reports of protective factors. *Prevention Science, 16*, 652–662.

34. Kim, B. K. E., Oesterle, S., Hawkins, J. D., & Shapiro, V. (2015). Assessing sustained effects of Communities That Care on youth protective factors. *Journal of the Society for Social Work and Research, 6*, 565–589.

35. Oesterle, S., Hawkins, J. D., Fagan, A. A., Abbott, R. D., & Catalano, R. F. (2010). Testing the universality of the effects of the Communities That Care prevention system for preventing adolescent drug use and delinquency. *Prevention Science, 11*, 411–423.

36. Oesterle, S., Hawkins, J. D., Fagan, A. A., Abbott, R. D., & Catalano, R. F. (2014). Variation in the sustained effects of the Communities That Care Prevention System on adolescent smoking, delinquency, and violence. *Prevention Science, 15*, 138–145.

37. Rhew, I. C., Oesterle, S., Coffman, D. L., & Hawkins, J. D. (2018). Effects of exposure to the Communities That Care prevention system on youth problem behaviors in a community-randomized trial: Employing an inverse probability weighting approach. *Evaluation & the Health Professions, 41*, 279–289.

38. Monahan, K. C., Hawkins, J. D., & Abbott, R. D. (2013). The application of meta-analysis within a matched-pair randomized control trial: An illustration testing the effects of Communities That Care on delinquent behavior. *Prevention Science, 14*, 1–12.

39. Brown, E. C., Hawkins, J. D., Rhew, I. C., Shapiro, V. B., Abbott, R. D., Oesterle, S., et al. (2014). Prevention system mediation of Communities That Care: Effects on youth outcomes. *Prevention Science, 15*, 623–632.

40. Rhew, I. C., Hawkins, J. D., Murray, D. M., Fagan, A. A., Oesterle, S., Abbott, R. D., et al. (2016). Evaluation of community-level effects of Communities That Care on adolescent drug use and delinquency using repeated cross-sectional design. *Prevention Science, 17*, 177–187.

41. Van Horn, M. L., Fagan, A. A., Hawkins, J. D., & Oesterle, S. (2014). Effects of the Communities That Care system on cross-sectional profiles of adolescent substance use and delinquency. *American Journal of Preventive Medicine, 47*, 196–205.

42. Kuklinski, M. R., Briney, J. S., Hawkins, J. D., & Catalano, R. F. (2012). Cost-benefit analysis of Communities That Care outcomes at eighth grade. *Prevention Science, 13*, 150–161.

43. Kuklinski, M. R., Fagan, A. A., Hawkins, J. D., Briney, J. S., & Catalano, R. F. (2015). Benefit-cost analysis of a randomized evaluation of Communities That Care: Monetizing intervention effects on the initiation of delinquency and substance use through grade 12. *Journal of Experimental Criminology, 11*, 165–192.

44. Washington State Institute for Public Policy. (2013). *Benefit–cost technical manual: Methods and user guide.* (Document No. 13-10-1201b). Olympia, WA: Author.

45. Washington State Institute for Public Policy. (2017). *Benefit-cost results.* Olympia, WA: Author.

46. Stith, S., Pruitt, I., Dees, J., Fronce, M., Green, N., Som, A., et al. (2006). Implementing community-based prevention programming: A review of the literature. *Journal of Primary Prevention, 27*, 599–617.

47. Merzel, C., & D'Afflitti, J. (2003). Reconsidering community-based health promotion: Promise, performance, and potential. *American Journal of Public Health, 93*, 557–574.

48. Peterson, P. L., Hawkins, J. D., & Catalano, R. F. (1992). Evaluating comprehensive community drug risk reduction interventions: Design challenges and recommendations. *Evaluation Review, 16*, 579–602.

49. Gruenewald, P. J. (1997). Analysis approaches to community evaluation. *Evaluation Review, 21*, 209–230.

50. Biglan, A., Ary, D. V., & Wagenaar, A. C. (2000). The value of interrupted time-series experiments for community intervention research. *Prevention Science, 1*, 31–49.

51. Farrington, D. P. (1997). Evaluating a community crime prevention program. *Evaluation, 3*, 157–173.

52. Braga, A. A., & Weisburd, D. L. (2014). Must we settle for less rigorous evaluations in large area-based crime prevention programs? Lessons from a Campbell review of focused deterrence. *Journal of Experimental Criminology, 10*, 573–597.

53. Fagan, A. A., Hanson, K., Hawkins, J. D., & Arthur, M. W. (2009). Translational research in action: Implementation of the Communities That Care prevention system in 12 communities. *Journal of Community Psychology, 37*, 809–829.

54. Grant, B. F., & Dawson, D. A. (1997). Age at onset of alcohol use and its association with DSM-IV alcohol abuse and dependence: Results from the National Longitudinal Alcohol Epidemiologic Survey. *Journal of Substance Abuse, 9*, 103–110.

55. Hingson, R. W., Heeren, T., & Winter, M. R. (2006). Age at drinking onset and alcohol dependence: age at onset, duration, and severity. *Archives of Pediatrics and Adolescent Medicine, 160*, 739–746.

56. U.S. Department of Health and Human Services. (2016, November). *Facing addiction in America: The Surgeon General's report on alcohol, drugs, and health*. Office of the Surgeon General. Washington, DC: Author.

57. Fagan, A. A., & Hawkins, J. D. (2012). Community-based substance use prevention. In B. C. Welsh & D. P. Farrington (Eds.), *The Oxford handbook on crime prevention* (pp. 247–268). New York: Oxford University Press.

58. Komro, K., Perry, C. L., Veblen-Mortenson, S., Farbakhsh, K., Toomey, T. L., Stigler, M. H., et al. (2008). Outcomes from a randomized controlled trial of a multi-component alcohol use preventive intervention for urban youth: Project Northland Chicago. *Addiction, 103*, 606–618.

59. Wilson, J. M., & Chermak, S. (2011). Community-driven violence reduction programs: Examining Pittsburgh's One Vision One Life. *Criminology and Public Policy, 10*, 993–1027.

60. Rosenbaum, D. P., & Schuck, A. M. (2012). Comprehensive community partnerships for preventing crime. In B. C. Welsh & D. P. Farrington (Eds.), *The Oxford handbook on crime prevention* (pp. 226–246). New York: Oxford University Press.

CHAPTER 9

1. Sussman, S., Valente, T. W., Rohrbach, L. A., Skara, S., & Pentz, M. A. (2006). Translation in the health professions: Converting science into action. *Evaluation and the Health Professions, 29*, 7–32.

2. Institute of Medicine. (1994). *Reducing risks for mental disorders: Frontiers for preventive intervention research* (P. J. Mrazek & R. J. Haggerty, Eds.). Washington, DC: National Academy Press.

3. Feinberg, M. E., Greenberg, M. T., & Osgood, D. W. (2004). Readiness, functioning, and perceived effectiveness in community prevention coalitions: A study of Communities That Care. *American Journal of Community Psychology, 33,* 163–176.

4. Feinberg, M. E., Greenberg, M. T., Osgood, D. W., Sartorius, J., & Bontempo, D. (2007). Effects of the Communities That Care model in Pennsylvania on youth risk and problem behaviors. *Prevention Science, 8,* 261–270.

5. Feinberg, M. E., Jones, D., Greenberg, M. T., Osgood, D. W., & Bontempo, D. (2010). Effects of the Communities That Care model in Pennsylvania on change in adolescent risk and problem behaviors. *Prevention Science, 11,* 163–171.

6. Rhoades, B. J., Bumbarger, B. K., & Moore, J. E. (2012). The role of a state-level prevention support system in promoting high-quality implementation and sustainability of evidence-based programs. *American Journal of Community Psychology, 50,* 386–401.

7. Butterfoss, F. D., Goodman, R. M., & Wandersman, A. (1993). Community coalitions for prevention and health promotion. *Health Education Research, 8,* 315–330.

8. Wandersman, A., & Florin, P. (2003). Community intervention and effective prevention. *American Psychologist, 58,* 441–448.

9. National Research Council and Institute of Medicine. (2009). *Preventing mental, emotional, and behavioral disorders among young people: Progress and possibilities* (M. E. O'Connell, T. Boat, & K. E. Warner, Eds.). Washington, DC: National Academies Press.

10. Catalano, R. F., Fagan, A. A., Gavin, L. E., Greenberg, M. T., Irwin, C. E., Ross, D. A., et al. (2012). Worldwide application of prevention science in adolescent health. *Lancet, 379,* 1653–1664.

11. Hawkins, J. D., Jenson, J. M., Catalano, R. F., Fraser, M. W., Botvin, G. J., Shapiro, V., et al. (2015). *Unleashing the power of prevention.* Discussion paper. Washington, DC: Institute of Medicine and National Research Council.

12. Spoth, R. L., Rohrbach, L. A., Greenberg, M. T., Leaf, P., Brown, C. H., Fagan, A., et al. (2013). Addressing core challenges for the next generation of Type 2 translation research and systems: The Translation Science to Population Impact (TSci Impact) Framework. *Prevention Science, 14,* 319–351.

13. Wandersman, A., Duffy, J., Flaspohler, P. D., Noonan, R. K., Lubell, K., Stillman, L., et al. (2008). Bridging the gap between prevention research and practice: The Interactive Systems Framework for Dissemination and Implementation. *American Journal of Community Psychology, 41,* 171–181.

14. Fixsen, D. L., Blase, K. A., Metz, A., & Van Dyke, M. (2013). Statewide implementation of evidence-based programs. *Exceptional Children, 79,* 213–230.

15. Rogers, E. M. (1995). *Diffusion of innovations.* (4th ed.) New York: Free Press.

16. Backer, T. E. (1995). Assessing and enhancing readiness for change: Implications for technology transfer. In T. E. Backer, S. L. David, & G. Soucy (Eds.), *Reviewing the behavioral science knowledge base on technology transfer* (pp. 21–41). Rockville, MD: National Institute on Drug Abuse.

17. Foster-Fishman, P. G., Nowell, B., & Yang, H. (2007). Putting the system back into systems change: A framework for understanding and changing organizational and community systems. *American Journal of Community Psychology, 39,* 197–215.

18. Durlak, J. A., & DuPre, E. P. (2008). Implementation matters: A review of the research on the influence of implementation on program outcomes and the factors affecting implementation. *American Journal of Community Psychology, 41,* 327–350.

19. Damschroder, L. J., Aron, D. C., Keith, R. E., Kirsh, S. R., Alexander, J. A., & Lowery, J. C. (2009). Fostering implementation of health services research findings into practice: A consolidated framework for advancing implementation science. *Implementation Science, 4,* 50.

20. Dariotis, J. K., Bumbarger, B. K., Duncan, L. G., & Greenberg, M. T. (2008). How do implementation efforts relate to program adherence? Examining the role of organizational, implementer, and program factors. *Journal of Community Psychology, 36,* 744–760.

21. Greenhalgh, T., Robert, G., Macfarlane, F., Bate, P., & Kyriakidou, O. (2004). Diffusion of innovations in service organizations: Systematic review and recommendations. *Milbank Quarterly, 82,* 581–629.

22. Johnson, K., Collins, D., & Wandersman, A. (2013). Sustaining innovations in community prevention systems: A data-informed sustainability strategy. *Journal of Community Psychology, 41,* 322–340.

23. U.S. Department of Health and Human Services. (2001). *Youth violence: A report of the Surgeon General.* Centers for Disease Control and Prevention, National Center for Injury Prevention and Control; Substance Abuse and Mental Health Services Administration, Center for Mental Health Services; National Institutes of Health, National Institute of Mental Health. Rockville, MD: Author.

24. Bennett, W. J., DiIulio Jr., J. J., & Walters, J. P. (1996). *Body count: Moral poverty and how to win America's war against crime and drugs.* New York: Simon & Schuster.

25. Office of Juvenile Justice and Delinquency Prevention. (1996). *Report to Congress: Title V incentive grants for local delinquency prevention programs.* Washington, DC: Author.

26. Campbell, L., & Bumbarger, B. K. (2012). Looking back, moving forward: The history & current state of evidence-based intervention in Pennsylvania. College Station: Pennsylvania State University.

27. Greenberg, M. T., & Feinberg, M. E. (2005). *An evaluation of PCCD's Communities That Care delinquency prevention initiative*. College Station, PA: College of Health and Human Development Center for Prevention Research, Pennsylvania State University.

28. Rhoades, B. (2011). *Building capacity for high quality implementation and sustainability of EBPs*. Tampa, FL: National Prevention Network Conference.

29. Elliott, D. S. (1997). *Blueprints for Violence Prevention*. Boulder, CO: University of Colorado, Institute of Behavioral Science, Center for the Study and Prevention of Violence.

30. Moore, J. E., Bumbarger, B. K., & Cooper, B. R. (2013). Examining adaptations of evidence-based programs in natural contexts. *Journal of Primary Prevention, 34,* 147–161.

31. Manger, T. H., Hawkins, J. D., Haggerty, K. P., & Catalano, R. F. (1992). Mobilizing communities to reduce risks for drug abuse: Lessons on using research to guide prevention practice. *Journal of Primary Prevention, 13,* 3–22.

32. Harachi, T. W., Ayers, C. D., Hawkins, J. D., Catalano, R. F., & Cushing, J. (1996). Empowering communities to prevent adolescent substance abuse: Process evaluation results from a risk- and protection-focused community mobilization effort. *Journal of Primary Prevention, 16,* 233–254.

33. Bumbarger, B. K., & Campbell, E. M. (2012). A state agency-university partnership for translational research and dissemination of evidence-based prevention and intervention. *Administration and Policy in Mental Health, 39,* 268–277.

34. Feinberg, M. E., Greenberg, M. T., Osgood, D. W., Anderson, A., & Babinski, L. (2002). The effects of training community leaders in prevention science: Communities That Care in Pennsylvania. *Evaluation and Program Planning, 25,* 245–259.

35. Feinberg, M. E., Greenberg, M. T., & Osgood, D. W. (2004). Technical assistance in prevention programs: Correlates of perceived need in Communities That Care. *Evaluation and Program Planning, 27,* 263–274.

36. Feinberg, M. E., Gomez, B. J., Puddy, R. W., & Greenberg, M. T. (2008). Evaluation and community prevention coalitions: Validation of an integrated web-based technical assistance consultant model. *Health Education & Behavior, 35,* 9–21.

37. Brown, L. D., Feinberg, M. E., & Greenberg, M. T. (2012). Measuring coalition functioning: Refining constructs through factor analysis. *Health Education & Behavior, 39,* 486–497.

38. Feinberg, M. E., Ridenour, T. A., & Greenberg, M. T. (2008). The longitudinal effect of technical assistance dosage on the functioning of Communities That Care prevention boards in Pennsylvania. *Journal of Primary Prevention, 29,* 145–165.

39. Gomez, B. J., Greenberg, M. T, & Feinberg, M. E. (2005). Sustainability of community coalitions: An evaluation of Communities That Care. *Prevention Science, 6,* 199–202.

40. Feinberg, M. E., Bontempo, D., & Greenberg, M. T. (2008). Predictors and level of sustainability of community prevention coalitions. *American Journal of Preventive Medicine, 34*, 495–501.

41. Brown, L. D., Feinberg, M. E., & Greenberg, M. T. (2010). Determinants of community coalition ability to support evidence-based programs. *Prevention Science, 11*, 287–297.

42. Brown, L. D., Feinberg, M. E., Shapiro, V. B., & Greenberg, M. T. (2015). Reciprocal relations between coalition functioning and the provision of implementation support. *Prevention Science, 16*, 101–109.

43. Cooper, B. R., Bumbarger, B. K., & Moore, J. E. (2015). Sustaining evidence-based prevention programs: Correlates in a large-scale dissemination initiative. *Prevention Science, 16*, 145–157.

44. Rhew, I. C., Hawkins, J. D., Murray, D. M., Fagan, A. A., Oesterle, S., Abbott, R. D., et al. (2016). Evaluation of community-level effects of Communities That Care on adolescent drug use and delinquency using repeated cross-sectional design. *Prevention Science, 17*, 177–187.

45. Bumbarger, B. K. (2015). *Promoting evidence-based prevention at scale: A state perspective.* Ogden, UT.

46. Campbell, E. M., & Bumbarger, B. K. (2012). *Youth placement and placement rates in Pennsylvania counties: The impact of evidence-based intervention programs.* University Park, PA: Evidence-based Prevention and Intervention Support Center, Pennsylvania State University.

47. Katz, J., & Wandersman, A. (2016). Technical assistance to enhance prevention capacity: A research synthesis of the evidence base. *Prevention Science, 17*, 417–428.

48. Greenwood, P., & Welsh, B. C. (2012). Promoting evidence-based practice in delinquency prevention at the state level: Principles, progress, and policy directions. *Criminology and Public Policy, 11*, 493–513.

CHAPTER 10

1. National Research Council and Institute of Medicine. (2009). *Preventing mental, emotional, and behavioral disorders among young people: Progress and possibilities* (M. E. O'Connell, T. Boat, & K. E. Warner, Eds.). Washington, DC: National Academies Press.

2. David-Ferdon, C., & Simon, T. R. (2014). *Preventing youth violence: Opportunities for action.* Atlanta, GA: National Center for Injury Prevention and Control, Centers for Disease Control and Prevention.

3. Woolf, S. H. (2008). The power of prevention and what it requires. *Journal of the American Medical Association, 299*, 2437–2439.

4. Hawkins, J. D., Jenson, J. M., Catalano, R. F., Fraser, M. W., Botvin, G. J., Shapiro, V., et al. (2015). *Unleashing the power of prevention.* Discussion paper. Washington, DC: Institute of Medicine and National Research Council.

5. Haskins, R., & Margolis, G. (2014). *Show me the evidence: Obama's fight for rigor and results in social policy.* Washington, DC: Brookings Institute Press.

6. Fixsen, D. L., Naoom, S. F., Blase, K. A., Friedman, R. M., & Wallace, F. (2005). *Implementation research: A synthesis of the literature.* National Implementation Research Network (FMHI Publication #231). Tampa, FL: University of South Florida, Louis de la Parte Florida Mental Health Institute.

7. Welsh, B. C., Sullivan, C. J., & Olds, D. L. (2010). When early crime prevention goes to scale: A new look at the evidence. *Prevention Science, 11,* 115–125.

8. Arthur, M. W., & Blitz, C. (2000). Bridging the gap between science and practice in drug abuse prevention through needs assessment and strategic community planning. *Journal of Community Psychology, 28,* 241–255.

9. U.S. Department of Health and Human Services. (2016, November). *Facing addiction in America: The Surgeon General's report on alcohol, drugs, and health.* Washington, DC: Author.

10. Farrington, D. P., & Welsh, B. C. (2007). *Saving children from a life of crime: Early risk factors and effective interventions.* New York: Oxford University Press.

11. Catalano, R. F., Fagan, A. A., Gavin, L. E., Greenberg, M. T., Irwin, C. E., Ross, D. A., et al. (2012). Worldwide application of prevention science in adolescent health. *Lancet, 379,* 1653–1664.

12. Kania, J., & Kramer, M. (2011). Collective impact. *Stanford Social Innovation Review, 9,* 36–41.

13. Quinby, R., Fagan, A. A., Hanson, K., Brooke-Weiss, B., Arthur, M. W., & Hawkins, J. D. (2008). Installing the Communities That Care prevention system: Implementation progress and fidelity in a randomized controlled trial. *Journal of Community Psychology, 36,* 313–332.

14. Shapiro, V. B., Oesterle, S., Abbott, R. D., Arthur, M. W., & Hawkins, J. D. (2013). Measuring dimensions of coalition functioning for effective and participatory community practice. *Social Work Research, 37,* 349–359.

15. Arthur, M. W., Hawkins, J. D., Brown, E. C., Briney, J. S., Oesterle, S., & Abbott, R. D. (2010). Implementation of the Communities That Care prevention system by coalitions in the Community Youth Development Study. *Journal of Community Psychology, 38,* 245–258.

16. Gloppen, K. M., Arthur, M. W., Hawkins, J. D., & Shapiro, V. B. (2012). Sustainability of the Communities That Care prevention system by coalitions participating in the Community Youth Development Study. *Journal of Adolescent Health, 51,* 259–264.

17. Brown, E. C., Hawkins, J. D., Arthur, M. W., Briney, J. S., & Fagan, A. A. (2011). Prevention service system transformation using Communities That Care. *Journal of Community Psychology, 39*, 183–201.

18. Rhew, I. C., Brown, E. C., Hawkins, J. D., & Briney, J. S. (2013). Sustained effects of the Communities That Care system on prevention service system transformation. *American Journal of Public Health, 103*, 529–535.

19. Gloppen, K. M., Brown, E. C., Wagenaar, B. H., Hawkins, J. D., Rhew, I. C., & Oesterle, S. (2016). Sustaining adoption of science-based prevention through Communities That Care. *Journal of Community Psychology, 44*, 78–89.

20. Brown, E. C., Hawkins, J. D., Arthur, M. W., Briney, J. S., & Abbott, R. D. (2007). Effects of Communities That Care on prevention services systems: Findings from the Community Youth Development Study at 1.5 years. *Prevention Science, 8*, 180–191.

21. Fagan, A. A., Hanson, K., Hawkins, J. D., & Arthur, M. W. (2009). Translational research in action: Implementation of the Communities That Care prevention system in 12 communities. *Journal of Community Psychology, 37*, 809–829.

22. Fagan, A. A., Hanson, K., Hawkins, J. D., & Arthur, M. W. (2008). Bridging science to practice: Achieving prevention program fidelity in the Community Youth Development Study. *American Journal of Community Psychology, 41*, 235–249.

23. Fagan, A. A., Hanson, K., Hawkins, J. D., & Arthur, M. W. (2008). Implementing effective community-based prevention programs in the Community Youth Development Study. *Youth Violence and Juvenile Justice, 6*, 256–278.

24. Fagan, A. A., Hanson, K., Briney, J. S., & Hawkins, J. D. (2012). Sustaining the utilization and high quality implementation of tested and effective prevention programs using the Communities That Care prevention system. *American Journal of Community Psychology, 49*, 365–377.

25. Fagan, A. A., Arthur, M. W., Hanson, K., Briney, J. S., & Hawkins, J. D. (2011). Effects of Communities That Care on the adoption and implementation fidelity of evidence-based prevention programs in communities: Results from a randomized controlled trial. *Prevention Science, 12*, 223–234.

26. Hawkins, J. D., Brown, E. C., Oesterle, S., Arthur, M. W., Abbott, R. D., & Catalano, R. F. (2008). Early effects of Communities That Care on targeted risks and initiation of delinquent behavior and substance use. *Journal of Adolescent Health, 43*, 15–22.

27. Hawkins, J. D., Oesterle, S., Brown, E. C., Monahan, K. C., Abbott, R. D., Arthur, M. W., et al. (2012). Sustained decreases in risk exposure and youth problem behaviors after installation of the Communities That Care prevention system in a randomized trial. *Archives of Pediatrics and Adolescent Medicine, 166*, 141–148.

28. Kim, B. K. E., Gloppen, K. M., Rhew, I. C., Oesterle, S., & Hawkins, J. D. (2015). Effects of the Communities That Care prevention system on youth reports of protective factors. *Prevention Science, 16*, 652–662.

29. Kim, B. K. E., Oesterle, S., Hawkins, J. D., & Shapiro, V. (2015). Assessing sustained effects of Communities That Care on youth protective factors. *Journal of the Society for Social Work and Research, 6,* 565–589.

30. Hawkins, J. D., Oesterle, S., Brown, E. C., Abbott, R. D., & Catalano, R. F. (2014). Youth problem behaviors 8 years after implementing the Communities That Care prevention system: A community randomized trial. *JAMA Pediatrics, 168,* 122–129.

31. Oesterle, S., Hawkins, J. D., Kuklinski, M. R., Fagan, A. A., Fleming, C., Rhew, I.C., et al. (2015). Effects of Communities That Care on males' and females' drug use and delinquency 9 years after baseline in a community-randomized trial. *American Journal of Community Psychology, 56,* 217–228.

32. Oesterle, S., Kuklinski, M. R., Hawkins, J. D., Skinner, M. L., Guttmannova, K., & Rhew, I. C. (2018). Long-term effects of the Communities That Care trial on substance use, antisocial behavior, and violence through age 21 years. *American Journal of Public Health, 108,* 659–665.

33. Hawkins, J. D., Oesterle, S., Brown, E. C., Arthur, M. W., Abbott, R. D., Fagan, A. A., et al. (2009). Results of a type 2 translational research trial to prevent adolescent drug use and delinquency: A test of Communities That Care. *Archives of Pediatric and Adolescent Medicine, 163,* 789–798.

34. Washington State Institute for Public Policy. (2017). *Benefit-cost results.* Olympia, WA: Author.

35. Coie, J. D., Watt, N. F., West, S. G., Hawkins, J. D., Asarnow, J. R., Marman, H. J., et al. (1993). The science of prevention: A conceptual framework and some directions for a national research program. *American Psychologist, 48,* 1013–1022.

36. Farrington, D. P. (2000). Explaining and preventing crime: The globalization of knowledge—The American Society of Criminology 1999 Presidential Address. *Criminology, 38,* 1–24.

37. Institute of Medicine. (1994). Reducing risks for mental disorders: Frontiers for preventive intervention research (P. J. Mrazek & R. J. Haggerty, Eds.). Washington, DC: National Academy Press.

38. Sampson, R. J., & Laub, J. H. (1993). *Crime in the making: Pathways and turning points through life.* Cambridge, MA: Harvard University Press.

39. Elder Jr., G.H. (1998). The life course as developmental theory. *Child Development, 69,* 1–12.

40. Patterson, G. R., DeBaryshe, B. D., & Ramsey, E. (1989). A developmental perspective on antisocial behavior. *American Psychologist, 44,* 329–335.

41. Catalano, R. F., & Hawkins, J. D. (1996). The Social Development Model: A theory of antisocial behavior. In J. D. Hawkins (Ed.), *Delinquency and crime: Current theories* (pp. 149–197). New York: Cambridge University Press.

42. Sampson, R. J., Raudenbush, S. W., & Earls, F. (1997). Neighborhoods and violent crime: A multilevel study of collective efficacy. *Science, 277,* 918–924.

43. Israel, B. A., Schultz, A. J., Parker, E. A., & Becker, A. B. (1998). Review of community-based research: Assessing partnership approaches to improve public health. *American Review of Public Health, 19,* 173–202.

44. Wallerstein, N. B., & Duran, B. (2006). Using community-based participatory research to address health disparities. *Health Promotion and Practice, 7,* 312–323.

45. Wandersman, A. (2003). Community science: Bridging the gap between science and practice with community-centered models. *American Journal of Community Psychology, 31,* 227–242.

46. Fetterman, D. M. (2005). Empowerment evaluation principles in practice. In D. M. Fetterman & A. Wandersman (Eds.), *Empowerment evaluation principles* (pp. 42–72). New York: Guilford Publishers.

47. Macaulay, A. C., Commanda, L. E., Freeman, W. L., Gibson, N., McCabe, M. L., Robbins, C. M., et al. (1999). Participatory research maximises community and lay involvement. *British Medical Journal, 319,* 774–778.

48. Holder, H. D., Saltz, R. F., Grube, J. W., Treno, A. J., Reynolds, R. I., Voas, R. B., et al. (1997). Summing up: Lessons from a comprehensive community prevention trial. *Addiction, 92,* S293–S301.

49. Meyers, D. C., Durlak, J. A., & Wandersman, A. (2012). The quality implementation framework: A synthesis of critical steps in the implementation process. *American Journal of Community Psychology, 50,* 462–480.

50. Flaspohler, P. D., Meehan, C., Maras, M. A., & Keller, K. E. (2012). Ready, willing, and able: Developing a support system to promote implementation of school-based prevention programs. *American Journal of Community Psychology, 50,* 428–444.

51. Supplee, L. H., & Metz, A. (2015). Opportunities and challenges in evidence-based social policy. *Social Policy Report, 28,* 1–16.

52. Kellam, S. G., Koretz, D., & Moscicki, E. K. (1999). Core elements of developmental epidemiologically based prevention research. *American Journal of Community Psychology, 27,* 463–482.

53. Neta, G., Glasgow, R. E., Carpenter, C. S., Grimshaw, J. M., Rabin, B. A., Fernandez, M. E., et al. (2015). A framework for enhancing the value of research for dissemination and implementation. *American Journal of Public Health, 105,* 49–57.

54. Spoth, R. L., Rohrbach, L. A., Greenberg, M. T., Leaf, P., Brown, C. H., Fagan, A., et al. (2013). Addressing core challenges for the next generation of Type 2 translation research and systems: The Translation Science to Population Impact (TSci Impact) Framework. *Prevention Science, 14,* 319–351.

55. Rogers, E. M. (1995). *Diffusion of innovations.* (4th ed.) New York: Free Press.

56. Hallfors, D. D., Cho, H., Livert, D., & Kadushin, C. (2002). Fighting back against substance use: Are community coalitions winning? *American Journal of Preventive Medicine, 23,* 237–245.

57. Fagan, A. A., & Hawkins, J. D. (2012). Community-based substance use prevention. In B. C. Welsh & D. P. Farrington (Eds.), *The Oxford handbook on crime prevention* (pp. 247–268). New York: Oxford University Press.

58. Jonkman, H. B., Aussems, C., Steketee, M., Boutellier, H., & Cuijpers, P. (2015). Prevention of problem behaviours among adolescents: The impact of the Communities That Care strategy in the Netherlands (2008–2011). *International Journal of Developmental Science, 9,* 37–52.

59. Brown, E. C., Hawkins, J. D., Rhew, I. C., Shapiro, V. B., Abbott, R. D., Oesterle, S., et al. (2014). Prevention system mediation of Communities That Care: Effects on youth outcomes. *Prevention Science, 15,* 623–632.

60. Chinman, M., Hannah, G., Wandersman, A., Ebener, P., Hunter, S. B., Imm, P., et al. (2005). Developing a community science research agenda for building community capacity for effective preventive interventions. *American Journal of Community Psychology, 35,* 143–157.

61. Mitchell, R., Florin, P., & Stevenson, J. F. (2002). Supporting community-based prevention and health promotion initiatives: Developing effective technical assistance systems. *Health Education & Behavior, 29,* 620–639.

62. Foster-Fishman, P. G., Berkowitz, S. L., Lounsbury, D. W., Jacobson, S., & Allen, N. A. (2001). Building collaborative capacity in community coalitions: A review and integrative framework. *American Journal of Community Psychology, 29,* 241–261.

63. Foster-Fishman, P. G., Fitzgerald, K., Brandell, C., Nowell, B., Chavis, D., & Van Egeren, L. A. (2006). Mobilizing residents for action: The role of small wins and strategic supports. *American Journal of Community Psychology, 38,* 143–152.

64. Durlak, J. A., & DuPre, E. P. (2008). Implementation matters: A review of the research on the influence of implementation on program outcomes and the factors affecting implementation. *American Journal of Community Psychology, 41,* 327–350.

65. Moore, J. E., Bumbarger, B. K., & Cooper, B. R. (2013). Examining adaptations of evidence-based programs in natural contexts. *Journal of Primary Prevention, 34,* 147–161.

66. Feinberg, M. E., Greenberg, M. T., & Osgood, D. W. (2004). Technical assistance in prevention programs: Correlates of perceived need in Communities That Care. *Evaluation and Program Planning, 27,* 263–274.

67. Feinberg, M. E., Bontempo, D., & Greenberg, M. T. (2008). Predictors and level of sustainability of community prevention coalitions. *American Journal of Preventive Medicine, 34,* 495–501.

68. Cooper, B. R., Bumbarger, B. K., & Moore, J. E. (2015). Sustaining evidence-based prevention programs: Correlates in a large-scale dissemination initiative. *Prevention Science, 16,* 145–157.

69. Gottfredson, D. C., Cook, T. D., Gardner, F. E. M., Gorman-Smith, D., Howe, G. W., Sandler, I. N., et al. (2015). Standards of evidence for efficacy, effectiveness and scale-up research in prevention science: Next generation. *Prevention Science, 16*, 893–926.

70. Stith, S., Pruitt, I., Dees, J., Fronce, M., Green, N., Som, A., et al. (2006). Implementing community-based prevention programming: A review of the literature. *Journal of Primary Prevention, 27*, 599–617.

71. Kreuter, M. W., Lezin, N. A., & Young, L. A. (2000). Evaluating community-based collaborative mechanisms: Implications for practitioners. *Health Promotion Practice, 1*, 49–63.

72. Butterfoss, F. D., Goodman, R. M., & Wandersman, A. (1993). Community coalitions for prevention and health promotion. *Health Education Research, 8*, 315–330.

73. Feinberg, M. E., Chilenski, S. M., Greenberg, M. T., Spoth, R. L., &Redmond, C. (2007). Community and team member factors that influence the operations phase of local prevention teams: The PROSPER Project. *Prevention Science, 8*, 214–226.

74. Roussos, S., & Fawcett, S. (2000). A review of collaborative partnerships as a strategy for improving community health. *Annual Review of Public Health, 21*, 369–402.

75. Zakocs, R. C., & Edwards, E. M. (2006). What explains community coalition effectiveness? A review of the literature. *American Journal of Preventive Medicine, 30*, 351–361.

76. Hanleybrown, F., Kania, J., & Kramer, M. (2012). Channeling change: Making collective impact work. *Stanford Social Innovation Review, 10*, 1–8.

77. Hawkins, J. D., Catalano, R. F., & Arthur, M. W. (2002). Promoting science-based prevention in communities. *Addictive Behaviors, 27*, 951–976.

78. Masho, S., Schoeny, M., Webster, D. W., & Sigel, E. (2016). Outcomes, data, and indicators of violence at the community level. *Journal of Primary Prevention, 37*, 121–139.

79. Gottfredson, D. C., & Gottfredson, G. D. (2002). Quality of school-based prevention programs: Results from a national survey. *Journal of Research in Crime and Delinquency, 39*, 3–35.

80. Rohrbach, L. A., Grana, R., Sussman, S., & Valente, T. W. (2006). Type II Translation: Transporting prevention interventions from research to real-world settings. *Evaluation and the Health Professions, 29*, 302–333.

81. Christoffersen, M. N., & Joshi, H. (2015). Can Rose's paradox be useful in delinquency prevention?. *Longitudinal and Life Course Studies, 6*, 397–419.

82. Rose, G. (1985). Sick individuals and sick populations. *International Journal of Epidemiology, 14*, 32–38.

83. Jonkman, H. B., Junger-Tas, J., & van Dijk, B. (2005). From behind dikes and dunes: Communities That Care in the Netherlands. *Children and Society, 19,* 105–116.

84. Perez-Gomez, A., Mejia-Trujillo, J., Brown, E. C., & Eisenberg, N. (2016). Adaptation and implementation of a science-based prevention system in Colombia: Challenges and achievements. *Journal of Community Psychology, 44,* 538–545.

85. Burkhart, G. (2013). *North Americans drug prevention programmes: Are they feasible in European cultures and contexts?* Lisbon, Portugal: European Monitoring Centre for Drugs and Drug Addiction.

86. World Health Organization. (2014). *Global status report on violence prevention.* Geneva, Switzerland: Author.

87. Catalano, R. F., Haggerty, K. P., Hawkins, J. D., & Elgin, J. (2011). Prevention of substance use and substance use disorders: The role of risk and protective factors. In Y. Kaminer & K. C. Winters (Eds.), *Clinical manual of adolescent substance abuse treatment* (pp. 25–63). Washington, DC: American Psychiatric Publishing.

88. Prinz, R. J., & Sanders, M. R. (2007). Adopting a population-level approach to parenting and family support interventions. *Clinical Psychology Review, 27,* 739–749.

89. Spoth, R. L., & Redmond, C. (2002). Project Family prevention trials based in community-university partnerships: Toward scaled-up preventive interventions. *Prevention Science, 3,* 203–222.

90. Institute of Medicine and National Research Council. (2014). *Strategies for scaling effective family-focused preventive interventions to promote children's cognitive, affective, and behavioral health: Workshop summary.* Washington, DC: National Academies Press.

91. Leslie, L. K., Mehus, C. J., Hawkins, J. D., Boat, T., McCabe, M. A., Barkin, S., et al. (2016). Primary health care: Potential home for family-focused preventive interventions. *American Journal of Preventive Medicine, 51,* S106–S118.

92. Estrada, Y., Molleda, L., Murray, A., Drumhiller, K., Tapia, M., Sardinas, K., et al. (2017). eHealth Familias Unidas: Pilot study of an internet adaptation of an evidence-based family intervention to reduce drug use and sexual risk behaviors among Hispanic adolescents. *International Journal of Environmental Research and Public Health, 14,* 264.

93. Molleda, L., Bahamon, M., St. George, S. M., Perrino, T., Estrada, Y., Herrera, D. C., et al. (2017). Clinic personnel, facilitator, and parent perspectives of eHealth Familias Unidas in primary care. *Journal of Pediatric Health Care, 31,* 350–361.

94. Prado, G., Pantin, H., & Estrada, Y. (2015). Integrating evidence-based interventions for adolescents into primary care. *American Journal of Preventive Medicine, 48,* 488–490.

95. Rhoades, B. J., Bumbarger, B. K., & Moore, J. E. (2012). The role of a state-level prevention support system in promoting high-quality implementation and sustainability of evidence-based programs. *American Journal of Community Psychology, 50,* 386–401.

96. Greenberg, M. T., Feinberg, M. E., Johnson, L. E., Perkins, D. F., Welsh, J. A., & Spoth, R. L. (2015). Factors that predict financial sustainability of community coalitions: Five years of findings from the PROSPER Partnership Project. *Prevention Science, 16,* 158–167.

97. Welsh, J. A., Chilenski, S. M., Johnson, L. E., Greenberg, M. T., & Spoth, R. L. (2016). Pathways to sustainability: 8-year follow-up from the PROSPER project. *Journal of Primary Prevention, 37,* 263–286.

98. Kramer, J. S., Philliber, S., Brindis, C. D., Kamin, S. L., Chadwick, A. E., Revels, M.L., et al. (2005). Coalition models: Lessons learned from the CDC's Community Coalition Partnership Programs for the Prevention of Teen Pregnancy. *Journal of Adolescent Health, 37,* S20–S30.

99. Rog, D., Boback, N., Barton-Villagrana, H., Marrone-Bennett, P., Cardwell, J., Hawdone, J., et al. (2004). Sustaining collaboratives: A cross-site analysis of The National Funding Collaborative on Violence Prevention. *Evaluation and Program Planning, 27,* 249–261.

100. Stirman, S. W., Kimberly, J., Cook, N., Calloway, A., Castro, F., & Charns, M. (2012). The sustainability of new programs and innovations: A review of the empirical literature and recommendations for future research. *Implementation Science, 7,* 17.

101. Scheirer, M. A. (2005). Is sustainability possible? A review and commentary on empirical studies of program sustainability. *American Journal of Evaluation, 26,* 320–347.

102. Johnson, K., Hays, C., Center, H., & Daley, C. (2004). Building capacity and sustainable prevention innovations: A sustainability planning model. *Evaluation and Program Planning, 27,* 135–149.

103. Brownson, R. C., Allen, P., Jacob, R., Harris, J. K., Duggan, K., Hipp, P. R., et al. (2015). Understanding mis-implementation in public health practice. *American Journal of Public Health, 48,* 543–551.

104. Annie E. Casey Foundation. (2013). *Lessons learned: community change: Lessons from Making Connections.* Baltimore, MD: Author.

105. Kellam, S. G. (2012). Developing and maintaining partnerships as the foundation of implementation and implementation science: Reflections over a half century. *Administration and Policy in Mental Health, 39,* 317–320.

106. Kingston, B., Bacallao, M., Smokowski, P., Sullivan, T. N., & Sutherland, K. S. (2016). Constructing "packages" of evidence-based programs to prevent youth violence: Processes and illustrative examples from the CDC's youth violence prevention centers. *Journal of Primary Prevention, 37,* 141–163.

107. Brady, S. S., Parker, C. J., Jeffries, E. F., Simpson, T. Y., Brook-Weiss, B. L., & Haggerty, K. P. (in press). Implementing Communities That Care: Challenges, solutions, and opportunities in an urban setting. *American Journal of Preventive Medicine*.

108. Manger, T. H., Hawkins, J. D., Haggerty, K. P., & Catalano, R. F. (1992). Mobilizing communities to reduce risks for drug abuse: Lessons on using research to guide prevention practice. *Journal of Primary Prevention, 13*, 3–22.

109. Groeger-Roth, F. (2016). Communities That Care in Europe: 2016 Update. CTC International Meeting, San Francisco.

110. Farrington, D. P., Jonkman, H. B., & Groeger-Roth, F. (Eds.). (in press). *Delinquency and substance use in Europe: Understanding risk and protective factors.* New York: Springer.

111. Axford, N., Sonthalia, S., Wrigley, Z., Webb, L., Mokhtar, N., Brook, L., et al. (2016). *What works in Europe? Developing a European Communities That Care database of effective prevention programmes.* Dartington, Totnes: Dartingon Social Research Unit.

112. Toumbourou, J. W., Rowland, B. C., Williams, J., Smith, R., & Patton, G. C. (2018). *Community intervention to prevent adolescent health behavior problems: Evaluation of Communities That Care in Australia.* Unpublished manuscript.

113. Rowland, B. C., Williams, J., Smith, R., Hall, J. K., Osborn, A., Kremer, P., et al. (2018). Social marketing and community mobilisation to reduce underage alcohol consumption in Australia: A cluster randomised community trial. *Preventive Medicine, 113*, 132–139.

114. Juvenile Court Judges' Commission and Center for Juvenile Justice Training and Research. (2015). 2015 Pennsylvania Juvenile Court Dispositions. Harrisburg, PA.

Index

Page numbers followed by *t* and *f* denote tables and figures. Page numbers followed by "n" and another number refer to endnotes.